MAKING MAINE

MAKING MAINE

STATEHOOD AND THE WAR OF 1812

JOSHUA M. SMITH

UNIVERSITY OF MASSACHUSETTS PRESS
Amherst and Boston

Copyright © 2022 by University of Massachusetts Press
All rights reserved
Printed in the United States of America

ISBN 978-1-62534-701-5 (paper); 702-2 (hardcover)

Designed by Deste Roosa
Set in Bell, Walbaum, and Alternate Gothic ATF
Printed and bound by Books International, Inc.

Cover design by Kristina Kachele Design, llc
Cover art by John S. Blunt, *Launching of the USS Washington, 1814–1815.*
Gift of Bertram K. and Nina Fletcher Little. Courtesy Historic New England.

Library of Congress Cataloging-in-Publication Data
Names: Smith, Joshua M., author.
Title: Making Maine : statehood and the War of 1812 / Joshua M. Smith.
Description: Amherst : University of Massachusetts, [2022] | Includes bibliographical references and index.
Identifiers: LCCN 2022022507 (print) | LCCN 2022022508 (ebook) | ISBN 9781625347022 (hardcover) | ISBN 9781625347015 (paperback) | ISBN 9781613769799 (ebook) | ISBN 9781613769805 (ebook)
Subjects: LCSH: Statehood (American politics) | Maine—History—War of 1812. | Maine—Politics and government—1775–1865. | Massachusetts—History—War of 1812. | Massachusetts—Politics and government—1812–1815.
Classification: LCC F24 .S655 2022 (print) | LCC F24 (ebook) | DDC 974.1/03—dc23/eng/20220708
LC record available at https://lccn.loc.gov/2022022507
LC ebook record available at https://lccn.loc.gov/2022022508

British Library Cataloguing-in-Publication Data
A catalog record for this book is available from the British Library.

To the Taylor family of Peaks Island

CONTENTS

Preface and Acknowledgments
ix

INTRODUCTION
1

CHAPTER 1
"An Exceedingly Dirty and Nasty People"
7

CHAPTER 2
War Comes to Maine
38

CHAPTER 3
"A Mongrel Breed of Soldier"
56

CHAPTER 4
War Afloat
77

CHAPTER 5
"Wicked War"
105

CHAPTER 6
"Hampden Races"
136

CHAPTER 7
"One against Another"
161

CHAPTER 8
Yankee Confusion
182

CHAPTER 9
Winter of Discontent
200

CHAPTER 10
Après la Guerre
215

PARTINGS
233

Notes
239

Index
297

PREFACE AND ACKNOWLEDGMENTS

Today Americans obsess about disorder in the nation. Politics have become bitterly partisan, the news media blatantly take sides, and urban elites and their rural counterparts vie for moral ascendancy. There are widespread concerns about riots, coups, and what role the states and federal government have in maintaining order or quelling dissent. Some alarmists even predict the end of American democracy. My message to the reader is: fear not. The republic has witnessed all these travails before and has not only survived but generally thrived. My evidence lies in a detailed analysis of Maine's search for a new identity separate from Massachusetts from roughly 1805 to 1820.

The choice of Maine may surprise many who know it as the land of quaint villages, Moxie, lobster rolls, and L.L. Bean, a political and economic backwater tucked in an obscure corner of the nation. But Maine in the early 1800s was a dynamic place, well placed for international trade with the British Empire, with a rapidly growing population. Increasingly its citizens sought independence from Massachusetts, ultimately becoming a separate state in 1820. Why did Mainers seek separation from a large, prosperous, and important state like Massachusetts? In part, its leading citizens decided that the time was ripe for them to take control. Another factor was a growing perception that Massachusetts treated Maine as a colony to be commercially exploited and its inhabitants disdained as uncouth rustics.

The timing of a resurgent statehood movement after 1814 also bears examination. Ronald F. Banks noted that the War of 1812 was the catalyst for Maine's statehood. That conflict left its citizens starving and humiliated by enemy occupation; businesses driven to bankruptcy; the people oppressed by taxes; and returning veterans maimed or disabled. Furthermore, the war demonstrated that the institutions of Massachusetts governance, such as the Congregational clergy and a heavily mythologized militia, could not protect Maine.

The reasons Maine sought statehood can be found in the catalog of miseries the war imposed upon its people. It is a story rooted in the darker side of human nature, with ambitious politicians, sly smugglers, venal officeholders, politicized clergy, semi-piratical privateersmen, and vainglorious militia officers playing outsized roles. The road to statehood was filled with plots and cabals, shouting matches, slanderous editorials, fistfights at town meetings, riots in the streets, and in one case, a dead skunk thrown into a meetinghouse.

Conversely, when statehood finally arrived, it was not acrimonious; it was orderly and consensual, a crowning achievement of what historians call the "era of good feelings." Ironically, Maine's founders immediately discovered that many of the Massachusetts principles they had so heartily disdained during the statehood movement now seemed sensible policy. As the Romans would say, *et sic vadit*.

This project originated while I was at Maine Maritime Academy in Castine in the early 1990s. I became obsessed with understanding the smuggling trade during the War of 1812 but discovered that secondary sources would not suffice. It would take deep archival research to uncover the names and frequently furtive activities of those involved in smuggling, which then demanded an understanding of the complex attitudes to the War of 1812, which led to researching the statehood movement. There were many diversions, dead ends, false leads, and countless revisions until I finally arrived at what I considered a book worthy of retelling the story of Maine's statehood.

Digging deep into primary sources in the United States, Canada, and Great Britain required the assistance of many persons, including some who have not lived to see its completion. Two Navy veterans and maritime historians with a penchant for database creation, Bill Wells and Ira Dye, generously gave me access to their materials even as they struggled with terminal illnesses. The late Danny Vickers persuaded me in the late 1990s to craft a database that proved crucial in pursuing this project. David Harris of Washington, D.C., shared documents from his collection, now deposited in the Clements Library at the University of Michigan.

Many contributors live in the great state of Maine. Larry Glatz was incredibly generous in sharing his meticulous notes and offering numerous editing suggestions. Many Maine librarians and archivists have helped—above all, Nicholas Noyes, Bill Barry, and Jamie Kingman-Rice of the Maine Historical Society, Nathan Lipfert of the Maine Maritime Museum, and Anthony Douin of the Maine State Archives. Local historical societies and individuals provided access to research materials, among them Barbara Rumsey of the Boothbay Historical Society, Tom Parker of the Bucksport Historical Society, Pam Dunning of the Wiscasset Public Library, Rosamond Rea of the Woodlawn Museum in Ellsworth, and Joel Eastman and Ken Thompson, who shared their knowledge of Maine's forts. Some families were kind enough to share records in their possession, such as Ruth McInnis from Eastport and her daughter, Pam Beveridge. Brittany Cathey, a graduate student at the University of Maine, generously shared research materials. Vice-Admiral George Emery, USN (retired), kindly permitted me to cite documents in his manuscript collection. Several people provided moral support, including Joe and Mary Mosier of Stockton Springs and Lincoln and Allison Paine of Portland. Lincoln also reviewed the manuscript and offered valuable suggestions. While he now lives elsewhere, Alan Taylor has been supportive of my research over the years, which has meant a great deal to me. Dawn Potter, also of Portland, was a terrific copy editor at several levels, including her knowledge of inland Maine.

Archivists and historians in Massachusetts were integral to this project. The Massachusetts Historical Society offered financial support in the form of a New England Regional Fellowship Consortium Award in 2010–11. Captain Michael Rutstein, master and owner of the re-created privateer schooner *Fame* of Salem, shared his research materials and even gave me tiller time on his fine craft. Professor Edward T. McCarron of Stonehill College provided information about Maine's early Irish immigrants. Rebecca Beit-Aharon, a graduate student at the University of Massachusetts, Boston, rendered valuable assistance by undertaking to mine the Massachusetts Archives for obscure references.

Librarians, archivists, and researchers throughout North America also assisted me. Paul O'Pecko at Mystic Seaport in Connecticut kindly located manuscripts and other sources. Dr. Shirley Tillotson of Dalhousie University in Nova Scotia and the independent scholar Dr. Faye Kert, also of Canada, shared research materials and kind words, as did Julian Gwyn, formerly of the University of Ottawa. Roger Drummond of the Provincial Archives of New Brunswick generously chased and caught several elusive documents. A special salute is due to some Canadian reenactors: Chris Laverton, Gareth Newfield, Eamonn O'Keeffe, and Ewan Wardle of the Seventh Battalion, Sixtieth (Royal American) Regiment Reenactment Group, who shared their insights about the British military.

The Border Historical Society of Eastport, Maine, deserves special gratitude for supporting the publication of this work. I am honored to be the latest addition to their respected publishing program, which promotes historical and archaeological research in the Passamaquoddy Bay region of Maine and New Brunswick. Among their titles are C. Donald Brown's *Eastport: A Maritime History* (Eastport: Down East Associates, 1968); *Eastport and Passamaquoddy: A Collection of Historical and Biographical Sketches*, compiled by William Henry Kilby (1888; repr., Eastport: Waterfront Research Committee, 1982); David Zimmerman's *Coastal Fort: A History of Fort Sullivan, Maine* (Eastport: Border Historical Society, 1984), and Neill DePaoli's *Beneath the Barracks: Archaeology at Fort Sullivan* (Eastport: Border Historical Society, 1986).

I also thank my wife, Jea, and daughter, Thea, for their patience during a lengthy and occasionally grumpy writing process. As a final aside, I owe debts of gratitude to many not mentioned here. However, any errors are mine alone.

Joshua M. Smith
AMERICAN MERCHANT MARINE MUSEUM
Kings Point, New York

MAKING MAINE

Introduction

Three themes run through this book: the changing relationship between regional and national identities in North America, war's inherent misery, and Maine's statehood movement.

Between 1783 and 1820, Americans struggled to sort out the meaning of the Revolution. Central issues were the conflicting local, regional, and national loyalties that many people now confronted and that drew complex responses from its citizens. The critical question was the relationship between the states and the national government. Were the states sovereign entities that had entered a compact willingly, or were they simply subordinate components of the nation? The question was thorny, and tracing its evolution is not easy. Even future presidents struggled with the problem. For example, in the late 1790s, Thomas Jefferson and James Madison favored state sovereignty. Fearing the arbitrary powers of the national government, Jefferson even devised a method whereby the states could "nullify" federal laws within a state. Notably, both men backtracked on this issue during their presidencies and sought more control over the nation.[1]

During these decades, the federal government was a remote institution that did not influence the daily lives of most Americans. This was true of both Boston sophisticates and Maine's backcountry settlers: all possessed only weak attachments to the nation before 1812. A regional identity prevailed in New England, one that James M. Banner, Jr., calls the "myth of New England exclusiveness." The historian Henry Adams, a great-grandson of President John Adams, believed that most Yankees of the period were uninterested in becoming American in thought or feeling. For his part, John Adams, though ostensibly a nationalist, frequently wallowed in his regional identity, which he thought offered the best example for the nation to emulate. When the rest of the nation refused to recognize Boston's political, moral, and cultural primacy, Massachusetts Federalists were nonplussed; and radicals such as Timothy Pickering retreated into a fantasy world of states' rights and secession. Maine's isolated settlers had an even more blinkered knowledge of the Constitution and the new national government, remaining largely indifferent to the politics of the Commonwealth of Massachusetts and even Maine's early statehood movements.[2]

The Commonwealth's political class had an exalted opinion of the state's importance, even as its political and economic influence waned. Many bitterly contested the policies set forth by Thomas Jefferson and James Madison, in particular those that concerned commercial restrictions and war with Britain. Many of the state's leaders loathed the vision of an expanding egalitarian republic. With the Commonwealth seemingly on a path to irrelevancy, some pondered disunion. The most radical actively promoted a regional identity that rejected the agrarian West and the slave-owning South. Beginning in about 1786, various people plotted a New England confederacy—notably Pickering in 1804. During the War of 1812, Governor Caleb Strong openly questioned whether a nation as vast as the United States could hold together, while the Massachusetts pamphleteer John Lowell, Jr., hoped that the West would secede.[3]

Maine's loyalty shifted in this contest between national and state government from a subservient appendage of the Commonwealth to a region demanding equal status as a state in its own right. Referred to as the District of Maine, it was politically a part of Massachusetts during these years, and familial, cultural, and economic ties bound it to the Commonwealth. Yet as the historian James Leamon has argued, Maine was "a colony, in every sense of the word"; and colonial relationships are complicated, combining elements of reliance and subordination with resentment. Historians have noted Maine's enduring love-hate relationship with Boston. The love portion mainly thrived in coastal towns that looked to Boston for its cultural cues. The hate smoldered in the backcountry, where agrarian settlers struggled to shake off absentee land speculators' economic and political domination. Maine communities protested that old Massachusetts had abandoned them during the Revolution. Between 1785 and 1789, a statehood movement supported by the District's first newspaper briefly flourished but ultimately collapsed due to a lack of popular support. But by the

1790s another statehood movement was brewing, and it began to gather strength in the first decade of the nineteenth century.[4]

The War of 1812 brought the national government and Massachusetts into conflict. The Madison administration and its followers supported the war, while Massachusetts vigorously opposed it. Maine served as a battleground in this political struggle, which devolved into arguments, lawsuits, riots, fistfights, shouting matches, and street theater as various parties attempted to influence friends, families, neighbors, and others to accept or adopt their feelings about the war. The military, including the militia, regulars, volunteer units, privateers, and even the navy, was a part of this disorderly discourse. Maine was home to the Commonwealth's strongest detractors of the war, such as the acid-tongued congressman Cyrus King. Yet while Samuel Eliot Morison has described Maine as "the hottest part of the antiwar bloc in 1813–1814," it also had the war's strongest proponents, such as William King, the elder brother of Cyrus. The misery that this conflict wrought within Maine's communities underscored both Massachusetts's indifference to its eastern counties and the national government's inability to defend the District. The British occupation of eastern Maine tested residents' loyalty to Massachusetts and to the nation, a dialectic that produced a third dynamic: a successful statehood movement. As Ronald Banks has found, the War of 1812 was the catalyst for Maine's statehood, a movement supported by both of the King brothers.

National, regional, and state politics in Maine before, during, and after the War of 1812 were complicated and contradictory. As Donald Graves has noted, there were many wars of 1812 within regional historiography; in other words, the War of 1812 had a different meaning to Maine than it did nationally. Scholars such as Donald Hickey have called for a study of Maine, and this book works to fill that void.[5] The story is not a triumphant one. The war brought enemy invasion and occupation, famine, and high taxation. Commerce came to a standstill, and veterans returned home crippled by wounds, disease, or accidents. Furthermore, its communities remained divided. While many had done their patriotic chore and supported the war, others thought it was unjust and bitterly opposed it. In eastern Maine, there remained the question of responding to those who had collaborated with the enemy. For Mainers, the War of 1812 must have felt something akin to a defeat. Some believed that only statehood would reduce the war's sting. Yet the leaders of the statehood movement were not heroes. Generally, their motivations were public office and personal ambition. Foremost among them was Maine's first governor, William King, a decidedly slippery character whose words should be carefully measured against his actions.

Many of the terms used in this work may confuse a twenty-first-century audience. In general, the term *Canadian* describes the inhabitants of British North America, even though it is ahistorical. Nova Scotians and New Brunswickers had no sense of being Canadian in 1812, but I have followed this convention for simplicity's sake. The term *American* describes U.S. citizens. *Yankee* denotes the English-speaking ethnic group in New England in the early 1800s, generally Protestant and white. *Native American* is used in preference to *Indians* when considering Indigenous peoples, although I use both terms. The same is true of *African American* and *Black*, with the occasional use of *Afro-Yankee*.

Some readers will be confused by the two political parties that dominated American politics. The *Federalists* were the minority party nationally but often held power in Massachusetts. The *Jeffersonians* opposed them but, for the sake of variety, are often referred to as *Republicans*. Maine's political issues often played out in the Massachusetts legislature before 1820. Many referred to the legislature by its ancient title, the *General Court*, or by its Revolutionary title, the *Assembly*. This work uses all three terms. Place names have changed over the course of more than two hundred years. Sometimes the changes have been minor, such as transforming Buckstown to Bucksport or Waldoborough to Waldoboro. Where changes have been more substantial, as with Balltown, which is now the towns of Jefferson and Whitefield, or Herring Gut, which is now Port Clyde, I have explained the change in parentheses. The Commonwealth of Massachusetts is variously referred to as the *Commonwealth* or *old Massachusetts* to distinguish it from its noncontiguous eastern counties, which formed the District of Maine, often referred to as the *District*. Canadian geography can be tricky to the uninitiated. Lower Canada is today known as Quebec Province. New Brunswick is the province to the east of Maine. While many referred to New Brunswick's largest port as *St. Johns* during the War of 1812, I have used the modern spelling, *Saint John*, to avoid confusing it with a similarly named city in Newfoundland.

Chapter 1

"AN EXCEEDINGLY DIRTY AND NASTY PEOPLE"

John Adams was vainglorious about his native Massachusetts, trumpeting it as a superior society that the world should emulate. In his estimation, repeated more than once in his diary and to foreigners and Americans alike, Massachusetts and New England were better than the rest of the nation. Other New England writers, such as the educator Timothy Dwight and the geographer Jedidiah Morse, validated his views. External observers, however, were not always impressed. When George Washington came to Massachusetts in 1775, he described New England's Yankees as "generally speaking the most indifferent kind of people I ever saw . . . an exceedingly dirty and nasty people." Even Loyalists in exile in Nova Scotia found their colleagues from Massachusetts obnoxious, noting their "superior *cunning*" and calling them *"great sticklers for the doctrine of saving grace."* This bumptious sectionalism disgusted Thomas Jefferson, who once grumbled that Massachusetts "would really be great, if she did not think herself the whole."[1]

Adams espoused a Massachusetts ideal that embraced unity and order, and he hardwired these values into the Commonwealth's 1780 constitution. It was arguably the most conservative state constitution of the era, creating a powerful executive with veto powers, a representational system that allowed Boston to dominate the legislature, and a state-supported church. Furthermore, Massachusetts, unlike other states, preserved the colonial capital instead of moving its government to a more central location.[2] Yet the ideals of an orderly and hierarchical state proved largely evasive in its eastern counties—the region known as the District of Maine. Isolated, impoverished, struggling to scrape together a living, few in Maine had the ability or desire to subscribe to the myth of a culturally and politically superior Massachusetts.

THE MASSACHUSETTS IDEAL

The Commonwealth's constitution bolstered a status quo wherein the wealthier and better-educated believed that poorer and less well educated citizens should subordinate themselves to the "natural rulers of society." Adams was typical of the Commonwealth's leading families in combining dedication to tradition and veneration for ancestors with a provincialism that saw Boston as the center of their identity. However, he (and later his son, John Quincy Adams) broke with this blinkered regional view by demonstrating a larger national vision that placed him at odds with other Massachusetts political leaders. The sectionalism of some was fierce. Timothy Pickering, for instance, repeatedly launched schemes in which Massachusetts would break away from the Republic and lead a union of northeastern states and possibly even the Maritime provinces. Little wonder, then, that Henry Adams, a great-grandson of John Adams and a grandson of John Quincy Adams, believed that Bostonians of the early national period were uninterested in becoming American in thought or feeling.[3]

The Commonwealth's constitution ensured that Boston dominated the state's legislature. While every incorporated town could send a representative to the legislature's house of representatives, larger towns could send more based on their population. Maine's small towns frequently could not afford to send a representative, while Boston alone could send almost fifty, although it sent far fewer in practice. The 1780 constitution also diminished Maine's influence, apportioning state senators by assessed property value and thus assuring that the impoverished District was underrepresented. On top of these injustices, the Commonwealth's tax structure discriminated against Maine, charging absentee landowners only one-third the rate that farmers paid. Based on these factors, some in the District argued that statehood would be more equitable and lower taxes.[4]

The Commonwealth became extremely sensitive to the issue of taxes after an uprising known as Shays's Rebellion broke out in its inland communities. The rebellion was triggered when the governor and the General Court raised taxes to address the Commonwealth's debts. In response, farmers in western counties revolted, demanding dramatic revisions to the constitution and calling for the capital to be moved to Worcester. In February 1787, the General Court declared a state of "open, unnatural, unprovoked, and wicked rebellion" and put down the uprising with armed force. While efforts to execute the leaders failed, it is clear that the Massachusetts polity would have shed blood to impose its vision of an orderly society on the Commonwealth.

While Maine's settlers did not revolt, an early push for the District's statehood arose about the same time as Shays's Rebellion. Governor James Bowdoin called the effort "a design against the Commonwealth, of very evil tendency," and the General Court agreed, noting the dangers of dismembering the existing state. In subsequent years, Massachusetts strove to bind Maine to the Commonwealth by incorporating new towns in the District, creating additional counties and courts to protect property rights, and commissioning civil and legal officials who owed their allegiance to Boston. The General Court also frequently suspended or abated taxes to Maine communities and gave some squatters title to their farms while encouraging land proprietors to compromise with backcountry settlers.[5]

Despite the Commonwealth's efforts, Maine's statehood advocates pointed out various injustices and inconveniences that the District's people were suffering; but as late as 1816, the Boston grandee Harrison Gray Otis noted a general indifference to the idea. In general, Boston's political class scoffed at the notion, claiming that Maine did not have enough learned or experienced men to govern a separate state adequately. Among them was John Adams. Though he had known frontier Maine well in his youth, by 1819 he was discouraging the idea of statehood, which, he said, would create a state "below mediocrity in the union." He advised that it remain a part of Massachusetts as long as possible.[6]

The Massachusetts ideal left little room for African Americans, Native Americans, or Maine. Although the Commonwealth banned slavery, its Black residents continued to live in a climate of institutionalized racism, and the state was actively negotiating with its Native peoples to deprive them of their ancestral lands. Massachusetts also looked down on its eastern counties. Separated from the main body of the Commonwealth by a sliver of New Hampshire coast, Maine remained a place apart, a frontier region to exploit for the benefit of Boston-based elites. While many Bostonians speculated in Maine lands, few understood why anyone would want to move there. A correspondent asked George Thatcher, a Maine resident and former congressman, how he could possibly prefer Maine to Boston: "Why do you not leave that region of ignorance, and vice, and Norwegian cold?" A move to Boston would, the writer claimed, give Thatcher access to a better class of people, "yet still you prefer plebians to patricians—Devils to Gods."[7] Maine residents reacted to this disdain by advocating for statehood. By 1806, Orchard Cook of Wiscasset, an early leader in the movement, was asked, "When shall the old State of Maine shake off its degradation of district?" He framed Maine's relationship to Massachusetts in terms of servitude, as a "kind of sub Colony."[8]

"I KNOW IT AIN'T RIGHT"

For nearly forty years after the Revolution, Maine was the Commonwealth's frontier solution for its excess population. Between 1784 and 1810, land-hungry Yankees from southern New England quadrupled the District's white population, swelling it from 56,000 to more than 250,000. Keeping track of this growth could be difficult, as one census worker recalled, recounting the suspicious reactions of a woman and her fisherman husband in York County:

> "Numbering the people!" exclaimed the good woman, "what do you want to number the people for? do you want to bring the judgments of God upon the land? don't you know what David did? I don't believe 'tis right," turning to the old gentleman and raising her voice, "do you father?" "What is it?" said the old man. "Why, here is a man taking the number of the people, and I don't believe 'tis right, do you father?" "Believe," said he, "I don't believe nothing about it; *I know it ain't right.*"

The only unusual aspect of this encounter was the age of the couple. Maine's population was notably young, and these newcomers were impatient to improve their circumstances.[9]

To oversee this restless population, Massachusetts sent forth a host of its better-educated sons to administer the region, impose order, and model deference and respect for property rights. Judges, county clerks, and sheriffs administered the law, including the Harvard-educated Silas Lee. The number of Massachusetts-born lawyers and judges increased in the District as the General Court created new counties. Many served long tenures: for instance, John Cooper, originally of Boston, moved to Machias and served as newly formed Washington County's first sheriff from 1789 until statehood. Yet even as the Commonwealth moved to consolidate its power in the District, its elite looked down on Maine's rustic settlers, despising their poverty, their leveling instincts, and their evangelical religion.[10]

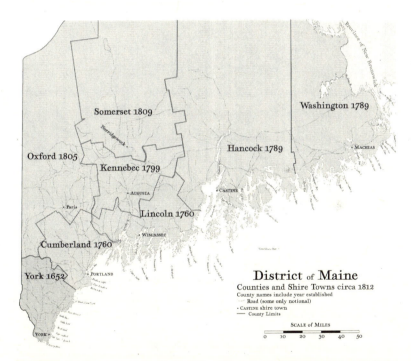

FIGURE 1. Maine comprised the eastern counties of the Commonwealth of Massachusetts. As the District's population grew, the Commonwealth created new counties to administer the region. County courts and jails were located in shire towns, and lawyers and jurists from old Massachusetts dominated the legal system, thus ensuring that the towns were in step with the Massachusetts ideal. Map by the author.

The Massachusetts ideal espoused the importance of religion in an orderly society and wove it into the state's 1780 constitution, which stated that "the happiness of a people, and the good order and preservation of civil government, essentially depend on piety, religion and morality." In Maine, therefore, the Commonwealth not only administered the law but also sought to control the settlers' souls via the Harvard-educated clergy who bullied them from the pulpit. Ministers such as the Reverend Samuel Deane of Portland, who served his parish for almost fifty-five years, promoted the vision of a unified, hierarchic, and godly society. Deane was affable, but some clergymen struck terror into their flock—among them Samuel Eaton of Harpswell. With his old-fashioned hat, wig, and a cane, he was an imposing and frightening figure who struck fear into the hearts of many. Likewise, the polymath parson, Jonathan Fisher of Blue Hill, was known to terrify children. On one occasion, he grabbed a schoolboy by the scruff of the neck and forced him to read aloud from the 139th Psalm: "Whither shall I go from Thy spirit? And whither shall I flee from Thy presence?" By the War of 1812, the generation of Deane, Eaton, and Fisher was growing old, but the pastorate still possessed significant influence.[11]

The militia was another institution binding Maine to Massachusetts. The Commonwealth had a long militia tradition and arguably the nation's best-organized force. For many residents, the militia was a guarantor of freedom. Congressman Elbridge Gerry (a future governor of Massachusetts and vice president during the Madison administration) explained in 1789, "What, sir, is the use of a militia? It is to prevent the establishment of a standing army, the bane of liberty." Gerry, who was a Massachusetts native, warned that "whenever Governments mean to invade the rights and liberties of the people, they always attempt to destroy the militia, in order to raise an army upon their ruins." Such beliefs were reiterated during Independence Day celebrations, when celebrants often expressed the hope that the militia could supplant "the curse of a Standing Army." As late as 1823, the Massachusetts adjutant general proclaimed that "the history of all ages proves that large armies are dangerous to civil liberty. Militia, however large, never can be; for it is composed of citizens only, armed for the preservation of their own privileges."[12]

Militias provided individual states with considerable coercive powers. After quelling Shays's Rebellion, Boston-based elites viewed the militia as a means to impose their sense of order. Military rank and uniforms reminded the masses that they lived in a hierarchical society, and militia service permitted young men to demonstrate their abilities as officers. Furthermore, it was seen as a way to teach "civility and respect for authority" and introduced "habits of subordination in society; . . . [to] impress, upon the younger part of the community a sense of that obedience to the laws, which influences all their conduct in life; and taken in connexion with our schools of education, and our establishments for moral and religious instruction, they make an orderly community."[13]

Militia reality, however, fell far short of the ideal. The heart of the militia was the un-uniformed sixty-four-man infantry company—known in Maine as "stringbeaners." Military exercises seldom started on time and were "then either dismiss'd or march'd thro the dusty streets an hour or two—in the course of which nothing is learn'd & the men retire no wiser than they came, fatigued & disgusted." Men regularly evaded duty or appeared for muster unarmed or with borrowed weapons. Sometimes soldiers launched picaresque protests against their officers or even incited minor mutinies. Non-attendance was rife, for reasons such as lack of time, religious qualms, disapproval of the heavy drinking that accompanied musters, and unpopular officers. The most significant complaint was the expense that militia duty imposed on white male citizens: many could not afford to arm and equip themselves as federal and state law demanded.[14]

On special occasions the Massachusetts judiciary, clergy, and militia came together to impress the people with the Commonwealth's power. The execution of Ebenezer Ball, which took place in the ruins of Fort George at Castine on October 31, 1811, was one such occasion. Perez Morton, the state attorney general, had prosecuted the case, which was presided over by three judges— Samuel Sewall, George Thatcher, and Isaac Parker—all deeply conservative advocates of the Massachusetts ideal. After a jury duly found Ball guilty of murdering a deputy sheriff, Reverend Fisher and other ministers attempted to save his soul. But though Fisher warned Ball of the "danger of falling into Hell," the condemned man replied, "there was no Hell but what was in this world." On the day of Ball's execution, the Hancock County sheriff rode into the old fort's parade ground, followed by a horse and cart carrying the prisoner's unpainted coffin, deputy sheriffs with drawn swords, the prisoner with several ministers, and a company of militia moving in step to a somber death march played by drum and fife. Here was social theater *par excellence*, a demonstration of the authority of the Commonwealth to punish criminals, even in the wilds of its eastern frontier.[15]

"A PEOPLE NATURALLY BAD AND VIOLENT"

Visitors to Maine came away with a general impression of poverty in the wilderness. A French nobleman described the District as being in a "languid and cheerless infancy," while a more charitable Italian nobleman described the settlers' homes as hovels. The French diplomat Charles de Talleyrand-Périgord called the people "ignorant and grasping, poor but without needs," and said that "they resemble too much the natives of the country whom they have replaced." Maine's first mapmaker, Moses Greenleaf, noted that the residents were poorer than their counterparts in old Massachusetts. An observer from the Commonwealth admired the region's forests but said it was not fit for cultivation and reasoned that the farmers tilling its soil should think themselves "curst."[16]

These judgments were harsh but not entirely inaccurate. Maine's Yankee populace was overwhelmingly rural and agrarian. Most people worked on hardscrabble farms that primarily produced Indian corn (maize), with lesser amounts of wheat, barley, and oats, most of which was intended for local consumption. Animal husbandry was common in inland communities such as Fryeburg, Paris, and Farmington. Settlers augmented their livelihoods by making shoes, brooms, shingles, potash, and maple sugar. Men often left home to work in timber camps, shipyards, and sawmills or served on ships engaged in coastal and foreign trade, returning with much-needed cash, store credit, or goods smuggled in sea chests or bed sacks. Women hired themselves out as servants, spun and wove wool or flax, taught children, or practiced midwifery. Maine produced vast amounts of yarn, thread, and textiles woven on an estimated 16,000 home-based looms. Yet it produced less wealth from manufactures than any other state on the eastern seaboard, except for tiny Delaware. Maine had only three cotton-manufacturing establishments, compared to fifty-four in old Massachusetts and twelve in New Hampshire. Except for nails, Maine had even fewer metalworking facilities, just a single ironworks located in Brunswick. Throughout the District there were some two hundred tanneries, two small paper mills, eleven rope walks, and numerous distilleries that produced more than 160,000 gallons of liquor per year, generally rum in port towns and potato whiskey in the backcountry.[17]

Fishermen and timbermen were proverbially poor and rootless, making them questionable exemplars of the Massachusetts ideal. Like the backcountry settlers, fishing families were impoverished and isolated, many of them on islands such as Georgetown, Monhegan, Matinicus, and Deer Isle. Boats primarily operated within sight of land, and most craft were small, under twenty tons. In 1810, Maine ports began to send fishing schooners to the Grand Banks, but more commonly fishermen worked the cod grounds off the southern tip of Nova Scotia or Grand Manan Island. Loggers were a particular problem for the Commonwealth government. They had no respect for landowners, whether they were Native Americans or Boston grandees. Lumbermen took the best mill sites without possessing titles, cut trees wherever they found them, and refused to compensate absentee owners. Timothy Dwight noted their "prodigality, thoughtlessness of future wants, profaneness, irreligion, immoderate drinking, and other ruinous habits" and thought they dissuaded more respectable farmers from emigrating to Maine.[18]

For Commonwealth elites, the squatters were Maine's most repugnant class. Land speculators such as Henry Knox were outraged when they learned that squatters had moved into some of their choicest real estate and were freely making off with its valuable timber. For their part, the squatters resented the proprietors' high land prices and the ability to buy vast swathes to enrich themselves. As Alan Taylor writes in *Liberty Men and Great Proprietors*, the squatters believed that winning the American Revolution had entitled them to cheap or free access to land, and they were willing to defend that idea with force if necessary. Maine's backcountry seethed with anger as agrarian resistance to the land speculators threatened law and order. The courts tried to enforce the speculators' property rights; but sheriffs, deputies, justices of the peace, land agents, and surveyors often found themselves threatened by settlers disguised as so-called "White Indians." The squatters were the antithesis of the Massachusetts ideal; they were, according to one observer, "a people naturally bad and violent." But Massachusetts also feared that the squatters would successfully agitate for statehood and thus break the proprietors' legal grip on the District's frontier lands. Within Maine, the squatters were often seen as admirable, and those opposed to the proprietors began to take up the label *squatter* as a badge of honor. Soon many people in old Massachusetts began to think of all Maine residents as squatters or squatter sympathizers.[19]

The evangelical Christianity that thrived among Maine's settlers and squatters was a further rejection of the Massachusetts ideal. By the 1780s, proselytizers such as Henry Alline were crossing from Nova Scotia into Maine, spreading a radical gospel that rejected temporal authority, including formally trained ministers, in favor of a populist and intensely personal theology. Maine's settlers recognized that Alline's life experiences mirrored their own, and many joined him in castigating establishment ministers as anti-Christian hirelings and rejecting entrenched notions of hierarchy, inequality, devotion to kinship, patriarchy, and patronage. Most astonishingly, the evangelicals rejected the most revered institution in Massachusetts: Harvard College. The divide was deep. Older religious groups viewed the evangelicals as apostates, while dissenters dismissed Congregational hegemony and deference in favor of religious pluralism and social leveling. Evangelicals even welcomed Black members as equals; in fact, a Black woman, Sarah Peters, was a founding member of her Baptist congregation in Warren, which had a substantial African American population.[20]

Mainers who did not adhere to Massachusetts's religious orthodoxy faced insults, discrimination, and occasional violence. George Thatcher derided evangelical meetings as "Bedlam," and Bowdoin College's president sneered that Methodist circuit riders were "illiterate vagabonds." John Neal of Portland recounted that other boys mocked and beat him on account of his Quaker clothes. When a Methodist attempted to preach at Castine's meetinghouse, a crowd armed with clubs gathered outside and drummed on tin pots to drown out his sermon. The preacher beat a hasty retreat out of town, lest the mob tar and feather him. The Massachusetts ideal reserved its most vehement reactions for Roman Catholics. The number of Catholics in the District was tiny, perhaps 2,500 compared to a quarter-million Yankees in 1810, but Maine had three out of the four Roman Catholic churches in New England. Advocating for Catholic rights, the Irish immigrant merchants James Kavanagh and Matthew Cottrill, along with the priests Francis Matignon and John Cheverus, filed to reclaim taxes that were supporting Newcastle's Congregational minister. The Massachusetts Supreme Court ruled against them, finding that only Protestant dissenters could claim a ministerial tax share. The judge opined that "Papists are only tolerated, and as long as their Ministers behave well, we shall not disturb them. But let them expect no more than that."[21]

Despite the sneers of the orthodox, evangelical preachers connected more effectively with backcountry settlers than their Congregationalist counterparts did. Often ill trained but always enthusiastic, they engaged closely with the lay population. One was the jovial Abraham Cummings, who traveled the Maine coast in a small boat; his published accounts of a ghost in Sullivan and a sea serpent in Penobscot Bay undoubtedly increased his popularity. Cummings was a rarity in that he had a college degree. Most evangelical preachers had little formal education, relying on emotional sermons that spoke to the spirit rather than parsing Scripture. To accommodate crowds, they often held open-air meetings, as one preacher did in 1805, a memorable gathering attended by seven hundred people in a "beautiful orchard by the sea," perhaps in the town of Old Orchard Beach. After the sermon, the group moved to a glassy cove, where the preacher baptized ten people by complete immersion, the scene illuminated by lanterns reflecting on the water.[22]

The Massachusetts ideal presupposed a social hierarchy with a complex web of social obligations among members of a natural aristocracy and ordinary people. Thus, the Commonwealth elite was irked by the leveling spirit prevalent in Maine, wherein "the President and the chimney-sweep are both on a level; the captain and the foremast hand are here upon perfect equality." In practice, this often meant that Maine's settlers refused to recognize the title deeds held by absentee proprietors. Old Massachusetts struggled mightily to tame the District's settlers and their leveling ways. Elitists such as David Cobb, who was a land agent and vigorous proponent of the Massachusetts ideal, flung the term *Yankee* as a pejorative as he decried the settlers' propensity for logging lands they did not own. He had many choice words for them, including "plunderers," "Yahoos," and "log stealers," and he criticized their hard-drinking ways.[23]

Cobb's outspoken politics verged on reactionary. During Shays's Rebellion, he had threatened to use militia artillery to clear crowds of protestors in old Massachusetts. "Away with your whining," he had growled as the crowd retreated. Intensely loyal to the Boston status quo and the Congregational orthodoxy, he opposed Maine statehood in the legislature, fearing that it would infringe on the property rights of the landed proprietors. In his milder moments, he noted that Maine's settlers would need time to become habituated to civil order. More typically, however, he bullied the squatters into compliance by prosecuting "every trespasser on these lands, that I can git my hold on." Cobb traversed the pioneer settlements east of the Penobscot River, preaching to the inhabitants that they must embrace and respect property rights, but to little avail. He tried to recruit settlers from southern New England, who would presumably import their appreciation of order and deference, but his efforts failed.[24]

Cobb's influential sons-in-law stood by him in defending land speculators' property rights. One of them, Judge Samuel S.

Wilde of Hallowell, noted, "There is a spirit in the people of Maine hostile to all correct notions respecting title to lands. To flatter this spirit would be the business of unprincipled and ambitious men." Like Cobb, he feared statehood would expose proprietors to physical violence and loss of their lands. Another son-in-law, John Black, was an Englishman who had come to Ellsworth to assist Cobb in overseeing the 2 million acres owned by William Bingham and later bought by Baring Brothers of London. After marrying Cobb's daughter, he rose in local politics and in 1805 received a commission in the Massachusetts militia, though he did not become a naturalized citizen until 1810.[25]

"BLACK SAL AND JEFFERSON"

The Massachusetts ideal was an offshoot of Federalism, a mode of political organization emphasizing order, stable commerce (especially with Britain), and social hierarchies. Like Alexander Hamilton, a leading proponent of Federalism, the Massachusetts polity decried the excesses of the French Revolution, believing that the masses lacked the requisite virtue to govern and suggesting that Jefferson and Madison were "servilely devoted" to France. Their conservative view prized harmony, unity, and order, yet even Hamilton thought that New England's Federalists were too "clannish." Some, such as the Massachusetts governor, Caleb Strong, had supported the Revolution that had swept away the colonial elite yet after independence espoused stability and order to secure their own places in society. Their goal was not to reinvent or improve upon that society but to exercise stewardship as a way to prevent the world from worsening. Disorder and tumult were anathema. In Maine, Congregationalist ministers such as Abraham Cummings of North Yarmouth preached that liberty and equality were false doctrines that led to anarchy and insurrection; Judge George Thatcher of Biddeford voiced a deep suspicion of mobs and demagogues; and Judge David Sewall of York summed up New England conservatism in his comment "one Revolution in an Age is quite Sufficient."[26]

Alden Bradford of Wiscasset encapsulates the complex strands of Federalism and how Massachusetts attempted to shape the Maine frontier into a simulacrum of itself. Like many officeholders in the District, he came from old Massachusetts, a proud descendent of the Pilgrims. Bradford was a graduate of Harvard College and an early member of the Massachusetts Historical Society. He served as Wiscasset's Congregational minister before resigning from his pulpit and becoming clerk of Lincoln County's courts. An accomplished public speaker, Bradford laid out his values in an Independence Day speech in 1804, cautioning his listeners against the excesses of liberty, which he claimed always led to licentiousness and anarchy. His illustration was the French Revolution, in which demagogues perpetuated bloody misdeeds in the name of liberty and equality. Bradford warned that "new-fashioned republicans" were threatening American liberty, "artful men" who were misleading the citizenry into questioning the wisdom of their betters. He urged his audience to depend instead on enlightened and virtuous characters such as Governor Strong, who could "discern the best means of promoting the interests of the nation; and who possess patriotism and fortitude." In Bradford's view, to preserve true freedom, Americans must embrace morality and religion and inculcate in the young the "necessity of subordination and obedience to their superiors."[27]

Massachusetts Federalists were not a monolithic bloc, but if they agreed on anything, it was on their loathing of Jefferson, whom they disparaged in the press, from the pulpit, and in speeches. Jefferson's advocacy of "leveling principles," his slave owning, his ill-disguised sexual relationship with the slave Sally Hemmings, his dismissal of formal religion, his relentless support of westward expansion: virtually everything he did or thought offended them. Those who opposed the Massachusetts ideal began labeling themselves *Jeffersonians* or *Republicans*; and to the dismay of old Massachusetts, Maine became the foremost Republican region in New England. The District's ambitious newcomers, religious dissenters, and landless farmers dedicated themselves to eroding Federalists officeholders' lock on the Commonwealth's polity. They did so by expanding the franchise, tapping into groups that had not previously voted, such as squatters and religious nonconformists, and by challenging Federalist control of the militia. In the process, they displaced Federalists such as Stephen Longfellow, a Portland attorney and father of the poet Henry Wadsworth Longfellow, as the leaders in Maine's statehood movement.[28]

The competition between Federalists and Republicans was bruising. Partisan newspaper editors engaged in shameless hyperbole during election seasons. Federalists decried their opponents as Jacobins, while Republicans tarred the Federalists as aristocrats. Both encouraged voter turnout, and both worked to evade the property qualifications required for voting, finagling even poor sailors and Afro-Yankees into casting ballots. However, the Republicans were more successful in expanding access to the polls, especially in Maine's impoverished interior communities. Their newspapers exhorted voters to "Turn out!"; they organized committees that urged "no man [to] remain at home on the day of the election who will give a republican vote." Republican runners traveled into communities to speak directly to the District's inhabitants, distribute flyers, and, as the Federalists angrily surmised, smear Federalist candidates. A letter to a Republican runner in Lincoln County instructed him to introduce himself to "every man, woman, or child that can in anyways help you." The runner was told to praise an unnamed candidate (probably William King), dismiss any accusations against him, persuade women of the candidate's Christian virtue, and talk to them "soft and pretty." He should speak to men about the candidate's capabilities and experience and emphasize his military ardor. The approach was effective, as the Federalists quickly recognized, and they adopted it for their own campaigns. In 1812, the District's Republican newspapers claimed that thirty or forty Federalist runners were operating in Maine seaports and in inland communities such as Cornish and Otisfield.[29]

Maine's Republicans grew in power and influence after 1801, in part because of Jefferson's election to the presidency in 1800. His administration installed Henry Dearborn of Pittston as secretary of war, a move that encouraged Republicanism in the District. Dearborn eschewed New England provincialism and embraced nationalism, even pulling his son from Williams College in Massachusetts and sending him to the College of William and Mary in Virginia. His apostasy annoyed Federalists such as Judge Samuel S. Wilde, who feared Dearborn would someday become governor of an independent Maine and thereby "make every honest man sick." As Jefferson's point man in the District, Dearborn ousted some Federalists from office, neutralized others, and installed his kin and political allies in their stead. The Federalist press mocked him for putting his sons-in-law into government positions, but Dearborn cared not.[30]

As secretary of war, Dearborn led Jefferson's "chaste reformation" of the military, which meant removing Federalist army officers or otherwise cowing them into submission. Among those officers was Amos Stoddard, an outspoken Federalist who commanded Fort Sumner in Portland. Stoddard remained in the service, almost certainly because Dearborn spoke up for him. However, there was a price: the secretary reassigned him to the remote banks of the Mississippi, far from New England. Dearborn also curtailed military contracts held by Federalists such as Henry Knox, whom he disliked. The Adams administration had favored Knox, giving him contracts linked to fort construction in Newport, Rhode Island, and purchasing lime for the project from Knox's estate in Thomaston, Maine. Dearborn, however, suspended construction after learning it was doing more to enrich his rival than to defend the port.[31]

Dearborn played a role in removing or muting Federalist customs collectors in Maine's port towns. He oversaw a similar transition in the District's post offices, installing his protégés as postmasters in Monmouth and Fryeburg. While such positions were not lucrative, they did control access to information. Politically partisan postmasters abused their office, sometimes curtailing delivery of opponents' newspapers. Bangor's Jeffersonian postmaster was even wont to read private letters for political content. The installation of Republican postmasters in Federalist communities could lead to considerable rancor, as in North Yarmouth, where unknown parties in 1806 vandalized the postmaster's docked sloop, slashing its lines and painting "Black Sal and Jefferson" on its hull. Then they painted over the post office's sign. The harassment continued:

in 1809, a brick thrown through a window wounded the postmaster's daughter. He offered a $500 reward for information about the perpetrators, but no one came forward.[32]

Dearborn was less effective at taming the District's federal courts, in part because virtually the entire legal community was composed of Federalists. Dearborn had served as the District's first U.S. marshal, and he was aware that Maine's single federal judge had repeatedly used the bench to bully Republican newspaper editors and sway voters. Furthermore, he was loath to tangle with the federal court's clerk, Henry Sewall, who had succeeded Dearborn as commander of the Eighth Militia Division. So the secretary and other Republicans conceived a more subtle approach to changing the balance of power: they invited the Federalist congressman Silas Lee of Wiscasset to serve as Maine's U.S. district attorney. Lee took the bait and resigned his seat to assume this lucrative post. This was not the only political office shuffle. In 1803, Jefferson allowed Maine's U.S. marshal, Isaac Parker, to complete his term in office before replacing him with Dr. Thomas G. Thornton. Thornton happened to be the brother-in-law of a Saco Republican, Richard Cutts, who had been elected to Congress during the first Jefferson administration. While in Washington, Cutts had wooed and married the sister-in-law of James Madison, then serving as secretary of state. The Madison and Cutts families lived under the same roof, a connection that gave Cutts extraordinary powers of patronage, especially after Madison became president. Predictably, the Federalists complained that Cutts, in becoming so entwined with the Jeffersonians, had forgotten his attachment to New England.[33]

As Dearborn and Cutts became more involved with Washington politics, William King of Bath rose to political prominence by tapping into the votes of the District's squatters. King was a complex and ambitious man. Noting his desire to become governor, one observer called him the settlers' "chief cook and bottle washer." In 1805 King challenged the great land proprietors in the General Assembly, pointing out that these speculators were not fulfilling the terms of their contracts, which required them to settle a stipulated number of people. The 2 million acres in Maine's interior, the so-called Bingham Purchase, formerly controlled by William Bingham but now owned by the London firm Baring Brothers, were particularly vulnerable because the owner's primary agent, David Cobb, had failed to bring in the required number of settlers. Boston Federalists resented King's machinations, which they regarded as an infringement on their property rights. King, however, signaled to Cobb his willingness to be bought off, and the speculators quietly transferred three entire townships to him for pennies an acre.[34]

In 1807 King fared better in pushing for land reform. The time for change seemed ripe as settlers had become increasingly violent toward surveyors and others employed by the speculators. In addition, Massachusetts had just elected its first Republican governor, the Maine-born James Sullivan, who had displaced the Federalist Caleb Strong thanks in no small part to the District's votes. With King's assistance, petitions and grievances flooded into the legislature, demanding that the state find a means to resolve the differences between landed proprietors and agrarian squatters in backcountry Maine. Armed with these complaints, King introduced the Betterment Act of 1808, which provided a legal mechanism whereby the proprietors had to compensate squatters for any improvements made on the land. If a squatter chose to purchase, a jury would determine the selling price. But neither the proprietors nor the settlers were satisfied with this solution, so King and his allies engineered an improved Betterment Act in 1810, which extended the time limit for squatters who were applying for an adjustment of the value of their improvements such as fences, wells, barns, and homes. The act was still imperfect, but the state had finally taken tentative steps toward placating the squatters.[35]

King also tapped into the militia to promote his political ambitions. Federalists and Republicans had long contested control of Maine's militia units; yet given the Federalist passion for order, it is surprising how many incidents involved cabals of junior officers combining to oust their superiors. Units in Hancock County were especially fractious, with the division's commander admitting that Federalist officers "put me to all the trouble they can."

Republican officers sometimes brought these troubles on themselves. For instance, after a Federalist was elected to company command, Colonel Jeremiah Wardwell of Penobscot responded, "damn him he is a Fed, shoot him." Subordinate officers pressed charges in a court-martial that stripped Wardwell of his commission. In another case, a Federalist captain felt that his Republican superior had unjustly denied him a promotion. The captain marched his company, drums rolling and fifes squealing, around the rest of the regiment, muttering contemptuously throughout the incident. A court-martial stacked with Federalists let the officer off with a reprimand, and Major General Henry Sewall blandly noted that he hoped the captain had acted by mistake.[36]

Republicans reciprocated by targeting Sewall, who commanded the Eighth Militia Division in Kennebec and Lincoln counties. Fond of military pomp, Sewall wore his militia uniform to Sunday church services and other public events. He was a dedicated Federalist, orthodox in his religious beliefs and rigid in his social views. He was also a martinet whose actions drew the ire of his stringbeaners, as at a muster in Nobleborough in September 1806. Sewall asked his commissioned officers to dine with him while the rank and file remained on duty under their noncommissioned officers. Many stringbeaners, especially those from Republican communities such as Balltown and Bristol, resented these kinds of class distinctions, While the bulk of the officers ate with Sewall, three companies led by their officers marched off the muster field in protest. Sewall sent mounted officers in pursuit, but some unruly stringbeaners threatened to shoot them while others drew their swords and pricked the officers' horses. A court-martial stripped the mutinous officers of their commissions, but Sewall did not emerge unscathed. Governor Sullivan carved a new militia division out of Sewall's in early 1807 and engineered the selection of William King as the division's commander. Federalists expressed outrage; King had no military background whatsoever, and they dubbed him the "Military Rocket" for his rapid rise. Sewall deeply resented the new division and its commander: he and King would remain implacable enemies.[37]

TUMULTS AND ARMED FORCE

Between 1807 and 1810, widespread unrest afflicted the backcountry squatters and port communities. As seaside communities protested Jefferson's embargo along the coast, the protests among inland squatters came to a head. In both instances, two questions arose: what were the limitations of the government's armed coercion of the populace, and who controlled the militia?

In June 1807, a British warship fired into the American frigate *Chesapeake*, nearly precipitating a war between Britain and the United States. President Jefferson responded by ordering British warships out of American waters and calling for 100,000 "minutemen." The Augusta Light Infantry was one of the units that stepped forward, with Henry Sewall declaring them "well appointed, armed, equipped, disciplined, uniformed & ready for service." However, Jefferson moved cautiously, hoping to avoid war. Reluctantly, Congress authorized fortifications for most of the nation's ports. Secretary of War Dearborn proposed numerous Maine fortifications, channeling the contracts to his son, who oversaw the construction of Forts Preble and Scammel in Portland Harbor, and to a son-in-law, who built a battery at the mouth of the Kennebec River. Congress also expanded the army, and Dearborn headed the new regiments exclusively with Republican officers.[38]

As an alternative to war, Jefferson asked Congress to legislate an embargo on all foreign maritime trade. Because Maine's port communities relied on timber exports to the West Indies and Britain, this embargo was hard on the District. Even large towns such as Portland faced an economic crisis as credit networks collapsed, while commerce in the settlements east of the Penobscot were paralyzed and the communities driven to famine. Predictably, sailors and merchants bridled against the commercial restrictions. As the embargo dragged on, they increasingly broke the law by smuggling goods out of their harbors, especially in easternmost Maine. The situation deteriorated so severely that Jefferson sent army and naval units to the District, invoking the Insurrection

Act of 1807, which empowered him to use the military to quell domestic unrest. On January 1, 1808, Dearborn ordered the army to assist civil authorities in enforcing the commercial restrictions, and in April the navy authorized commanders to stop vessels. As the historian Leonard Levy writes, Jefferson's embargo avoided a foreign war by waging a domestic one.[39]

The embargo was a quandary for Massachusetts Republicans. Many publicly supported the measure but privately had reservations. The foremost example was Governor Sullivan, who paid lip service to the wisdom of the restrictive measure even as he undermined it by issuing permits to carry cargoes of flour and other provisions to eastern Maine. Smugglers landed thousands of barrels of flour at previously sleepy ports such as Eastport before surreptitiously taking it aboard British ships. The legal community split on the issue in surprising ways: sometimes Jeffersonian attorneys challenged the embargo as unconstitutional, while a Federalist judge ruled it legal. The Republican Massachusetts district attorney was lax in enforcing the embargo, whereas Maine's Federalist district attorney earned praise from Washington for his efforts. Maine's sole federal district judge, David Sewall of York, was a firm Federalist but nonetheless instructed juries that the embargo was legal. In both Maine and Massachusetts, juries frequently favored embargo breakers.[40]

At first the situation in Portland remained quiet, so much so that the navy refused to activate any of the gunboats laid up in Clay Cove. Lieutenant Charles Morris confessed he spent most of his time at the naval station "dozing or sleeping the whole day." But things took a serious turn in July 1808, when four vessels escaped from the harbor bound for the West Indies. In October there was a rash of violence: smugglers overwhelmed a customhouse boat crew; and a mob took over a Portland pier, loaded two ships, and sailed for parts unknown. In another incident, men with blackened faces snatched an informant from his bed, stripped him naked, smeared him with tar and feathers, and lashed him to the deck of a ship at Union Wharf. Alarmed, the Navy activated a single gunboat, *No. 79*. It was a fast sailor, its cannon was a massive thirty-two-pounder, and the armed crew was supplemented with soldiers from

Fort Preble. Locals no doubt took note. Sleepy Lieutenant Morris, who commanded the gunboat, proved to be firm but diplomatic in enforcing the embargo.[41]

In Penobscot Bay, smugglers murdered a customs guard on Isle au Haut, and a mob released the suspects from Castine's jail. The customs officers begged the navy to send a ship: "The lives of those employed by the Collector are now in imminent danger as they are fired upon—by english vessels." However, the Federal government did not possess the coercive power to enforce the embargo, and Portland's garrison feared that mobs of angry citizens would descend on it. Fort Preble's soldiers disliked enforcing the embargo, and many deserted. One went a step further while on leave in Freeport. After his neighbors filled him with "frightful stories" about having to fight his friends and countrymen, he contrived to be dismissed from the army by slicing off part of his hand.[42]

Congress responded to resistance with the draconian Second Enforcement Act, passed in January 1809. This law authorized customs collectors to call out militia units without going through a judge, a governor, or an adjutant general. Jefferson realized that this provision could lead to trouble, so he asked each governor to "appoint some officer of the militia, of known respect for the laws," to support the customs collectors. Had Sullivan still been governor of Massachusetts, his response to these instructions probably would have excited little criticism, but Sullivan had died while still in office, on December 10, 1808. His successor, Levi Lincoln, was a far more doctrinaire Republican who immediately complied with Jefferson's request. The Massachusetts House of Representatives took Lincoln to task, complaining that he had written directly to officers who shared his Republican views rather than transmitting his orders through the adjutant general. The legislature condemned them as "irregular, illegal, and inconsistent with the principles of the constitution . . . subversive of the militia system, and highly dangerous to the liberties of the people." As an added insult, the legislature mimicked Jefferson's own words in the Virginia and Kentucky resolutions of 1798, calling the embargo's provisions "unjust, oppressive, and unconstitutional and not legally binding on the citizens of this state." Massachusetts Federalists, led by Timothy Pickering, began to discuss disunion again. For his part, Jefferson, with the concept of nullification thrown in his face, believed that Massachusetts's opposition "amounted almost to treason and rebellion."[43]

Some misgivings about the militia's use were less abstract: William King found himself calling out troops to enforce an embargo that was beggaring himself and his constituents. The stringbeaners were not eager to perform this duty; Henry Sewall reported, "some of the men say they will not go if it is to support the Embargo." When militia units turned out, they proved to be miserably equipped; and when they attempted to enforce the embargo, they often faced legal proceedings in local courts. For example, in February 1809, a militia captain and six privates accompanied by a customs officer boarded the brig *Betsey* in York harbor. The vessel's owner verbally abused them and threatened to raise a mob to rescue the ship. The militiamen doggedly held on but two days later were dragged before a local justice, who declared both the embargo and the militiamen's actions illegal. The Federalist press did its best to discourage militiamen from turning out. One article asked, "Can you quit your social, happy firesides, your wives, your smiling infants, to point the bayonet and level the musket at the breasts of your fellow beings?" At town meeting, the citizens of Belfast, Maine, resolved that any militiaman who supported the embargo was an enemy "to the constitution and to the liberties of his country, and ought to be treated as such." They declared that using the militia to enforce the law was one of "the most preposterous, oppressive, and despotic acts that ever disgraced a civilized nation."[44]

Republicans found themselves caught between economic cataclysm and their loyalty to the Jefferson administration, and their support for the embargo waned. King estimated that it was costing him $5,558 every month, and Richard Cutts claimed that he had lost $28,000 in its first year. In vain, Congressman Orchard Cook pleaded to King and others that the embargo must continue, urging them to rise above parochial business interests: "the Dis't. of Maine has interests different from the other parts of the U.S.— admit it—can you expect that all other parts can, or ought to yield to the Dis't. of Main[?]" But even as Cook admonished King to "look to the whole," King was pressuring Cook to vote to repeal the embargo and even threatened to turn Federalist. Publicly, however, King continued to supported it, as his remarks in meetings in Bath and the legislature attest.[45]

On Jefferson's last day in office, Congress repealed the embargo. Townspeople in Wiscasset and other ports held raucous celebrations:

> This town is in an *uproar* "the Embargo is off" is all the cry; the President's proclamation was received this evening—every man, woman, boy, girl, horse, dog, cat, pig, hen, duck, and all living things are rejoicing, huzza'ing guns firing Bells ringing flags flying not a Wiscasset but what is merry—you cannot imagine anything more noisy than this town—I expect that by 1 o'clock everything that can swallow, will be *how fairs ye jolly boys.*

The end of the embargo had ramifications beyond epic hangovers. The Commonwealth's Federalists reaped a political harvest in April 1809. While Maine counties remained Republican, the Federalist candidate, Christopher Gore, swept into office as governor, with David Cobb as lieutenant governor.[46]

During these same years, long-simmering debates about using the militia against the inland squatters came to the fore. The militia units that had refused to enforce the embargo turned out to defend their communities against the largely imaginary threat posed by the squatters. In January 1808, the sheriff of Kennebec County asked Henry Sewall to call out four hundred militia in Augusta in response to squatters' assaults on his deputies. However, Governor Sullivan dismissed the militia detachment and removed the sheriff from office. Less than a year later, a suspicious fire broke out in Augusta and reduced the county jail to ashes, and Sewall again called out the militia. The first unit he called upon was the Augusta Light Infantry, composed of young Federalists who could be counted on to protect their families' property and wealth. This was class warfare: the armed and uniformed sons of privilege, marching under a silk banner proclaiming "Victory or Death," opposed ragged backcountry squatters disguised as Indians.

The rural settlers wisely refused to offer battle; but in September, rumors of an attack to free squatters from jail again transformed Augusta into an armed camp. Three hundred militia remained on duty for several weeks at an expense to the Commonwealth of more than $11,000.[47]

Given these disorders in Maine, the Federalist-controlled legislature passed a law in early 1810 that permitted judges to call out the militia without applying to the governor or adjutant general. The law mimicked the enforcement acts of the embargo in that the justice could pick the officer of his choice. A few months later, Judge George Thatcher ordered five hundred men from William King's Eleventh Division to protect surveyors in Bristol. He chose Colonel Samuel Thatcher (no relation), a reliable Federalist, a son-in-law of the late Henry Knox, and King's political opponent. Samuel Thatcher was a well-known adversary of the squatters, who had once left an open coffin on his doorstep as a warning. On the day appointed for the militia to gather, the men deserted en masse. Judge Thatcher defended his decision in a letter to the Republican governor Elbridge Gerry; and while Republicans called for the judge's removal, the motion died in the Federalist-controlled state senate. Predictably, the now Republican-controlled legislature soon repealed the obnoxious elements of the law, and no stringbeaners faced prosecution.[48]

THE GERRYMANDER DOWNEAST

Abigail Adams knew and liked Elbridge Gerry, but she also pitied him, noting he "always had a wrong kink in his head." Highly intelligent, he had signed the Declaration of Independence and participated in creating the Constitution. At the same time, he was capricious, contrary, and deeply suspicious of military power, to the point of paranoia. In 1810 he won the Massachusetts governor's seat on a platform of restraint and nonpartisanship, sweeping every county in Maine except for Washington. In Gerry's first year in office he worked with the Republican lower house of the legislature on some modest reforms, while the Federalist state senate kept Republican measures in check.[49]

In 1801 there were 258 legislators in the lower chamber. This was a sizable representative body, but for reasons of distance and cost only 30 percent of the members regularly attended sessions. Federalists liked this situation because it allowed Boston and its environs to dominate the General Court. But Gerry and the Republicans took measures to increase the number of representatives. In 1810 the number grew to 650 as the legislature incorporated plantations into towns, and by 1812 the chamber had 749 members. Many of these new representatives came from Maine, which became home to 26 percent of the legislators. Previously, many of the District's impoverished communities could not afford to send their members to Boston for sessions. But in 1811, Republicans had passed a law to address this problem, requiring the Commonwealth, not the towns, to pay representatives' expenses. This move cemented their majority, and attendance at sessions reached a startling 85 percent. Residents of old Massachusetts resented this influx of Maine representatives; one Boston newspaper scoffed, "The shoals of Representatives that pour out of the District of Maine are just fit to rob hen roosts." This hauteur did nothing to endear the Commonwealth to Maine's growing populace.[50]

Gerry easily won reelection in 1811, carrying every county in Maine except for Washington again. But even though his margin of victory was wide, the acrimonious campaign left him "bristling with anger at the Federalists." Encouraged by Jefferson via Henry Dearborn, Gerry abandoned his attempt at moderation and became extraordinarily partisan in cooperation with the legislature, both of whose houses were now Republican. The majority ran roughshod over the Federalists, whom Gerry accused of being "out-and-out monarchists." Federalists such as former lieutenant governor David Cobb of Gouldsborough reciprocated the vitriol, referring to the Gerry administration as "harpees & cutthroats."[51]

One of the most significant reforms under Gerry's watch was a law sponsored by King and other Republicans who were allied with religious dissenters. Religion had become increasingly politicized as the Congregational establishment pushed back against the rising numbers of new religious groups, and Maine was a center of this battle. In a conversation with the Baptist minister Daniel Merrill, the orthodox Cobb opined that those who disobeyed the Commonwealth's religious laws should be burned like any other rebels against the state. Republicans made hay of Cobb's hasty words and in 1811 scored a significant legislative victory. Known as the Toleration Act in Maine and as the Religious Freedom Act in old Massachusetts, the new law undermined previous laws that had recognized religious dissent only after the General Court had incorporated petitioning groups as separate religious societies. Once officially recognized, the group would qualify for tax relief. However, there was no guarantee that the General Court would approve such petitions; for instance, in 1810 it turned down a group of twenty-eight men who were seeking incorporation as the "First Baptist Society in Machias." Without recognition, the law compelled these Baptists to continue to financially support their community's Congregational minister.[52]

This religious discrimination worsened when the state judiciary rolled back recognition in the 1810 case of *Barnes v. Falmouth*. The case involved the ability of a deceased man's estate to donate to an unincorporated or "voluntary church," in this case the Unitarian congregation in Falmouth, Maine. The trial commenced in Maine's Cumberland County courts but wound its way through the system to Theophilus Parsons, the Federalist chief justice of the Massachusetts Supreme Court and a staunch defender of the status quo. Parsons mocked the idea of voluntary churches, calling the idea "too absurd to be admitted." The Commonwealth, he said, supported churches as way to secure "all the social and civil obligations of man to man, and of citizen to the state." Parson reasoned that an individual had no more right to be exempt from supporting a church he did not attend than to be exempt from school taxes because he was childless. Parsons refused to allow the Falmouth Universalist church to accept the donation because it had no legal standing. This was the last victory for the Commonwealth's religious establishment. Parsons's reactionary approach galvanized Republicans, who pushed back with legislation that permitted dissenters to opt out of ministerial taxes. Notably,

Maine's delegation to the General Court favored the Toleration Act by a margin of four to one.⁵³

More notoriously, Massachusetts Republicans redrew senatorial districts in a way that guaranteed electoral victory. While Gerry had little to do with the redistricting, Federalists termed the practice *gerrymandering*, and the label stuck. Furthermore, Gerry deviated from past practice by sweeping Federalists from office. Jefferson confided in Dearborn that he approved of the "rasping" that Gerry had given to the Federalists, whom he described as a "herd of traitors." Among those removed from office was Wiscasset's senior selectman, Alden Bradford. In that position, he had been at the heart of a squabble over voting lists, with Republicans accusing him of altering them illegally in favor of the Federalists. After Gerry dismissed him as Lincoln County's clerk of the court, Bradford published a lengthy protest in the Boston newspapers, expressing shock and outrage that party loyalty had led to his dismissal. He also accurately predicted that Gerry's partisanship would cost him the governor's seat in the 1812 election.⁵⁴

Gerry also instigated a militia version of gerrymandering that created six new divisions within the Commonwealth, ostensibly because of the growing population but really to break Federalist control. Two of the new divisions were in Maine, and a look at one of them, the proposed Seventeenth Division, reveals their politicized nature. The Republicans carved the Seventeenth from Henry Sewall's Eighth Division as a way to humiliate him and deprive him of prestige and patronage. The new division included virtually all of the artillery, cavalry, and uniformed companies on the west bank of the Kennebec River, leaving Sewall with the stringbeaner companies on the east side—home of the troublesome squatters who hated him. According to one observer, Sewall was left "the name without the substance" of command. The Seventeenth's new commander was John Chandler, an ally of King and a protégé of Dearborn. Gerry bragged about the new divisions in a letter to President Madison: "When I came into office there were seven federal[ists] of eleven Major Generals, & now there are but six of seventeen; being the number of existing militia divisions. The increase I effected as an indispensable measure."⁵⁵

"AN EXCEEDINGLY DIRTY AND NASTY PEOPLE"   35

To the surprise of Richard Cutts and other Republicans, Gerry lost the April 1812 gubernatorial election in a contest that saw extraordinary turnout from an unprecedented 68 percent of eligible voters. Maine's Republicans failed to deliver: only Portland-dominated Cumberland County voted Federalist, but turnout in the other counties could not overcome Federalist sentiment in old Massachusetts. The election went to the Federalist candidate Caleb Strong, who had previously served as governor from 1800 to 1807. Why did Gerry lose? Alden Bradford said it was because he had accused Federalists of being monarchists. The historian James M. Banner, Jr., has since posited that the Toleration Act drove a wedge between Republicans and Congregationalists. Accusations of gerrymandering, his attempts to prosecute critical newspaper editors, and his dismissal of Federalist officeholders were contributing

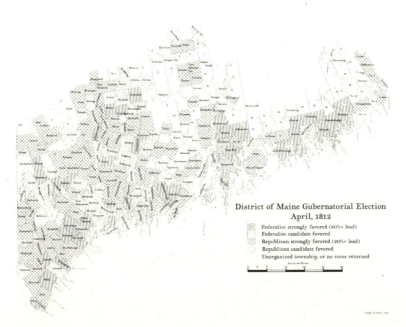

FIGURE 2. A study of the gubernatorial election of 1812 reveals Maine's overall voting patterns before statehood. Shire towns and seaports generally voted Federalist, especially if they had a well-established Congregational church. Inland agrarian communities, especially those with a strong Baptist presence, tended to vote Republican. Map by the author.

factors; another may have been the federal embargo that Congress declared in April, just before the election. This measure, a standard preparation for war, restricted commercial ships to harbors in order to prevent their capture. But the pro-war sentiment in Washington was unpopular throughout the Commonwealth, and the Federalists successfully convinced the electorate that a vote for Gerry was a vote for "Taxes, Embargo, and War." Gerry's running mate for lieutenant governor, William King, may also have been a crucial factor in his loss. The partnership was curious, as Gerry had long been an opponent of Maine statehood, while King was its foremost advocate. King probably did bring votes from Maine, but the Commonwealth's Congregationalists undoubtedly recalled that he had been responsible for passing the Toleration Act, and many Federalists loathed King as a demagogue.[56]

Humiliated by his defeat and bedridden by illness, Gerry had plenty of time to fantasize about Strong's potential treachery. He had already developed the habit of describing his opponents as "british federalists," and now he imagined that they were monarchists courting English assistance to establish a separate country. He invented numerous plots, among them that the Federalist militia was planning to seize control of Boston's fortifications.[57]

The new Federalist governor, Caleb Strong, was an attorney and an experienced administrator with a reputation for moderation, Congregationalist views, and an austere lifestyle. Strong preferred to let Republican officeholders disappear via attrition rather than dismiss them outright. For example, when George Ulmer resigned his command of Maine's Tenth Militia Division to take a commission with the national government, Strong installed the outspoken Cobb in his place. Strong did remove a few officeholders, such as Orchard Cook, whose incompetence as Lincoln County sheriff merited dismissal. He also rewarded Alden Bradford by making him the Commonwealth's secretary of state. Bradford ultimately reciprocated this kindness by publishing a laudatory biography of Strong in 1820.[58]

The Federalists began dismantling Gerry's reforms, including the new militia divisions he had created. A "Committee on

Militia affairs" recommended abolishing three of them, including the Seventeenth. With a stroke of a pen, Strong restored Sewall's Eight Division, and in response many Republican officers resigned their commissions in disgust. Chandler, who had headed the now defunct Seventeenth, did not receive the militia commission he coveted, but his old friend Dearborn arranged to make him a brigadier general in the army. The Federalists also repealed the legislation requiring the Commonwealth to pay for representatives' attendance at the General Court, thus ensuring that Maine would send far fewer members to the sessions. In short, the election of 1812 was momentous. Governor Strong undid his predecessor's reforms, squashed support for the war, and put Massachusetts's management of the militia at odds with the national government's military priorities. It also put Maine on a course for statehood.[59]

Chapter 2
WAR COMES TO MAINE

On the last day of 1811, William Widgery, a freshman legislator from Portland, rose to speak in the U.S. Congress in response to Speaker of the House Henry Clay's call for an army of 25,000 men to invade Canada. Widgery supported most war preparations but not this one. Asking why Clay had said nothing about the militia, he boasted that "the militia of New England was an army well equipped, and would fight—would take Canada immediately, if authorised." Widgery brayed, "I will engage to take Canada by contract. I will raise a company and take it in six weeks."[1]

An early convert to Jeffersonian politics, Widgery had supported the unpopular embargo to the bitter end, and he deplored the British practice of impressment, which he deemed "manstealing." In 1810 he had challenged Portland's Federalist dominance to run as a Republican for its congressional seat. The bitterly contested election was a draw, but he won a runoff in April 1811. Widgery was rough around the edges: the Federalists mocked his home-spun speech patterns, and even Portland's Republican newspaper, the *Eastern Argus*, admitted that his speaking style was "unvarnished." Nor was he a conventional Republican; like many Federalists, he advocated for expanding the navy. But when Congress attempted to organize the militia, his populist suspicions came to the fore. He declared that the measure violated his constituents' freedoms and rights and predicted that the northern states would never stand for it.[2]

In 1812 Congress made few preparations for war. While it did raise soldiers' pay and abolished the army's practice of flogging, it authorized only a few new regiments. For his part, President Madison pardoned deserters who returned to service, and he persuaded Henry Dearborn to return to active duty as the army's senior general, with headquarters in Boston. But neither Madison nor Congress focused on building up the navy, even though the naval secretary, William Jones, had long warned that the American fleet was unprepared for war. Jones proposed funding repairs to existing vessels and financing the construction of twelve seventy-four-gun ships of the line and ten new frigates. Congress authorized the repairs but not the new ships.[3]

Dearborn selected Republicans as officers for all of the new regiments, among them Eleazar Wheelock Ripley, an attorney from Winslow, Maine. Ripley was an outspoken defender of the embargo, and Dearborn rewarded his loyalty with a lieutenant colonel's commission in the army's newly raised Twenty-first Infantry Regiment. Recruiting officers appeared in commercial villages such as Gardiner and Hallowell, and recruitment advertisements were printed in the District's Republican newspapers. Not many men signed up, but most Republicans did not see this as a problem. They imagined that conquering Canada was a mere matter of marching.[4]

FREE TRADE AND SAILORS' RIGHTS

On June 1 President Madison asked Congress to declare war on Great Britain. He enumerated five reasons justifying his request: the impressment of American seamen, illegal blockades, the sovereign's Orders in Council British spies operating in America, and the encouragement of Native American war on American settlers. Madison's emphasis was overwhelmingly maritime, and at first glance one might assume that his reasoning intersected with the needs and opinions of coastal Maine residents.

First as secretary of state and then as president, Madison had long been frustrated by the impressment problem. Between 1803 and 1812, the Royal Navy impressed an estimated 10,000 American seamen into service. Many of them were from the District. By 1812, hundreds of Maine seamen had served on British warships against their will. A few escaped; others were discharged with injuries—for instance, John Allen of Wiscasset, who returned home with a pegleg after being disabled in combat. The experience of John Nichols of Durham was typical. While he was ashore in Liverpool, England, a press gang seized him. When he presented papers proving that he was immune to impressment, the officer swore at him and tore up the documents.[5]

American newspapers grumbled about impressment on British soil and on the high seas, but impressment in U.S. waters provoked outrage, as when the British frigate *Guerriere* stopped the Portland brig *Spitfire* off New York City in 1811. British sailors boarded the *Spitfire* and impressed an apprentice shipwright from Cape Elizabeth named John Diggio. Thomas Barclay, the British consul-general, engineered Diggio's return but not before a bloody encounter took place between the American frigate *President* and the British sloop of war HMS *Little Belt*. On reading about Diggio's impressment, Captain John Rodgers, commander of the *President*, sailed north to find the offending British warship. Instead, he stumbled across the much smaller *Little Belt*, which he pummeled into surrender in a confusing night action. Although Rodgers had attacked the wrong vessel, the American public heartily approved of his actions.[6]

British harassment of American trade was another long-standing issue for Madison. Since 1803, most of the European countries and their colonies had been at war. Markets and ports opened and closed with fantastic rapidity, leading to seizures of vessels that were ostensibly engaged on innocent business. The British Privy Council redoubled its economic war against France after 1805, blockading most of continental Europe in 1806, and an 1807 Order in Council required neutral shipping to put into a British port for inspection before proceeding to European ports. The Orders in Council primarily targeted American trade with France. Royal Navy warships enforced the edicts by stopping and searching American merchant ships for contraband cargoes, which were liable to seizure. The French dictator Napoleon also seized American ships suspected of trading with the British. The Madison administration had long protested such actions, but Maine's merchants and shipowners understood that risk and profit were two sides of the same coin. Though they knew that the American flag offered only flimsy protection, they aggressively sent their ships into foreign markets. If their gamble paid off, they could build elegant homes and join the District's elite. William King was both skilled and lucky at this game, but others overplayed their hand. Edward Emerson, Jr., of York lost four ships to the French and consequently shot himself. A few years later his brother Bulkeley, also faced with shipping losses, followed suit.[7]

Madison was on firmer ground when he complained that British navy ships were hovering along the American coast and harassing shipping. Several had been sighted on the Maine coast, where smuggling was common. In 1807 the Royal Navy schooner *Porgey* launched a campaign to "discourage and punish" these smugglers. It sailed into Passamaquoddy Bay firing its cannon, and one of the cannonballs rolled among some children. During another incident in bay, HMS *Columbine* underwent a near mutiny, and its sailors deserted en masse, with many taking refuge in Eastport.[8]

Madison also complained about British espionage in American territory. The object of his ire were men such as John Henry, who had once commanded Portland's Fort Sumner. Henry had immigrated from Ireland in the 1790s and had persuaded President Adams to give him a commission in the army, but he resigned from service in 1801, suspecting he would be a victim of Jefferson's chaste reformation. Henry eventually settled in Montréal, and by 1808 he had become a British spy, traveling throughout New England. In 1812 Henry sold false intelligence to Madison, convincing him it would expose Federalist treason. Madison squandered $50,000 on the useless papers, and Henry wisely fled before anyone could uncover his ruse.[9]

Unbeknownst to Madison, a British spy had visited Maine as early as 1807. William Girod was a native of Switzerland and a lieutenant in the British army, and he spied under the code name "Nancy." Girod was a shrewd choice; his accented English undoubtedly disarmed even the most suspicious American. His first stop in Maine was Penobscot Bay, where he was tasked with verifying rumors of a secret American invasion force gathering there. Girod found "not the smallest appearance of any hostile preparations," just a few schooners hauled up on Castine's shore. He quickly determined there was no such threat here or anywhere in Maine, claiming the "whole coast & every Town is in an utterly defenceless state."[10]

CAPTAIN NYE DEFENDS HIS SLOOP

On June 18, Congress complied with Madison's request, declared war, and sent express riders to carry the news to every state. The Massachusetts government spread the alarm around the Commonwealth and off the coast, sending dispatch boats to warn American shipping and the fishing fleet. Captain Ansel Nye, a resident of Hallowell and master of the coasting sloop *Washington*, was one of the first Mainers to hear the news. His vessel put into Boston, where many ships were flying their flags at half-mast to protest the war. Nye, however, continued to fly *Washington*'s colors at the masthead, one of only four vessels in the harbor to do so. A crowd gathered and demanded that he lower the flag, which they found offensive on two counts. First, the flag represented support for the recently declared war. Second, the sloop's name was stitched onto the flag and thus was a slight on the reputation of George Washington, the personification of Federalism. Confident in their numbers, the crowd rushed the sloop, but Nye and his crew successfully defended it, tossing one of the attackers into the harbor. The flag remained flying, and Nye returned to Hallowell, acclaimed as a hero by the war's supporters.[11]

Despite Nye's triumphant procession through Hallowell's streets, many Mainers remained, at best, ambivalent about the war. Even in his home port, protesting vessels displayed their flags at half-mast. From Kittery to Eastport, news of the war provoked a variety of responses, including street theater, flight away from the vulnerable coast, and politicking in town meetings and county conventions. In Portland, news of the war arrived with a clatter of hoofs. A messenger delivered the information to the garrison's commander, who immediately sent the message to other posts. When the courier arrived in Wiscasset, Fort Edgecomb's commander responded by raising the post's largest flag and firing cannon. The rider pressed on, and fifty-six hours after leaving Portland he arrived in Eastport and roused Fort Sullivan's commander from his bed. The messenger received a princely $250 for this service, and even the pinchpenny Henry Dearborn had to admit he had performed with great dispatch.[12]

In Augusta, the war news almost precipitated a riot. "Alas! Alas!" proclaimed the town's Federalist paper, "a dark day has commenced—sorrow, gloom and deep distress are visible in the countenances of our wisest and best citizens." A crowd hanged President Madison in effigy and flew a flag at half-mast. A party of recently recruited soldiers took down the flagpole, locals re-raised it, and the soldiers returned with the intention of cutting it down as a final solution. They found a crowd determined to defend the flagpole, and town officials intervened before a brawl erupted.[13]

Overall, response to the war was gloomy. A Portland diarist wrote, "Without resources, with scarcely anything of a navy, an exhausted treasury . . . we are involved in a war with a nation whose navy sweeps the ocean, who has millions of our property in her possession, who can blockade our whole coast, & burn our seaports from Maine to Georgia." A Bangor merchant fretted in his journal about what he considered an "unjust, partial & unpolitic war." A Buckstown woman recorded, "Our fears are realized—War—a most unreasonable war is openly declared, and what will be the consequence God only knows." Frightened communities bombarded the federal government with requests for military support. Portland's citizens pointed out that the port was open to a naval attack, as had happened in the Revolutionary War. Midcoast communities requested gunboats for protection, often offering to provide the crews. Dearborn recalled that it had once been "fashionable for many people to laugh at gunboats" and was delighted that they now clamored for them. Rather than planning the invasion of Canada, he dwelled on how many dozen tents he should send to Maine and fretted about whether to send field pieces to Camden or gunpowder to Machias.[14]

On the border, news of the war created consternation. Eastport residents "unanimously agreed to preserve a good understanding with the Inhabitants of New-Brunswick, and to discountenance all depredations on the property of each other," even as women and children fled to Portland, Portsmouth, and Boston. Canny merchants used the confusion to smuggle goods across the border before the war stopped all trade, but they need not have worried: Eastport remained a center of illicit trade throughout the war. On the Saint Croix River, parishioners from both sides of the border flocked to the Methodist meetinghouse in Saint Stephen, New Brunswick. The minister recorded that his congregation sobbed loudly, "thinking withal that this should be the last time they could see each other in peace." In Houlton, the Yankee settlers feared that the British and Indians would attack. Some proposed fleeing westward to the Penobscot River, but cooler heads prevailed. A representative met with British agents in New Brunswick and agreed to neutralize the settlement in return for promises of safety. As for the Madawaskans on the upper Saint John River, there is little reason to think they took much notice of the war. The undoubted highlight of their year was a visit from the bishop of Quebec, Joseph-Octave Plessis.[15]

Backcountry settlers dreaded a Native American attack. In Foxcroft, residents discussed preparations but did nothing beyond barring their doors at night. The arrival of a party of Penobscots in East Pond Plantation (now Newport) caused panic until the Indians assured them of their peaceful intentions. Yankee settlers feared attack by Mohawks from Canada more than from local Indians, expressing their concerns to Governor Strong in a petition that pointed out their proximity to Quebec and Native Americans who "might easily destroy our whole settlement." Meanwhile, the area's militia general ordered his command to cultivate harmony with the tribes and individual members.[16]

Native communities sensed the settlers' fears and receded into the interior. They also sought one another's counsel in a meeting at Saint Andrews, New Brunswick. British colonial officials agreed to protect the chapel at Pleasant Point, while Massachusetts officials doubled down on whites who illegally logged on Native American lands, securing the Penobscots' neutrality. Borderland individuals, such as the eccentric proprietor of Campobello Island, assured the Passamaquoddy that the British government would not harm them: "Francis! You called last at my house, in great sorrow—wives (squaws) and your children (papoos) were flying to the woods for safety. . . . Now by our right hands, let peace be between British-men, and Indian-men. They will keep peace with you.—Welcome!"[17]

In a war fought ostensibly for sailors' rights, even the responses from impressed sailors were mixed. Elias Hutchins of Arundel had been impressed in 1803, and in 1812 he was serving on the North American station on the frigate HMS *Belvidera*. On June 23, an American squadron attacked his ship, and *Belvidera*'s captain wisely chose to flee. In a running engagement, the British frigate suffered casualties but escaped. Once in port, Hutchins reported himself as an American who was unwilling to fight against his country, and the Royal Navy ultimately released him. In late October, the impressed sailor John Nichols learned of the war and asked his captain to treat him as a prisoner of war. The captain threw him in irons for twenty-four hours, then had him flogged. When asked if he would return on duty, Nichols replied that he would rather die. The process was repeated for the next three days until the captain gave up and Nichols went to a British prison. At least he lived to tell his tale. John Cand of Woolwich was an impressed sailor on board the British frigate *Macedonian* when it fought an American frigate. The British suffered heavy casualties, including Cand.[18]

Several hundred British subjects in the District faced discrimination because of the war. The 1798 Act Respecting Enemy Aliens demanded that Maine's federal marshal register enemy aliens. In response, U.S. Marshal Thomas G. Thornton posted advertisements calling for British subjects to report themselves, even the 120 Irish immigrants whose ship had happened to enter Portland harbor. In total, about three hundred aliens stepped forward, most in seaports such as Saco or Wiscasset. Not all aliens self-reported; Eastport's deputy marshal found 164 enemy aliens but estimated the actual number at higher than two hundred, more than a quarter of the island's population.[19]

Many British subjects became naturalized American citizens, ranging from modest laborers to community leaders such as the Congregational minister of Deer Isle. The Vaughan family, for instance, were British expatriates living in the District. The brothers Charles and Robert Vaughan had established themselves in Hallowell, where they headed a small colony of Britons. No newspaper editor dared cross swords with the wealthy, powerful, and highly connected clan, and their activities remained almost entirely out of the press. The fact that Robert Vaughan's son was prominent in Hallowell's militia but spent much of the war in England conducting family business went without remark. The Vaughans were Federalists, opposed the war, and engaged in illicit trade with Britain. When federal officials caught one of their ships entering the United States illegally, the family used its connections to squash the case, despite Waldoboro's customs collector's efforts.[20]

In the end, little came of the Enemy Alien restrictions because Marshal Thornton balked at the order to remove British expatriates from coastal areas. Having registered them as enemy aliens, he knew their numbers were small, that many were poor tradesmen and mechanics, and that some had even enlisted onboard U.S. privateers. Nonetheless, a handful of British subjects left the District, including Anthony Holland, the owner-editor of the Buckstown *Gazette of Maine*. Holland was a Nova Scotian by birth who operated the most ardently Federalist newspaper in the District. Just before the war broke out, he returned to Nova Scotia, and in 1813 he commenced publishing the highly successful *Acadian Recorder* in Halifax.[21]

THE STORM OF CIVIL DISCORD

The Federalists thumped the Republicans in the November 1812 elections: three out of four Maine congressmen lost their seats, while the fourth declined to run. Out of the Commonwealth's twenty-two counties, only Maine's Oxford County returned a majority for Madison in the presidential election. It was the first time towns such as Bangor had voted Federalist.[22]

The most senior congressman who lost his seat was Richard Cutts, who had been tarred in Federalist newspapers as "all for War." The victor was the Federalist Cyrus King, a Columbia College–educated attorney from Saco. King was surprised by his victory but rose to the occasion as a critic of the Madison administration.

It helped that he was the youngest half-brother of Rufus King, a well-known diplomat and Federalist senator. Intriguingly Cyrus was also the youngest full brother of William King.[23]

Among the defeated congressmen, William Widgery suffered the most. As they returned to Maine in July, Widgery and fellow congressman Francis Carr of Bangor were repeatedly insulted and threatened by Federalist crowds. In Newburyport, Massachusetts, a militia company publicly hissed at them, and local newspapers lambasted Widgery as a traitor. Crowds gathered outside his Portland home at night, beating drums, blowing horns, shouting threats, and eventually forcing him to move his family elsewhere. George Bradbury, a Federalist attorney and a graduate of Harvard College, took Widgery's seat. Carr, who had assumed his seat in June 1812 may have regretted his vote for war more than anyone else, after British forces sacked his hometown in September 1814. John Wilson of Belfast, another Harvard-educated attorney and a vocal war opponent, defeated Carr in the November 1812 election. Only Peleg Tallman of Bath had dared to vote against the war, but he declined to run again. Abiel Wood, a Republican merchant from Wiscasset, took his place.[24]

Many communities sent letters directly to President Madison. Some towns declared their support for the war, such as Frankfort, whose leading Republicans scolded Governor Strong and resolved to "protect and defend our own government against all its enemies, whether external or internal." York County citizens warned Madison that the Federalists would reintroduce British rule, dramatically forecasting that "The storm of civil discord is gathering; the thunder roars at a distance; the lightning gleams on the dim mantle of night." Federalist towns such as Lyman wrote to Madison to "most harttily say, that we Disaprove of the Present war." John Low's signature topped Lyman's petition; he became a leading critic of the war. Among his fears was the war would lead to an alliance with Napoleon Bonaparte, "from which Evil may the good Lord Diliver us." Seaborne trade was a common theme; Biddeford's selectmen invoked the memory of prosperous times, asking, "why has our Gold become dim? Why are those happy, thrice happy times changed? We see no sufficient Reason for it." The town of Wells echoed Biddeford's concerns and accused Republicans of having impoverished the nation. Columbia in Washington County considered the war "unnecessary, unjust, and ruinous," while North Yarmouth argued that the war would introduce poverty and wretchedness and that "Maine, ere long, will have nothing left but 'rocks, ruins and demagogues.'"[25]

Both Federalists and Republicans convened county-level conventions. Lincoln County's Federalists met at Wiscasset, complaining that the war had crushed Maine's "Navigation, the lumber trade, the fishery & all other sources of prosperity" and lauding Governor Strong's measures to obstruct the war's prosecution. Delegates from more than thirty towns met at Buckstown, where they focused on the national government's anticommercial bias and dismissed claims about impressed sailors. They argued that the embargo had "nearly exhausted" the District, leaving little specie in circulation and exposing shipping to the British navy, and they foresaw heavy taxation. York County's Republicans expressed their confidence that party factionalism would give way to patriotism. Their criticism of the Federalists was a straightforward (if long-winded) accusation of treason: "What then is to satisfy the opposers of government? Power! Power! under the auspices and guarantee of Britain! For this they would barter the dearest rights of the country. For this they would wade thro' blood." The York convention urged communities to arm themselves "to support the laws, suppress insurrections and repel invasions!" Based on such rhetoric, some predicted a civil war.[26]

"THIS INFAMOUS TRAFFICK"

Overall, the war brought economic stagnation to Maine's export-based economy, which relied heavily on British markets. Some sought to cash in on the war, especially the shipbuilders who offered to build vessels for the navy, but they had no luck. Denied conventional exchange, many traded with the enemy. Inflated war prices, a demand for British manufactures, and the promise of payment in silver tempted many Mainers, no matter what their politics were—from herdsmen to fishermen to the wealthiest merchants in the District.[27]

The heavily wooded upper Kennebec Valley was the first region to report cattle smuggling during the war. The border with Quebec was undefended and unsettled, and people from both sides crossed back and forth searching for work, among them Roger Chase of Caratunk. Acquaintances in Quebec convinced Chase of the easy profits in cattle smuggling. In September, he crossed from Canada to Maine, collected thirty to forty cattle, and headed back toward the border, accompanied by ten armed confederates and their dogs. Chase had promised to kill anyone who pursued them. Still, a posse of about fifty men set out after them and soon captured the slow-moving cattle, although all but two smugglers escaped into the woods. As the posse drove the cattle back to the town of Solon, its size grew to almost 120 men. Nonetheless, twenty armed smugglers shadowed them the entire way, waiting for an opportunity to take back the cattle. Villagers taunted the posse, and the cattle's original owners attempted to repossess the animals through a judicial order, but to no avail. The guards stood firm and turned the cattle over to federal authorities. As a result of the incident, Bath's customs collector traveled to Somerset County and appointed inspectors in settlements such as Anson, Solon, and Sandy River to stop "this infamous traffick." But the cattle drives persisted, with the smugglers shifting their track west into New Hampshire, where John Page, Jr., a future governor, led militia in a campaign to stop these "Maine cow-boys."[28]

In coastal communities, merchants such as the Spofford brothers were known for their willingness to resort to violence against federal officers who interfered with their smuggling. In 1812 Charles Spofford was on the lam in New Brunswick, while Frederick and Pearl remained on Deer Isle. Frederick complained bitterly that the war had halted business and correctly predicted, "it will wax worse instead of better." Another well-known smuggling merchant was William King. When an American privateer boarded two of his ships, officers found evidence that they had been trading with the enemy. One of King's captains informed the privateersman that "the ship belonged to General William King, that no person dared to seize her, if they did, Mr. Madison was the friend of Mr. King & would order her released." The other captain claimed, "'Every body' to the Eastward acted in this manner." The privateersman concluded, "I know Gen'l King to be what is called a good Democrat, and friendly to the Executive." Understanding that the matter would cause complications, he released King's ships.[29]

LIABLE TO THE ATTACK OF THE ENEMY

Some militia officers demanded that "all party spirit should be done away!" Nonetheless, partisan politics remained a problem throughout the war. The Madison administration gave lip service to the militia's effectiveness, and Dearborn thought that Maine's militia could invade New Brunswick, confidently writing, "The whole might be effected, in two, or three months, with very little expence, or risk." American spies reported on New Brunswick's geography and garrison, and one American in the province encouraged an invasion, claiming that the colony's poor would rise and assist the American forces. The idea was pure fantasy: the militia was incapable of such operations, even had Governor Strong been inclined to support them.[30]

The Madison administration was well aware of the shortcomings of the militia, and Dearborn agreed, writing to the president, "The sooner we can dispense with their services, the better." However, some thought that the militia could replace regulars in coastal fortifications. Toward this end, Governor Strong ordered out forty-one companies of militia, seventeen of them in coastal Maine, with the largest concentration in Portland. However, there were signs that Federalist militia officers would not heed the federal government's call: Henry Sewall was one Federalist officer who refused to mobilize his men. In contrast, the Republican George Ulmer made preparations to receive an enemy he was sure would strike at Castine.[31]

Backed by the General Court, Strong refused Dearborn's request to activate the Commonwealth's militia. While the Constitution provided the executive with the power to call out the militia, it was vague on how or when the president could do so. In the wording of the day, the federalized militia would be "detached" from the state militia and put under federal control and pay, but there were questions about how this might work in practice. Could detached militia cross the border into Canada? Would they serve under their elected militia officers or under appointed regular officers? Who determined when the president could call them out? Ever the attorney, Strong covered his actions by submitting two questions to the Massachusetts Supreme Court for consideration. First, he asked who had the power to determine if an emergency was sufficient to mobilize the militia—state governors or the president? Second, he asked whether state- or federally appointed officers commanded militia when they were called into national service. The justices found that state governors were tasked with determining if it was appropriate for the federal government to activate the militia. They also found that the militia must serve under state-appointed officers. Governor Strong duly informed the War Department that he would not detach any militia, based on this advice.[32]

The subtext of this quibbling was the animosity between Massachusetts Federalists and Republicans. Both parties believed that the Commonwealth was on the verge of a civil war in which the militia would play an essential role. Elbridge Gerry thought that Strong had left the state open to a British invasion and worried that local "tories" would seize Boston's under-garrisoned fortifications. His fears infected Dearborn, who became so obsessed with the idea that he did little to prepare to invade Canada. Secretary of War William Eustis ordered Dearborn away from Boston three times before he reluctantly departed for the front.[33]

Governor Strong's refusal to detach militia left some coastal posts completely ungarrisoned and others severely undermanned. Among these was the battery overlooking Machias Bay. Alarmed by the port's vulnerability, customs collector Jeremiah O'Brien personally hired men to garrison the battery and pried munitions from the War Department. It was well he did: in early July, a privateer landed British prisoners at the battery, and more followed. In August, an actual invasion seemed likely when British boat parties fought a sharp action with three privateers and a revenue cutter at nearby Little River. Only then did Machias's militia companies activate, standing watch for two days in preparation for an attack that never came. Other posts barely had enough soldiers to act as caretakers. Captain Binney of the army's Fourth Infantry noted to his brother, "I shudder when I think a privateer with 100 men could destroy every port from Eastport to Portsmouth." Binney had only thirty-three soldiers scattered in five batteries between the Kennebec's mouth and Castine. He needed at least five hundred soldiers "to make a respectable defence, but I shall endeavor to do my duty."[34]

Militia turned out only when there seemed to be a threat. On July 15, Colonel Oliver Shead ordered several companies to defend Calais, Robbinston, and Eastport, and they remained on duty for some weeks. This duty severely curtailed regular economic activity, so Shead devised a system whereby half the men remained on duty, allowing the others to harvest crops, mow hay, or otherwise pursue a living. Despite his sensitivity to their plight, he was not a talented officer, and boys taunted him in Eastport's streets.[35]

Governor Strong hit upon a unique response to Eastport's defense needs. In observance of President Madison's order, he activated a militia battalion from the Penobscot Bay area and stationed it on the border. He did so to twist and subvert the purpose of the detached units. His orders emphasized that "disorderly persons may attempt to disturb and annoy the peaceable inhabitants in that neighborhood and endanger their lives and property." Furthermore, the men were "not only called forth to defend the frontier against any invasion of a foreign enemy, but to prevent the depredations of any lawless banditti who may be disposed to rob and plunder, whether they belong to our own Territories or those of the enemy." Adjutant General William Donnison's orders also indicated that the detached militia's mission was to deter "Lawless plunderers," proclaiming that such pirates or bandits "occasion distress and misery to the exposed inhabitants, and have no tendency to produce an equitable peace, which is the only justifiable object of war." Donnison's orders reflected Strong's hostility to the war effort, slyly condemning privateering, the invasion of Canada, and the army's use to further partisan aims. The pirates or bandits were a veiled reference to privateersmen from Essex County, north of Boston, who harassed ships suspected of smuggling. Republican militia officers such as George Ulmer reported that the detached militia "appear to be ordered there to protect the smugglers from the American privateers—but not to prevent supplying the British subjects with Provisions."[36]

Some two hundred detached militia marched to Eastport in early September after a "long & tedious march" from the Penobscot River. They found no barracks, supplies, or equipment, and the officers had to buy their men's provisions at retail prices. Many soldiers had worn out their shoes, and only about half had muskets in working condition, a chronic problem in militia units. Understandably, desertion commenced almost immediately. Compounding their problems, Governor Strong refused to supply them because they were now in federal service, and Major General Sewall echoed the sentiment. Lieutenant Samuel Maclay, the regular officer in command of Fort Sullivan, also refused to feed them. The general in Boston insisted that he had no official notification of their service. The detached militia remained in this uncertain situation for weeks. Adding to their misery was the post's precarious situation: one officer claimed that 10,000 men could not defend it if a British fleet were to attack.[37]

The actual threat of invasion seemed slight. One of the unit's officers crossed over to Saint Andrews, New Brunswick, and reported he was "politely treated." This cordial behavior was not unusual for militia officers or even state officials who were anxious to preserve peace on the border. John Brewer of Robbinston was one example of this borderland comity. He held high rank as a brigadier general in the militia, yet some Americans suspected he could not be trusted. An Eastport attorney wrote, "No man in this part of the country has manifested more inveterate hostility to the country than he has." Washington County's sheriff John Cooper also raised the suspicions of some. He made such traitorous statements during after-dinner toasts at Saint Andrews that even English observers thought he should have displayed more loyalty to his nation.[38]

Miserably provisioned, two militia companies remained in Eastport and one at a newly constructed barracks in Robbinston throughout the autumn. Their commander, Major Jacob Ulmer, incurred the locals' wrath by assisting the customs collector in preventing trade with the enemy. Despite their hardships Major Ulmer and his troops were eager to join the federal service. Meanwhile, the British watched Eastport carefully, stationing a half company of regulars at nearby Saint Andrews but avoiding any hostile moves.[39]

"ALL POSSIBLE FORBEARANCE"

Britain did not seek this war, but it did not act swiftly enough to prevent it either. In 1812, the Admiralty ordered its officers to exercise "all possible forbearance" toward American mariners and to keep ships clear of the American coast to preclude any incidents. The British government offered substantial trade concessions that opened European trade to American ships and even repealed the obnoxious Orders in Council on June 16, just two days before Congress declared war. This news briefly ignited hope that reason would prevail, but the efforts were too little and too late to stop the conflict.[40]

Provincial officials in the adjacent colonies wanted to preserve comity on the border. New Brunswick's newly arrived military governor, Major General George Stracey Smyth, refused to call out any militia, claiming they would interfere with the province's crops, and advised the inhabitants to pursue "a reciprocal forbearance from Hostilities." Smyth's superior officer in Halifax, Sir John Coape Sherbrooke, issued a proclamation ordering all parties to abstain from harassing Americans in eastern Maine or bothering unarmed coasting vessels. These officers had good reason to act with forbearance. The news of the war had not yet reached Britain, and there was hope that the two nations could avoid a full-blown war. Furthermore, the Maritime provinces could not provide enough food for their populace and garrisons and relied on American flour from the Chesapeake region. The British were anxious to keep the flow of foodstuffs into Saint John and Halifax, a trade that was highly profitable for American merchants. The British were fully aware that the war was unpopular in New England and saw their continued trade with the Northeast as a way to divide the Americans further. The Royal Navy even issued licenses to Americans who were "WELL INCLINED TO THE BRITISH INTEREST," including the Federalist Jabez Mowry of Eastport and Republicans such as William King. In short, the United States was unprepared for war, Britain was a reluctant enemy, Massachusetts was an unwilling participant, and the war divided Maine, bringing misery to the entire District.[41]

Chapter 3

"A MONGREL BREED OF SOLDIER"

The War of 1812 had its share of farcical moments, most provided by the American military. One involved Captain Joseph Westcott, who commanded a company stationed at Castine that had not received pay since arriving in December 1812. In March, Westcott traveled to Portland to collect his unit's payroll and returned on the coasting sloop *Harriet* carrying some $1,500 in bank bills in his coat pocket. Coasting sloops had no toilet facilities. Men generally went to the lee rail to urinate, but defecation was a more complicated process. Sailors squatted in the front of the vessel, which became known as the "head." The weather was blustery; and while Westcott was at the head, the jib sheet nearly knocked his hat into the icy waters. As he was reaching to save it, the carefully bundled payroll popped out of his pocket and fell into the sea. The sloop's master launched a boat to recover the bundle, which remained tantalizingly visible, but the craft immediately filled with water. So Westcott returned to the battery empty-handed. The loss of the money was a grievous blow for the garrison, many of whom came from impoverished families.[1]

Westcott was in financial difficulty even before the war started. He likely joined the military to revive his sagging fortunes, but his army career was a disaster from the start. The regular army officer in charge of the Castine battery initially refused to hand over the post. There were no supplies available, and Westcott had to advance money to procure provisions, straw, blankets, and firewood because local merchants would not offer him credit. Then the payroll disaster occurred, an event that haunted his life for years. In July, a final tragedy befell him when his soldiers attacked the Hancock County jail to free a comrade, nearly precipitating a battle with the local militia.[2]

It would be easy to dismiss Westcott as a bumbler, but nearly all of his regiment's officers were equally untalented. Commanding this lackluster regiment of twelve-month enlistees was George Ulmer of Lincolnville, and the unit was known as "Ulmer's Volunteers." In a war in which the American army was notably inept, this regiment stood out for its poor performance. Ultimately its hapless commander would be disgraced and the unit disbanded, not because it failed on the battlefield but because of civilian animosity on Maine's home front. Ulmer regretted this "strange war" in which he had to fight other Americans, "for we have no other real enemies on this frontier." But Ulmer, as usual, did not get the situation quite right: the biggest menace to officers such as Westcott and himself was their own incompetence.[3]

"THE MOST EFFECTIVE SOLDIERY"

Before declaring war, President Madison and Congress created a new corps known as "U.S. Volunteers" or "twelve-month Volunteers." These were temporary units raised for wartime service, less expensive to maintain than regular regiments but more efficient than the detached militia. In January 1812, Congress authorized 50,000 volunteers, with the proviso that the state governments organize the units and select the officers. The Madison administration rejected that approach because it wanted to weed out Federalists. Congress did not amend the Volunteer Act until July 6, authorizing the administration to select officers. Later that month, Henry Dearborn wrote to leading Maine Republicans, asking them to raise volunteer units, pinning his hopes on William King to organize them.[4]

The Madison administration did not have a clear vision for the volunteer program. Republicans naïvely assumed that farmers and other laborers would leap to arms to invade Canada yet provided little incentive for them to do so, other than the vague hope that they would demonstrate republican virtue. Many Americans viewed the regular army as a potential threat to their liberties, and the volunteer program was a means to raise troops that posed no threat to the republic. King reinforced this point: "The service of a Volunteer Corps is always considered more honorable (to the men in particular) than it would be in the ordinary line of the army, notwithstanding by the act that the pay and emoluments will be about the same." The pay was a mere $6 per month, raised to $8 before the end of the year. The Madison administration talked of using the District's volunteers to attack Lower Canada via the Kennebec River, as Benedict Arnold had done in 1775, or marching into neighboring New Brunswick, but nothing came of these schemes. For his part, King wanted the volunteers to serve in the District's coastal forts to prevent British seaborne attacks. Like Elbridge Gerry and Henry Dearborn, he feared allowing the Federalist-dominated militia into coastal forts, suspicious they would hand them over to the British.[5]

The Madison administration expected Mainers to respond enthusiastically to the call for volunteers. Dearborn appealed to the citizenry in advertisements in Hallowell's *American Advocate* and other newspapers, but the results were disappointing. Several companies did form in communities along the Kennebec and Androscoggin rivers. They marched to Vermont and eventually served on the Canadian border after combining into a regiment with companies raised in New Hampshire. Another understrength regiment was formed from men in Hancock and Washington counties and remained in the District to defend the "Eastern Frontier"—that is, the border with New Brunswick. In August, King set out to persuade Eastport's collector of customs, Lemuel Trescott, to command the regiment, though Dearborn, Secretary of the Treasury Albert Gallatin, and Secretary of War William Eustis had already failed to convince him. Trescott remained adamant that he was too busy running the customs house to accept the command, and King's trip to Eastport was a failure, one made worse when he fractured his leg in a fall from his horse. Eventually King approached his ally George Ulmer, who agreed to take charge of the regiment, although he had hoped to command a whole division.[6]

Three other volunteer regiments failed to coalesce. Several prominent Republicans jockeyed to command a third regiment based in Cumberland County, but nothing came of it. John Blake, Jr., of Brewer proposed raising a fourth regiment from along the Penobscot River, but the Madison administration refused his proposal because he was a Federalist. Blake protested, to no avail, that he and his compatriots would proceed "without any Riguard to Political Charicters—and of such as we are willing to risk our Reputation and Honour of our contray." Isaac Lane, a well-connected Republican from York County, began to recruit a fifth regiment in late 1812 but ceased when Congress abandoned the volunteer concept as impractical. Massachusetts proper raised a few volunteer companies but no regiments.[7]

At first King held no federal commission and drew no pay, but he nonetheless put considerable effort into organizing the volunteer units. The national government sent him blank commissions to appoint the officers directly, giving him considerable patronage. The British in nearby Nova Scotia watched King's movements, noting that while he was a "violent democrat" the volunteers themselves were no threat. King had a relatively easy time finding company-level officers. Typically, militia officers mustered their companies, gave a small speech, and asked those who were willing to serve to step forward. A few Federalists offered their services as volunteer officers. Among them was Abel Atherton of Portland, who had military qualifications although a "Violent Fed" and made overtures to both the volunteers and the regular army. Unsurprisingly, the administration rebuffed him, and Republicans expressed astonishment that he had even tried to serve, given how frequently he denounced Madison. Men who pursued a commission generally were motivated by social status and an officer's pay. Few seem to have undergone the intense introspection of one law student, who wrote to his elder brother seeking advice on raising a company of volunteers. The elder assured the younger that he had the qualities to "secure the respect & love of your inferior officers & soldiers & to command them with satisfaction & applause." Though a military career was out of the question, the brother agreed that one might choose to be a "temporary soldier, again to become a peaceful citizen." Despite this advice, the young man did not offer his services, and less thoughtful officers filled his place.[8]

The recruitment process went slowly. One potential officer complained that the "volunteer business is unpopular"; another tried but was unable to raise a full company. Many men did not want to serve far from home, let alone invade Canada. State authorities worried that the creation of volunteer units would deplete the militia, and these concerns forced Dearborn to promise Massachusetts authorities to station volunteers in coastal fortifications rather than march them to Canada. King thought this was the only way to recruit successfully, and some companies tendered their services with the proviso that they serve only within U.S. borders. By the time the volunteer program ended, 1,377 Mainers had signed up, 122 of whom refused to march when so ordered and had to be dismissed.[9]

Intriguingly, there is evidence that a volunteer ideal was positioning these soldiers as morally superior to regular troops. In October 1812, an article titled "Plan for an efficient Volunteer Corps" appeared in Hallowell's *American Advocate*. Its proposed model was "as liberal as republicanism could devise." First, "every member shall treat his fellows in sickness and distress, with the same tenderness he would treat a brother." Furthermore, officers should treat enlisted men as equals, except when good discipline required a stricter approach. Those who "misused" enlisted personnel would receive a $50 fine. Finally, the article called on every soldier to act as an instructor to the others in their leisure hours. The article promised that this plan would make military service "a school of morals and literary and general improvement where friendship, union and harmony unmolested may dwell." For as the writer claimed, "Volunteer corps are the most effective soldiery."[10]

"KEEP THE FEDS IN ORDER"

Federalist opposition to the volunteers was fierce. Ideologically, they opposed the war as folly, resented the partisan nature of volunteer units, and feared that the volunteers allowed the federal government to circumvent state control of the militia. Others suspected that the Madison administration had raised volunteer units to overawe Federalist opposition to the war, a rumor founded on William Widgery's supposed claim that the units would "KEEP THE FEDS IN ORDER." These were more than rumors. John Chandler wrote to William King, "it is not improbable they may be wanting to put down a Tory Rebellion." One Republican directly suggested that the company of volunteers in Anson should "cow down toryism." A few weeks later, he again stressed the need for local volunteers because the streets were "full of tories and they are full of treason." The *American Advocate* encouraged readers to enlist in the volunteer units, calling it the duty of "every legitimate American" given that "enemies of our country both internal and external, are prostituting the American name by treasonable resolutions and seditious resolutions." Leading Jeffersonians in the District confided to one another that it was probable they would have to use the volunteers to put down a "Tory Rebellion." Even the British commander in Halifax reported that the units were intended to overawe the Federalists.[11]

Little wonder, then, that Federalists assumed that the Madison administration would use the volunteers to suppress them. Boston newspapers pointed out the supposed unconstitutionality of these units, one calling them an "ARMED MOB to '*hush all disaffection*' and to destroy all freedom of speech and opinion in the country." John Lowell's pamphlet *Perpetual War*, with the loaded subtitle "The Establishment of an Immense Standing Army of Guards and Spies, Under the Name of a Local Volunteer Force," compared the volunteers to Napoleon's paramilitary police force, the *gens d'armes*. According to Lowell, just as Napoleon had selected the gens d'armes for their zealous loyalty to him, the volunteer officers were composed of "only the *most bitter*, and *violent*, and *persecuting*, and *blind*" friends of the Madison administration. This, in fact, was largely true. Lowell lambasted the volunteers as a "mongrel breed of soldier citizen" and continued his comparison to Napoleonic France:

> The French gend'armerie seldom or never fight a publick enemy—they live in and near home—lead an idle life, and draw great pay. Our volunteers, Mr. Madison recommends, should not be obliged to *leave home*—If the enemy comes to their houses, perhaps they might fight, but they are to be paid for living in idleness—paid for their *loyalty*—paid for their votes—paid for watching the opposition—paid for cutting their fellow-citizen's throats (if need should be) or if Madison should so order.

Lowell was essentially correct. Many volunteers were glad to stay at home and draw military pay, and their officers were happy to bully Federalists. Although the Madison administration did not envision the volunteers as a gendarmerie, Dearborn and King had no such qualms. As a result, Governor Strong excluded volunteer officers from the militia on the pretext that they were liable to be called away on federal service. This decision created fear among socially insecure Republicans, who craved the prestige associated with militia rank, and made it more difficult for King to convince men to associate into volunteer companies.[12]

Apart from political feelings, Federalists opposed recruitment because it hurt them financially, or so they said. A popular claim was that poor men enlisted to escape prosecution for debt. Federalists sometimes arrested indebted soldiers, hoping to sow confusion among the volunteers. One ended up in the Somerset County jail, and his release two months later required the best efforts of his captain as well as a federal court order. A Federalist merchant from Camden groused that local men joined the army to escape their debts, which he doubly resented because impoverished soldiers' families also looked to the town for support. Yet though he complained when the soldiers—the "scouring of God's Earth"—marched away to war, he sourly told his brother, "it is a public benefit to have them gone." Other Federalists resented the labor costs that rose as their workforce marched away, even as they wondered about their quality as soldiers. As one Portland diarist wrote:

> Very few will prefer the perils, fatigues, & abstinence of the camp to the ease & felicity of domestic life. A few of the offscourings of the earth, dissolute, ignorant, & poor, may be induced to enlist in the army; but what can we expect from such men? Without attachment to country, neither friends nor property to defend, no character to support, no respect for superiors, no fear of shame or love of honor, they will neither acquire discipline nor courage, they will only fight where fear of punishment drives them, & wage war as readily with friends as with foe.[13]

Little wonder that one volunteer officer found Federalist towns such as Castine "not very friendly to the Volunteer troops." The Federalist press was contemptuous about these officers. A Boston paper called them "the refuse of society." The *Portland Gazette* mocked them as those who, "by idleness, vice and incapacity, are starved out at home; unable to provide for themselves and families; and wanting ability and honesty to pay the smallest bill when presented—these are sent to fatten on the bounties of government, riot in folly and wantonness, and *command armies*! and this merely *because they are thus vile*; because they are *unprincipled*; because they are DEMOCRATS."[14]

"THE HARDY YEOMEN OF THE DISTRICT"

The volunteer movement did not start in earnest until the autumn of 1812, far too late for the new units to participate in the invasion of Canada. In October the first company went into active service as the garrison of Portland's Fort Sumner. Unactivated units remained at home, receiving pay and rations and drilling infrequently, and this squandering of resources angered many observers. Once in actual service, the volunteers rarely felt welcome, for most of the regular army officers disdained them as amateurs. A volunteer officer stationed at Fort Scammel complained that his men had no supplies, poor food, no bedding, and inadequate housing and said that his requests for supplies had been met with profanity. Regular officers raised tensions by enlisting volunteers into their own regiments. As early as October, the army's recruiting advertisements stated that volunteers who joined a regular regiment would be released from their old units and receive a $25 bounty and a land bounty of 160 acres. These powerful incentives sapped enlisted personnel from the volunteer companies.[15]

Among the regulars, Captain Binney at Fort Edgecomb was an exception. He welcomed the volunteers, writing, "It will afford me much pleasure to be of service in calling out and arming the hardy yeomen of the District." He went out of his way to find supplies and build barracks for them, and he was relieved that the volunteers were reinforcing his meager command. However, he confided to his brother that he did not think many would step forward to enlist in the regular army and expressed disappointment in their performance.[16]

The volunteers remained scattered across the district that winter, with the largest concentration in Portland. Living conditions were grim, and there were many complaints about provisions, which a volunteer described as "one pound of salt beef, one pound of bread, and one gill of potato whiskey per day." Many soldiers purchased meals at a cellar on Fish Street, where the one-legged proprietor sold food and drink on credit. Miserable quarters, poor diet, and tedium resulted in low morale, which plummeted further in January, after a cartel ship carrying sick prisoners of war from Canada was driven into Casco Bay by foul weather. The worst cases disembarked in Portland. Ill and emaciated, many could barely stand, and their condition shocked civilians and soldiers alike. Although military officials set up hospitals for their care on Munjoy Hill, several died, sparking rumors that the British had poisoned them.[17]

Maine's coastal volunteers occasionally assumed policing roles, as when they seized a fisherman from New Brunswick who had landed at Boothbay. The volunteers insisted he was a spy, but the fisherman claimed he had been born in Boothbay and was returning to buy a home and bring his family back to the United States. The District's U.S. marshal, Thomas G. Thornton, appealed for the man's release to the secretary of state and the U.S. attorney general, who finally freed him after months in confinement. Understandably, the man returned to New Brunswick and never came back.[18]

As winter waned, volunteer morale continued to decline, especially when it became clear that the troops would soon have to march to Vermont. Several men complained that the government had promised them garrison duty in coastal posts and had not paid them. Some soldiers deserted individually; and in one incident a group of thirty men decamped simultaneously, claiming they had no obligation to serve without pay. Pushing past Fort Sumner's sentries, they set out westward toward Hebron and Poland. An armed party pursued them in sleighs and persuaded them to return, promising leniency. In March, the army ordered the volunteers stationed west of the Penobscot River to march to Burlington, Vermont. Slogging through snow, slush, and mud, the companies made their way to Fryeburg and then crossed the White Mountains, often accompanied by women camp followers. By this time, the units had abandoned their egalitarian ideals: the enlisted men slept in barns and stables, while their officers enjoyed warmer quarters in public houses.[19]

Some volunteers remained behind to defend the approaches to Maine and New Hampshire. Two companies guarded the approaches from Quebec, building barracks at Caratunk on the Kennebec River's upper reaches, while another took quarters at Stewartstown, New Hampshire. These posts served a dual purpose, discouraging profiteers from driving cattle to Quebec while also guarding against an attack from the province. In their spare time, the soldiers raided local hen coops; otherwise, they did little more than report a group of Indians who had robbed hunters of their traps and furs. Two companies remained in the Boothbay region, repelling a Royal Navy landing party and taking two prisoners.[20]

Congress soon recognized that the volunteer program was a disaster. The chair of the House Select Committee on Military Affairs asked, "Shall we any longer deceive ourselves by a further dependence on the absurd volunteer acts?" Maine Republicans also knew that the program was failure. As the influential politician John Holmes admitted, "Should the war continue, temporary armies, will, I fear, be found inadequate to the purposes of the war." When astute would-be volunteer officers such as Isaac Lane saw that the program was in trouble, they offered their services as short-term regulars instead.[21]

The volunteer program failed because many saw the Volunteer Act as a threat to constitutional freedoms and because army officers thought it was insulting to their professional abilities. One Maine man wrote to President Madison, "I Shall observe that a *regular* Army has become the *only* Safety and bullwork of our Country, and that the *drafted* Malitia and Volunteer Corps are more fatal and dangerous than our open Enemies." Congress repealed the Volunteer Act on February 6, 1813, but permitted the units to serve until their enlistments expired. Many men transferred into regular regiments, but Ulmer's Volunteers continued to guard Maine's eastern border against illicit trade with the enemy. It failed almost completely in this task, as civilian resistance to the mission ultimately led to its colonel's arrest and disgrace.[22]

MODUS VIVENDI

During the war, the Maine border with New Brunswick was known as the Eastern Frontier, and the military posted volunteers there to suppress smuggling by "avaricious unprincipled citizens, & English agents." George Ulmer seemed like good choice for leading these units. He was a loyal Republican and a Revolutionary War veteran who had served in Washington's army and had wintered at Valley Forge. In Maine, he had prospered for a time as a land agent and a sawmill operator and served as both a militia major general and the sheriff of Hancock County. When lawsuits and business failures drove him to the brink of bankruptcy, he turned to federal service, which he hoped would restore his fortunes and shelter him from his creditors. In late July 1812, Ulmer corresponded with William King about taking command of a volunteer regiment, and he soon organized several companies in the Penobscot Bay area, with the understanding that they would remain in the District. He began his new enterprise by resigning as sheriff and giving up his militia commission. (Governor Strong happily appointed Federalists to fill those posts.) But then he dragged his feet on traveling to his command, which would be headquartered in Eastport, until he learned about a skirmish between American privateersmen and British forces in Passamaquoddy Bay. Reluctantly, he mounted his horse on November 29 and picked his way eastward from Lincolnville. The roads were miserable. Three days later, Ulmer was only in Buckstown, thirty miles away from his home, and he did not arrive at the border until December 9.[23]

Many of Ulmer's troops were from the Penobscot Bay area, including the three companies of detached militia already at Eastport under the command of his nephew. These companies joined Ulmer's regiment, along with two companies raised in the border region.

Eastport's Fort Sullivan served as his headquarters for subsidiary posts. The battery in Castine was the westernmost post, and a company of volunteers relieved its garrison of eight regulars. Ulmer described the battery near Machias as useless: "very small, badly contrived." The volunteers also built barracks at Robbinston and later at Calais to control border crossings.[24]

Colonel Ulmer realized he had a nearly impossible task. He described the people of Calais, Maine, and Saint Stephen, New Brunswick, as "like one family," whose members continued to cross the border as though there were no state of war between their nations. Robbinston's postmaster permitted mail to cross into enemy territory without inspection, and Eastport swarmed with armed smugglers who sold provisions to the British military. Ulmer had directions to observe the border's *modus vivendi*, which translates

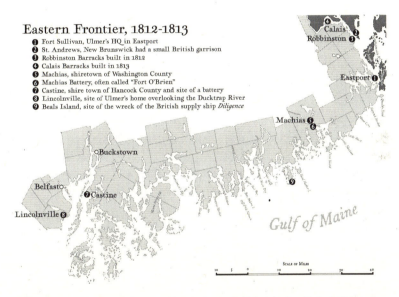

FIGURE 3. The Eastern Frontier was the U.S. military's term for Maine's border with the British province of New Brunswick. The region offered numerous opportunities for smuggling between locals on both sides of the border, with the tacit approval of British commanders. A few small military posts were located on the American side, but George Ulmer and other military officers found it impossible to control trade with the enemy. Map by the author.

from Latin as "way of living." In military terms, a modus vivendi was an arrangement whereby conflicting parties agreed informally to coexist peacefully. Such arrangements were common in European wars, used to create temporary, localized ceasefires. But if Ulmer were to chase smugglers into British waters or fire on a British unit, the delicate arrangement would crumble: and he had specific orders to exercise extreme prudence. For their part, some British officers wanted to attack Ulmer's command, but cooler heads prevailed in Halifax.[25]

Ulmer soon learned that the Eastern Frontier was a chaotic mess. Fort Sullivan's regular army commander refused to have anything to do with the detached militia, even denying them entry into Fort Sullivan. These men slept in rented barracks that were "scarcely fit to shelter cattle," and after three months of duty they were "generally almost naked, ragged, and filthy." In contrast, Fort Sullivan's garrison of seventeen regulars lived in a barracks designed to hold 150 men. The fort's commander refused to share its stockpile of supplies and weapons, vowing he would never hand over the post except to another regular officer and that he would not take orders from a volunteer officer. For the time being, Ulmer left the lieutenant alone and wrote for instructions. In the meantime, volunteers began to arrive, but there were few supplies for them, and the provisions were substandard. Ulmer wrote that the pork was "all heads and the Beef all bones," a claim the provisions contractor vehemently denied.[26]

Ulmer was at the end of a long and tenuous supply chain; even without British interference, getting provisions and other necessities proved to be extraordinarily difficult. Transportation and communication were problematic, depending on boats that ducked from one cove into the next, from Penobscot Bay east to Machias, always in fear of being captured by the Royal Navy. From Machias, the supplies traveled over bad roads to Eastport. The colonel requested an armed schooner and gunboats to protect his supply lines and patrol nearby waters, but this request went unanswered. His underfed, poorly clad men suffered cruelly in the winter weather, occasionally collapsing during morning parade. Ulmer bought pots, kettles, straw, stationery, and provisions at his own expense. He discovered that one company was composed mainly of underaged boys, children "that ought to have nurses come with them to take care of them and cannot with prudence be suffered to be out in the night, and seldom on days, in a cold blustering climate like this." He toyed with sending these youngsters home, but he badly needed troops to control the border.[27]

Ulmer found the modus vivendi frustrating. He could generally see one or more British warships stationed in Passamaquoddy Bay. However, under the terms of the modus vivendi, those warships could pass Fort Sullivan with perfect impunity, so long as they lowered their flags as a signal that they were not engaging in hostilities. Ulmer wrote of watching HMS *Rattler* and HMS *Nova Scotia*, both loaded with soldiers, float close up to the fort: "The tide brought them so near that my grape shot could have cleared their decks and my round shot would have bored them through. I having no orders to act other than on the defensive as respects hostilities, they were permitted to pass." The sight of these British warships was doubly frustrating because the same ships were capturing the supply vessels that were bringing food to his hungry troops. The only silver lining was that they also captured Lieutenant Samuel Maclay, the officer who had refused to allow Ulmer to use Fort Sullivan. In another incident, HMS *Boxer* briefly detained Ulmer's wife and three other women. Fortunately, its commander did not realize who the women were or that the fifteen men accompanying them were members of Ulmer's volunteers. The volunteers had no uniform other than a cockade pinned to their hats, which they had thrown overboard, along with their muskets, to conceal their identity. *Boxer*'s captain released the boat after having coffee with the ladies.[28]

"WILDNESS AND INCONSISTENCY IN HIS ORDERS"

Ulmer estimated that, since the declaration of war, contraband worth more than $1 million had entered Maine from the British side of the border, a staggering sum in 1812, considering that the federal budget for 1811 had been $8.6 million. The colonel believed there were almost two hundred smugglers in Eastport, an overwhelming number for his garrison to handle. Determined to stop trade with the enemy, he composed a draconian proclamation demanding that all non-U.S. citizens in Eastport either take a loyalty oath or depart in six days; otherwise, they would be imprisoned. He required anyone crossing the international boundary to carry a pass and ordered his officers to read all cross-border mail. In the spirit of the modus vivendi, Ulmer shared his proclamation with the British commander at Saint Andrews, who urged Ulmer not to be too strict until word of the new regulations could be disseminated. In the meantime, many smugglers fled from Eastport, while others threatened to tar and feather the colonel.[29]

Ulmer aggressively patrolled the waters of Passamaquoddy Bay, sending boatloads of soldiers in pursuit of smugglers. They caught several, and for a while the colonel seemed to be getting the upper hand, despite squabbles with the federal officials who should have been his allies. For example, the wreck of the British transport *Diligence* on Beals Island, southwest of Machias, should have been a windfall. Ulmer and a company of troops braved bitter wintry conditions to salvage cannon, blankets, muskets, camp kettles, and other much-needed supplies, though not before locals hid some of the cargo in barns and the woods. However, Machias's customs collector insisted that the wreck was under his authority and claimed the salvage rights. The customs officers in Eastport, especially the deputy collector, William Coney, also clashed with the colonel, interfering with his seizure of a sloop loaded with British manufactured goods reportedly worth $100,000. Ulmer ordered the goods to be taken to the blockhouse in Fort Sullivan, safe from civilian control, but then Maine's federal district court ordered him to hand the contraband back to the customs officers. Even more devastating was the secretary of war's decision that Ulmer should abandon his extreme measures. The colonel's only comfort was that his wife had joined him.[30]

Meanwhile, the logistics situation had worsened after a supply vessel sailed directly for New Brunswick, where its master enraged the colonel by selling the provisions to the British. Ulmer continued to pay out of pocket for straw, firewood, hospital stores, stationery, and lead for musket balls. Provisions were the only thing he did not have to purchase because a local merchant (and prominent smuggler) provided them on a contract basis. Unfortunately the unscrupulous contractor provided Ulmer's soldiers with spoiled rye flour, substandard meat, and biscuits said to be hard enough to break soldiers' teeth. One volunteer complained, "my god if this be the case we must die, and it may as well be by sword as by Famin." The contractor also informed the British how many men Ulmer had on the Eastern Frontier. By the middle of March, 1813 Ulmer learned that Captain Westcott had lost the payroll overboard and that another officer had misappropriated almost $2,000.[31]

Resistance to the colonel's measures grew as smugglers united against him, bribing his volunteers with liquor and money. In one bold act, smugglers stole nine barrels of tobacco from a wharf and rowed them across the border. In a related incident, soldiers captured several smugglers and a boat, but the prisoners overwhelmed their guards and handed them over to the British. Washington County officials also harassed the troops. When one of Ulmer's soldiers shot and wounded a smuggler, the sheriff arrested the soldier and sent him to jail in Castine to await trial for attempted murder. Ulmer was now deeply in debt, thanks to the supplies he had bought on credit; and his opponents arrested him and incarcerated him in the Machias jail. Ulmer meekly submitted, declared the jail to be his headquarters, and brought a clerk in so that he could continue his administrative duties. He remained in jail for a month until he persuaded local judges that it was illegal to prevent a military officer from performing his duties during wartime. The colonel begged King for help: "I am not a little mortified, that you appear to decline doing anything more for the Volunteers. They do, and will consider you, their Creator in this quarter; and of course will consider you their preserver, and protector." As time passed, he became increasingly morose, writing to a subordinate, "I am an old man and came to this frontier to die."[32]

While in jail, Ulmer learned that civilians and foreigners were entering the post without challenge and passing information to the British. He ordered sentries to deny entry to unapproved civilians. He also ordered his officers to prevent civil magistrates or deputies from arresting or imprisoning any of his soldiers—a somewhat ironic command, given his own situation. During his absence in jail, the campaign to stop smuggling ceased, and Eastport returned to its former state—in the words of one officer, "filled with speculators, spies & smugglers." Ulmer's enemies further eroded his authority with a poison-pen campaign that complained about his conduct. After his release and return to duty, he discovered that several officers had turned against him, led by Lieutenant Sherman Leland. Ulmer upbraided Leland for neglecting his duties in order to continue his Eastport law practice, and Leland told one private that "Ulmer was a rascal" and encouraged other soldiers to make official complaints. They did. The regimental surgeon called Ulmer's behavior "very irregular" and told King that "the discharge of Col. Ulmer would conduce to the honour & interest of the service and the satisfaction of the troops—he drinks so hard and there is such wildness and inconsistency in his orders & conduct that he has become perfectly contemptible in the sight of his troops, and the consequence is insubordination and all the train of evils which naturally follow."[33]

Yet not everyone agreed with such statements. Ulmer was known to be concerned about his men: on frigid nights he personally checked on the sentinels; he diligently inspected the troops every Sunday afternoon; he shared their privations while salvaging the wreck of the *Diligence*, huddling under an old sail for shelter at night. He repeatedly asked his officers to let him know, in a friendly manner, if he had erred. His defenders called him "an able, correct, and vigilant officer." A subordinate said that he was "indefatigable in promoting the good of the Army." Yet even though some observers credited the colonel with doing as well as anyone could have in managing the difficult situation at the border, his supporters also recognized that his orders were erratic. In mid-May, the secretary of war reported "much confusion" among the Eastern Frontier's volunteers.[34]

Shortly after returning from jail, Ulmer learned that Leland and two others had sought and gained commissions in the Thirty-fourth U.S. Infantry. With these commissions in hand, they immediately commenced recruiting privates from the volunteers, offering generous amounts of alcohol and furloughs as incentives. Alarmed, Ulmer wrote to the secretary of war for direction, after first attempting to arrest the officers and refusing to recognize their commissions. But greater embarrassments yet awaited the unfortunate colonel. His power to control the region had slipped away, and his command was rapidly eroding.[35]

"THE RAGE OF VOLUNTEERS"

A series of tumults in the summer of 1813 marked the end of Ulmer's command. The first occurred in Castine, where Captain Westcott's troops remained unpaid. At the end of June, a trial took place in the Hancock County courthouse involving the soldier at Eastport who had shot and wounded a smuggler. A jury found him guilty of assault, fined him $40, required a bond for two years of good behavior, and ordered him to pay all court costs. The verdict did not sit well with Westcott's disgruntled company, and one night thirty armed soldiers forced their way into the jail and released their colleague. The jailer recognized several of the men and informed the Hancock County sheriff, Moses Adams, who deemed the jailbreak an "insurrection" and called out the militia to patrol Castine's streets.[36]

County officials issued warrants against several soldiers, but they were no longer at the fort: Captain Westcott claimed he had given them furloughs before the jailbreak. Nonetheless, sheriff's deputies apprehended three volunteers, and a judge committed them to jail without bail. The townspeople and Wescott feared another assault, so the sheriff called on the Ellsworth Light Infantry to patrol the village. They were an unfortunate choice, being notoriously Federalist in politics, and clad in British-style red uniforms. and led by an English land agent who worked for the wealthy landowners whom poor settlers widely hated. His name was John Black, and despite being the son-in-law of General David Cobb, who commanded the militia in Hancock and Washington counties, he had to explain to his troops that he was a naturalized citizen who had renounced his allegiance to England and was completely loyal to his adopted country. Despite Sheriff Adams's provocative moves, no further incidents plagued Castine, other than an increase in Republican ire.[37]

The next crisis occurred in Eastport on Independence Day. The town's Federalists had gathered at the schoolhouse to read the Declaration of Independence and George Washington's Farewell Address. Volunteers disrupted the proceedings by firing muskets, throwing stones and bricks, and screaming obscenities. The locals ignored the taunts, and many gathered in a tavern to propose holiday toasts, which included praising the judge in Castine for not submitting to "the rage of volunteers," a reference to the recent jailbreak. Meanwhile, the volunteers continued to rampage, stealing the celebrants' cannon, throwing rocks and gravel at the inn's windows, burning an effigy of one of the civilians, and screaming threats. Finally, Ulmer arrived on horseback and ordered the men back to their barracks. The men did return to quarters but continued firing their muskets in celebration and defiance. So Ulmer ordered an officer to point two cannons at the barracks, commanding him to load them with canister shot, a lethal munition designed to mow down large groups of people. It was a bold move and was meant to intimidate, but it failed when the soldiers called the colonel's bluff. Ulmer left the scene and within minutes of departing could hear musket fire. Despite Ulmer's orders, the officer of the guard refused to fire the cannons on the drunken volunteers.[38]

The Independence Day disorders were too much for Leland, who circulated a petition among the regiment's officers. Enough of them signed it to encourage him to write a damning letter to Colonel Joseph D. Learned in Portland. Among the complaints were falsifying muster rolls, misappropriating weapons, wrongfully arresting an officer, concealing underaged soldiers from an inspecting officer (one drummer boy was only nine years old), and letting the regiment slip into a state of anarchy. Learned and Leland, both attorneys, seem to have been friendly beforehand. Learned had even advocated for Leland's promotion to lieutenant colonel, and he now passed the complaints about Ulmer on to headquarters in Boston. In the meantime, Ulmer had realized that Leland posed a threat, and the colonel tried to convince him to move his troops to Machias.[39]

But Ulmer was dealing with increasingly disorderly behavior among his troops as well as resistance from locals. Soldiers broke into Fort Sullivan's blockhouse and stole supplies, including ammunition. Civil authorities continued to arrest his men, despite his orders. In one particularly fraught incident, locals refused to cooperate with Ulmer after an escaped Canadian privateer captain named Solomon Jennings appeared in Eastport. When Ulmer learned of his presence, he sent soldiers to arrest him, but Jennings escaped in a boat to Indian Island, on the British side of the border, with the colonel and his troops in hot pursuit. Ulmer tried to negotiate with the Indian Island people, with the goal of convincing them to give up Jennings. The islanders refused but agreed to travel with Ulmer under a flag of truce to Saint Andrews, where the British commander would sort out the privateersman's status the next day. When Ulmer returned to Indian Island the next day, he found a crowd assembled and learned that Jennings had fled to Saint John. This was the last of many embarrassments for the colonel. General Thomas H. Cushing relieved him of command, arrested him, and encouraged the volunteers to join regular regiments. Mortified, Ulmer expressed his wish to die on a battlefield in Canada.[40]

After Ulmer's dismissal, the number of volunteers in the District shrank dramatically, and they became little more than a constabulary that pursued cattle smugglers. Volunteers on the upper reaches of the Kennebec joined the Thirty-third U.S. Infantry, leaving their officers with only a handful of soldiers. Many of Ulmer's enlisted in the Thirty-fourth U.S. Infantry. Having jumped from one unit to another, at least a few found it easy to keep moving, deserting Leland's company and crossing the border into New Brunswick, where they signed up on a Canadian privateer.[41]

With the volunteer program's collapse, William King also found himself on the defensive. In June 1814, a committee drawn from both houses of the Massachusetts legislature asked if he had held any federal commission, received any federal arms, or recruited any soldiers. King denied holding a commission or controlling arms belonging to the national government. However, he readily admitted to raising volunteers, claiming he could have organized three more regiments without difficulty. He concluded with a bit of bravado, assuring the committee that "as a Citizen of the U. States

I have duties to perform, as well as those of this State; and while I shall endeavor not to neglect the latter, the former will most unquestionably claim my attention."[42]

Though King announced that his primary loyalty lay with the United States, not with Massachusetts, he continued to trade with the enemy, sending loads of lumber and potatoes to Bermuda, the site of a Royal Navy base. British merchants and commissary officers paid his captains in silver, meaning that little or no cargo returned to Maine, just specie deposited in a bank in Bath. King was able to continue this commerce because he had purchased British licenses notifying Royal Navy warship commanders that he had permission to pass. Now, with Ulmer out of the way, King also began smuggling at Quoddy, shipping livestock to Bermuda for sale at inflated wartime prices.[43]

King was not the only Mainer engaged in illicit trade with Bermuda. Many Bath merchants were also involved, facilitated by former congressman Peleg Tallman, who had procured an appointment as Swedish vice-consul that allowed him to register Bath ships under Swedish colors. Bath's Republican merchants increasingly adopted this ruse, which gave legal cover to their illicit trade with the tacit approval of the port's customs collector. The U.S. Navy wanted to put a stop to it. When Captain Charles Stewart of the frigate *Constitution* discovered that one of Tallman's Swedish-flagged ships was involved in the Bermuda trade, he reported the matter to his superiors. Yet even though Stewart knew that the vessel was supplying the Royal Navy, he had no legal grounds to hold it and had to release the brig. Merchants in Downeast communities also engaged in the illicit Bermuda trade. Like their Bath counterparts, Federalists such as John Crosby, Sr., of Hampden used Swedish-flagged vessels. But Castine's merchants did not bother with such stratagems: they simply sailed straight to Bermuda. In April 1813, five brigs and a schooner from Castine and nearby ports arrived at the island, loaded with lumber, shingles, spars, and barrel staves. Like their fellow traders, they returned to Maine with little cargo, preferring specie or credit.[44]

Chapter 4

WAR AFLOAT

The British assumed that a negotiated peace would prevent full-blown war, so they worked to avoid escalations in the Gulf of Maine in 1812. The Royal Navy made every effort to accommodate New England merchants who were shipping flour to British forces in Spain and timber to the forces in Nova Scotia. Nonetheless, they did capture American vessels. HMS *Belvidera* seized the first, the brigantine *Malcolm* of Falmouth, Maine, carrying a cargo of Madeira wine. Admiral Sir Herbert Sawyer released *Malcolm* and subsequent prizes as a goodwill gesture, promptly paroled American seamen, and permitted coasting and fishing vessels from communities such as Eastport to pass back and forth unmolested. As mentioned in chapter 3, the British even issued licenses that allowed American ships to carry crucial provisions and naval stores to their colonies as well as timber from Wiscasset, Portland, and Hallowell to the naval shipyard at Halifax.[1]

INVESTING IN PRIVATEERS

The most active units afloat in 1812 were American privateers that operated in the approaches to the Bay of Fundy. Many were mere fishing or coastal craft, hastily armed and sailing in pursuit of profit. Their operations seldom had much military value but were essentially elaborate plundering or smuggling schemes. The idea behind the privateer units was that commercial vessels with government commissions could block or slow Britain's seaborne supplies and thus bring conflict and confusion to the enemy. Thomas Jefferson saw them as a cheap, ideologically sound auxiliary fleet that could damage the British economy as well as a way to avoid relying solely on an expensive navy. Philosophically, privateering was analogous to the volunteer program in that it emphasized Republican zeal and parsimony. On June 26, 1812, Congress passed an act laying out specific instructions and provisions for licensing privateers. Within a week, privateering commissions arrived in New England ports; and with these documents on board, several vessels immediately sailed.[2]

Most privateers belonged to Republican shipowners who bought shares in several vessels, which spread the risk among several families, should a vessel be lost. In the summer of 1812 James Jewett, a Portland merchant and ardent Republican, applied for a commission for his brig *Rapid*. It seemed to be a good candidate: a fast sailer and only three years old. Armaments were scarce, so Jewett borrowed cannons, and *Rapid* set sail in August. Twenty-eight people purchased shares in the brig, including his nephew Joseph and his mother, Ruth Jewett, the only Maine woman known to invest in privateering. Most of these investors never bought shares in another vessel. The Jewetts dropped out of privateering after *Rapid*'s capture, as did William Crabtree, the brig's commander, who left the vessel after two voyages. Joseph Cross, Jr., briefly persisted, investing in the *Mars* that summer but then withdrawing. Robert Ilsley did reinvest in privateers, but not until 1814. Lemuel Weeks, Jr., never took shares again but served as a lieutenant on the privateer *Superb* in 1813 and commanded the *McDonough* late in the war.[3]

The privateering brothers Samuel and Seward Porter of Portland were heavily engaged in maritime trade. They were typical of the American merchants who came of age during the Napoleonic wars, accustomed to running high-risk cargo past the Royal Navy to French continental and colonial markets. As Federalists, they were not drawn to privateering immediately, instead preferring to have their vessels commissioned with letters of marque. That is, their armed vessels were licensed to act as blockade runners. The French West Indies was their primary trading partner, and their goal was to carry cargo into inflated wartime markets. If they came across a likely prize, their ships had the legal authority to capture it. The Porters' vessel *Dash*, well known for its speed, made three successful voyages to Haiti, returning with valuable cargoes of coffee despite being chased by British warships. Yet despite *Dash's* good luck, the Porter brothers had business problems. The declaration of war left them, like many other merchants, with large amounts of British merchandise on the wrong side of the Canadian border, and they had to scheme to bring it into the United States via Eastport. After the Porters' Portland warehouse burned, and with it a cargo of coffee, the partnership teetered on the brink of insolvency. Only then did the Porters commission *Dash* as a privateer.[4]

Most privateers were small vessels, simple two-masted schooners able to be rowed if becalmed. They were nicknamed "shaving mills," a derogatory reference to their size. But their shallow draft allowed them to enter small harbors, hide among islands, and run onshore to avoid capture. Many carried under a dozen crewmembers. Before the war, Maine shipyards had built few vessels for speed: at that time, most shipowners had preferred a boxy design that maximized cargo capacity and freight revenue. This was not the case in other ports. Both New York and Baltimore were ahead of New England shipbuilders in constructing fine-lined schooners with raked masts that carried a large press of canvas. Yankee shipowners such as the Porter brothers recognized this rig's utility and began building vessels such as *Dash* along similar lines. However, the low freeboard, sharp entry, and lofty rig that made these vessels speedy sometimes also led to problems, and *Dash* may have capsized on its last voyage in January 1815.[5]

"GOING A PRIVATEERING"

While some privateersmen acted out of patriotism, many people, especially Federalists, equated them with disorder and immorality. As a Portland diarist grumbled in the summer of 1812,

> Every petty boat which can find patronage & men, is fitting out to take part in this disgraceful & barbarous species of warfare. The petty fishing boats, which are frequently going out, can do nothing but rob & steal from the helpless; their only hope is from such kind of depredation, as ought to be regarded by every civilized nation as absolute piracy. Larger privateers may secure their profits by fighting manfully those who are able to look out for themselves;

but these [craft] will even steal along shore by night, & plunder families & shops.

Even seafarers doubted the morality of privateering, some referring to it as "a species of piracy." Moses Adams, a Federalist physician from Ellsworth and a representative to the Massachusetts General Court, was more outspoken. He demanded that privateer prizes be burnt at the wharf and proposed to pull privateersmen from their beds at midnight to be tarred and feathered. The Republican press lambasted Adams for such talk, but Governor Strong rewarded him by making him sheriff of Hancock County in place of George Ulmer. Adams was a graduate of Harvard College and the son of a Congregationalist minister, from whom he had inherited his Federalist politics. Strong must have thought him a perfect representative of the Massachusetts ideal, who could impose order on Maine's frontier, including curbing the excesses committed by the shaving mills.[6]

Young men who signed onto these vessels were often quickly corrupted. Henry Ingraham's journal records that his nineteen-year-old brother Charles badgered their parents for permission to sign onto a privateer. The parents finally conceded, but Henry noted that "father & mother very much against his going a privateering. He is a poor fellow inexperienced [and] knows but Litle what a place he has put himself in. But we hope for the Best." Charles Ingraham survived his first cruise but came home a changed person: "Charles went up To the Store Drinking & swearing. wicked Boy allmost ruined–having his own way & going a privateering."[7]

Privateer crews were relatively diverse: African Americans commonly served on these vessels and were just as unruly as their white counterparts, as when the commander of the *Lilly* of Portland noted in his logbook that "Richard Bell 'a culler'd man,'" had deserted. Foreigners, including Spaniards, Portuguese, and even Englishmen, also signed onto American privateers. However, most privateersmen in Maine waters were white Yankees from the District or from Essex County, Massachusetts.[8]

These polyglot crews often proved challenging to handle. The logbook of the *Rover* of Portland records, "In consequence of the badness of the vessel the pepple groan but by the pursuasion of the officers they agree to go." Conditions on the vessel remained unhappy. A few days later, its officers broke up a fistfight between the gunner and the boatswain. Shipboard fisticuffs were frequent on shaving mills such as the *General Pike* of New York. This craft reportedly spent four days in Portland, with the privateersmen "*bunging up* each others eyes." The men of the tiny *Swiftsure* spent more time brawling among themselves than fighting the enemy. Sometimes this everyday violence escalated. The first lieutenant of the *Wasp* of Salem, Massachusetts, ordered his men to fire on a deserter as he fled the vessel at Machias. They shot him dead, and the entire crew attended his funeral ashore. The privateer's captain, flummoxed by the affair, sought Colonel Ulmer's advice on what to do. Ulmer, in jail himself, thought the captain should arrest the lieutenant and sail for Salem to seek legal advice.[9]

Provisions were a problem on small privateering craft, which had large crews but little storage space. The logbook of the *Fame* of Salem frequently mentions fishing, an activity that would have served as good cover for the vessel's real business as well as a source of fresh food. Its crew also went ashore to dig clams. Logbooks sometimes portray these voyages as pleasure cruises: one noted that the crew "had fine amusement fishing & fowling." But the *Favorite* of Portland was so ill provisioned that its master had to sell gunpowder to buy food, and he later pawned a musket in the Cranberry Isles for the same reason. Sometimes privateersmen stole shipboard provisions and had to be punished or went ashore and filched calves or chickens, much to the ire of coastal farmers. When the bosun of the privateer *Frolic* discovered that the vessel's provisions were spoiled, he threw the bread pan overboard, earning a $5 fine. When the crew of the privateer *Salisbury* of Newburyport, Massachusetts, found themselves low on food and water, its commander and another officer went ashore in Digby, Nova Scotia, to reprovision. Locals quickly captured the feckless men and killed another crewmember as the *Salisbury* hoisted anchor and fled. As a Newburyport Federalist sourly noted in his journal, "May the cruise of the *Salisbury* prove a good lesson to all privateersmen."[10]

Many coastal communities resented the privateers, who commonly seized American vessels, robbed the crews, and invited reprisals from the Royal Navy. Eastport's Committee of Safety asked American privateers to leave without taking prizes from nearby waters. When privateersmen did bring prize vessels to that town, they often fell victim to nocturnal pranks, as when someone drilled a hole through the bottom of a prize schooner, which sank at the wharf. Privateersmen responded to Eastport's hostility with threats, so it was little wonder that its harbor was an unsafe place for them to linger. Castine's residents feared that privateers would instigate retaliatory raids and publicly denied that a shaving mill conducting shore raids in New Brunswick had come from there. Portland's selectmen refused to let the *Rambler*'s captain land a mortally sick sailor, fined him when two of his crew got drunk ashore, and even refused to let him take water on board.[11]

PRIVATEERS IN ACTION

The first privateers to arrive in Maine waters came from Essex County, Massachusetts. In the ports of Gloucester, Marblehead, and Salem, vessels had prepared and armed before the declaration of war and were waiting impatiently for their commissions. On July 1, the commissions arrived, and the privateers sailed immediately, anxious to pounce on British shipping before it became aware that a state of war existed. Their destination was the Bay of Fundy, where they intended to capture ships coming out of Saint Andrews and Saint John, New Brunswick. The first to arrive was the *Jefferson*, a twenty-two-ton sloop. When it anchored at Eastport, on its way northeast, a committee immediately ordered it to leave without molesting any shipping in Passamaquoddy Bay. *Jefferson*'s commander ignored them, hoisting anchor and seizing two British vessels in Snug Cove on Campobello Island, within sight of Eastport but lying in the province of New Brunswick. Eastport's deputy U.S. marshal wrote, "This day is a day of gloominess. We had been able to live peaceable until this morning when the American shaving mill *No. 46* from Salem cut out of Snug Cove on the British side of the water a British schooner, Capt. Swain, cargo $1500 and we expect the like treatment from the British in return—Everything in Confusion on both sides of the water. God grant we may see no more of those [shaving] mills."[12]

Throughout the summer of 1812, Saint John newspapers complained about swarms of American privateers in the Bay of Fundy: "so numerous are the privateers around the coast, that we consider it very imprudent for any vessel to sail from this port unless under convoy." These vessels carried names such as *Jefferson*, *Madison*, and *Elbridge Gerry* to advertise their political loyalties, and they captured several valuable prizes—for example, the British military transport brig *No. 50*, which beat off an attack from the *Jefferson* while sailing near Grand Manan Island but later surrendered to the *Madison* of Gloucester. Its cargo was a trove of military supplies, including gunpowder, new uniforms for the British 104th Regiment, drums, trumpets, and other camp equipment estimated to be worth $50,000.[13]

By November 1812, Canadian privateers were harassing American shipping. The infamous *Liverpool Packet* was raiding the coast, possibly with an American pilot's help; and it was rumored that the crew had landed at York, Maine, and had posed as Salem privateersmen in a local tavern. Other Canadian ships joined the *Liverpool Packet* in 1813, paralyzing ports such as Portland for days and intercepting supplies. On one occasion they captured the sloop *Mary*, which was carrying $5,000 worth of goods destined for Augusta, including gunpowder and cannonballs for Hallowell's militia.[14]

The government had commissioned the privateers not to fight the enemy but to attack commercial shipping. Consequently, they usually had puny cannons or even smaller swivel guns. Sometimes the privateersmen had only muskets or blunderbusses and crude cutlasses made from farm implements. Nonetheless, they were occasionally involved in combat. Privateers generally engaged with one of four opponents: a prize vessel, a naval vessel, militia units, or an enemy privateer. Merchant ships often defended themselves, especially larger vessels with more valuable cargoes. On occasion, a potential prize offered dogged resistance, as when the Salem privateer *Revenge* pursued the ship *Ned* off Grand Manan in a running battle that ended when the Yankees overwhelmed the ship by boarding. In contrast, the *Fame* captured a British merchant ship off West Quoddy Head on July 4 without a fight. *Fame* was a mere thirty-one tons and armed with two cannons; its target was a three-hundred-ton ship with four real guns and several dummy ones. Undaunted, *Fame*'s commander demanded that the vessel surrender; and when the merchant ship refused, the privateersmen boarded it. The British crew promptly ran below deck. As one Salem correspondent reported, "It was a brave thing in going along side so warlike a looking ship."[15]

Sometimes resistance to privateers was more subtle, as when the *Fame* attempted to seize a sloop alongside a Campobello pier and found that the owners had chained it to the wharf. The local militia peppered the crew with musket fire, so they had to abandon their effort. At other times resistance was more lethal, as when the one-legged American captain of a captured schooner killed the sole Canadian seaman placed on board as prizemaster. The captain brought the vessel into Narraguagus, where locals buried the prizemaster's body.[16]

But even the doughtiest privateers generally fled if they spied a British warship. The Portland brig *Rapid* led the frigates HMS *Maidstone* and *Spartan* on a chase that lasted for eight hours. Its commander, Joseph Weeks, Jr., did everything possible to lighten the ship, throwing overboard eight cannons and an anchor and cutting loose the ship's boat, but to no avail. When the *Maidstone* approached within musket shot, he surrendered. The British officers admired the commander's seamanship and returned his sword to him as a token of esteem. They were not the only adversaries who praised him: Weeks had an impressive bearing and an intelligent mind but suffered from bad luck. When the British captured him again two years later, a Royal Navy officer recorded that he was the "best informed and most respectable man in his situation that I ever met with."[17]

American privateers sometimes ran afoul of Canadian militia, as when the *Fame* tried to capture a schooner in Beaver Harbour,

New Brunswick. The privateers ran in close to the schooner, but contrary winds prevented them from capturing the vessel "before we should have been all killed by the inhabitants. There was about 30 men with their rifles right over our heads where we could not bring one of our guns to bear upon them; therefore, we thought it prudent to heave up and leave them." Likewise, a boat from the *St. Michael* of Portland found itself under fire from Canadian militia who were patrolling Indian Island's waters in guard boats. One American was wounded in that incident; in another, Campobello militia wounded two American privateersmen as they sailed past their island.[18]

Canadian privateers also encountered American militia units, as when the tiny sloop *Fly* captured three small coasting vessels near Owl's Head on Penobscot Bay and then crossed to Vinalhaven, anchoring near its prizes. The sloop's crew looted the captured craft throughout the night, attempting to allay suspicions by flying an American flag. Locals saw through the ruse, however, and the militia gathered overnight on the shore. As dawn broke, the Yankees opened fire, killing the sloop's captain, shooting off the mate's jaw, and wounding others. The sloop narrowly escaped by cutting its anchor cable and drifting out on the tide, and the militia returned the three American vessels to their owners and captured four privateersmen. The history of the *Fly* is itself representative of how often privateers changed hands. Built in Virginia in 1797, the sloop went to sea as the American privateer schooner *Buckskin* in 1812, until HMS *Statira* captured it off Halifax. Canadian investors procured a privateering commission for it under the name *Fly*, and rerigged it as a single-masted sloop. It cruized Maine waters in 1813, managing to elude Vinalhaven's militiamen, only to fall prey to USS *Enterprise* off the Isle of Shoals that summer. By late 1814, still named *Fly*, the sloop operated out of Portland, despite having once sunk at its moorings.[19]

The least common form of combat was privateer against privateer. The best-known example occurred in 1813, when a group of men from Bristol, Maine, gathered under the leadership of Captain Samuel Tucker, a veteran of the Continental Navy. They armed the sloop *Increase*, borrowing cannons and ammunition from Fort Edgecomb. *Increase* patrolled the coast for two days seeking the elusive Royal Navy schooner *Bream*; but crewmembers were anxious to return to their spring plowing, so they returned the borrowed cannons and sailed for home. En route, they spied a suspicious schooner, and Tucker ordered all but a few of his men to hide while the craft approached.[20]

The other vessel was the Canadian privateer *Crown* of Halifax, only forty feet long and armed with a single carronade. Its commander, too, had hidden his men. When the *Crown* came near Tucker's sloop, the Bristol men leaped up and opened fire. The schooner replied in kind and attempted to hoist its British flag, but musket fire cut the halyards and the jib sheet. Tucker and his men overwhelmed the *Crown* with small-arms fire and then boarded and captured it. Remarkably, the affair was bloodless: as the Canadian captain marveled, "there is above 300 balls in our hull and spars, the sails and rigging of both vessels wonderfully cut to pieces, a number of balls through our hats and cloaths, yet there is not a man either killed or wounded on either side." Tucker landed the prisoners and marched them to Wiscasset, where he handed them over to federal authorities. His crew returned to their farms, leaving the old captain to complain, "all was clamour with my People to get home & get into the ground their sowing & planting and the instant the prize was secured and taken care of my command was dissolved."[21]

The privateer *Young Teazer* sailed from Portland in June 1813 and operated near Halifax, an incredibly bold plan, given that the town was a Royal Navy base. *Young Teazer* was a purpose-built 124-ton privateer schooner notable for its figurehead, an alligator with gaping jaws. It took a number of prizes until it was cornered by several warships in Mahone Bay, adjacent to Lunenburg, Nova Scotia. The British warships sent armed boats after the privateer, but the *Young Teazer* exploded as they approached. Rumor had it that the schooner's first lieutenant, Frederick Johnson, had fired the magazine to escape capture. According to his widow, Johnson was a "man of violent passions" with a burning hatred for the British. Before the *Young Teazer* had left New York, he had declared that "he would rather blow up the vessel sooner than he would be taken a prisoner by the British." He had experience with that fate; the British had already captured him twice. Although he had been paroled from his second imprisonment in Bermuda, Johnson had not been formally exchanged. This meant that the British could execute him if they were to capture him again.[22]

The *Young Teazer* sank immediately. Some twenty-five crewmembers died; the few who survived went into captivity. The lieutenant's desperate act horrified the British and the Canadians, and even the American press claimed that "he must have been possessed of the disposition of the devil, to plunge such a number of his friends into eternity." However, survivors of the incident testified that the *Young Teazer* was pulling away from the pursuing British boats when the explosion occurred. They believed it had resulted from an accident by crew members working in the magazine.[23]

"YOU DAMNED RUFFIAN"

In practice, privateering seldom fulfilled the government's goal of bringing the war to the enemy. Legal scholars have concluded that it was more of a business opportunity to profit from a war than a patriotic activity. Furthermore, the privateersmen frequently engaged in excesses that violated federal and state laws. Its major deviations were related to trade. First, many privateers, especially those from Essex County, assumed a policing role, searching American-flagged vessels for contraband or for evidence that they were trading with the British. Yet American privateering commissions made no mention of this authority, and numerous merchants protested in newspapers and lawsuits until the Supreme Court validated their policing role. Second, many shaving mills engaged in collusive capture, the prearranged sham capture of a vessel loaded with British merchandise. These schemes could be lucrative if they were undetected, but a number went awry, and federal officials learned about them, sometimes by accident. Third, privateersmen were occasionally involved in petty theft, both ashore and afloat. Incidents involving roughed-up passengers, pilfered cargo, and at least one cold-blooded murder occurred—the kind of violence one might expect of armed, undisciplined, and poorly led men under the influence of alcohol and adrenaline.[24]

Privateers' policing actions commenced within days of the war's declaration, when a crew from Marblehead, Massachusetts, fired on and boarded the American schooner *Enterprize*, terrorizing its crew and passengers with pistols and cutlasses. A few days later, the crew of a Newburyport privateer shouted curses at the master of a vessel bound for Portland and then fired cannons, muskets, and pistols at the ship, leaving its sails full of holes. On another occasion, Essex County privateersmen boarded a schooner in Cranberry Harbor, pointing a cutlass at the captain's chest, threatening to "run him through," and promising to shoot him if he did not cooperate. In addition to terrorizing and damaging the ships of fellow Americans, the privateers frequently helped themselves valuables, as when they took $1,100 in gold coins from a coaster's passengers. Little wonder that some Federalist newspapers described these abuses as "pirateering."[25]

There was an ideological element to these boarding actions. American privateering officers were nearly all Republicans. The Salem privateer *Dolphin*'s commander was a noted Anglophobe who even refused to wear British clothing. An officer from the shaving mill *Swiftsure* described himself as a born Englishman but claimed that, having lived in the United States for six or seven years, he "was now a *true American*, and meant to detect and punish smugglers and tories." Politically motivated privateersmen committed many misdeeds in their pursuit of contraband traders, the same transgressions that many had feared the volunteers would commit on land. Their acts often revealed a class-based animosity, particularly their ire against merchants who continued to trade with the British. Still, sometimes the ships they targeted resisted, as when the Portland privateer boat *Partridge* chased the Portsmouth brig *Friendship* into George's River. *Friendship*'s master sent word ashore, and soon armed locals appeared and ordered the privateersmen off the brig and out of the river. The *Friendship*'s owners subsequently pursued a court case against the privateersmen.[26]

A vivid example of resistance occurred when the privateer *Jefferson* seized the American schooner *Lively* near Machias. A passenger on the *Lively* had made some trouble overnight, cursing at his captors and uttering threats. He became so unruly that privateersmen put him in irons before extracting a promise of good behavior. The following day, as the prize crew sailed the *Lively* up Machias Bay, a sentry at Fort O'Brien hailed the vessel with the usual questions about the ship's name and where it was bound. The troublesome passenger took this opportunity to begin shouting "pork & molasses" and similar nonsense to attract attention. Confused, the sentry demanded that the vessel halt or be fired on. The *Lively* came to anchor, and the *Jefferson* soon arrived on the scene. When the privateer's commander came ashore at the fort's wharf, the *Lively* passenger shouted, "Here comes that damn ruffian who stole my schooner from me," and "Well, you damned ruffian, I am ashore now, and have got friends." The privateering captain asked a crewman to fetch his pistols from the *Jefferson* and offered one to the troublesome passenger, inviting him to a duel, which the passenger refused, even as he continued his verbal abuse. The captain proceeded to the customhouse, where, to his chagrin, the collector told him that *Lively*'s papers were in order. But the privateersmen took the *Lively* anyway, leaving the seething passenger behind.[27]

Sometimes mariners and merchants sued privateersmen in state courts, where Federalist judges fined or imprisoned overzealous Republican privateersmen. After the crew of a shaving mill threatened to run him through with a cutlass, ransacked his cargo, and pointed a loaded pistol at his chest, the master of the *William & Anne* had their captain thrown into jail and sued him for damages. The *Dart* of Salem's officers bullied and threatened the master of the coasting schooner *Traveller* while it lay anchored at Little River (today known as Cutler). He sued in Essex County courts, which awarded him $160 for his trouble. In another case, men from the privateer *Germantown* of Marblehead took trade goods from a passenger's trunk. The aggrieved party went ashore at Machias and had a warrant sworn out. A deputy sheriff boarded the privateer, recovered the looted items, and forced the commander to post a bond to appear in court.[28]

Actions involving collusive capture also started in the first weeks of the war, and they continued throughout the conflict. In one of the earliest incidents, the owners of the Boston privateer *Friendship* had instructed its captain to proceed to the Bay of Fundy and drop off an agent referred to as "Mr. A." He would go to Saint John, purchase a small vessel, and load it with a cargo of wine, cloth, and hardware. He would then sail to a predetermined point and fly a signal flag. The pink-sterned *Friendship* would fire a sham volley or two, take possession of the vessel, and send it to a friendly port. The instructions admonished the captain to keep this illicit activity secret from the crew. But the owners had already promised to pay them double wages, a dead giveaway that this voyage was not on the up and up. Unfortunately for the owners, HMS *Indian* captured the *Friendship*, interrupting the elaborate plan. The Royal Navy discovered that its captain was a British subject and imprisoned him at Halifax, where he eventually died. Collusive capture schemes were not limited to American privateers. Canadian shaving mills also made sham captures of American craft loaded with provisions. Officials in Saint John would pay for the cargoes and then return the vessels to their owners, allowing them to repeat the process. By 1813, the scale and sophistication of collusive capture schemes had increased. Now they always involved high-priced British goods. For instance, the *Eliza Ann*, captured at anchor in Passamaquoddy Bay, carried almost six hundred boxes of tin, 5,000 pounds of steel, fifty-eight kegs of paint, a box of hardware, and seven bales of woolen goods.[29]

Seward Porter, an owner of the privateer *Dash*, was eager to become involved in collusive capture. He wrote to Halifax's British naval and military commanders proposing a grand scheme, even offering $50,000 in specie to guarantee good behavior. In his letter, Porter identified himself by name and stated his position in the Massachusetts legislature. He pointed out that the war was unpopular, writing that "altho' the Merchants of the State of Massachusetts are unwilling to engage in any measures of direct hostility to the General Government of the United States yet forc'd as they have been against their consent into a War which they consider unnecessary and unjust they feel no reluctance, but on the contrary are desirous of continuing and extending their commercial intercourse with Great Britain." He proposed that his privateer make sham captures of vessels loaded with West Indian and European goods. In return, he promised to provide American flour, beef, and pork to the Royal Navy and conjectured that this trade could be worth millions of dollars. Halifax merchants supported the idea, but there is no evidence of a reply.[30]

A major collusive capture scheme fell apart due to the efforts of the Robinsons, a family of fishermen who worked the waters between Deer Isle and Mount Desert. The Robinson men were well respected among their neighbors, who claimed they feared "neither God man or the Devil." In August 1813, the family discovered the *Lydia*, a suspicious-looking vessel anchored in nearby Eggemoggin Reach. They suspected it was a Canadian privateer, armed themselves, and boarded the vessel before the crew could mount a defense. Once in possession of the schooner, the Robinsons realized that there was something odd about the *Lydia*. It certainly looked like a typical fishing boat, with lines hanging off its rail, but only one line had a hook, and the Robinsons found no more hooks on board. Furthermore, no name was painted on the stern, as federal law required, nor were there any flags, except for a signal flag they found sewn up in a ruffled shirt. The schooner's commander claimed that the boat was a privateer, yet it had no weapons on board other than a few muskets. Oddest of all, one of *Lydia*'s crewmembers had slipped below and then reemerged on deck with something concealed under his hat, an object he threw overboard. Instead of sinking, the item bobbed to the surface, and the Robinsons, now thoroughly alarmed, plucked it out of the water. Their concerns grew when the mysterious schooner's captain offered them a bribe to set the vessel free. The fishermen may have been fearless, but they knew they were in over their heads. They took the retrieved package to Castine's customs collector, Josiah Hook, Jr., who discovered that it contained documents written in code.[31]

The Robinsons had unwittingly stumbled across a collusive capture ploy involving wealthy and influential merchants who were seeking to introduce contraband into the United States. The smuggling ring was based in Bath and included the pious Boston merchant John Tappan as well as Joseph F. Wingate, Jr., a confederate in William King's smuggling business. Hook decoded the documents, alerted customs officers in neighboring districts, and successfully broke up the ring. In the process, he netted at least $100,000 for himself, but the Robinsons received a mere $1,000 for their efforts. As the war continued, so did collusive captures, but federal officials had become increasingly alert to these ploys. Maine's customs officers had long been suspicious of small craft, and they asked the president for help. In response, President Madison revoked the commissions of shaving mills in November 1813, and Congress banned privateers with crews of fewer than twenty in January 1814.[32]

"MUCH ABUSED & MOST PIRATICALLY TREATED"

Both Canadian and American privateers broke the laws of war by pilfering from prize vessels, among them two craft with almost the same name: the Canadian privateer *Weazle* and the American shaving mill *Weasel*, which both operated in the summer of 1813. The crew of the *Weazle* of Halifax stopped and boarded a schooner just east of Portland. According to a passenger, "both passengers and crew were Robbed of Everything [the crew] could lay their hands on under American Colours." The privateersmen robbed this passenger of his gold watch and $500 in silver coins: "we were also much abused & most piratically treated & left without any kind of Provisions." Pilfering a prize ship's stores, especially its liquor, and shaking down passengers for their possessions seem to have been standard behavior for privateersmen.[33]

Shore raids, which American law expressly forbade, were rare but not unknown. The *Weasel*'s crew demonstrated uncommon viciousness in this regard, landing at an isolated New Brunswick port, breaking into homes with a crowbar, and reportedly even stealing children's clothing. Canadian militiamen in boats from Campobello chased the *Weasel* ashore onto Grand Manan and presumably retrieved and returned the stolen goods. The Federalist press took great delight in pointing out that this craft's commander was a Baptist preacher from the Penobscot River area.[34]

The war's worst atrocity involving enemy noncombatants took place on Sheep Island, Nova Scotia. A landing party from the American privateer *Wily Reynard* shot Lydia Clements's husband and then knocked at her door. When she did not answer, they smashed a window and demanded "who was within? She answered: A friend—Upon which one of them said—Damn you if you are a friend, open the door!" Clements let the armed men inside, and they interrogated her, asking if there were any other men on the island before departing with two of her pigs. The following day her children found their father's corpse. Now a widow with nine children, Clements probably drew little satisfaction from HMS *Shannon*'s capture of the *Wily Reynard* two days later. The privateer's crew testified that their lieutenant was the murderer, and British officials retained him for trial.[35]

Privateersmen did commit a few acts of kindness. For instance, the crew of the Canadian privateer *Fly* returned trunks to the passengers of a coasting vessel it had seized, and a Salem privateer captain returned $900 in specie to a female passenger. Yet these were rare: a few months later this same gallant captain "thoroughly fisted" a prisoner in the streets of Salem. Among Canadian privateersmen, James Archibald had a particularly vicious character. When not stealing from his neighbors, he sailed on the privateer *Lunenburgh*. His evil ways spiraled out of control, and ultimately provincial authorities executed him for murder in early 1815.[36]

NAVAL WAR IN THE GULF OF MAINE

Given the rampant privateering in American and Canadian waters, Admiral Sir Herbert Sawyer found himself on the defensive in the early months of the war. He focused his energies on protecting British seaborne commerce, instituting convoys and patrols to guard colonial shipping, especially the valuable mast ships sailing from New Brunswick. There were several actions between American privateers and British warships in the approaches to the Bay of Fundy.

Experienced and innovative Royal Navy officers such as Commander Henry Jane of HMS *Indian* were not above perpetrating a *ruse de guerre* to confuse the enemy. Jane disguised his brig by painting the hull a different color on each side, giving it the appearance of two vessels. He also rearranged the vessel's boats, unsquared the yards to make it look like a merchant ship, and flew an American flag, thus luring one unwary American sea captain on board. The Americans, for their part, worked to fool Commander Jane. When he sent a ship's boat to inspect a large sloop that proved to be a Salem privateer, the Americans opened fire with muskets and swivel guns, wounding three British sailors before disengaging.[37]

Sawyer had too few frigates to patrol the region's waters regularly, but they were highly effective when they did appear. In a sweep of the Bay of Fundy in August 1812, two frigates bagged almost a dozen privateers, sometimes sending boat parties into harbors and landing marines to capture grounded vessels, as at Little River. Here the crew of the revenue cutter *Commodore Barry* and three privateers beached themselves and hastily threw together a firing position out of cordwood to defend their craft. They did so successfully, and the British had to send a second landing party of marines and sailors to capture the vessels. Most of the American sailors escaped while the British looted waterfront homes.[38]

Toward the end of 1812, Admiral Sir John Borlase Warren took charge of the Royal Navy's North American Station with instructions to negotiate a peace or, if that failed, to wage a more aggressive war. When diplomatic efforts collapsed in November, he focused his energies on neutralizing the American navy, blockading the Chesapeake and Delaware bays, and continuing economic warfare against American shipping. In early 1813 Warren reassessed the strategic situation in the Gulf of Maine. Like Sawyer before him, he had to defend British and colonial shipping, and he regarded privateers as the main threat. He had three options: patrol, convoy, and blockade. He chose the first two, claiming that he had too few ships to blockade the entire coastline. Things began badly: the gun brig *Plumper* wrecked in the Bay of Fundy with significant loss of life, and the supply ship *Diligence* was stranded near Beal's Island with a cargo of cannons and munitions destined for Saint John. Warren also misinterpreted Ulmer's arrival at Eastport as the first element of a force of 3,000 intending to invade New Brunswick. The Admiralty shared his concerns and ordered him to establish a force in the Bay of Fundy to convoy British and colonial trade.[39]

Warren ordered five small warships to protect New Brunswick, a force known as the Fundy Squadron. *Rattler* was the largest but oldest vessel, and its commander, Alexander Gordon, served as the squadron's commander for a time. The squadron's two brigs had been American vessels until their capture. *Emulous* had been the American warship *Nautilus*, while HMS *Nova Scotia* was formerly the Portland privateer *Rapid*. The two schooners were Bermuda-built; *Bream* was the most successful of its class, *Herring* more typical in that it foundered with the loss of all hands in July 1813. That same month, *Boxer*, a newly built gun brig, arrived from England under the command of Samuel Blyth. None of these vessels was impressive, but their officers had a wealth of experience after decades of service in wars against France. All had gone to sea in their early teens, all had seen combat, and several had distinguished themselves as aggressive officers.[40]

Warren left operations on the Maine coast to Rear Admiral Edward Griffith, who arrived at the North American Station in 1813. Griffith oversaw the Halifax navy yard, attended to the Maritime provinces' defense, and protected commercial shipping, thereby freeing Warren to direct the war in American waters. Griffith was an experienced and competent sea officer, one whom Warren knew well and respected. The Fundy Squadron's activities primarily consisted of convoying merchant ships between Saint John and Halifax, a thankless and tedious duty. Still, these convoys proved to be effective; while the British occasionally lost a ship or two to American privateers, they never lost an entire convoy during the war.[41]

Patrolling, known as cruizing, was more exciting and profitable. The Fundy Squadron patrolled as far west as the Isle of Shoals, taking many small coasting vessels, entering American harbors to cut out ships, and sometimes skirmishing with American land forces. One of those skirmishes took place in March 1813, after U.S.

volunteers stationed at Boothbay manned three fishing boats and recaptured a schooner that *Bream* had taken, along with its prize crew of two sailors. The prisoners revealed that their warship would anchor in Boothbay Harbor that night to join the larger and more powerful *Rattler*. Forewarned, the Yankees prepared for a raid and called for reinforcements. When a landing party from the *Rattler* came ashore, the Americans easily repulsed them in a bloodless skirmish. In May, *Rattler* and *Bream* chased the large American privateer *Alexander* onto the beach at Kennebunk. The privateersmen hastily abandoned ship, some in boats and others by diving into the chilly waters to swim ashore, with at least one drowning in the process. Local militia companies assembled on the beach to protect the stranded ship. However, *Alexander*'s captain made a deal with Commander Gordon of the *Rattler* to let his crew go free in exchange for handing the vessel over to the British. The militia officers quickly determined that it was not prudent to intervene, and Gordon retrieved the privateer, describing it as a "remarkably fine ship, four years old, and . . . considered the fastest sailing privateer out of the United States." In another action, *Young Emulous* assisted a Canadian privateer in pursuing a vessel entering the Kennebec River. During a running battle, the American vessel, reinforced by soldiers from the Kennebec battery, fought until the crew ran out of ammunition. Finally, they abandoned the ship to the British and escaped ashore.[42]

A favorite tactic for American privateers was to beach themselves. For example, the tiny American privateer *Lilly* ran itself onshore to evade *Bream*, its logbook recording, "we histed English collers under American cullars and took the trumpet and told them to come in and take them downe we was so near we could hear them talk." Beaching forced the British vessel to send in a boat after its quarry, while the privateersmen hid behind trees and rocks and blazed away at them. Discretion being the better part of valor, boat parties carefully appraised a situation before coming within gunshot and sometimes broke off their attack. In October 1813, when *Bream* pursued the *Holker* into a creek, the privateer's logbook related that "we then got on all our arms on shore &

prepared to give them a warm reception but she bore away & went to their old anchorage." Seaborne combat became rarer between privateers and Royal Navy vessels in 1813. However, *Bream* pursued the Salem privateer *Wasp* for nine hours while the American captain tried every sailing trick possible to shake the Royal Navy schooner. Finally, *Bream* closed with the privateer, and a fierce half-hour battle resulted in *Wasp's* surrender.[43]

The Fundy Squadron captured dozens of American vessels in 1813, typically defenseless schooners of less than one hundred tons with cargoes of timber or cordwood. The squadron also captured three Yankee privateers and burned three more after removing valuables. Other captured craft went unreported because they carried foodstuffs to the British at Saint John. In June, *Bream* escorted three such vessels into Saint John, where its commander was undoubtedly compensated for his kindness. While the practice was illegal, Royal Navy officers sometimes ransomed vessels, as *Bream's* commander did. The brig *Boxer* proved to be an especial scourge to American shipping, sending nine prizes to Halifax, exclusive of vessels burnt or ransomed. An officer from HMS *Tenedos* noted that *Boxer's* success was due to its innocuous appearance: "'twas impossible for any one to know her for a man of war, having her sides varnish'd, and altogether the appearance of a Yankee."[44]

By early 1813, the Fundy Squadron had brought hardship in Maine's port communities, choking off food supplies to the point that many feared starvation. Desperate pleas from communities such as Biddeford attest to the squadron's success: "The enemy's cruisers have hovered on our coast in such great numbers of late as to entirely cut off our coasting trade, which has reduced the inhabitants to great distress: they are almost in a state of starvation, and the evil is still growing." Newspapers reported shortages and inflated prices, and a Camden man claimed that hundreds were without bread or potatoes because of the Royal Navy. In the beginning of May, a Blue Hill pastor recorded the deaths of four people due to starvation. A hatter in Damariscotta Mills wrote to a sibling in mid-April, "I know of many families that has not tasted bread of any kind for these two weeks past." Even the better-off, such as the lawyer George Herbert of Ellsworth, feared that their families would starve to death.[45]

The American counterpart to the Fundy Squadron was the Eastern Station, based in Kittery, at Portsmouth Harbor. As the Royal Navy cruized the Gulf of Maine almost freely, the U.S. Navy focused on building a ship of the line. By early October 1812, the navy was reconsidering the long-neglected shipyard in Kittery and noting that it possessed advantages: Portsmouth Harbor never froze, and the area had numerous shipbuilders and nearby timber supplies. The navy sent Captain Isaac Hull to oversee the warship's construction. Hull, who was best known for commanding USS *Constitution* during its famed battle with the British frigate *Guerriere*, saw great potential in the facility, even though its staff initially consisted of only himself and seventeen others.[46]

He soon had laborers and shipwrights swarming over Seavey's Island, building a smithy, a powder magazine, a mast shed, a sail loft, a house for Hull's family, and the massive warship. Timber, however, was in short supply, and by midsummer 1813, Hull laid off dockyard workers for lack of wood. Other problems included the civilian ship constructors who were overseeing the shipbuilders. The first constructor proved to be insufficiently experienced and had a drinking problem. Hull fired him and hired a new constructor from Boston. He also received permission to build an enormous ship house to cover the warship's hull, thus allowing work to continue year round and concealing progress from prying eyes. Hull's workmen completed the structure in December, just as the weather was worsening.[47]

Hull was worried because Portsmouth Harbor had inadequate defenses. Fort McClary in Kittery was without troops, and Fort Constitution in Portsmouth had only a token garrison. Hull had no marines to guard the shipyard, although he did have two gunboats. His concern was that the British would send a force of boats up the Piscataqua River or perhaps land in nearby York, march overland, and burn the shipyard. He also feared that the militia would not turn out and concluded that he would have to defend the navy yard himself. He procured a few cannons, threw up earthworks to create a battery, and eventually received a few marines. Furthermore, the secretary of the navy allowed him to activate two more gunboats.[48]

While the Kittery navy yard grew, the Portland gunboat station shrank. In March 1813, Hull withdrew the gunboats from Casco Bay and laid them up at Kittery, dismissing seamen "such as are worthless" and transferring those who were "good and fit for service." One sailing master, Nathaniel Stoodley, a politically well connected smuggler, took charge of the laid-up gunboats, while another, William Harper, "a young man whose connexions are very respectable," remained at Portland on recruiting service. Harper proved to be able at this task but gave extravagant promises that he could not keep, earning a reprimand from Hull.[49]

The navy withdrew Portland's gunboats just as Canadian privateers and British warships were appearing along the coast. The Federalist press fretted that, in peacetime, the nine gunboats lying at Portland had been used to enforce the hated embargo. "But now, when the country is at war, and the town liable to an attack from the British Marine, even this defence, is taken away." Local Republican William Widgery pointed out that Portland alone had sent 350 seamen into the navy, and he asked the government for gunboats and brigs to defend the long coastline. Federalists, too, demanded protection: in April, the *Portland Gazette*'s editor bemoaned the British depredations and asked why the American navy was doing nothing to protect coastal commerce.[50]

The navy bowed to political pressure and dispatched the brig *Enterprise* to protect the coasting trade. Hull relayed the news to Portland's citizens, but Widgery was suspicious: "if by that is ment off Portsmouth, they might as well be in Boston, for all the good they will do us." He pointed out that Maine had a long coastline without a single ship to defend it, while New Hampshire had a revenue cutter and two gunboats. As it turned out, the brig's presence along the coast was a mixed blessing. HMS *Rattler* appeared off Portsmouth Harbor almost immediately after *Enterprise* arrived there, blockading it in port. Hull worried the brig would become a target. Nonetheless, in July, it managed to slip from Portsmouth up to Portland, where HMS *Rattler* blockaded it again.[51]

In August, Hull was made responsible for intercepting smugglers, per an order that decried the practice as one "carried on with great subtility and treachery by profligate citizens, who . . . find means to convey succors or intelligence to the enemy and elude the penalty of the law." He ordered *Enterprise* to cruize as far east as the Kennebec River's mouth to protect the coasting trade and intercept vessels that were doing business with the enemy. The brig had some luck, capturing the small Nova Scotia privateer *Fly* off the Isle of Shoals in August. However, a few days later its commander, Lieutenant Johnston Blakely, received orders to construct a sloop of war at Newburyport. His successor on the *Enterprise* was Lieutenant William Burrows, an odd duck in the eyes of his peers: very serious in demeanor, yet thirsting for fame.[52]

SEA FIGHT OFF MONHEGAN

In early September, the *Enterprise* lay at anchor in Casco Bay when a fishing vessel reported that a British naval brig was lying off Pemaquid Point. Burrows leaped at this opportunity for action and put to sea immediately. The British vessel was the *Boxer*, whose commander, Samuel Blyth, had become entangled with Saint John's smuggling community. He agreed to take part in an elaborate collusive capture plan masterminded by an American, Charles Tappan, and a New Brunswick merchant, William Black, who paid Blyth with a note of exchange worth £100. The plan involved bringing high-value British manufactured goods from Saint John to the Maine coast, escorted by *Boxer*. On arrival, the escort would depart, and American privateers would conduct sham captures. At least two privateers were involved. The first was the shaving mill *Lark* of Frenchman's Bay, captained by the notorious smuggler Jonathan Haskell III, nicknamed "Long Metre" because of his great height. Haskell conducted a sham capture of the sloop *Traveller*, separating it from a convoy under *Boxer*'s ostensible protection. The privateer *Lydia* should have made a second sham capture, this one of the Swedish brig *Margaretta*, also in the convoy. However, the Robinson family captured *Lydia* before the plan could be enacted. So *Boxer* escorted the vessel to the Kennebec River's mouth and fired a few blank cannon shots to give the appearance of pursuing the Swedish brig. Of course, what it was really doing was allowing the *Margaretta* to enter the river.[53]

Early on September 5, *Enterprise*'s lookouts spied *Boxer* getting underway near Pemaquid Point and gave chase. The British warship headed out to sea, with *Enterprise* following. In an act of bravado, Blyth ordered his crew to nail the British flag to the mastheads, a signal to them that there would be no surrender. At 3 p.m., the two vessels shortened sail and approached one another. *Boxer* opened fire within a half pistol shot (roughly thirty to forty feet). The senior midshipman on board the *Enterprise* recalled that the British seamen then mounted their guns and gave three cheers. While they were cheering, the American vessel returned fire, with devastating effect. Blyth was among those struck early in the battle: a cannonball ripped off his left arm and opened his belly, killing him almost instantly. The *Enterprise* also had casualties. After a cannon shot to the chest mortally wounded its captain, William Burrows, he lay on deck bleeding but refused to let his sailors carry him below. *Enterprise* clinched the battle when it pulled ahead of *Boxer* and poured cannon fire down the length of the brig's hull. After this devastating broadside, Lieutenant Edward McCall of the *Enterprise* hailed *Boxer* and asked if it was surrendering. A British seaman leaped onto a gun and shook both fists at the American warship, shouting "No, no, no!" and a string of profanity. However, *Boxer* was now a complete wreck. Cannons had shot away much of its standing rigging, the mainmast hung over the side, three feet of water lay in the hold, and it carried no surgeon to care for the wounded. As *Enterprise* again maneuvered into a raking position, the surviving British officers agreed to surrender. Still, they needed time to get the message to the Americans, who continued to fire until a British seaman reportedly cried out, "Ain't you going to give quarter, we have surrendered." The British had been unable to haul down their flags as a sign of surrender because Blyth had nailed them to the mastheads.[54]

The Americans boarded the *Boxer* and took possession of the battered brig. Someone picked up Blyth's sword from the quarterdeck where it had fallen and presented it to the dying Burrows, who reportedly clasped his hands and uttered, "I am satisfied, I die contented." Between twenty and twenty-five British sailors were dead, with another fourteen wounded. *Enterprise* suffered much lighter casualties; only one sailor was killed in action, although its commander and the carpenter's mate died soon afterward and another eleven sailors were wounded, some badly.[55]

The American warship took its prize in tow and slowly made its way back to Portland, arriving on the following day. A Portland schoolteacher boarded the *Boxer* that morning and described the grim scene, including Blyth's shattered corpse still lying on the quarterdeck. Despite the gore, a business associate of Charles Tappan managed to remove the bill of exchange from the late commander's trouser pocket, replacing it with $500 in coins. Blyth would not need the money anymore, but his widow in England would. Upon hearing of the battle Captain Hull rushed to Portland and was amazed at how American cannon fire had torn up the British brig. Other observers were less enthusiastic. After visiting the two warships, a young man reported, "I have just returned from an awful scene produced by Maddison's wicked & unnecessary war." Meanwhile, up the coast in Wiscasset, news of the victory sparked drunken revelry. Celebrators broke windows, and even Federalists conceded they were pleased.[56]

Two days later, Portland hosted a remarkable burial for the two dead captains. The event was a carefully orchestrated street theater piece. Shops closed, ships flew their colors at half-mast, and church bells solemnly tolled. Respectful crowds lined streets, rooftops, and windows. Sailors rowed the flag-draped coffins ashore as the two vessels fired salutes. On land, the coffins were transferred into hearses, and a long procession began wending its way through the streets. First came three uniformed militia companies; then the town's selectmen, other town and county officials, and the presiding minister; then Burrows' hearse surrounded by pallbearers and followed by Captain Hull and the officers and crew of *Enterprise*. Blyth's hearse came next; then *Boxer*'s officers and crew; followed by shipmasters, the U.S. marshal, the navy agent, the customs collector, army officers, congressmen, judges, members of the Portland Marine Society, and bank and insurance company directors. The procession wound its way to a church service, then continued to the Eastern Cemetery, where the officers were interred side by side. Captain Hull was pleased with the ceremony but was soon outraged to learn that the city fathers now expected to be reimbursed for the lavish affair. They dunned the U.S. Navy for more than $300 for Burrows's burial and charged the British government the same amount for Blyth's. Hull protested that he would have arranged a far more modest ceremony had he known the navy would have to pay for it.[57]

In the aftermath of the battle, many were concerned that the British might launch a retaliatory attack on Portland. Indeed, HMS *Rattler* and two smaller ships arrived off the port a few days later, and a lieutenant landed at Fort Scammel. He asked for the return of *Boxer*'s crew, offering in exchange a like number of American seamen who were being held at Halifax's Melville Prison. Portland's military commander politely refused, claiming he did not have the authority to make this decision. *Rattler* left empty-handed, and there were hard feelings about the situation in the Fundy Squadron, leading to talk that *Emulous* or even the little *Bream* should challenge *Enterprise* to another one-on-one fight. These proposals came to nothing, in part because the Admiralty forbade such actions.[58]

Enterprise's crew continued to suffer psychologically and physically long after the battle was over. The navy charged Sailing Master Harper with cowardice for allegedly hiding behind a mast during the battle, and for months he remained under arrest in Portland, the butt of dirty looks and "remarks of levity & Malice." After a court-martial found him innocent, he returned to naval service as a recruiter. Isaac Bowman of Woolwich, a captain's clerk, had fled below decks during the battle, but Hull forgave him because of his youth. British cannon fire had mortally wounded sixteen-year-old midshipman Kervin Waters, but he took almost two years to die. Several young men from Portland took turns sitting by his bed, trying to bring him what comfort they could. After he finally died in 1815, they buried him next to his commander in the Eastern Cemetery.[59]

For the remainder of 1813, there was little naval action in the Gulf of Maine other than minor skirmishes against shaving mills off the coast of Washington County. The Fundy Squadron, now under Commander Henry Fleming Senhouse of HMS *Martin*, continued to patrol Passamaquoddy Bay; and in October, boats from *Bream* and *Emulous* burned a privateer near Machias. Later that month, the British destroyed two beached shaving mills near Lubec, brushing aside the crews' resistance. There was only one other notable action: when HMS *Fantôme* captured the American privateer *Portsmouth Packet* off Matinicus.[60]

On November 13, a hurricane struck Halifax Harbor, driving nine warships ashore. Although the damage curtailed operations, no ships were permanently lost. Despite foul weather, a sloop of war was usually present in Passamaquoddy Bay to watch Fort Sullivan. The winter of 1813–14 was relatively peaceful, but this was merely the calm before the storm. As Britain's war against Napoleon wound down, forces stationed in Europe were sent across the Atlantic. When the spring campaign season opened, the Royal Navy had more ships in American and Canadian waters and a far more aggressive leader, one with a known hatred for Americans. Vice-Admiral Sir Alexander Cochrane was a hot-tempered Scot whom a superior had once described as "a crackheaded unsafe man." Cochrane planned to bring the war to the Americans by sending his vessels into bays, harbors, and rivers. The naval war was going to start in earnest.[61]

Chapter 5
"WICKED WAR"

With the collapse of the volunteer program in early 1813, Congress had to expand the army. On January 29, lawmakers authorized twenty additional infantry regiments, intended to remain in service for the duration of the war. Maine housed two of them, the Thirty-third and Thirty-fourth, which were joined by a third, the Forty-fifth, in 1814. Their regimental depots were in Saco, Portland, and Bath, respectively. Congress was aware of the war's unpopularity in Massachusetts proper so based only one new regiment there: the Fortieth, headquartered in Boston and led by Joseph Loring, a Republican stalwart who had repeatedly fallen out with Massachusetts militia establishment. Old Massachusetts underperformed as a recruiting ground: while Maine produced an estimated 424 recruits per 10,000 eligible males enlisted, in old Massachusetts the number was 288. While these new regular regiments ostensibly represented a fresh start, they remained connected to the volunteer units in spirit and in the politicized selection of officers.[1]

The officers of the new regiments ranged from mediocre to completely incompetent. There were widespread complaints about drunken officers who imposed harsh punishments on their enlisted personnel. Their appointments had more to do with political credentials and family connections than with their military abilities. Officers from older regiments generally held them in low regard, referring to them as "bloodsuckers" who should be sent back to their "dram shops and saw mills." Petty jealousies were rife, advancing to bickering and frequent courts-martial. Many officers, confronted with the realities of military life, soon resigned.[2]

Nonetheless, competition to command these units, especially the Thirty-fourth, was fierce. The Portland attorney Joseph D. Learned was ruthless in pursuing its command, eliminating his competitors via a vicious letter-writing campaign. With the support of Joseph C. Boyd, the District's paymaster, as well as Congressman Richard Cutts, Learned landed the position, but he turned out to be a poor choice. A military officer remembered him as a "haughty, imperious, proud foppish man, about five feet five inches in height, weighing about 140 lbs. looking like a lady dressed in mens clothes." The colonel was seen as "mean effeminate and fond of flattery" and was believed to be jealous of taller and better-looking subordinates. Officers in other units commented on the Thirty-fourth's "General disaffection with their Colonel," observing that the regiment was "convoluted with quarrels and disputes." Yet while many held Learned in contempt, the regiment's adjutant considered him "as fine a fellow as any in the army" and "as fine an officer as ever wore a plume."[3]

Learned established his headquarters in Portland, where his troops quartered in rented barracks or at Fort Sumner, which he described as "a most miserable place, totally unfit for a garrison." He recruited four hundred men and repaired Forts Scammel and Preble, appealing to Portland's citizens for support and materials. When George Ulmer's command collapsed, Learned took charge of Fort Sullivan, too, thus taking charge of every post from Casco Bay to the Canadian border. Learned built his reputation by puffing his regiment in the Republican press. The *Eastern Argus* described it as being "composed of fine, vigorous, active, hardy youths, as have ever measured their steps to the music of the field." Captain Sherman Leland, who was commanding a company of the Thirty-fourth at Fort Sullivan, published another paean, one that praised Learned's influence in restoring order in Eastport. Leland's article criticized Ulmer's command, claiming that it had been "without order, discipline, and almost without control," while the "coming of Colonel LEARNED has moulded the clay deposited here, and given it martial form and character."[4]

The Thirty-third U.S. Infantry's command went to Isaac Lane of Buxton. Lane was a stalwart Republican who in 1813 had resigned as York County's sheriff to join the military. He moved the regimental rendezvous from Hallowell to Saco, closer to his home. It was a wise choice: almost all of his officers were from York County, and the Saco rendezvous was an unusually healthy post. Lane was lucky to have his brother Daniel serving as a major, and some of his subalterns were also capable, especially Captain Isaac Hodsdon. According to family tradition, Hodsdon's appointment had been a matter of sheer luck. The two Isaacs had happened to meet over breakfast at a Saco tavern and became immediately friendly, leading Lane to offer Hodsdon a commission.[5]

Another Republican stalwart with a history of militia service commanded the Forty-fifth. Denny McCobb of Bath was a protégé of William King and had commanded a volunteer regiment in 1813, seeing active service in Vermont and Canada. When the volunteers disbanded, many personnel from that unit enlisted in the new regular regiment, where McCobb was now colonel. Throughout the spring and summer of 1814, the Forty-fifth coalesced slowly at its Bath rendezvous.

"NONE BUT HARDY MEN"

From the start, the recruiting system was chaotic, and numerous attempts to reorganize it failed to produce satisfactory results. Even before the war started, recruiting parties were establishing themselves in village taverns and plastering leaflets that promised glory and increasingly lucrative bounties. Recruiters such as Josiah Vose of the Twenty-first U.S. Infantry vowed that "None but hardy men, of steady habits and sound constitution will be enlisted." Yet despite appeals to manly pride and patriotism, extravagant amounts of liquor, and steadily increasing cash bounties, recruiters routinely missed their goals. The army remained understrength throughout the war, partly because families and communities discouraged enlisting. Confrontations between recruiters and the populace frequently descended into shouting matches, fistfights, and lawsuits. There were also tensions between military branches. The navy complained that the army was stealing away recruits with bounties, while the army protested that its deserters were joining the navy. Both branches complained that the prize money offered by privateers made recruitment a challenge, but the privateers had difficulty too.

In one instance, three sailors signed up to serve on the privateer *Frolic*, received their cash bounties, and then absconded. An officer griped, "we never saw the varlets again."[6]

Officers regarded recruiting as a plum duty because it often meant that they could live at home. Noncommissioned officers also sought this duty, hoping to earn a commission if they brought in enough men. For each new enlistee, the recruiter would receive a cash incentive, originally $2 at the beginning of the war but more as the conflict dragged on. As one officer explained to his sister, "there is some profit in it." Typically, a recruiter would set up shop in a rented house or a tavern. Josiah Vose operated out of Burbank's tavern in Augusta, while Isaac Hodsdon worked out of his home in Corinth. Though state authorities frowned on the practice, militia musters were good places to recruit because their atmosphere of drunken military ardor often led young men to drop their caution. Alcohol also flowed freely at recruiting rendezvous, as one pension applicant confessed decades after the war. He had enlisted in the army under a false name while intoxicated but deserted and joined the navy after he sobered up. Many recruits deserted from their rendezvous, in part because they often had to wait there for weeks before marching to join their regiment. Even Republicans complained that this system was wasteful and suggested that recruits should be forwarded more quickly: "They are too long idle on expence and created a dissatisfaction among the inhabitants where they are stationed." An example of this mischief occurred in Hallowell, where one of Captain John Fillebrown's recruits got into a brawl with a local and the matter spilled into the street. Fillebrown waded into the fray and tried to pull the two men apart. When that failed, he kicked the civilian, as he had sworn to protect his soldiers. Fillebrown avoided severe legal consequences and soon left Hallowell, but not before someone filched his wallet.[7]

Generous bounties attracted recruits, as did a lull in other economic opportunities. There was a seasonal, agrarian tempo to recruiting; many officers focused their efforts on the periods after crops or hay were harvested. The end of winter was a popular time to enlist. For men who were tired of being cooped up in the house and facing rapidly depleting larders, the military offered the possibility of adventure as well as regular meals. Recruiters welcomed almost everyone who stepped forward; their standards were low. Recruits had to be between eighteen and forty-five years of age, with those under twenty-one requiring parental permission. Physicians inspected them for "sore legs, scurvey, scalled heads, ruptures and other infirmities." This work could be lucrative: an Augusta doctor earned between $40 and $50 per month to attend to recruits. After receiving physical clearance, the recruits would appear before a justice to establish that they were joining of their own free will. Foreigners, including deserters from the British military, were welcome to enlist. However, most recruiters rejected African Americans, although one in Brunswick asked permission to enlist a "Nigro

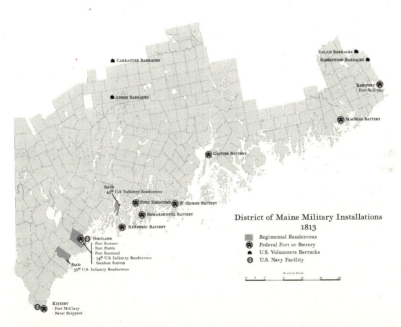

FIGURE 4. Maine's military installations were generally small. Some were mere barracks hastily thrown up to shelter soldiers who were attempting to stop trade with the British. Coastal fortifications were usually small batteries that housed recruits and sometimes prisoners of war. Maine generated more recruits than old Massachusetts did and produced three regiments of regulars. Map by the author.

fellow," apparently because he was an excellent drummer. The navy had regulations against enlisting African Americans, but officers eager to crew their vessels ignored those rules. Privateers had no such qualms and eagerly recruited Afro-Yankees.[8]

Men were supposed to receive a uniform and a musket promptly upon enlisting, and recruiters saw their ability to immediately issue these items as a significant draw. The uniforms, in particular, were highly important to some recruits. One new enlistee at Castine strutted before his comrades in his uniform, asking them "how his coat fitted." On one occasion, the Forty-fifth Infantry duplicated this strutting en masse: after the regiment received uniforms in May 1814, Colonel McCobb ordered his troops to march through Bath's streets to impress the populace with their appearance. Yet the quality of the uniforms was often poor. Colonel Learned complained that they were "almost worthless," "one part blue, the other brown, or nearly black." Coat sleeves were often too short, and pantaloons soon fell apart. The shoes were shoddy and pinched soldiers' feet; the socks were too small for a "child ten years old." The blankets were especially miserable, some only a little over five feet long, "scarcely sufficient to cover a child in the cradle."[9]

Many parents did not want to see their sons march away. Samuel Tyler pestered his parents for a year before they allowed him to sign up at age sixteen. Recruiters frequently enlisted minors such as Samuel, and irate parents often demanded their return. One father traveled from Hancock to Portland to recover his underage son, a trip of roughly 165 miles each way. A number of single mothers also successfully petitioned for the return of their sons. Officers usually complied with such requests so long as the recruit returned all clothing and bounties. Those who refused to return sons risked a lawsuit; in one case, a York County court awarded a parent $115.27, which came out of the recruiting officer's pocket. The navy's Captain Hull was also the target of parental ire. By the war's end, Massachusetts courts were requiring both parents to sign consent papers. Yet determined youngsters could elude this regulation by enlisting under false names, probably with a wink and a nod from their recruiters.[10]

Another concern was that recruiting deprived families of their primary breadwinners. This created burdens on towns when the families looked to the community for relief. There were attempts to solve the problem. For instance, Camden's overseers of the poor tried to garnish soldiers' wages, but apparently without success. The community burden was even worse when a soldier died. Massachusetts law decreed that individual towns had responsibility for caring for paupers, orphans, the ill, and others incapable of caring for themselves. Smaller communities did so on a contract basis, assigning the indigent to the lowest bidder. This cruel system left the paupers in a situation of involuntary servitude, as when a Monmouth woman saw her three children auctioned off to the lowest bidder after her husband allegedly died in military service. Yet in this instance the husband had not really died; he eventually returned home after surviving for several years in Britain's dreaded Dartmoor prison.[11]

Sometimes other parties discouraged enlistment, either from prejudice against military service or because of concerns about debts. Participants in Castine's town meeting openly discouraged citizens from enlisting, and Federalists actively interfered with recruiting throughout the District. In Wiscasset, a recruiter complained that meddling Federalists were claiming an enlistee had been drunk and in poor health when he signed up. Near Fryeburg, a Federalist deputy sheriff struck a recruiter with the butt end of a whip handle, knocking him senseless for two days, and made off with a recruit whom the deputy claimed was a minor. Many Federalists considered the regular army to be nothing more than mercenaries in Madison's pay and were glad to see recruiters fail. A Machias man gleefully noted that enlisting was not a popular option among his community's young men. Many preferred to find seasonal work in Saint John, New Brunswick, muttering complaints about the Madison administration as they traveled into enemy territory.[12]

The most common method of harassing recruits and recruiters was through legal prosecution for debts, an issue that predated the war. Debtors frequently sought refuge in the army because it paid a cash bounty that could solve immediate financial problems.

Furthermore, Congress had passed laws making it illegal to issue a writ of habeas corpus against soldiers, thus preventing their arrest and incarceration for debt. Creditors frequently ignored this law, and recruiting officers often found themselves powerless to resist. Sometimes sheriffs or deputies arrested and jailed a recruit as part of a moneymaking scheme: a man would enlist, collect his bounty, and then have himself arrested, with a friend or relative available to bail him out. The recruit thus remained at home and kept the enlistment bounty while the recruiter and the unit marched to war. Yet despite such obstructions, recruits continued to sign up, with new soldiers moving from east to west in the District, generally bound for the Canadian border in Vermont or New York, sometimes in groups of as many as two hundred. As the Thirty-third prepared to march in late August 1814, the war's opponents attempted to detain both officers and soldiers through legal writs and even to claim the unit's baggage as a way to satisfy debts. But Colonel Lane swept aside the deputies, and the unit marched to the Canadian border.[13]

"OUR DUTY IS NOT HARD"

Life in Maine's military posts was not arduous. One recruit wrote, "Wee fare well as to Provisions. Our Duty is not hard." A few weeks later, he crowed to his parents, "I am hearty as A Buck.... I am verry well Contented. Wee have Good Bread, Beef & whiskey and Good Barracks." Yet military life was grim. Disease, boredom, drunkenness, and disorder were common, as were harsh discipline, disease, and injuries. Then there was homesickness: one young recruit recalled spending most of his time crying.[14]

A garrison's day typically began with the discharge of a cannon before dawn, after which drummers beat reveille, the signal for every man to turn out. Noncommissioned officers combed the barracks for sleepyheads. The men lined up for morning parade, which was followed by drilling on the post's cannon until 6 a.m., drilling with small arms from 8 to 9 a.m., then a dress parade and roll call, then another hour on the cannon from 10 to 11 a.m. Between 3 and 5 p.m., there were more drills, then a dress parade at sunset, and a final roll call. Drills were unpopular and widely evaded by both officers and men. In small posts such as Machias, officers neglected drills, instead letting their troops work for locals, who often paid them in potatoes. A sergeant major in the Thirty-fourth who had started his military career in the Prussian army noted another problem: "hardly two sections of men within the District are drilled alike, the soldier is bewildered by experiments. Confidence in his Superiors is lost, and Confusion is apparent in every movement except the daily routine of morning Parade."[15]

Soldiers dedicated much of their days to cleaning, an essential part of recruits' training and one reinforced by garrison orders: "[a] dirty soldier is a disgrace to his profession." Daily inspections reinforced cleanliness, but keeping the crowded posts sanitary was difficult. Garrison orders at Fort Preble warned, "No soldier will choose a Place near any of the buildings or round the walls of the Garrison for personal convenience & any found Guilty of such a filthy Practice as heretofore has been Discovered will be severely Punish'd." Nonetheless, the problem persisted. A few weeks later, these orders were repeated, reminding the garrison they were not to relieve themselves near buildings and instructing that slops and "filth of every kind must be carried out of garrison & thrown over the Bank near the Battery." The orders threatened that anyone "found guilty of the filthy practice of throwing filth & dirt in and about the Garrison will be considered as disobeying orders and dealt with accordingly."[16]

Crowding and poor hygiene commonly led to disease, especially measles and mumps, both of which could kill, disable, or permanently blind a soldier. Larger posts had hospital facilities overseen by surgeon's mates, but smaller posts often relied on local physicians. Accidents were common, especially those related to construction activities such as moving buildings or heavy timbers. Firing the forts' cannon was also hazardous, as when a gun fired at Fort Scammel leaped backward with such power that it tumbled off its platform and injured a soldier, whose toes had to be amputated. At the Robbinston barracks, a swivel gun exploded while firing a salute, killing one man and severely wounding another.[17]

Tedium was a significant problem for garrison troops. The surviving "Order Book for Portland Forts" instructs that "No one will be allowed to scuffle, make bad noises play at cards dice or any unlaw[ful] game." Drunkenness was frequent, given that the military issued each man a quarter pint of spirits (five ounces, termed a gill) per day. Soldiers often received additional liquor during construction duty and were allowed to buy up to another gill per day from the post's sutler. Nonetheless, garrison orders treated intoxication as both "unsoldierly & beastly." The punishment for drunkards was confinement to the garrison for fifteen days and no whiskey ration. Officers and enlisted men alike suffered from alcoholism. The Thirty-fourth's surgeon was a confirmed drunkard who survived a court-martial over the matter but resigned soon afterward.[18]

While Congress outlawed flogging in the army in 1812, penalties for infractions continued to be painful and humiliating. After a private sassed his company commander, a court-martial ordered him confined to the garrison for one month, with no whiskey ration. He had to wear a ball and chain for ten days, appear in front of the paraded garrison at the morning and evening drills, and face a daily public admonishment. For enlisted men, other common punishments included consignment to the "black hole," literally a hole in the ground with no room to stretch out. While incarcerated, they received only bread and water for rations and painful and humiliating punishment such as being made to ride a "wooden horse." Officers' punishments were milder and never corporal. For example, one officer who spent many hours "lurking in an ungentlemanly & scandalous manner" outside of a young woman's quarters received a mere official reprimand.[19]

As the tale of this amorous officer demonstrates, garrison life did not mean complete separation from women. Regulations permitted a few wives to follow their husbands and receive rations. The wives and families of officers and senior noncommissioned officers often lived in quarters adjacent to the post. References are fleeting, but there is evidence that one pregnant woman followed her husband to Fort Edgecomb in 1813, where she gave birth to a healthy daughter. Women performed vital jobs for the garrison, such as washing clothes, for which the soldiers paid them directly. Fort Preble's garrison orders forbade soldiers from entering the "Womens rooms except on wash-days" and reminded them not to dally chatting. But not all women were welcome: two were drummed out of Fort Sullivan in 1814 for fraternizing with its garrison.[20]

The soldiers' day ended with the drummers beating the tattoo as sentries received their passwords and were ordered not to allow anyone in or out of the post without challenge. Guard duty could be hazardous. On a dark and foggy night, a sentinel fell off Fort Scammel's ramparts and was maimed for life. In another instance, a sentry at Bath complained that an unseen and unknown person had assaulted him at midnight with a blow to the head. The sentry suspected one of the "many sailors and other evil-disposed persons at Bath, by whom the soldiers were frequently annoyed . . . or other persons lurking about the barracks and hostile to the soldiers." The congressional committee investigating this matter was skeptical, speculating that the sentry had received the blow while robbing a hen roost, garden, or nearby orchard and that he had concocted the story to escape the taunts and jeers of his comrades.[21]

"CELL OF DARKNESS AND DESPAIR"

Federalists grumbled that the coastal garrisons served no purpose other than to "help waste the public property." In fact, however, they served various purposes, the most underreported of which was holding prisoners of war captured by American privateers. Sometimes commanders shifted the responsibility for prisoners to federal customs collectors or the local U.S. deputy marshals, who shunned the duty for the same reason that military officers did: caring for them was troublesome and expensive.

Jailers frequently quarreled with U.S. marshals or their deputies about the matter, but the heart of the problem was states' rights. The federal government wanted to use state-controlled jails to hold federal prisoners, and local and Massachusetts authorities resented and resisted that idea. For example, the District's U.S. marshal thought the Wiscasset jail was an ideal place to hold prisoners. The purpose-made granite and brick structure had opened in 1811 and was solidly constructed. By mid-1813, however, local resentment against the war had grown, as had resistance to housing prisoners of war in a state facility. In August, Lincoln County officials ordered an inquiry into the damage that federal inmates were doing to the jail and "by what authority the gaoler has or can receive into the County gaol United States prisoners of war." Furthermore, county officials did not want to provide federal prisoners with blankets or clothing, and the local army post did not have any to spare, which threw the problem onto Wiscasset's deputy marshal. In September, the jailer, William Bowman, refused to hold prisoners of war for more than one night before handing them back to federal officials. He also inflated his expenses, charging the government forty cents every time the prisoners went into the yard for exercise and for every physician's visit—a total of about $74 for simply opening and shutting doors. Bowman billed extravagantly for food, charging the government more than forty cents per ration though soldiers' rations across the river at Fort Edgecomb cost just twenty cents. Yet the jail provided miserable fare; the prisoners complained that their bread was so hard it had to be split with an ax and held in the mouth to soften.[22]

The arrival of prisoners of war exacerbated tensions between military and civil officials. Often they appeared by ones and twos, but sometimes they arrived by the dozen, as when the privateer *Thomas* dumped twenty-eight all at once in Wiscasset. The town's deputy marshal despaired over cramming this new batch into a facility that was already at capacity with twenty-six other prisoners. Marshal Thomas G. Thornton sent the prisoners to Massachusetts proper as soon as possible. This was not unusual: coffles of men in irons were often seen on the District's roads.[23]

Conditions in the jails were primitive at best. A Canadian privateersman held in Wiscasset described his noisome stone cell:

> we found dung or dirt enough on the floor to load a cart; however, they were so kind as to get some lime and spread over the floor,

also a bundle of hay, which was divided into two parts, and laid in the corner for four of us to sleep on. The room was ten feet square, with a hole cut in the wall 18 inches long, and 4 wide; this was to give us light. In this Cell of darkness and despair, we remained six weeks, and at one time, were so long neglected by the Keeper, that we were almost afloat in our own ******.

He warned his readers, "If any of you are taken [by the Americans], run-away if possible, if you love your liberty; or you may be caught as I was, and find a hell before you leave this world."[24]

These poor conditions encouraged prisoners to escape, and many succeeded, both singly or in groups. Castine's tiny, undermanned battery was the site of multiple escapes. Within a month of the declaration of war, the tiny post was holding six prisoners of war, a number almost equal to the garrison of six enlisted men and a junior officer. More than a year later, the battery held sixteen prisoners. Authorities paroled five of the prisoners, another five escaped (one on his second attempt), and six remained. The Popham battery held twenty-eight prisoners that the privateer *America* had deposited there on July 21, 1813. Escape apparently was easy; by August 24 only twelve remained.[25]

Authorities and citizens were concerned that prisoners of war might overwhelm their guards and seize coastal forts. William King saw Fort Edgecomb as particularly vulnerable, and others were concerned that the *Boxer* prisoners would seize Fort Preble. This latter fear had some foundation, as the *Boxer*'s crew was troublesome. Relying on their honor, Marshal Thornton had paroled the officers, and they took up lodgings at Burnham's Hotel in Portland. However, Captain Isaac Hull discovered that locals were allowing the officers to visit the Portland Observatory and freely use its spyglass. This was a grievous miscalculation, as the view from the observatory included the harbor forts and coastal shipping. The *Boxer*'s enlisted personnel also caused trouble. When a military barge landed some of them at Fort Scammel, the prisoners seized the craft and escaped into the night. They spent the night rowing around Casco Bay, unable to find a way out, and soldiers in another boat recaptured them in the morning. The escapees resisted, with one of them attempting to grab a soldier's musket, though he relented when an American officer drew his sword and threatened to cut off his hand. In response to these hijinks, Thornton sent the crew to Salem's floating guard ship and the officers to Boston; only the wounded remained behind.[26]

Both the British and the Americans were anxious to divest themselves of troublesome prisoners. Early in the war, an exchange system existed whereby licensed cartel ships would return British prisoners to Halifax and American prisoners to Boston. In return for their release, the prisoners would swear not to take up arms again until receiving formal permission. In practice, however, the cartel system was complex and unwieldy. In the spring of 1813, Wiscasset's deputy marshal waited for a British cartel ship to pick up his sixty prisoners, but the vessel never got farther east than Portland. In another case, the British cartel *Agnes* left Portland Harbor without permission after Marshal Thornton treated the captain rudely. An alert sentry discovered the ship's movements, and Fort Preble's cannon fired on the vessel, but the *Agnes* got away, to the chagrin of Thornton, who now had to find a new way to dispose of his many prisoners.[27]

Guarding prisoners became a crucial issue in the late summer of 1813, when the federal government withdrew virtually all of its troops from Maine. Fort Edgecomb's garrison shrank to six or seven "invalid soldiers" under the command of a second lieutenant. Thornton ordered civilian guards to move the fort's twenty-seven prisoners to Portland, which they did just a few hours after the federal troops marched for New York. A few days later, five prisoners arrived in Wiscasset, but the jailer refused to take them in for more than one night, so the deputy marshal paid a fisherman to transport them to Portland. In early 1814, the Federalist-dominated Massachusetts legislature prohibited county jails from holding British prisoners. Lincoln County officials must have been relieved. Just recently, British prisoners had broken the hinges off the Wiscasset jail door, and two had escaped. After that incident, two soldiers from Fort Edgecomb stood guard duty at the jail.[28]

"FAT OFFICERS AND MEAGRE SOLDIERS"

The fortifications guarding Maine's ports had strict orders to challenge all boats and ships entering or leaving, especially at night. In July 1813, an order forbade any vessel from entering Portland Harbor after 8 p.m. Any craft arriving after that hour had to spend the night anchored under Fort Preble's guns, and sentries would fire on vessels that ignored the command. In August, soldiers at Fort Scammel fired a shot across the bow of a boat whose occupants, probably intoxicated, refused to identify themselves properly. Local boat operators were resentful about such aggressions. One pleasure boater grumbled in his diary that Portland's forts "at present seem to be commanded by boys, who know [no] more of their duty than school children would of battle. Their chief object seems to avenge neglects of civility, not to watch for enemies." But the situation could be terrifying. When a father and son attempted to enter Portland Harbor in a boat after dark, sentries spied them and forced the boat to remain under the guns of Fort Preble all night. The pair recalled the night as the longest in their lives. They were justified in their fear, for tragedy was not always averted. In January 1814, a marine sentinel at the Kittery Navy Yard shot and killed a man in a boat. York County authorities arrested the sentinel and held him for trial. Fearing that Massachusetts authorities would hang him, Captain Hull gave strict orders that sentries should carry unloaded guns during the day and hail approaching boats at least three times before firing. Thanks to his efforts to placate the civilian judiciary, the jury was able to find the sentry not guilty, and Hull quietly discharged him from the service, claiming he was underage.[29]

In addition to their sentry duties, both coastal and inland garrisons took part in anti-smuggling operations. In Castine, a detachment from the port's battery was tasked with guarding contraband goods seized by the town's customs collector, which required the ill-dressed men to remain outdoors in a snowstorm all night. Sometimes the garrisons faced violent resistance, as when smugglers stabbed a soldier in a confrontation in Machias. To stop the cattle smugglers who were providing beef to the British military, Captain Isaac Hodsdon's company of the Thirty-third Regiment undertook aggressive anti-smuggling operations in Stewartstown, New Hampshire, on the Canadian border. Hodsdon's vigilance made him unpopular with the locals who were engaged in this illegal but lucrative trade with Lower Canada. After Hodsdon arrested several men driving cattle across the border, the smugglers initiated legal proceedings against him. New Hampshire's Supreme Judicial Court ordered his arrest, but a party of soldiers freed him, and he returned to Maine.[30]

Individual posts varied in how they acted against smugglers. Whereas Hodsdon was vigilant, Captain Sherman Leland of the Thirty-fourth was erratic at best. In November 1813, his troops at Fort Sullivan opened fire on the smuggling vessel *Venture*, intercepting a valuable contraband cargo but also potentially upsetting the border modus vivendi. When the commander of HMS *Martin*, who witnessed the seizure, asked Leland if the incident had ended the arrangement, Leland assured him otherwise. His report eventually went to President Madison as evidence of borderland smuggling. In fact, however, Leland usually ignored Eastport's smuggling trade. An anonymous letter reported that his garrison displayed "indifference and almost total disregard" to illicit trade and claimed that "No regard is paid by the centinels stationed on the wharves." Colonel Learned, Leland's superior, denied these accusations, even taking a dig at a fellow Republican by suggesting that Portland's customs collector was in cahoots with smugglers.[31]

Trigger-happy sentries and clashes with smugglers signaled a degree of alienation between communities and military posts. Even more alarming, however, was the breakdown in cooperation between garrisons and militia units, which heightened in the spring of 1813, when the number of regular soldiers in Maine was dramatically reduced. The national government stripped coastal garrisons of troops in the spring of 1813 for a summer offensive in Canada. An officer in the Light Artillery left the District without even saying goodbye to his mother. He apologized in a letter: "Perhaps

I did wrong to deceive you—forgive me, for the motive was good. I shall march hence in a few days for Canada, and may the God of Armies grant that this war be short and glorious for our arms." Other officers responded less nobly: one drank wildly on his march to Vermont, and a court-martial dismissed him from the service.[32]

The dearth of soldiers became serious in August of that year, after most of the Thirty-fourth Infantry marched for the front. A half-dozen invalids held Fort Edgecomb, two privates were stationed at the Damariscotta River battery, and a single officer manned the Kennebec battery. The Saint George battery was left completely ungarrisoned. Because the posts held munitions, this unilateral withdrawal put militia officers on the spot. For instance, the battery at Saint George held a ton of gunpowder in its magazine, guarded by a caretaker who was a notorious drunkard. Even Portland now had no regular troops, and its citizens were forced to ask Governor Strong for militia to guard the town and even garrison the federal forts, which were virtually empty when the *Enterprise* towed *Boxer* into Casco Bay.[33]

During this crisis, Colonel Learned of the Thirty-fourth continued to respond rudely to his militia counterparts. Initially, he let them take possession of the Jordans Point battery, a work thrown up in the summer of 1812 at the foot of Portland's Munjoy Hill, as well as the old gunhouse that stood behind it. However, he changed his mind later that same day, evicting the militiamen from the structure and even insisting that they could not train with the battery's cannon. Nonetheless, after Learned left town to inspect the troops at Eastport, militia officers built barracks and a parade ground at the battery, using donated materials and their soldiers' labor, which they rewarded with extra liquor rations. One unit consumed a whopping four hundred gallons of rum within sixty days. The barracks were completed by the end of November, and 134 militiamen and eight women moved in. Captain Abel Atherton dubbed the post "Fort Burrows" in memory of the fallen captain of *Enterprise*. On his return to Portland, Colonel Learned was outraged to discover state troops building on a federal post. He sent his soldiers to take possession as soon as the militia left the barracks in December, even evicting the caretaker's family. For the rest of the war, the post remained a point of contention; militia officers invariably referred to it as Fort Burrows, while regulars called it the Jordans Point battery."[34]

Militia officers also bickered among themselves. Major General James Merrill, Jr., had commanded the Twelfth Division of militia since 1811. He was an ardent Republican but not a dynamic officer, and his subordinate, Brigadier General James Irish, Jr., regularly outshone him. Irish, too, was a Republican; but unlike his superior, he wanted to make the militia a capable force, even if this meant cooperating with Federalist officers. In September, when Portland's Committee of Safety called on him to order his troops to defend the town, Irish obliged, and the troops remained on duty until December. Merrill took offense, claiming that Irish had acted without orders and demanding a court-martial. But the court-martial, headed by Major General Henry Sewall, vindicated Irish, further embarrassing Merrill, who resigned his commission. Undoubtedly this move delighted Governor Strong, who replaced Merrill with the Federalist Alford Richardson, thus further rolling back Republican influence in the militia.[35]

Between 1813 and early 1814, the army's forces earned little credit for themselves. Federalist newspapers complained of "Fat officers and meagre soldiers stalking through the country, annoying the inhabitants whom they are bound to protect, and violating the civil authority, as well as the laws of decency." Portland's Federalists mocked the army's officers—Learned, in particular: they found a man who had recently been dishonorably discharged and, in a bit of street theater, dressed him in an officer's uniform, dubbed him "Colonel," gave him a sword, and paraded him in the streets. Not everybody was so hostile. Citizens sometimes banded together to support the troops, as when several Fryeburg families whisked a company of the Thirty-third Regiment through town in their sleighs. However, these demonstrations became increasingly rare as the war dragged on and it became apparent that the regulars offered no guarantee of protection. As the *Portland Gazette* pointed out, they might be here today but gone tomorrow.[36]

"CURSE YE MEROZ"

In January 1814, farmers in Monmouth, Maine, witnessed an ominous harbinger of the coming year. They reported seeing dark shapes in the sky marching across the horizon, each perfectly shaped like a coffin, surely a portent of dire events to come. Many people who viewed the war as divine punishment also predicted calamity. A Buckstown woman noted in her journal, "War is rolling its thunderbolts on our frontiers and seaboard our interior in many places is desolated by sickness, our commerce dead, our Revenue cut off, all this has com upon us because of our departure from the God of our Fathers." She was far from alone in her dread. Among the District's religious, especially the Congregational clergy, the war had always represented God's punishment, manifesting as a disease sweeping through Maine. The disease was more than metaphorical. In Wiscasset, "spotted fever" or "cold fever" carried away several people, including the U.S. district attorney, the wife of Fort Edgecomb's long-time commander, and the wife of Congressman Abiel Wood. The family of Francis Cook, the port's customs collector, was especially hard hit, losing three adult children in two days. Most of the stores in the village closed, and many people fled to other towns. To combat the disease, the selectmen burned barrels of tar through the night to purify the air. The eerie atmosphere of illness disquieted many, and their anxieties were compounded by the sudden, premature death of the Commonwealth's chief justice as he presided over a court in Wiscasset in June. To some, the shire town seemed to be cursed.[37]

The spiritual aspect of the war spilled over into formal religious practice, mainly among Federalist Congregational ministers, who took their cues from Boston. In 1812, Governor Strong declared a statewide fast day as a means of begging pardon for the nation's sins. Republicans found the proclamation obnoxious, especially its reference to Britain as the "bulwark of religion" against the atheist dictator Napoleon. But Congregational ministers took up Strong's words and used their pulpits to blast the war. Fryeburg's minister reminded his flock that wars created a disregard for the Sabbath and led to profanity, intemperance, and many other disorders. In Brunswick, Winthrop Bailey's sermon took issue with a war that he believed benefited Napoleon, whom he identified as the antichrist. The Reverend Nathan S. S. Beman of Portland cataloged the evils of war. He bewailed the loss of property due to taxes and the destruction of shipping, either by enemy action or because it rotted in blockaded harbors. He warned that agriculture would also suffer, leading to famine. He addressed war's immorality, how it was linked to robbery and murder as well as to military camps polluted with oaths, intemperance, and licentiousness. Attending all of these evils was the loss of fathers, sons, brothers, and husbands on the battlefield. Like many such sermons, Beman's also praised Britain as a Christian nation. His published version went even further than his spoken one, questioning President Madison's morality and piety prominently on its back cover.[38]

Republicans responded with disgust. The *Eastern Argus* called such ministers "heralds of discord, the low instruments of sedition." Later in the war, another Republican newspaper published a toast to "Our Clergy—May all those who preach sedition or treason from the pulpit, be branded with eternal infamy and left to earn their bread by the sweat of the brow." Congregationalist ministers sometimes found themselves abandoned by their parishioners because of their politics, among them the English pastor of Deer Isle's Congregational church, who was a vocal opponent of the war. The few Congregationalist ministers who supported the war, such as John Cayford of Norridgewock, were soon dismissed from their posts for too much political talk. Cayford entered politics and abandoned Congregationalism for the Baptist faith, where he was free to support the war effort—a change made all the more peculiar because he was English. Waterville's Congregationalist minister was another supporter of the war. He resigned his pulpit in 1814 after a fiery Fourth of July oration in which he accused the Federalists of treason.[39]

In general, Baptist and Methodist clergy supported the war. Baptist minister Samuel Baker of Thomaston urged his parish to arm themselves and support the government. Timothy Merritt, a Methodist, took umbrage at a Congregational antiwar sermon based on the text "This year thou shalt die." He refuted it by preaching to newly recruited soldiers at Hallowell, quoting a text from the King James Bible that was often used in times of crisis: "Curse ye Meroz, said the angel of the LORD, curse ye bitterly the inhabitants thereof; because they came not to the help of the LORD." The Reverend Daniel Merrill of Sedgewick, a Congregational minister who had taken most of his parishioners with him when he defected to the Baptists, was probably the most outspoken critic of the Federalist-Congregationalist alliance. Having forsaken Federalist politics to become a Republican, he declared, with a convert's fervor, that "Governor Strong and the New-England clergy, are, generally, downright hypocrites and enemies to their country."[40]

Among Federalists, the war was commonly reviled as "wicked" or "wickedness." These words, connoting obstinacy without compromise, were common in the writings of both private individuals and members of Congress. A Bowdoin College professor recalled receiving a letter that described the war as an uninterrupted series of calamities: "none but infidels can deny the solemn tokens of Divine displeasure against this wicked & murderous war—still our cup of suffering is not filled I fear." A Bangor merchant attributed his financial losses to the "wickedness of our Government, for they have bro't a dread foe upon us by declaring War." He continued:

> A foe who is as insatiable as the grave, as destructive as the pestilence that wasteth at noonday—whose tender mercies are the most horrid cruelties—whose trade is War, whose profession is devastation, whose gain is the spoil of conquered and destroyed nations. How long these things are to be, God, the righteous Judge, only knows—but our wicked rulers are more guilty, in my opinion, than the worthless foe.

Newspaper editors picked up on the usage, as when one writer blasted Congressman Widgery for voting for war: "The wickedness and folly of the members of Congress from this section of the Union, who voted in favour of War, will be handed down to posterity as an example of treachery towards the people, unparalleled in the history of republicks."[41]

In 1814, Maine's Federalists again took up the language of wickedness when Congress imposed a draconian embargo act that completely stopped all maritime trade. Legislators had passed the measure over the protests of Cyrus King of Saco, who had floated the idea that an embargo on the coasting trade was unconstitutional. Federalist newspapers decried the Republican legislation as a threat to liberty: "This *Embargo*, like the *War*, is made to weaken the power of New-England, by *starving* a *portion* of its *citizens*, and *annihilating* the *whole* of its *commerce*." The writer continued:

> what a *wicked* and *weak* pretext the government have for stopping our coasting trade with the District of Maine. I think I have by the foregoing remarks proved that the *Embargo* is UNCONSTITUTIONAL, and if persisted in, this state is no longer *sovereign and independent*; and if not *resisted*, the *government* may go on from one un-constitutional act, to another, till the *conscription forces* from us, our *sons and brothers*, to be driven at the *point* of the *bayonet* to the Canadas.[42]

Many Federalists agreed. A Machias man declared, "The wicked war into which our national rulers have plunged us, and to which they added their abominable embargo restrictions, has caused general distress in this part of the country." George Thatcher of Biddeford wrote to Cyrus King that Congress needed to change its policies or, "be assured, a civil war is as certain as the vegetation of returning spring." Several coastal communities sent remonstrances to the General Court about the embargo. These complaints came mostly from the Federalist strongholds of Brunswick, Buckstown, Castine, Ellsworth, and Gouldsborough, but less politically homogeneous towns such as Belfast and Deer Isle also joined in.[43]

Wickedness took local, sensational form in the Commonwealth in late 1813. Nicholas Crevay, a Penobscot living in Quebec, had returned to the United States after the declaration of war. In

November, white factory workers shot and murdered him in his sleep and left his wife severely wounded. The assaults occurred in Stoneham, Massachusetts, far from the war on the Canadian border, and Crevay had been well known as a member of the "friendly" Penobscot Nation. Massachusetts authorities tried the accused murderers, and the judge pronounced them to be wicked in thought and deed, sentencing the two "to be hanged by the neck, until dead, dead, dead—and may God have mercy on your soul." In New England this was first time that whites had been convicted of murdering a Native since 1676. Yet in early 1814, hundreds of Yankees, many of them residents of Frankfort, Maine, where one of the murderers had lived, signed a petition asking the governor to reconsider the case. Strong responded by creating a committee to reexamine it, and committee members recommended commuting the executions to life in prison. Strong followed this recommendation, but a second petition campaign from Frankfort and towns in old Massachusetts led to the two convicts' release in January 1818. The Penobscots long remembered this injustice, and they would invoke the memory of Crevay after the war ended.[44]

"RAVINGS OF A POLITICAL MANIAC"

Maine's most outspoken Federalists became famous or notorious for their objections to the total embargo the Madison administration imposed in late 1813 in an effort to cut off trade with the British. Unfortunately the embargo also halted the coastal vessels that brought provisions to Maine. Samuel Fessenden, a lawyer from New Gloucester and a representative to the General Court, was infuriated by it and in early 1814 took up the language of wickedness to publicize his views. He thundered before the General Court that the "distress of the District of Maine was intolerable—the children were naked and barefoot—their families were deprived of bread for six weeks together, and they were entirely dependent on other parts for that article." He threatened to "take the SWORD in one hand and the State constitution in the other, and demand his rights." Complaining that the war was "wicked and unjust—that our goods were stopped on the roads and searched—that we had petitioned Congress for redress, and they had refused to consider it," he concluded "That the State of Massachusetts had not courage to assert her rights, and that Congress thought so from the tameness of our conduct—that it was time to take our rights into our own hands." This was radical talk indeed, not only critical of the war and but also accusing the Massachusetts elite of being too timid to oppose it. The Boston Federalists approved of Fessenden's rant, glad to see their rural colleagues leading the charge; and the more sophisticated, such as Harrison Gray Otis, took the opportunity to frame themselves as the voice of reason. After Fessenden finished speaking, Otis rose and complimented him on his eloquence and spirit but then declared "we were not yet ready to proceed to those extremities, indicated by his honorable friend." In other words, the Boston party leaders were not prepared to secede, but they enjoyed Fessenden's legislative antics and knew they could use him as a cat's paw to further their political goals. Republicans, however, regarded his speech with horror, deeming it the "ravings of a political maniac."[45]

Critics such as the Reverend Beman were correct when they predicted that the war would bring hunger to Maine. Maine had always needed to import food, especially flour and salt, from elsewhere in the nation. Even in the best of times, spring was often referred to as the "starving time," when winter stores dwindled and fresh food was scarce. But as the war continued to disrupted trade patterns, famine now stalked the region. The cost of provisions skyrocketed. The price of flour doubled to $20 a barrel, and even low-quality cornmeal could cost as much as $2.25 a bushel. Few families had cash, and little credit was available because Mainers could not transport their usual trade items, such as timber, to markets in Boston.

But even as Maine families starved, provisions continued to flow through the District and across the border to British agents, who paid handsomely in silver. Army officers complained bitterly that speculators were draining the countryside of food in order to enrich themselves and feed the enemy. This included animals.

Herders would drive cattle up along the Penobscot River, through the woods to Houlton, Calais, or Lubec, and then across the border. Federal officials stopped several such drives in autumn 1813, but one herd of twenty-five cattle got through to Canada after the drovers fought off customs officers with staves. The smugglers later sued the customs collectors in state court for assault, while the customs collectors sued the cattle drovers in federal court on the same charge.[46]

The spring of 1814 was as hungry a season as 1813's had been, and the embargo was compounding the crisis by restricting all ships to port and halting exports and the coasting trade. Jeffersonian newspapers declared that the embargo was good for Mainers, ensuring that they would have plentiful food at lower prices because provisions would not be going to the British in Halifax. But this boosterism was cold comfort to the starving. In April, Congress finally relented and ended the embargo. However, the Royal Navy continued to plague the coasting trade, making it almost impossible for vessels to move flour and other provisions. For many hungry and impoverished families, the obvious solution was to send their sons to a recruiter. Cash bounties could pay property taxes, recruits were promised regular meals, and diminishing family larders would have fewer mouths to feed. As many observers noted, "scarsity of provisions serves to recrute for the army."[47]

TAX REVOLT

A flurry of new taxes deepened the District's misery. As the national government struggled to finance the war, Congress imposed an excise tax on furniture, timepieces, and carriages; doubled import duties; and required retailers to acquire licenses to sell liquor or foreign goods. It also levied a direct tax of $3 million on real estate and structures. The Federalist press blamed Madison's war for these new financial burdens, and even the well-off complained about taxes.[48]

The excise tax as well as other fees and duties targeted merchants, shop owners, distillers, and banks in commercial villages and seaports, thus revealing intriguing details about the concentration of wealth and economic activity in Maine. Backwoods communities in central parts of the District, such as Farmington, Paris, and Foxcroft, often had one or more distilleries that produced a fiery concoction known as potato whiskey. Cumberland County had larger distilleries that used imported molasses from the West Indies to produce rum. Tax records are also revealing as they relate to a tax that Congress levied on horse-drawn carriages. Because Washington County had only one carriage, it reaped a single tax dollar in 1814. In contrast, Cumberland County had 825, which brought in $1,800 in taxes. As mentioned, retailers of wine, spirits, and other goods now had to pay for licenses, although the fees were substantially less for those in communities with fewer than one hundred families per square mile. A small tax imposed on auctions raised comparatively little money from custom house sales of contraband goods and cargoes captured by privateers. Banks and lawyers paid most of the stamp tax, which applied to legal documents and paper money. In impoverished rural Washington County, the revenue collector netted only $791.52 for the U.S. Treasury, but collecting that sum cost $315.39 in pay and other expenses. Citizens resisted paying the new taxes, and there is anecdotal evidence that many tavern keepers, storekeepers, and others refused to pay. Prosecutions were rare, but a ferryman in Perry, who retailed alcohol, found himself dragged into federal court.[49]

The direct tax of 1813, which targeted improved land and structures, was just one of many new federal taxes, but taxpayers resented it above all others. The law allowed individual state legislatures to pay the tax as a lump sum, with the national government offering a 15 percent discount if they did so. Alternatively, federal tax officials could assess and collect the tax. Over the opposition of Republican communities such as Paris, the Massachusetts General Court chose the latter option because it opposed the war. However, this decision made the tax, which amounted to less than $75,000 for Maine's eight counties, more expensive to collect and ensured that the revenues would come in slowly. Federalists supposed that collecting Oxford County's share of $5,559.60 would cost $1,050, but in a rare demonstration of competence, it seems to have only cost a few hundred dollars. Inevitably, individuals and even entire communities delayed or refused to pay the new taxes. Massachusetts as a whole paid $316,272.98 of the direct tax; the counties in Maine shouldered $74,220.01 of this burden. One wag calculated that Massachusetts's share of the direct tax (including Maine's) could pay for two days, four hours, forty-one minutes, and forty-three seconds of the war. The impoverished District's share would have covered fewer than twelve hours. Nonetheless, the federal direct tax meant that Maine's counties paid about 330 percent more in taxes in 1814 than they did in 1812. Communities such as Thomaston slashed their school budgets to compensate for wartime purchases such as arms and ammunition.[50]

Resisting the tax was consistent with Federalists' argument that anything supporting an immoral war was also immoral, although they admitted that Congress had the authority to collect the tax. At a local level, neighbors, friends, and relatives often interceded to pay the taxes of those unable to bear the expense of often nominal sums. Inevitably some defaulters could not pay, and some decamped as a result. There were instances in which properties lost value—say, to an accidental fire. Tax receipts came in slowly. By the end of 1814, 344 property owners in York County had not paid their direct tax, even though the average sum was less than $1. The tardiness was a show of resistance against the war and a product of weak legislation that failed to punish those who dithered. By the end of 1814, tax collectors had received only two-thirds of Maine's total, a rate slightly less than the rest of the country, which averaged roughly 74 percent of the expected yield.[51]

Residents of North Yarmouth were notably reluctant to pay the direct tax, though it was a large and wealthy town by Maine standards. The community's Federalists consistently outvoted Republicans by more than four to one and led delinquencies on the direct tax throughout the war. By early 1815, North Yarmouth had 140 delinquent households out of 477 and an average tax of $2.90. The delinquents included community leaders such as selectmen and a militia major general. Smaller adjacent towns such as Freeport only had twenty-three delinquents, while Falmouth, a more populous community, had only twenty. The source of North Yarmouth's resistance is unknown, but a likely suspect is the town's Congregational minister, Francis Brown. He repeatedly decried the war in sermons such as "The Evils of War," in which he asked, "To what are we to attribute those enormous exactions, which are imposed . . . in the various forms of impost, excise, stamp duties, licenses, and direct taxes?" He answered himself with another question: "To what, but war?" The Reverend Brown did not have to pay the tax because he lived in a rectory. However, his influential deacon, Dr. Ammi R. Mitchell, was one of the town's biggest taxpayers. Mitchell had led North Yarmouth's antiwar meeting and moderated Cumberland County's antiwar convention in 1812, served as a representative to the General Court, and notably was among those who refused to pay his taxes.[52]

Woodbury Storer, a Republican lawyer and Cumberland County's federal tax collector, efficiently crushed North Yarmouth's tax rebellion. He coolly and methodically followed the law and listed all of the county's tax delinquents in the *Eastern Argus*. Posting names was standard practice, but Storer also included addresses and descriptions of property. Nearly all of North Yarmouth's recalcitrant citizens, including Dr. Mitchell, soon paid their taxes. In the end, there were only five holdouts, all of whom owed nominal amounts.[53]

In 1815 the direct tax grew to $6 million. Moreover, tax collectors were now required to enter homes and assess the value of furniture and timepieces, including clocks and silver or gold watches. Taxpayers grumbled and resisted, among them a Camden woman who concealed a clock from a visiting tax collector. When the hidden clock chimed in another room, the official saw the distress on her face and departed without correcting his records. As late as 1817, tax collectors were still collecting the direct tax of 1815.[54]

Though the revenue collectors did not net much for the United States, they made a tidy profit for themselves. The growing number of federal officials tasked with squeezing the citizenry angered Federalists, who knew that only loyal Republicans were receiving these positions. The *Portland Gazette* groused, "The times were 'never more prosperous' for assessors, assistant assessors, collectors, and deputy collectors." One editor fumed about "Pimps and spies of the customs running their noses into their neighbor's barns and stables, ware-houses, and other *necessary* appurtenances [that is, privies or outhouses]." Frustrated by the regime of heavy taxes and big government, the District's inhabitants were rude to the collectors, making the job, as one official complained, "very fatiguing and unpleasant." Many towns refused to share their records with collectors, and one official recalled frequent insults, verbal abuse, and unpleasant pranks, as when someone cut his horse's harness and turned it loose. A woman showered him with "insolent and abusive language"; another drove him out of her home with a broom. Some of these situations felt dangerous, and at least one tax collector was robbed at gunpoint.[55]

Nonetheless, Republicans continued to step forward for these positions. James Irish, Jr., wrote directly to President Madison for an appointment and received a commission as the principal assessor for Cumberland County. He justified his application by claiming that his surveying business had come to a standstill because Federalists refused to employ him. Other applicants were perpetual office seekers, such as former congressman Orchard Cook, who spent much of his adult life seeking federal and state positions as sheriff, military agent, postmaster, and ultimately revenue collector for Lincoln County.[56]

Many of the District's citizens resented, and in some cases, resisted the taxes, tariffs, duties, and commercial restrictions imposed on foreign goods imported by sea, much as they had during the embargo of 1807–9. Trade prohibitions and high tariffs created incentives for illicit trade in tea, textiles, porcelain, and hardware. Much of this trade came into Maine through isolated coves, beaches, or spots like Roque Island, but new inland routes developed to avoid customs authorities on the coast. A Bangor merchant noted in the summer of 1814 that smugglers were bringing goods worth thousands of dollars in birchbark canoes via inland waterways from New Brunswick. A growing number of customs officers searched for contraband, men whom the merchant derided as a "hungry set of wolves." These officers drew their neighbors' ire because they received both a substantial salary and a share of anything seized. The arbitrary and self-serving manner in which many customs officers applied the law also angered people. Some of the officers were outright corrupt, turning a blind eye to smuggling or even actively facilitated it.[57]

The customs officers who patrolled Maine's highways were also irksome. They performed heavy-handed searches of sleighs and wagons, and Federalist newspaper editors delighted in lampooning them, relaying anecdotes about officers stopping travelers and finding nothing, often after an exhausting chase. In one instance, mounted customs officials pursued a carriage for several miles on the highway between Wiscasset and Bath. After finally bringing their quarry to a halt, one inspector cried out, "I am a United States officer, I won't see the United States Laws trampled on, I am determined to do my duty, I am not [a]feared." The inspector, reportedly trembling with fright, demanded that the carriage driver open a box. The driver refused, and the inspector forced it open himself. He was humiliated to find only a horse blanket and an old coat.[58]

Federalist newspapers also took delight in printing fatuous articles, such as one titled "Horse Marine List," which treated carts and wagons as if they were ships: "*Port of Kennebunk, Oct. 16*—Passed this port since our last, about twenty sail of Horse and Ox Waggons, with dry goods, from Bath and Portland bound to Boston." The point of such pieces was to emphasize that the Madison administration had destroyed American maritime commerce; instead of ships full of valuable goods arriving in port, ox carts were carrying what remained of American trade.[59]

Some smugglers resisted customs officers with force, as when a group in Steuben thrashed two customs officers with staves. After customs officials seized a vessel from Kennebunk in Boston Harbor, a gang boarded the sloop at night, tied up the guards, and removed the smuggled goods. On Portland's Union Wharf, a half-dozen smugglers scuffled with customs officers. More typically, however, they fled when government officers approached, as happened when authorities surprised a group on a beach near Prout's Neck. The officers found five abandoned sleighs loaded with contraband worth $30,000.[60]

War brought hardship to the District. Under the burden of taxes, corrupt officials, famine, disease, and disorder, Yankee society further fell away from the Massachusetts ideal of a unified, orderly society. Some New Englanders began to talk of seceding from the rest of the country. As a Portland diarist recorded, "We have reason to fear our union is not to be everlasting; there is a discord among us." A man confided to his sister, "Still our damn democrats are crying at what fine times and one half of them are a starving and I wish they were all in canady [Canada] surrounded by Indians." Faced with incidents such as the brawl that broke out at a Fryeburg election, even Republicans had to admit that "discord reigns and triumphs among us." A Camden man observed, "As to the times they are very hard. The District of Maine is going [to] wreck as fast as ever a country did." If Maine's citizens had known more about the character of the British naval commander newly arrived in Halifax, they would have been even more worried.[61]

Chapter 6
"HAMPDEN RACES"

Two minor skirmishes in early 1814 signaled Americans' increasing willingness to resist Canadian privateers and British warships. Both took place off the coast of Washington County. The first was an affray in what is now Jonesport. In late February, the Canadian privateer *Hare* chased a customs boat ashore. Aided by local stringbeaners, the customs men fought back from the water's edge. Ultimately, they captured the boat that *Hare* had sent in to seize the customs boat, killing one Canadian and taking the others prisoner. The second took place in late April, when the tiny British warship *Bream* pursued a schooner into Pigeon Hill Bay. The schooner's master, John Allen, beached his vessel and prepared to defend it. When an armed boat from *Bream* approached, Allen and his crew fired into it, killing two sailors, wounding two others, and capturing the survivors. *Bream*'s commander entered into negotiations with Allen for the return of his crew. Buoyed by the sight of a militia unit that had now arrived to aid him, Allen drove a hard bargain, demanding and receiving $25 for each prisoner and keeping the *Bream*'s boat and weapons. It was quite a coup for a humble Yankee skipper, and it was later capped by a ceremony in Boston, where a group of worthies awarded Allen an engraved sword. It remained his prize possession for the rest of his life.[1]

"A MESS OF YOUR OWN COOKING"

These minor skirmishes exemplified hardening attitudes. American vessels began regularly resisting British capture, often with the militia's assistance. For their part, the British swooped in to seize every sail in sight, even the humblest coaster, such as the sloop *Mary* of Waldoborough, laden with firewood for Boston. The sailors burned the sloop and carried its crew to Melville Prison in Halifax.

Things got worse for *Mary*'s crew, who were eventually transferred to Dartmoor Prison in England, where they rotted until the war ended. The Royal Navy also began burning fishing boats in retaliation for American privateers' harassment of Nova Scotian fishermen. When an American skipper asked a warship's commander if this was an honorable mode of warfare, the captain gruffly replied, "it was a mess of your own cooking." Other British officers were more sympathetic, viewing the conflict as "an ungenerous war against the poor, & unworthy of Englishmen." Nonetheless, in September 1814, the Royal Navy banned American fishing vessels from the offshore banks and scuttled all fishing vessels exceeding thirty tons.[2]

This aggression was part of Vice-Admiral Sir Alexander Cochrane's strategy. Cochrane had declared the entire American coast under blockade, including the New England ports that the British navy had previously spared. Now he was escalating the

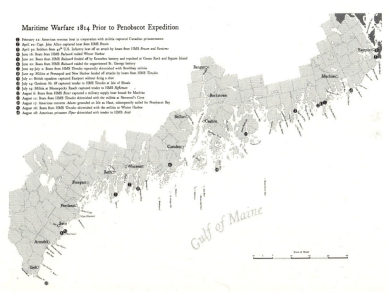

FIGURE 5. In the spring and summer of 1814, Royal Navy ships frequently raided coastal communities and seized any shipping they could find, even wood coasters and fishing boats. Increasingly, Maine's militia and mariners fought back. These actions kept coastal communities in a constant state of anxiety. Map by the author.

war through raids along the coast, hoping to force the Americans to defend their ports rather than invade Canada. As he explained, "I have much in heart to give them a complete drubbing," and he ordered his ships to "destroy and lay waste such towns and districts upon the coast as may be found assailable."[3]

Cochrane disliked Americans, whom he described as a "whining, canting race, totally lacking in courage." Many of his officers agreed. A fellow Scot, Captain David Milne of HMS *Bulwark*, summed up New Englanders as a "sad despicable set" ruled by greed. Another officer said they were "Proud ignorant vain cowardly unfeeling & revengeful set of people, divided among themselves and incapable of acting with liberality or honor even toward those whom gratitude ought to have obliged them to respect." Yet another claimed that the Federalists were only pretending to be friendly to the English and only opposed the war because it prevented their pursuit of gain. Even Boothbay's Jeffersonian fishermen earned British contempt when they decried President Madison.[4]

British officers reserved their greatest disdain for Yankee collaborators, among them Tyler Porter Shaw, a mariner from Lincolnville. Shaw had landed a lucrative government contract to ship supplies to military posts in eastern Maine. Instead, he sailed down the coast, heading directly for the British blockading force off Cape Ann, Massachusetts, where he sold the supplies to the Royal Navy. One British officer accused Shaw of forfeiting his honor, national fidelity, and Christian morality for money and predicted that he would hang before his next birthday, a prophecy that came very close to fulfillment. American authorities apprehended him, tipped off by his decision to sail for Maine against an unfavorable wind and returning with an empty vessel after only one night away. They found incriminating documents, including a letter from the captain of HMS *Nymphe* with details on a future rendezvous to buy more supplies. Shaw faced treason charges, but sword-wielding kinsmen rescued him from custody, and he escaped to New Brunswick, despite a $300 reward for his capture.[5]

In 1814, Cochrane instituted a *guerre de razzia*, or raiding warfare, on Maine's coast, commencing with HMS *Bulwark*'s sacking of Winter Harbor (modern-day Biddeford Pool) in mid-June. The seventy-four-gun *Bulwark* was the largest British warship that had yet appeared on the Maine coast, but its danger lay less in its powerful battery than in the boats it carried. Captain Milne's approach was to send boat parties into harbors, where they would burn anchored vessels and raid homes, warehouses, and stores. At Winter Harbor, they burned a brig belonging to Thomas Cutts (father of former congressman Richard Cutts), torched two coasters loaded with lumber, and destroyed a ship under construction. The area's militia offered little resistance to the raiding party, arriving just in time to watch the marauders sail away. The *Bulwark* invaders took Cutts's full-rigged ship *Victory* with them, although he soon ransomed it for $6,000, with the assistance of Congressman Cyrus King.[6]

Milne next appeared off the Kennebec River, on June 20. From this chokepoint, he captured vessels moving up or down the coast or emerging from the Kennebec or Sheepscot rivers. *Bulwark*'s presence sent Lincoln County into a panic: a visitor described the inhabitants as "all very much flustrated there expecting the enemy to Destroy & Burn them up every minit." Militia units assembled and marched for the coast, while shipowners brought their vessels as far upriver as possible and banks sent their specie inland. William King estimated that forty thousand tons of shipping worth more $1 million was hiding in the rivers.[7]

The federal government's coastal fortifications did little to hinder the British raids. While the midcoast region had several batteries guarding harbors or rivers, there were only thirty regulars at Fort Edgecomb, six at Damariscotta, none at Saint George, and fewer than two dozen at Hunnewell's Point. Militia proved to be more agile in defending against boat parties, in one case repelling Milne's craft as they approached Bath via the Back River at Goose Rock. The boat party retreated and next proceeded up the Sheepscot River, where the British brushed aside some stringbeaners on Squam Island (Westport) before encountering more on the Edgecomb side of the river. At this point, faced with Yankee militiamen plinking away at them from trees and brush, the British boats prudently retreated. Casualties were light on both sides: three militia members were wounded, one of them a mixed-race man who was injured when a signal cannon fired prematurely, while the British casualties included a lieutenant and two sailors, all lightly wounded, and a third sailor killed when a musket discharged by accident. Recognizing that the area had been alerted to his presence, Milne sailed *Bulwark* further east. A few nights later, its boats raided the battery on the Saint George River, which was manned only by a civilian caretaker. The British spiked the battery's guns and carried off the gunpowder and four coasting vessels.[8]

No sooner had *Bulwark* left the area than the British frigate *Tenedos* anchored off Boothbay. Its boats probed the waterways for a few days and found militiamen guarding every approach. In one encounter, boats from *Tenedos* fired a carronade at some militiamen. The shot hit a nearby house, and a British officer recorded seeing the militiamen inside jump out the windows and retreat into the woods, tumbling over an old woman in their haste. The stringbeaners had reason to be alarmed: the shot had taken off the head of a man, splattering his brains and blood onto the front of his father's house. The boats of *Tenedos* also probed the shores of nearby Bristol, where they again encountered resistance, with alert militiamen at Pemaquid opening fire after hearing the sound of oars on a foggy night. The British returned fire but retreated and rowed around the peninsula into New Harbor; yet again, the militia fended off the boat party, and only one stringbeaner was wounded.[9]

Tenedos shifted its operations to the waters of Mount Desert Island, where its boats encountered militiamen at Norwood's Cove. The frigate's surgeon described the stringbeaners' wildly inaccurate gunfire as they fought from behind rocks and bushes: "it is certainly strange that they did not either kill or wound the whole of our people. Our getting off so cheaply must be attributed to a kind Providence and the unsoldierlike conduct of the Yankees who would not expose their precious cascases [carcasses] long enough from the cover of the rocks to enable them to take a deliberate aim." The British suffered three wounded, one severely, but the militia suffered no casualties.[10]

The boat raids conducted by *Bulwark* and *Tenedos* also disrupted inland communities as militia companies mustered and marched toward the sound of the guns. In coastal communities, alarmed families evacuated, carting off as many valuables as possible. But even a temporary evacuation was not without risk. In Boothbay, neighbors plundered the gardens of those who fled during British raids. Worse, as Boothbay's militia skirmished with the boats of *Tenedos*, the militiamen's neighbors came alongside the frigate in "bumboats" and sold potatoes, butter, and vegetables to eager buyers among the officers and crew.[11]

Many of the few available regulars and the more numerous militiamen showed pluck in fending off British boat parties, but not all behaved well. In a letter to his mother, a militia officer at Wiscasset wrote of seeing "many pale cowards" in his company. In Bath, militiamen dragged a cowering stringbeaner from an attic. Individual bravery, however, was not the point: collectively, the militia often fended off boat raids. One of the reasons was that the Royal Navy's officers were loath to risk casualties. Experienced seamen were precious commodities, and officers were not quick to throw lives away.[12]

Not everybody supported the militia's actions, including Congregational clergymen such as the aged Reverend Samuel Eaton of Harpswell. Eaton was preaching at Bowdoin College when several militia companies marched by on their way to respond to *Bulwark*'s boat raids. The air was filled with the sound of drums and fifes as Eaton prayed with the congregation "that our ears might not be stunned in the sanctuary by the sound of musical instruments exciting men to deeds of death; for every battle of the warrior is with confused noise and garments rolled in blood." The behavior of the Reverend William Jenks was even worse. When the Bath clergyman heard that British boats were approaching the port, he set out to save the town from destruction by offering up the port's shipping in return for a British pledge not to torch the village. Local authorities apprehended the minister in a boat carrying an unauthorized flag of truce. Because Jenks was a militia chaplain, a court of inquiry investigated his conduct. The timely intercession of an influential friend (almost certainly William King) persuaded the court to acquit him of treasonous intent.[13]

MOOSE ISLAND CAPITULATION

There were few regulars in the District in 1814, but most that remained belonged to the newly raised Fortieth U.S. Infantry. Two of its companies garrisoned Castine, Machias, Fort Sullivan, and the barracks at Robbinston. Another manned Lincoln County's posts. Still others garrisoned Portland's harbor forts as well as those around Portsmouth Harbor, such as Fort McClary. Eastport was the Fortieth's most tenuous position. It lay at the distant end of a weak supply chain, and the companies' heavy baggage and supplies moved by open boats, which had to dart from cove to cove to avoid Royal Navy vessels. One got as far as Lubec when it encountered boats from HMS *Bream* and *Fantôme*. The soldiers ran their vessel ashore and formed ranks on the beach, driving off the British in an action that lasted for several hours.[14]

Relations between the militia and regular officers remained tense, as William King discovered when he spoke with Fort Edgecomb's commander, Captain James Perry. When King asked how many soldiers were needed to defend the fort, Perry replied one hundred, but he had only eight. King offered militiamen to assist, but Perry replied that he did not have any instructions to request assistance. King was shocked that "we are not only not defended by the United States, but that there is no disposition to do it."[15]

The lack of coordination between the state militia and federal forces was alarming because the British seemed likely to invade the District that summer. Communities devised elaborate signal systems to raise the alarm up and down the coast, including cannon fire, flags, and lanterns. Governor Strong reluctantly agreed to Dearborn's request to detach five hundred militia to be paid and supplied at federal expense. The detached militia assembled in the first week of August, but they were poorly armed and their numbers too small to help much. For example, Castine received forty-six militia infantry and forty artillerymen to join a garrison of about two dozen regulars. This number might discourage a raiding party but could not hope to resist a large force.[16]

Where would the attack fall? The District's most critical military target was the Kittery Naval Yard, and rumors abounded that the British would raid the vulnerable facility. Captain Isaac Hull persuaded the six activated gunboats to defend it, the army sent an engineering officer to repair the harbor's forts, and New Hampshire's governor, John Gilman, called out five hundred militia. Unfortunately, bickering over who would control and feed these troops led Governor Gilman to send the militia home in mid-July, leaving only 230 soldiers to defend Portsmouth Harbor. Kittery was not the only potential focus of attack. Portland's populace had feared one throughout the war. Now only a handful of recruits, invalids, and administrative officers remained in the harbor's forts, under the command of Colonel Joseph D. Learned: the others had marched to the front on Lake Champlain. But in August 1814 the army arrested Learned for fraud, embezzlement, and conduct unbecoming an officer, accusing him of defrauding the government in a crooked contract to provide cartridge boxes and belts for his regiment. A court-martial found him guilty of most of the charges and cashiered him. Portland's Committee of Safety pleaded with Major General Alford Richardson to activate the militia, but he claimed to lack the authority. Despite this roadblock, Portland's militia did put the final touches on Fort Burrows and worked on a battery on Fish Point. For their part, William King and Henry Dearborn thought a British attack would most likely occur on Penobscot Bay. Concerned about their vessels, Castine's shipowners sent them up the Penobscot or into the Bagaduce River for shelter. At the same time, Brigadier General John Blake, Jr., of Brewer ordered his command to prepare to march at a moment's notice. Yet rumors circulated that Castine's militiamen had declared they would not fight, though the town's leaders denied this.[17]

William King had already observed that the federal government had little desire to defend Maine, but Massachusetts was equally unlikely to assist, given that Governor Strong opposed the war. One of Strong's most reactionary councilors, David Cobb, wrote of almost wishing that the British would take Hancock and Washington counties so that their "wretched inhabitants" could restore their connections to British markets. Within a few weeks, his offhand remark nearly became a reality.[18]

The British invasion of Maine came in July, and it happened in Eastport. The decision was linked to diplomatic border concerns. The British had long claimed that Eastport, on Moose Island in Passamaquoddy Bay, was part of New Brunswick. For years, Nathaniel Atcheson, the province's agent in London, had been keeping New Brunswick's claims alive via pamphlets with aggrieved titles such as *American Encroachments on British Rights* (1808) and *A Compressed View of the Points to be Discussed with the United States* (1814), the latter even included foldout maps. In early 1814, New Brunswick's assembly made an attempt to resolve various border issues, focusing primarily on the Madawaska region, though Atcheson remained more concerned about Passamaquoddy Bay. In response to both the assembly and Atcheson, the British government ordered Nova Scotia's military commander, Sir John Coape Sherbrooke, to occupy Moose Island.[19]

Sherbrooke placed Lieutenant Colonel Andrew Pilkington in command of an expedition with orders to "occupy and maintain the possession of the Islands in the Bay of Passamaquoddy" and provided an engineering officer to assist in constructing additional fortifications. Pilkington linked up with troops that had been sent from Bermuda in a small convoy, including the ship-of-the-line HMS *Ramillies* under the command of Captain Sir Thomas Hardy, an officer famous for fighting in the battle of Trafalgar.[20]

On July 11, a British fleet rounding Campobello Island headed directly for Eastport while HMS *Borer* moved west of Moose Island to prevent Fort Sullivan's garrison from escaping. As the fleet anchored, Lieutenant Oates, a relative of Sherbrooke's and his aide de camp, came ashore under a flag of truce and delivered a note demanding surrender, "As we are perfectly apprized of the Weakness of the Fort & Garrison under Your Command." Fort Sullivan's commander, Major Perley Putnam, was a political appointee with little military experience, whom the army recorded as "thought little of by the officers generally—wants experience, talents, and many other qualifications." Eastport's leading citizens approached Putnam and begged him not to resist, arguing that his situation was hopeless and that resistance would lead to civilian casualties. After consulting with his officers, Putnam ordered the fort's flag to be lowered to prevent a needless "Effusion of Blood." The British paroled Putnam and his officers and transported enlisted personnel to the prison on Melville Island in Halifax. Several soldiers fled rather than face imprisonment, eventually finding their way to Portland.[21]

Within a day of Eastport's fall, Pilkington informed the local militia commander that he had reclaimed Moose Island as British territory and would not attack the mainland. Neither the federal government nor Massachusetts expressed any interest in retaking the island, and Adjutant General John Brooks asked militia leaders to suppress any attempts to wage war. The biggest threat the British faced was a lack of provisions; the garrison required a thousand pounds of fresh beef per day. British commissary officers overcame this by paying inflated prices in silver, and soon Yankee drovers arrived with herds of cattle and other provisions.[22]

MORRIS ON THE ROCKS

Only one American warship operated on Maine's coast in the summer of 1814, the corvette *Adams*, often referred to as the "little *Adams*" by its crew, returning from a cruise against British shipping. It had been largely unsuccessful, destroying a few British merchant vessels and taking their crews prisoner. Furthermore, scurvy had broken out on board, disabling many in the crew. Charles Morris, the sleepy lieutenant who had commanded Portland's gunboats during the embargo, now commanded *Adams*, an assignment he saw as "far from being perfect." Nonetheless, it was his first independent command, with a hand-picked crew primarily from Maine, including his executive officer, Alexander Wadsworth of Portland. Morris hoped to evade the British blockade and enter Portsmouth to resupply and refit, but the weather did not favor *Adams*. Morris was renowned for his seamanship, yet constant fog and cloud cover meant he could not determine his position. In the early morning of August 17, *Adams* ran its bow hard aground on a ledge, and the vessel came to a sudden and wrenching halt.[23]

Morris discovered, however, that the stern was in seven fathoms of water. After transferring the prisoners and the sickest sailors into open boats and sending them off to seek safety ashore, Morris assessed his position. He guessed that the ledge lay off Cape Neddick, about ten miles up the coast from Kittery. Eventually a rising tide lifted the warship off the ledge, and Morris shaped a course for Portland; but after sailing all night, he discovered he had miscalculated his position and was approaching Mount Desert Island. *Adams* had been sailing away from Portland, not toward it. Morris immediately reversed course, only to discover that a most unwelcome guest, HMS *Peruvian*, was following him. The British warship shadowed the larger but stricken American vessel, staying out of cannon range. Noting the steady stream of water flowing over *Adams*'s sides from its pumps, *Peruvian*'s commander recognized that it was severely damaged. Morris, for his part, could do little to shake the British warship. His surgeon warned that the crew, weakened by scurvy, would die from the slightest wound. Furthermore, the shock of firing the guns would probably further open the leaks that already required constant pumping. So Morris put into Penobscot Bay, after which *Peruvian* bore off to relay the exciting news of a nearby American warship.[24]

Penobscot Bay did not provide much of a welcome for the *Adams*. Castine's small fort offered little protection, so Morris sailed up the Penobscot River as far as Crosby's wharf in Hampden. There the crew removed the ship's armament and stores and dismantled its masts and rigging to make repairs. Meanwhile, the sick crewmembers who had rowed off in the open boats rejoined their shipmates and communicated a strange story about the ship's prisoners of war. Forty-nine of the prisoners had arrived at Camden in the ship's boats, including five officers. But as a militia guard prepared to march the prisoners to Wiscasset, they discovered that the officers were missing: they had bribed a pilot to take them to the border in his open boat. Militiamen pursued and recaptured the prisoners near Eggemoggin Reach, including the pilot, who went to jail to await federal prosecution. Morris was undoubtedly glad to have his sailors back and the prisoners secured, but now he had another concern: the British were coming.[25]

SHERBROOKE'S PLAN

The town of Madawaska, which on today's maps is tucked at the top of Maine against the New Brunswick border, seemed very far away to many of the District's Yankees. However, it was part of a vital British communications route that connected the commander-in-chief of British North America in Lower Canada to his subordinates in New Brunswick, Nova Scotia, and ultimately London. The problem was that the American government claimed the entire Madawaska region and beyond, and British anxiety about the route's security grew after two worrisome incidents. In 1813, an American attempted to entice a courier to desert and hand over the mails. Then, in 1814, another American tried unsuccessfully to pay a Native American to intercept the mails. The British responded by sending soldiers to escort the couriers and even settled ex-soldiers and their families in Madawaska to anchor the region's loyalty.[26]

The route's importance grew as the British sent reinforcements from the Maritime provinces to Lower Canada in an unprecedented and risky movement of unprecedented scale. In early 1813, after some rudimentary training on snowshoes, the 104th Regiment marched up the frozen Saint John River, through Madawaska, and into Lower Canada (Quebec Province). It was an arduous journey in subzero temperatures, but the 104th lost only one man out of 550. The next year, in February 1814, most of the Eighth Regiment followed the same difficult but now proven route. In an even more surprising move, the Royal Navy sent experienced seamen from Saint John, New Brunswick, to Lake Ontario via Madawaska.[27]

In early 1814 the British moved to secure the Madawaska route and address New Brunswick's demands to resolve its boundary with Maine. Earl Bathurst, the secretary of state for war and colonies, ordered Sir John Coape Sherbrooke to occupy that part of Maine, "which at present intercepts the communication between Halifax and Quebec," and promised him two additional regiments. Sherbrooke leapt at the chance, seeing it as an opportunity to bring the war to American soil via a plan that was both daring and economical. Rather than occupying Madawaska, he proposed to occupy Maine east of the Penobscot. Sherbrooke even floated the idea that the campaign might result in a permanent border alteration. New Brunswick's London agent agreed, declaring that the Penobscot River should be the province's western border.[28]

The cautious Sir George Prévost, who held overall command in British North America, was not sure that so few troops could occupy eastern Maine. However, Sherbrooke pointed out that his approach would fully defend the communications route while creating strategic pressure on the Americans. Besides, with winter on the way, it was too late to send troops to Madawaska. Prévost, undoubtedly aware of British military plans to occupy Castine since the war scare of 1807 in the wake of the *Chesapeake* incident, conceded the point. Though Earl Bathurst supported the proposed invasion, Sherbrooke nonetheless asked his subordinate in New Brunswick, George Stracey Smyth, for his approval. Smyth could provide some intelligence and was well connected to the monarchy, so his backing was essential. Among the Royal Navy commanders, Admiral Sir Alexander Cochrane liked the plan, as did his subordinate at Halifax, Rear Admiral Edward Griffith. While Griffith admitted that he had no intelligence on the Penobscot region, "there is no harm in going to *look at* it." Because Griffith proposed to go with the fleet, Sherbrooke also joined the expedition.[29]

Sherbrooke speedily assembled what Griffith called "our little expedition." Troops from Europe arrived at Halifax on July 15, 1814, and 2,500 veteran soldiers reembarked on ten troopships in late August. The force included a company of Royal Artillery and their field pieces; two companies of the Sixtieth Regiment, armed with accurate Baker rifles; and three regiments of foot (the Twenty-ninth, Sixty-second, and Ninety-eighth), along with various staff officers, including engineers. On August 31, additional Royal Navy warships joined the force off Matinicus Island. The fleet had intended to attack Machias, until HMS *Peruvian*'s commander relayed the news that the *Adams* had taken refuge up the Penobscot River. Without hesitation, General Sherbrooke and Admiral Griffith decided to seize Castine and destroy the *Adams*. That night the British fleet swept up the eastern side of Penobscot Bay. A Royal Navy lieutenant recalled, "I do not think I ever saw a more gratifying light by night. The Moonbeams striking through the trees which covered both sides of the river [he meant *bay*]. The stars appearing in full lustre." Locals were quick to notice the invasion fleet: a man on Vinalhaven reported it, others took note as well, and word reached militia officers in Wiscasset that same night.[30]

Arriving off Castine at daybreak, Griffith sent an officer to demand the fort's surrender. The American commander, Lieutenant Andrew Lewis of the Fortieth U.S. Infantry, replied that he "would defend his fort to the last extremity." These were brave words, but Lewis had no intention of keeping them. When a British schooner came forward to reconnoiter, he fired his battery's cannon before setting fire to the magazine and retreating up the Bagaduce River. The detached militia under Captain Isaac Perry also retreated, taking two small cannons with them. Captain John Fillebrown, who was in the village on recruiting duty, also fled. He had more reason than most to evade capture, as he had been taken prisoner at Eastport and was on parole. A paroled officer was allowed to undertake recruiting duties, but being captured twice within six weeks would have been awkward.[31]

When they discovered that the Americans had decamped, Sherbrooke and Griffith quickly decided to attack and destroy the *Adams*. One force would occupy Castine, another Belfast, and a third would go up the Penobscot River. In the early evening of September 1, the frigate *Bacchante* and two transport ships anchored off Belfast and landed officers under a flag of truce. They explained to the selectmen that they would occupy the town for a few days and would require provisions, for which they would pay. Powerless to resist, the selectmen agreed, and soon soldiers from the Twenty-ninth

Regiment of Foot came ashore, along with its band of Black musicians. A Royal Navy officer wrote that the inhabitants received them "most cordially," with the soldiers quartering in schools and meetinghouses and the officers staying in private homes.[32]

Simultaneously, a force drove up the Penobscot River, seeking to destroy *Adams*. The naval commander was Captain Robert Barrie, who had ample experience in leading similar expeditions in Chesapeake Bay. Admiral Griffith provided Barrie with many of the fleet's larger armed boats, each of which had a small carronade in the bow to cover landing operations. Another open boat was equipped with Congreve rockets, which, while very inaccurate, were good for terrifying inexperienced troops. Lieutenant Colonel Henry John of the Sixtieth Regiment led the army units, a mixed force of six hundred soldiers composed of the flank companies of the Twenty-ninth, Sixty-second, and Ninety-eighth as well as a company from the Sixtieth Rifles. Most of these riflemen were Germans whom the British had recruited from prisoner of war camps; few spoke English. A Royal Artillery detachment with a 5.5-inch howitzer completed the army's complement, while Captain Barrie also stripped all eighty marines from HMS *Dragon* to join the expedition. Many officers thought the Royal Marines were poor troops, but Barrie believed that their experience with landing operations might come in handy. While this force might have looked like a hodgepodge, these units were, in fact, the pick of Sherbrooke's force and a perfect example of British expeditionary warfare, an approach that combined the Royal Navy's mobility with fast-moving light infantry.[33]

The third force occupied Castine. On September 2, Sherbrooke sent out a patrol to disperse some militia who had gathered at the muster grounds on the road to Blue Hill; they scattered the stringbeaners with a few shots. The Twenty-ninth remained in Belfast, "biting our nails," as one officer put it, keenly aware that militia had collected outside town. Fears of conflict were rife in Belfast. Women and children fled the town, and the British warships landed their marines one night because of a rumored militia attack. Meanwhile, Barrie and his little squadron struggled up the Penobscot River, firing on anything that looked even vaguely threatening. Troops landed briefly at Orrington to disperse two militia companies, killing one American before reembarking. Among the militia they fired upon was Captain Perry's detached unit, which had retreated from Castine. With difficulty Perry's men had dragged along two artillery pieces in their march up the east bank of the Penobscot. Now, confronted with the British landing party, they retreated to Buckstown, hid the field pieces, and took a roundabout route away from the river. The British ships continued up the Penobscot and fired on another party of militiamen at Frankfort, quickly driving them off. By late afternoon the flotilla had reached Bald Hill Cove, where it drove off militia dragoons by lobbing Congreve rockets at them. By 10 p.m., the landing force was all ashore, and the soldiers spent a rainy and chilly night in houses and barns vacated by the fleeing inhabitants.[34]

"BLACK JACK, BY GOD!"

As soon as he heard that the British had taken Castine, Captain Morris prepared to defend the *Adams*. He asked Brigadier General John Blake, Jr., to call out his militia, and Blake promptly ordered his brigade to assemble at Hampden, where the militiamen could hear the British ships firing their cannon as they sailed up the river. Blake had had a distinguished combat record in the American Revolution. On April 19, 1775, he had responded as a minuteman to the "Lexington Alarm," and he had taken part in the siege of Boston. Blake joined the Continental Army as a sergeant in 1776 and fought with distinction. His friends referred to him as "Black Jack"; and while the exact origins of that name remain unclear, it does appear in two stories dating from the Revolution. According to one account, Blake and his soldiers crept up on a remote farmhouse. As Blake listened below a window, he heard a British officer ask, "what's trump?" Blake immediately understood that the officers were playing whist, a card game in which a trump suit has the power to beat all other cards. Blake burst in on the surprised officers, exclaiming, "Black Jack, by God!" and captured them without a struggle. In another incident, George Washington assigned Blake to capture Colonel James

De Lancey, a prominent Loyalist officer. Blake and his troops burst into the house where they thought De Lancey was sleeping. As a Loyalist soldier shouted out, "Who in the name of God are you?" Blake, who had been wounded in the side by a Loyalist bayonet, growled, "Black Jack of the 5th Massachusetts Regt. Lay down your arms instantly, or you will all fall beneath the bayonets of my soldiers!" Six Loyalist officers and thirty soldiers surrendered, as did Lancey's servant, though the Loyalist colonel evaded capture.[35]

What stands out in Blake's record are his daring and initiative. Yet he had not seen active service since 1780. In 1812 he dutifully asked his command to "draw out old rusty swords" but did little to prepare his brigade. Given his Federalist politics and the fact that his commander remained in Boston for the entire war, his inaction is unsurprising. His age also undoubtedly contributed to his lethargy: he had just celebrated his sixty-first birthday on August 29; and with his hair pulled back in a queue, he looked every bit the Revolutionary War veteran. There is no record of what he thought as his militia joined the seamen and marines from the *Adams*. If he despaired, he did not show it.[36]

Blake understood that the terrain favored the defense because of the plentiful obstructions and chokepoints at bridges and hilltop positions. The problem was that he could not use the best hill because he had to defend the *Adams*, which lay at Crosby's pier just south of Souadabscook Stream. The northern bank of the stream would have been better, but its bridge could not support the ship's cannons. Blake therefore placed his defensive line south of the hill where Hampden's meetinghouse stood, overlooking a small stream. The British called it a "very strong & advantageous position." Morris's men, assisted by locals with oxen, dragged nine of the ship's cannons to the hill overlooking the helpless *Adams*. Fourteen more guns on Crosby's wharf pointed down the river. Blake stationed another in the highway under Lieutenant Lewis, who had arrived from Castine with his handful of regulars. The Bangor artillery company placed its two brass fieldpieces just west of the road, commanding the bridge across Pitcher's Brook. Moving all of this artillery created confusion, as when Blake ordered one company to fetch some cannons from a privateer at a wharf. The stringbeaners complied, but only until another officer ordered them to go to General Crosby's brick store, where they remained all day, leaving the cannons on the wharf.[37]

On the night of September 2, Blake convened a council of war at Hampden Academy with Captain Morris, the town's selectmen, and others. Blake did not discuss field fortifications, which, while not unknown, were rare during this period. Instead, he opted for a static defense because he understood that his poorly armed stringbeaners were not capable of much more than standing in a line and firing their motley collection of muskets. Any sort of maneuver in combat would have quickly devolved into chaos. Neither Morris nor Blake emerged from the council confident of victory. Morris arranged to destroy the *Adams* if necessary and ordered his sick seamen to hide in the woods in case of defeat. As Morris and Blake went to their respective quarters, they must have scowled as they watched rain and fog envelop Hampden. The stringbeaners, sailors, soldiers, and marines spent the night in the open, the cold rain sapping their morale. Many of the stringbeaners lacked muskets and had arrived with little ammunition. Morris tried to remedy the situation by distributing muskets from the *Adams* while his seamen retained only cutlasses and boarding pikes.[38]

"MY HONOR IS GONE"

Both sides awoke to find the Penobscot River hidden under dense fog. By 5 a.m., the British were on the march, pausing only to land an artillery piece. Boats loaded with sailors and marines moved up the Penobscot while the soldiers marched up the road. The warships sailed behind the boats, firing their cannons whenever a target presented itself. One cannonball killed an Orrington man by ripping his left arm off, while another sailed through a Methodist meetinghouse. The land force moved cautiously in the mist, with the riflemen taking the lead. Before long, they encountered militia at Hampden Corner and captured a stringbeaner named Tobias Oakman. Tradition has it that they compelled Oakman to serve as their guide to Blake's position.[39]

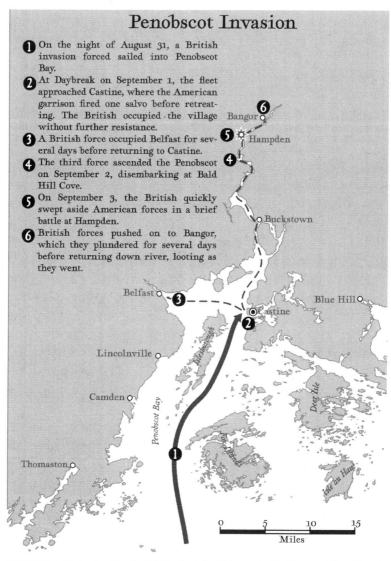

FIGURE 6. In September 1814, the British seized all of Maine east of the Penobscot River. The only serious resistance they encountered was a militia force at Hampden, augmented by the crew of the warship *Adams*. The veteran British troops quickly routed the American force, plundering both Bangor and Hampden in the following days before returning to Castine, which they fortified and held for the rest of the war. Map by the author.

Blake appeared on the field at dawn. His aide, Francis Carr, asked him for orders in case the line broke, to which Blake replied, "The line shall not be broken." Carr persisted in asking what to do in case of a retreat. Blake finally replied that each company commander should take the best possible position to annoy the enemy. Hampden's selectmen, fearful that the hungry troops would raid nearby hen coops and gardens, approached the brigadier general and asked how he intended to provision his troops. Blake told them he planned to dismiss all of his troops after the battle, a surprising statement, given his responsibility to defend the region.[40]

Blake's five hundred militiamen stretched across the road from the meetinghouse to the bluff overlooking the river. The uniformed light infantry companies took position on either flank, while the stringbeaners occupied the center. Blake tried to keep his forces calm as the British approached. He exhorted them to be cool, and one sergeant replied, "I am as cool as a cucumber." Blake told Lieutenant Lewis to take careful aim, an instruction that somewhat annoyed the young officer, who reportedly said that he would fire when he pleased. Major Joshua Chamberlain's horse became restive, and Blake offered him his own horse, which Chamberlain declined. Soon the sound of gunfire could be heard, and the militiamen from Hampden Corner streamed up the road toward Blake's line, with the British following close behind.[41]

While the main British force advanced up the road, barges fired Congreve rockets at the *Adams*. One or two bounced off the hull, with no effect other than unnerving the militia. The sailors on Crosby's wharf fired a cannon at the rocket boat, but it was just out of range and they only harmed themselves: the recoiling guns crushed the toes of one and broke the leg of another. At about that time Morris heard British bugles sounding as the landing party charged Blake's militia.[42]

Partially veiled by the fog, the British crossed the bridge, formed a line, and ascended the hill while the American artillery fired on them. Blake resolved to reserve his musket fire until the enemy was at close range, but the stringbeaners lost their nerve, and men fired without orders. The British soldiers advanced at the double-quick and fired several volleys. While the light infantry companies on the flanks held up, the stringbeaners broke and fled, many without firing. As the line dissolved, Blake shouted to his aide, "Carr, for GOD's sake! Form the line!" The militiamen did not respond, abandoning some thirteen wounded as well as their flags and leaving Blake and his officers to fend for themselves. Artillery captain Charles Hammond ordered every man to take care of himself while a handful of cavalry covered the rear of the retreating mob.[43]

With the militia in flight, Morris and his crew realized they must flee. He ordered his sailors to spike their cannons and retreat across the bridge, and Morris set the *Adams* on fire. He was last to leave the wharf. Before reaching the bridge, the enemy arrived on the hill above him. In danger of being cut off, Morris and the last of his sailors forded Souadabscook Stream as the British fired down on them. They emerged unscathed, and the *Adams* exploded when flames reached the magazine, destroying the warehouse on the wharf.

After retreating a quarter-mile, some militia officers contemplated taking another stand. Oliver Leonard found General Blake, who appeared to be "cool, deliberate, and objected." Blake's aides asked if they should find another hill where they could rally; and after hesitating a moment, he simply replied, "go." That effort failed: the enemy's barges peppered the men with gunfire, and the militia broke again. Asked if they should rally again in Bangor, Blake replied, "No, it is of no use, I am done, my honor is gone." Many would come to agree with Blake, who became a widespread object of scorn in the following decades. The engagement was often referred to as "Hampden Races," a derisive comment on the speed with which Blake's command had run away. Even the British complained that the Americans had been too nimble and had escaped into the woods.[44]

The firing lasted perhaps fifteen minutes. Casualties had been light, with two Britons killed, eight wounded, and one missing. On the American side, two militiamen died, including the unfortunate Tobias Oakman; eleven were wounded, and the British captured eighty. One civilian died, struck by a stray bullet as he watched the battle from his doorway. As the ranking officer at Hampden, John

Blake bore responsibility for the defeat. While he had repeatedly exposed himself to enemy gunfire and was among the last to flee the field, Black Jack had also been dealt a lousy hand. Even had he placed his troops on the north bank of Souadabscook Stream, his raw militia would have stood little chance against the seasoned British veterans.[45]

The British failed to capture the crew of the *Adams*, who passed through Bangor before heading west overland to the Kennebec River. Bereft of provisions, Morris ordered his men to take several different routes so as to better forage for food. The sailors met with a mixed reception as they retreated through the woods. While most locals tried to assist them on their march, one Federalist reportedly refused to let the sailors pick potatoes from his fields, despite Morris's pleas. A sailor suggested to Morris that the men should pull the man's house down, but the officer refused to permit this. Eventually, the captain's party made its way to a cabin without floor or window glass. The young couple who lived there gladly slaughtered their sheep to feed the hungry sailors, and Morris gave them a musket for their kindness. Other backwoodsmen drew a different conclusion when they saw the sailors. When five or six strangely dressed men approached one cabin, the family fled to Waterville, claiming that Natives were murdering everyone in their path. As one correspondent described the scene, "Messengers were dispatched in all directions, and for 2 hours our good people here thought of nothing but Tomahawks & scalping knives.—The women and children in some instances ran screaming for miles without daring to look behind them.—In some towns the Militia were actually under arms, before they discovered the real cause of the alarm." After locals discovered who the men were, fear turned to pity as they watched hungry, barefoot sailors filter through the village, "limping thro' like scattered sheep." Once he arrived in Waterville, Morris took out a bank loan to buy provisions for his men. He reported with some pride that not one of his crew had deserted during their retreat to the Kittery Naval Shipyard. He should not have been so surprised. One-half of the crew had come from southern Maine: they were simply heading home.[46]

MACHIAS FALLS

After the battle at Hampden, the only U.S. garrison east of the Penobscot River was Fort O'Brien at Machias. The officer in charge, Lieutenant Samuel A. Morse, commanded twenty regulars augmented by thirty detached militia, all of them housed in a ramshackle barracks and blockhouse. About thirty more soldiers from the Fortieth Infantry joined him after Lieutenant Enoch Manning abandoned the barracks at Robbinston on July 16. Members of the Passamaquoddy tribe led Manning and his starving troops through the woods to Machias. Unfortunately, their arrival compounded an already grim supply situation, as Royal Navy vessels had intercepted supply boats bound for the little fort. Furthermore, Manning and Morse had very different ideas about soldiering. Morse seldom drilled his troops and let the garrison soldiers (and even prisoners of war) hire themselves out as laborers, which irked Manning, whom his superiors called a "pretty good soldier, but not much of the gentleman."[47]

Morse knew that local support was not forthcoming. Worried about an invasion, many of the area's families had fled. Though one Machias man claimed, "I know of only three men in the town who would not meet the enemy at the water's edge," this was an idle boast. Washington County's sheriff John Cooper had a more pragmatic response, alleging that he would meet the British with open arms and a "low bow." After the battle at Hampden, Cooper rode through the countryside to suppress resistance. When an army officer (probably Morse) suggested that the people had a duty to resist, the sheriff sneered, "none but a scoundrel or a blockhead would propose such a thing."[48]

After the small Salem privateering vessel *Viper* stumbled into an ambush near Roque Island, Morse became aware that the Royal Navy was tightening a noose around Machias. During their fierce skirmish, the privateersmen could hear the British sailors crowing, "you damnd Yeanckey rebiles, we got you." *Viper* fought for an hour and a half before breaking off the engagement. After the battle, the privateer's lieutenant counted almost a hundred bullet holes in the ship's sails, masts, and hull. Only *Viper*'s gunner died during the fight, and the crew buried him in Machias before sailing westward. The ambush was unnerving news, but there was one ray of hope at the little fort: the steady trickle of British deserters passing through town. Morse interviewed them and discovered that the British on Moose Island were suffering from food shortages. Aware that Yankee drovers were bringing cattle to the British, Morse's troops intercepted two herds and impounded them in the fort.[49]

Sir John Coape Sherbrooke and Rear Admiral Edward Griffith were indeed preparing to attack Machias. Sherbrooke again chose Lieutenant Colonel Pilkington to lead the expedition. The British flotilla arrived from Castine on September 10, piloted by a local man, and anchored at Bucks Harbor. Pilkington determined to make a night attack on the American positions from the landward side. But the thick brush was challenging to pass through; a British officer described the march as "feeling their way through the night," and a party of sailors dragging two howitzers further slowed progress. At dawn Pilkington's troops arrived behind the fort and drove off its sentries. As one British officer recorded, "we charged into the Fort at Daybreak . . . before they had time to discharge their ready primed Guns or to put on their Cloaths however they all escaped by firing their Barrack." The British captured the "well stored" magazine and the cattle that Morse had seized, leading a British officer to jest that this was the first time he had captured a fort garrisoned by bullocks.[50]

The Yankees' low morale was apparent in their timid surrenders when apprehended. For example, five British sailors spotted and pursued two soldiers escaping in an open boat. The Americans beached their craft and ran ashore, with the seamen in hot pursuit. The sailors were closing fast, and one of the soldiers turned around and threatened to "shoot the first man dead who advanced." Nonetheless, the headmost sailor seized the soldier by the collar while his comrades took the other without resistance. Remarkably, the sailors were unarmed, and the soldiers had loaded muskets.[51]

Morse and his troops began a long, hungry, westward march to Portland, while the detached militia returned to their homes. The local stringbeaner companies had never turned out. Far from resisting the invaders, the selectmen and Sheriff Cooper met the British outside the village and agreed to provide them with food and quarters. While there is no record that the sheriff made a "low bow" to Pilkington, he did lodge the British commander in his own home. He also encouraged locals to sign a document acknowledging their capitulation, with his name topping the list. The Republican customs collector Jeremiah O'Brien signed at the bottom, reflecting his reluctance to admit submission.[52]

Because the village surrendered without a fight, the British limited themselves to seizing the militia fieldpieces, several schooners they found in the river (including one loaded with valuable silks), and government property. Their enlisted personnel did not harm the citizens but did slaughter cattle, sheep, and poultry; dug potatoes, pulled up vegetables; and burned fence rails. The soldiers also brutally ripped apart a cat that crossed their path, an act that deeply impressed an observing eleven-year-old girl. Yet she also recalled that the British officers tipped their hats to women, even to girls such as herself.[53]

Within a day, Sherbrooke and Griffith arrived to examine the position. Sherbrooke wanted to garrison the town, but Griffith felt that the place was too difficult to evacuate. So on September 13 the British blew up the battery's magazine and burnt the blockhouse. The demolition was not without accident: when the magazine exploded, a piece of masonry struck HMS *Pictou*'s rigging. After loading their plunder, the troops reembarked and sailed for Castine on September 15. A local pilot received eighteen Spanish silver dollars for guiding British warships and transports up and down the Machias River and led the ships out of the bay, including the captured schooners. While they suffered no combat casualties, one British officer reported, "six Rascals have deserted since we arrived."[54]

Chapter 7
"ONE AGAINST ANOTHER"

Military defeat left communities exposed to the depredations of the British military and naval forces. Inhabitants responded in various ways, some collaborating with the British, others declaring themselves neutral, still others fleeing, and many attempting to profit. The common thread was that the Yankee populace preferred property to pride. If the price of opposition was the loss of their homes, barns, stores, boats, and warehouses, then it was too high a price, especially given the federal government's feeble efforts to defend coastal Maine. The impact of enemy occupation divided communities: as a teenager in Saint George commented, "Some a trading with them [the British] and some a fighting them. Strang[e] war and people we are one against another."[1]

Bangor's residents were flabbergasted by the appearance of the British in their village. Initially, the law clerk Joseph Williamson was impressed by their looks, which he described as "truly martial & splendid. A finer set of fellows never were embodied." The riflemen made the biggest impression on him, "dressed in black," resembling "a banditti of devils direct from the infernal regions." Six officers lodged with his brother William Williamson, a Republican attorney and postmaster. The unwelcome guests arrived on September 3, 1814, shortly after the battle at Hampden and forced William to hand over all post office funds, but later that day both brothers sat down with the officers at dinner and engaged in conversation. Joseph found them courteous, "gentlemanly in their manners, free, open & agreeable." The redcoats claimed the war would be over in four months. The Williamsons disagreed, but the officers insisted the Americans would be forced into a treaty now that Britain had defeated Napoleon.[2]

The British officers were correct that the war was nearly over, and the Williamson brothers were equally correct that the United States would wrangle a favorable treaty. Their civilized conversation occurred even as soldiers and sailors were plundering Bangor's stores and homes, publicly humiliating its leading citizens, and wantonly destroying property. Bangor and Hampden suffered the worst depredations, but all of eastern Maine had to contend with enemy occupation and its attendant miseries. Many, such as the destruction of personal property, were material and obvious; more enduring were the loss of pride and the shame of defeat. As Joseph Williamson noted, "We are completely in their hands, & they can do with us as they please."[3]

PLUNDER

Common patterns emerged as each village's selectmen hastened to mitigate the effects of enemy occupation. The British had clear-cut responses to the choices that communities made: they ruthlessly pillaged those that resisted but respected private property in those that capitulated without a fight. Selectmen rushed to find provisions and quarters for the enemy soldiers and mounts for officers, and they confiscated weapons from their townsfolk. The British were eager for plunder, which took place both unofficially, as officers lost control of their men in the immediate aftermath of combat, and officially, via a ponderous legal process that took years to sort out.

Unofficial plunder was chaotic, violent, and humiliating. British army regulations forbade it under pain of death, but its soldiers expected to loot the communities they took by storm. Rapine was catharsis for the enlisted personnel, who vented their many frustrations on a defenseless civilian population. In Bangor and Hampden, soldiers and sailors smashed windows, crockery, and anything else they could not steal. Undoubtedly many were drunk. Although Bangor's selectmen promised to deny spirits to the British troops, the men soon managed to find some, compelling Captain Robert Barrie of HMS *Dragon* to order the destruction of liquor supplies. Sailors gleefully smashed barrels of rum and brandy and looted stores. They repeated the process in Hampden: soldiers and sailors fanned out, stealing what they could carry, indiscriminately slaughtering animals in the streets, and gorging themselves on food and drink. According to one report, they "took every cent of property and broke every window." Frankfort suffered somewhat less, though Captain Barrie and Lieutenant Colonel Henry John demanded cattle, sheep, and fresh vegetables, which village committee members provided as best they could.[4]

The British took particular delight in forcing Bangor's most prominent men to perform menial tasks, singling out Federalist war opposers as the butt of their antics. Even Republicans were shocked to witness these purposeful humiliations, which included making a Federalist attorney draw water from a well and destroying a Congregational minister's books and papers. One observer noted that the Federalists could expect no mercy because "Love of country is almost the only virtue an Englishman possesses. And they respect that spirit wherever they find it." In contrast, the British did not harass Francis Carr, who as a Republican congressman had voted for the declaration of war. Captain Barrie was particularly inclined to bully Americans. Joseph Williamson described him as a "churlish, brutal monster." Quick to anger and crude of mouth, Barrie punched a man he discovered serving brandy to soldiers and then kicked over the cask; he also allegedly horsewhipped a Bangor physician and threatened to "bury the village in ashes." At Hampden, Barrie imprisoned sixty of the town's leading figures in a stifling ship's hold, ignoring their pleas for water and air. When one man asked Barrie for leniency, he replied that "He had none;—that we had come to the wrong person;—that his business was to burn, sink and destroy;—that he had taken the town by storm;—that according to the rules of war, we ought not only to have our houses burnt, but ourselves put to death;—that he should spare our lives, but meant to burn our houses."[5]

In contrast, the occupation of Buckstown exemplified how the British rewarded cooperation. While Barrie was plundering Bangor and Hampden, General John Sherbrooke was sending a force to Buckstown. After the selectmen surrendered the two cannons hidden there, the town's shipping was left alone and, at Sherbrooke's request, "every kindness and protection" was given to its inhabitants. Though Mary Sewall Buck found her parlor filled with British officers and her outbuildings occupied by soldiers, she took comfort in religion, giving thanks because God had "sent His Angels to encamp about our bed and no evil has come nigh our dwelling."[6]

Official plunder included confiscated militia weapons, funds or bonds in post offices and customhouses, and property owned by nonresidents, including real estate and goods in warehouses and stores. British officers collected and recorded official plunder, which then underwent an adjudication process that could last for years. Part of the proceeds would go to the Crown, the remainder to the officers, sailors, and soldiers who had been directly involved in the operation. Yet while the practice was officially sanctioned, it was not necessarily gentle. Ellsworth's customs collector lost the cash in his office, which the British confiscated under threat of destroying his home if he did not surrender it. They also captured Eastport's customs collector as he attempted to flee with his papers, including actionable bonds worth roughly $100,000. Castine's customs collector, Josiah Hook, Jr., received much rougher treatment. He fled from Castine with all of his official papers and cash before the British occupied the village. Infuriated by his flight, the soldiers seized his furniture, household goods, and real estate. As mentioned, official plunder included property owned by nonresidents, which the British identified by locking the Hancock County registry of deeds so that they could examine the records at leisure. They also seized goods in warehouses, such as the nearly $80,000 worth of smuggled goods found at Machias. The smugglers tried to hide their contraband in the woods, and Sheriff John Cooper assured locals that the British soldiers scouring the area would not harm those who remained indoors. Nonetheless, locals pilfered the hidden goods, and others bought the plunder from soldiers who sold it in the streets.[7]

Official plunder also applied to the many boats and ships found between the Penobscot and Saint Croix rivers, including those still under construction. In mid-December, the Halifax vice-admiralty court adjudicated dozens of seized vessels. British officers preferred ransoming vessels to simplify the lengthy and expensive judicial process. Shipowners who paid a relatively small sum in specie, say 10 percent of its actual value, received their vessels back. Ellsworth's customs collector bought back the customhouse boat for $50; the owners of the *Penobscot Packet* also ransomed their vessel and even received permission to resume service on the Penobscot River. Nonetheless, seized vessels crowded Castine's harbor, including the schooner *Washington*, which had belonged to Jeremiah O'Brien of Machias. Nova Scotia's vice-admiralty court condemned the schooner on December 17, 1814, yet the captors did not auction it until March 10, some weeks after the war ended. Hoping that the return of peace meant that he could reclaim his vessel, O'Brien petitioned for its return, but in vain.[8]

Vessels still under construction went through a slightly different legal process whereby the vice-admiralty court condemned them *jure corone*, or to the Crown's benefit. In this process, the British forces compelled locals to post a bond payable by a specific date; if they refused, the British would set the vessels on fire. Captain Barrie burned roughly a dozen vessels in the Penobscot River and three under construction in Brewer, a waste of private property that Joseph Williamson found "truly humiliating & distressing." Barrie threatened to burn four more ships in Bangor's shipyards, but the selectmen begged him to stop when they realized that the village would also catch fire. Bangor posted a bond of $30,000 for the uncompleted ships, and Hampden posted $12,000, with both towns promising to deliver them to Castine at the end of September.[9]

There was yet another category of official plunder: salvage for recaptured British ships. In early 1814 the Portland privateer *Hyder Ally* set sail for the East Indies in hopes of surprising British shipping on the far side of the world. It captured only three prizes before being captured itself, but two of those prizes got as far as Mount Desert Island. HMS *Alban* recaptured the brig *Favorite* on September 2, and HMS *Pylades* recaptured the 330-ton ship *Betsy* and its Lascar crew near Bass Harbor on September 7. Admiralty courts usually awarded the recapturers 10 percent of the value of the ship and cargo as salvage, which would have been a tidy sum, especially *Betsy*'s cargo of pepper, which was worth an estimated $56,000.[10]

Official plunder did not reap much profit: Captain Barrie expected a mere £100 from the Penobscot River expedition. Sailors and marines probably received just £1 each. The army's share of official plunder amounted to £11,417. When the British government finally doled out the prize money in 1820, a private received the equivalent of about $5, roughly the same as a laborer's weekly wages. A quarter of the enlisted personnel never claimed their share because they were either dead or unaware the money was available. The surplus £3,000 eventually benefited the Royal Chelsea Hospital, which catered to veterans. Officers did much better: Sherbrooke received more than £989, while lieutenants garnered slightly more than £17 each.[11]

Official plunder led to the only violent resistance to British rule in the occupied portion of the District. There were two incidents, both related to the brig *Kutusoff,* which the American privateer *Surprise* had captured off the Azores in April 1814. It was a large and valuable vessel, a former American privateer with an expensive coppered bottom and a cargo of more than one hundred bags of coffee, some hides, and a staggering one hundred tons of cocoa beans. The *Surprise*'s captain assigned prize master Alexander Milliken of Frankfort to take the vessel back to the United States. Assessing his chances, Milliken made for the Maine coast, which was only lightly patrolled by the British. Even so, as he approached Mount Desert, a Royal Navy ship pursued him. Milliken escaped and brought *Kutusoff* up the Penobscot River to his hometown. Boston merchants purchased the brig and its cargo but had not moved them by the time the British invaded. Although agents for the owners concealed the cargo ashore and took the brig upriver to Hampden, the British were nonetheless able to capture it. They recovered some cocoa, but many tons remained hidden.[12]

Rear Admiral David Milne soon learned about *Kutusoff*'s hidden cargo and warned Frankfort's selectmen that they must surrender it. A sloop with a Royal Navy crew arrived to recover the cocoa and take one hundred muskets that Massachusetts had loaned to the town. Unfortunately for the British, Lieutenants Enoch Manning and Samuel A. Morse of the Fortieth U.S. Infantry, now retreating to Portland, learned about their presence. They surprised the landing party at the wharf and found the sloop's lieutenant and midshipman at a nearby tavern, where the Americans captured them without firing a shot. Manning and Morse now had a quandary: what to do with the muskets and cocoa? They offered to give the weapons back to the selectmen, who, fearing British retaliation, refused. So the soldiers took the best muskets, threw the remainder into the river, and burned the sloop with many tons of cocoa still on board before resuming their march, now escorting fourteen prisoners. On hearing of the party's capture, Milne demanded his men back, but General Henry Dearborn responded that the party's flag of truce was a "mere cover" for plundering and that their capture was therefore legitimate. Meanwhile, Frankfort's residents filched the remaining cocoa, frustrating the efforts of the legitimate owner in Boston to recover it.[13]

After the cocoa incident, the British only went up the Penobscot River in force, as when they returned to carry away the *Kutusoff*, whose owners refused to pay a ransom. With some difficulty, the gun brig *Adder* ascended the river in November 1814, its crew using sweeps to fight the current. Forty soldiers augmented the crew to ensure sufficient force if they met resistance. They took possession of *Kutusoff* without incident, and both ships dropped down the river until *Adder* "received 4 shots from the bank from Yankees hid in the wood." The soldiers immediately returned fire, as did the *Adder*'s cannons, and "the crew cont'd firing round shot at all the houses we passed on the Starboard bank of the River, one good house got three 12 lb. shot thro' it." The message was unmistakable: the British would punish resistance with overwhelming force. *Kutusoff* arrived safely at Castine, where it remained all winter.[14]

ACCOMMODATION

Defeat led to personal humiliations. In Bangor, the British compelled men to report as prisoners of war for parole, meaning they could not bear arms until they were formally exchanged. General John Blake signed the same parole that about two hundred others did.

In Machias, Sheriff Cooper shamelessly negotiated the militia's surrender, summoning Washington County's two highest-ranked officers to ratify an agreement that gave their brigades' parole in return for "the safe and full enjoyment of our private property." Even Houlton's settlers had to swear an oath and surrender their arms. But Yankees outside of the occupied area were unsympathetic about such concessions. One wrote, "those people the best gunners in the Union are giving up their Arms, unconditional submission—I shall never take the Oath to the British come what will."[15]

Initially, Sherbrooke was not keen on compelling Americans to take an oath: "The time was when oaths were considered sacred, but I am sorry to say their frequency has in part done that away—and I will not introduce them here." After returning to Halifax, however, he reversed his earlier decision and required all men to swear to behave peaceably, not carry arms, and cooperate with British officials in a proclamation that laid out how the British would rule eastern Maine. He also demanded that strangers purchase a pass to enter the occupied zone. Sherbrooke did allow maritime trade to resume, validating Admiral Edward Griffith's order permitting vessels from any part of British North America to sail to Castine. Local craft could resume the coasting trade or fishing if their owners bought a permit. As a result, Castine was in business again, though now as a British port integrated within the Maritime provinces' trade network. Merchants in Saint John and Halifax soon sent cargoes to Castine; and in October, Halifax customs officials arrived to oversee and tax the blossoming trade.[16]

Sherbrooke's proclamation placed Major General Gerard Gosselin in charge of all of eastern Maine, except for Eastport and Houlton, which fell under New Brunswick's military authority. Sherbrooke tasked Gosselin with compelling all males above age sixteen to take an oath of allegiance or neutrality before December 1. Gosselin asked each town's selectmen to administer the oath, but many delayed or resisted. Sedgewick's selectmen refused because the proclamation bore the royal seal, which would make them "Culpable as Traitors to our Country." Few were as bold as the Sullivan selectman who debated the issue in person with Gosselin.[17]

Those who refused to take the oath had permission to leave the occupied zone. Perhaps a third of Eastport's population decamped. Paul Dudley Sargent of Sullivan decided that occupation was more than he could bear and moved to Hampden. Others debated the issue, among them a Buckstown man, who reasoned:

> My real estate is worth 5 or 6 hundred dollars and to leave it will come hard. My possession has cost me 400 dollars in cash besides a great deal of produce and hard labour. But before I will be to[o] much oppress'd by Brittish power I will leave the whole and flee to the land of liberty if such is to be found. But to leave this place at present might be like jumping from the frying pan into the fire for our scrimage is over for the present and my life is spared and if I should move to another place I might be again called into battle and loose my life.

Even on the west bank of the Penobscot, many families left. Hampden's Methodist minister withdrew to New Hampshire, while Bangor merchant Joseph Leavitt moved to a farmhouse five miles up Kenduskeag Stream.[18]

"CONQUERED EASILY BY KINDNESS"

Sherbrooke had landed in arguably the most pro-British areas of the entire District. Castine, Buckstown, Orland, Blue Hill, Deer Isle, and Ellsworth deeply resented the war, and the local leadership proved to be very accommodating. Many Hancock County attorneys and judges had ties to the British firm Baring Brothers, which owned a large swathe of eastern Maine. William Black of Ellsworth and his father-in-law, David Cobb, worked as agents for the firm. Furthermore, members of the region's mercantile community had continued selling timber to the British throughout the war, including John Crosby of Hampden and the Perkins family of Castine.[19]

During his time at Castine, Sherbrooke noted two types of Americans: Federalists and Democrats. He deemed Federalists "the people of property and respectability," while Democrats were "a lawless set of plunderers," and he described "a most irreconcilable hatred between them." Sherbrooke naturally favored the Federalists but found they feared the "lower orders" whom he considered "lawless Banditti." His source was George Herbert of Ellsworth, a Federalist attorney who met with the general to enable "such measures for the safety of themselves, their families & their property, as may become necessary & proper." Herbert suggested that "New England may be conquered easily by kindness" and argued that the inhabitants needed firearms to defend against "Desperadoes made up of our own people [who] would invade every night on defenseless houses with impunity." Sherbrooke and Admiral Griffith agreed to Herbert's request to retain firearms "in order to secure the quiet and unoffending against Violence and Outrage from their less peaceable neighbours," but insisted that their possessors must sign a certificate promising not to use them against the British.[20]

Local farmers supplied Castine's garrison with ample amounts of fresh meat and other provisions, often delivering them by boat. Customs officers in Belfast seized one such boat, laden with "8 quarters beef, 1 leg pork, a quantity of butter, eggs, & other articles." Provisions passed by land, too; according to a militia officer, cattle, grain, and other supplies passed into Castine daily. He requested permission to stop the trade, but his superiors ignored it. Alexander Milliken was one customs officer who attempted to stop cattle bound for Castine. In October, he crossed to the Penobscot's eastern bank to investigate, but a deputy sheriff attempted to arrest him for not possessing a British pass. Infuriated with the deputy for collaborating with the British, Milliken informed him that he was under arrest for interfering with a federal officer. A shouting contest ensued until bystanders intervened, thus allowing each official to depart with the matter unresolved.[21]

Republicans such as George Ulmer, now back at his Ducktrap home, were outraged by the open trade with the enemy. He raged about Americans cooperating with British agents in buying up all available corn, grain, and cattle, claiming that the region would "be soon drained of every article of provision, Supplies are going to them from all quarters, as far west as Waldoborough." Another

Republican wrote, "Cattle and sheep going daily to the British, wheat and rye bought up by speculators, penury & starvation staring us in the face." Other reports verified that the British were paying extravagant prices, driving up the cost of food for the poor and making it difficult and expensive to provision militia units. While the scale of the provisions trade with Castine is impossible to measure, it was more than sufficient for the garrison. By November, shiploads of provisions were leaving the port destined for Bermuda's naval base. One of these vessels, the New Brunswick schooner *Sheffield*, carried a cargo of root vegetables, peas, beans, eggs, butter, cheese, hams, salted beef and pork, smoked fish, and live sheep, geese, and hens, in addition to shingles, oars, timbers, and handspikes.[22]

Castine's customs collector, Josiah Hook, Jr., tried to stop the provisions trade after reestablishing his office in Hampden. In September, his officers seized twenty-three cattle bound for enemy territory. However, their owner initiated a successful legal action that cost Hook more than $1,000. In another instance, after customs officers seized a herd of forty cattle in Bangor, an armed crowd of smugglers took the herd back across the frozen Penobscot River to Brewer. The pursuing officers caught up with them, and a skirmish on the ice wounded several men, including a smuggler who was shot in the face.[23]

COLLABORATION

The British encouraged selectmen and magistrates to enforce civil law, and some inhabitants bridled because the Federalist leadership in the occupied portion of the state seemed to be collaborating with the British so readily. William King received an anonymous letter from Machias listing "the traitors that sold this place & invited the Briton; I think their names ought to be known as they have acted Benedict Arnold to perfection." Topping the list was Washington County's Sheriff Cooper.[24]

Cooper had opposed the war from the start. When the British seized Moose Island, he quickly lauded their "magnanimity, moderation, and justice." In Machias, he urged the townspeople to cooperate with British soldiers, boasting to Governor Strong that the British had left without hurting anyone and thanking them for their conduct. The British understood Cooper's utility and even dispatched a Royal Navy vessel to bring him to headquarters in Castine. A day after his return to Machias, notices requiring the neutrality oath appeared at the local tavern. But Cooper's collaboration sat ill with many. An open letter in a Boston newspaper warned him that the British "heartily despise disloyalty as any people on earth. They may cherish you, and encourage you by some trifling office, while you subserve their interest; but you never need to look for an office of honor or responsibility."[25]

Sheriff Moses Adams in Hancock County also worked closely with General Gosselin in Castine. Adams required his deputies to examine strangers to see if they were carrying British passes that allowed them to enter occupied territory. He also crossed Penobscot Bay to arrest debtors and confined them in the Castine jail in enemy-occupied territory. In October 1814, however, he had a humiliating experience in Wiscasset. While Adams relaxed in front of a tavern fireplace, an alert customs officer discovered that the sheriff had concealed British textiles under a double bottom in his wagon. Adams claimed he had hidden the goods because he feared British deserters and the "many ferocious inhabitants" on the Penobscot River, who "exultingly proclaimed that 'now there was no law' and openly committed many acts of violence and plunder." Yet testimony revealed he had bought the goods from the notorious smuggler Jabez Mowry while Eastport was in enemy hands, making the merchandise contraband.[26]

Caught in forces beyond their control, most people honored their neutrality oaths and simply waited for the war to end. The American privateers prowling the coast were the biggest challenge to neutrality, especially in Federalist communities such as Machias and Deer Isle. Machias's inhabitants complained of their embarrassing predicament: although the privateers plundered their vessels, they did not dare "oppose them by Arms, for fear of being considered traitors to their Country." Deer Isle's response to a fight between an American privateer and an armed British merchant vessel illustrates this fastidious concern. In early January 1815, *Paul Jones* chased the British brigantine *Danzic* aground in Small's Cove. The British master appealed to the people on the shore for assistance, but they replied that "they were Neutrals and could give no assistance to either party." Yet they did not interfere when some of the British crew escaped onshore, probably because the *Danzic*'s mate was a local. The next day the American privateer captain came ashore and compelled them at gunpoint to hand over the mate, which they reluctantly did.[27]

The neutrality oaths left eastern Maine's demoralized populace with mixed feelings about the national government that had failed to defend them. Many resisted demands for taxes, recruits, and cooperation. A curious example involved U.S. Navy captain Isaac Hull's attempt to recoup items salvaged from the wreck of *Adams*. The community of Hampden had formed a committee to salvage the wreck, with the ostensible goal of selling what they could recover and distributing the proceeds among those who had been impoverished by the British sacking of their village. Hull was astonished at this conduct and ordered his agents to report those who were concealing salvaged materials. Nonetheless, a large amount of copper went missing, some of which reappeared in Portland, where the local navy agent seized three hundred pounds of the metal from merchants. These storeowners complained they had bought it on the open market and threatened to sue the agent if he did not release the metal. Meanwhile, the Hampden committee protested to Hull that the British had permitted them to salvage the wreck and that they had petitioned Congress for its consent. More disingenuously, one committee member claimed that people from the eastern side of the Penobscot River had taken the scrap metal, while others whined that they had gone to great trouble to conduct the work. Nonetheless, the committee handed over perhaps $1,500 in salvaged materials to the navy, which hauled them inland to the presumed safety of Dixmont.[28]

Bangor and Hampden were facing another problem: the penal bonds they had posted for ships still under construction were due at the end of September 1814. By October, General Gosselin was reminding both towns of their responsibility. They sent delegations to him seeking relief, or at least a reduction in the amounts due, but Gosselin remained adamant and threatened to dispatch soldiers to extract the money. Suitably alarmed, the towns asked John Crosby, Sr., of Hampden and Amos Patten of Bangor to meet with General Sherbrooke in Halifax to renegotiate the bonds. Sherbrooke, however, refused to assist them, instead laying out three bleak options: they could destroy the vessels; they could auction them and send the proceeds to Castine; or they could deliver the completed ships to General Gosselin in the spring. By the time Crosby returned to Hampden, the British had taken matters into their own hands and had carried off the prize ships *Victory* and *Kutusoff* to Castine, thereby liquidating half of that town's bonds. The war's end in 1815 made the issue moot.[29]

Like their Yankee neighbors, members of the Penobscot Nation also sought neutrality. General Sherbrooke had asked them "on no account to injure or make war upon the Citizens of the United States." Far from waging war, the Penobscots looked to Massachusetts to protect them from settler encroachment and provide an annual grain supply through the local Massachusetts Indian agent, the disgraced General Blake. But the Commonwealth found it nearly impossible to fulfill its treaty obligation to provide flour and corn to the Penobscots due to the British blockade and control of the Penobscot River, so in February 1815 a Penobscot delegation went to Castine to see if the British would help. Gosselin would not assist them, but he did give them a little money and some small gifts. In return, the Penobscots promised to return in three or four months with bear, sable, and otter furs.[30]

SMUGGLERS

Smuggling threatened the national government in several ways. It sapped revenue, undercut the war effort, and created a crisis in specie circulation. More importantly, it subverted the loyalty of ordinary citizens. According to one military officer, "our citizens are, by their ready communication with the Enemy, becoming familiar with treason, corruption & purgery, which with their characteristic avarice, will soon annihilate every estimable quality they may have possessed as Citizens & prepare them for submission." Vice President Elbridge Gerry agreed, suspecting that the British were seeking the "recolonization of Maine" and that the smuggling trade was preparing the inhabitants' minds for "voluntary submission" to British rule.[31]

Castine became the center of a roaring smuggling trade. British manufactured goods and West Indian produce flooded into a market hungry for consumer goods. A multinational group of adventurers, including English, Irish, and Scottish merchants well versed in avoiding troublesome regulations, was behind this trade. John G. Brown was representative. Born in Dublin, he departed for the United States in 1805, where he worked as a merchant but never sought citizenship. In January 1814, he traveled to Nova Scotia via Eastport and New Brunswick. In Halifax, he was questioned by the magistrates, who thought he and his business were suspicious. Brown appeared next in Saint John, where he became involved in the smuggling trade in Passamaquoddy Bay before moving on to Castine. Brown came to the attention of American customs officers after they seized his trunk in Brewer. In response, he rode to Hampden one moonlight night with a sleighload of confederates and demanded his right to search a customs officer's home for his trunk, firing a pistol into the air to emphasize his point. The official reluctantly admitted Brown into his house and proved that the trunk was not there. Another representative smuggler was the Scottish merchant John Young, who wrote to his son from Castine, "We are you know creatures of imitative habits & as all around me are smuggling I am beginning to smuggle too."[32]

Some adventurers exploited their neutral status to facilitate illicit trade. Constantino Llufrio (sometimes spelled *Lefrio*) was a Spanish Floridian who had commenced his smuggling career at Amelia Island, which lay on the border with Georgia. Somehow he ended up in Saint John, New Brunswick, and became involved in the fraudulent neutral trade between that port and Eastport. After the British occupation, he moved to Castine. Another well-known smuggler, Stephen J. M. Peillon, was a native of Lyon, France. The Tappan brothers, however, had New England roots. John Tappan was a Boston merchant, a "verry religious man," who smuggled goods through Wiscasset and Hampden. Arthur Tappan traded in Portland until Jefferson's embargo and then moved to Montreal. When the war broke out, Arthur left Quebec because he refused to accept British allegiance. His biography, written by another Tappan brother, Lewis, completely omits his activities during the War of 1812, but customs officers sometimes intercepted Arthur's smuggled merchandise from Castine.[33]

By October, an elaborate system evolved whereby merchants would land British manufactured goods legally at Castine, transport them to Buckstown or Orrington, and load them onto the Swedish-flagged sloop *Christina*. When the sloop crossed the Penobscot River, federal customs authorities would permit the entry based on the legal fiction that *Christina* was a neutral vessel. It was a thin ruse. Before October 14, the *Christina* had been the old and leaky thirty-ton sloop *Union*, owned by Samuel Bartlett of Buckstown, who had sold it to William P. Unger, a Swedish subject. Unger repeatedly crossed the Penobscot River in the *Christina*, fully laden with British manufactured goods. The scale of the trade was massive. According to British customs records, roughly $1.25 million in goods entered Castine during the occupation. To put that number into context: the value of legitimate imports into the entire country was $13 million in 1814. American merchants paid for the merchandise in specie, leading one man to complain that Buckstown's bank contained more gold and silver than it ever had in peacetime. Maine's Republican and Federalist newspapers both bemoaned the drain of the nation's specie in trade with the enemy, but it proved impossible to stop.[34]

Another measure of the trade at Castine was the crowding of the District's roads. So many smugglers hastened to Castine that an enterprising individual established a regular stagecoach route from Hallowell to Castine via Belfast, a service unknown before the war. Customs officers estimated that three hundred wagonloads of contraband left Hampden before the end of 1814, destined for Portland, Portsmouth, Boston, and even New York, with each wagon carrying two to three tons of contraband. Customs officer Alexander Milliken stumbled across sixty wagons at Hampden ready to receive cargo, then crossed the river to find fourteen more. The teamsters openly told him they had carried British merchandise from Castine. Milliken returned to Hampden and seized the packages when they landed in American-controlled territory, angering Unger and his partners, who persuaded the District's deputy collector, Charles Tebbets, to allow the goods to enter after paying duties. Seeing that he could not defeat the smugglers, Milliken quit the customs service and fitted himself out as a privateer.[35]

Milliken's patriotism was at odds with government policy. The neutral trade took advantage of a loophole permitting neutral vessels to land cargoes in the United States. The secretary of the treasury confirmed that this was legal, as did the Swedish vice-consul, who verified Unger's citizenship. With official permission, on November 28, 1814, the Swedish merchant Johan Nyman imported roughly $28,000 in British goods at Hampden, paying more than $10,000 in duties, revenue that the national government desperately needed. However, the merchants involved declared only a fraction of the imported merchandise, perhaps as little as 10 or 20 percent; and some intimidated or bribed customs officers to look the other way. Another ruse involved allowing customs officers to make phony seizures of cargo. The officers would then submit a ludicrously low evaluation of the contraband, allowing the claimants to post a small bond before taking their wagons or sleighs to Boston, where they sold their goods at a fabulous profit.[36]

The outrage of honest customs officers also indicated the smuggling trade's scale. Waldoborough's collector reported that "the revenue laws have been shamefully violated and trampled upon, & that our means for preventing it are extremely feeble & inadequate." He described Castine and Buckstown as "thronged with Englishmen & Americans walking hand in glove & transacting business as if no war existed." He raged, "The inhabitants on both sides of the river are (with some few exceptions) so favorably disposed towards this intercourse that the civil & revenue officers find it difficult to get along—indeed it is utterly impossible to enforce the laws." Yet Republican complaints about the trade did not mean that they were bystanders. When William King wrote to Secretary of War James Monroe, disgusted by the "free and unobstructed" illicit trade with Castine, he reported that the British were giving every facility to smugglers. He wrote on good authority, for in late 1814, King himself smuggled a substantial quantity of textiles via Castine. One wonders if he gave himself a wry smile as he penned his letter.[37]

The smugglers behind the neutrality ploy might have gotten away with their schemes had it not been for the vigilance of a customs inspector named Amos Proctor. Though he lived in New Hampshire, he had permission to travel to smuggling hot spots; and in late 1814 and early 1815, he entered Castine three times to spy on smugglers. Proctor discovered written evidence of various smuggling plots, but during his last visit someone informed the British about his activities, and he barely escaped with his hard-won intelligence. Armed with that information, customs officials seized wagons in South Berwick, close to the New Hampshire border, that were loaded with smuggled goods reportedly worth more than $100,000. Proctor's boldness reinvigorated the District's customs officers. In early 1815 they seized contraband in cellars, barns, warehouses, and coves stretching from Hampden down to Kittery. Isaac Ilsley raided Portland's auction houses and found large amounts of British manufactured goods. Josiah Hook, Jr.'s, officers even crossed into the occupied zone, seizing crockery and window glass on Islesborough, tea in Orrington, and cloth in Brewer. Smugglers sometimes resisted but were more likely to rescue seized goods or use trumped-up charges against customs officers in state courts.[38]

"HALF A LOAF IS BETTER THAN NO BREAD"

Privateers and other craft harassed British shipping from October 1814 until the war's end in 1815, picking off stragglers from British convoys and driving up insurance rates. A unique example was the seizure of the Nova Scotia letter-of-marque schooner *Ann*. Unbeknownst to the vessel's master, two of his crew were American privateersmen who had escaped captivity and found their way to Halifax, where they had signed on board the schooner. One of them, Jonathan Low, Jr., had even talked his way into a position as lieutenant. The American privateersmen convinced their shipmates to seize the vessel as it entered Penobscot Bay in mid-October; and after securing the officers and crew, they sailed *Ann* into South Thomaston. A squabble between the local customs collector, Joseph Farley, and *Ann*'s captors followed. Farley seized the vessel as enemy property, initially agreeing to split the profits with Low and his confederates. Low and his companions reneged on the deal and attempted to exclude Farley's share in federal court. Farley tried to reason with Low, arguing that "Half a loaf is better than no bread." Unfortunately for Low and his shipmates, Judge David Sewall ruled in Farley's favor. He received $5,000 while Low and his sailors received nothing.[39]

While some Republicans took part in the Castine smuggling trade, others were genuinely outraged and took action. In an infamous case in November 1814, several Lincolnville men captured the British sloop *Mary* under dubious circumstances. The incident began when Noah Miller, who had served in Ulmer's Volunteers at Eastport, rented a boat, armed himself and a few neighbors, and set off to intercept vessels bound for Castine, despite having no official sanction. The men boarded the *Mary* because its master thought they were pilots. He discovered his mistake too late; and despite being offered a £10,000 bribe, Miller carried the prize into Camden. He unloaded the sloop and carted its cargo to Portland before sailing the empty *Mary* to Thomaston.[40]

Miller's act infuriated the British. The day after he captured the sloop, the frigate *Furieuse* anchored off Camden and threatened to destroy the village if Miller and his men did not return the *Mary*. The frigate's captain gave the selectmen one hour to respond. Representatives went on board *Furieuse* to explain that the cargo and sloop were gone, but the captain insisted that they had two hours to pay £20,000, or he would level the town. The representatives returned ashore and called an impromptu meeting. The selectmen decided the town could not pay the ransom and two went back to

Furieuse to plead their case. At the same time, militia units arrived, bolstering Camden's will to resist. Eventually, *Furieuse* set sail for Castine without the ransom but with the two selectmen. When the men finally returned home, one was enraged to find a customs officer demanding to inspect his trunk. The furious selectman damned the federal officer, "took him by the neck and hitch'd him out of doors & told him if he wanted to search his trunk to git a search warrant." [41]

Adding to the farce, the Russian consul in Boston claimed that *Mary*'s cargo was his personal property and thus not liable to seizure. Maine's U.S. district attorney took great pleasure in pointing out the clothing the consul claimed was many sizes too small for him and even bore another man's initials. Nonetheless, Miller and his confederates did not derive much benefit from *Mary*'s capture. Castine's customs collector, Josiah Hook, Jr., convinced them that their action had been illegal because they had had no official sanction. He offered Miller an antedated customshouse commission as legal cover, with the proviso that he and the others surrender their claim to the *Mary*. They accepted these terms, and the government auctioned the cargo for $62,829.86. Miller received $14,106 and his confederates $1,000 each, while the canny customs collector received a sum equal to Miller's. Eventually, they realized that Hook had hoodwinked them. The crew spent decades trying to get their fair share from Congress, which opined that "it would seem that Miller beat the bush, and the collector caught the bird."[42]

Now employed by Hook as a customs officer, Miller persisted in his determination to curtail smuggling, despite threats against him. In one episode, a Belfast innkeeper assaulted him. In another instance, as Miller attempted to stop a boat from carrying beef to Castine, a smuggler stabbed him, permanently crippling his right hand.[43]

Alexander Milliken, who had been so frustrated as a customs officer, found greater satisfaction in commanding the privateer *Fame* of Wiscasset. In a bold act of defiance, he nailed a document to the flagstaff in the burned shell of Fort O'Brien on November 17. His "PROCLAMATION" declared that eastern Maine had been liberated except for Castine and Eastport and that he was placing the coast in a state of rigorous blockade, and he signed it with his name.

Milliken fared well when he captured the richly laden schooner *Industry* bound for Castine. He brought it into Thomaston, where the locals assisted him in unloading its cargo.[44]

Sometimes small privateers joined forces, as when several attacked the British cutter *Landrail* off Mount Desert Island on Christmas Day. For forty-five minutes the American vessels tried to overwhelm the cutter with gunfire, but the British repeatedly repulsed them with grapeshot and musket fire. The privateers abandoned the fight, and the battered but triumphant British vessel limped into Castine, though much of its rigging had been shot away and its sails were in near tatters. Yet the small American privateers remained persistent—for instance, the *Fly*, which operated in Penobscot Bay even during the coldest weeks of a remarkably bitter winter. For five days it was locked in ice north of Isle au Haut off Stonington, and the enterprising captain took the opportunity to board other ice-locked vessels to ensure that they were not carrying British supplies. After *Fly*'s crew cut their own craft out of the ice, they joined *Jefferson*'s crew in marching ten miles across the sea ice to board a vessel in Eggemoggin Reach. But unfortunately for the privateersmen, the ship was on legitimate business and not subject to seizure.[45]

Chapter 8
YANKEE CONFUSION

Mounted messengers spread the word that a British force had seized Castine. They reached Portland on September 2, 1814, and Boston the next day. Coastal communities responded to the news by sending women, children, and valuables into the interior, leaving many homes stripped of their furniture. Stringbeaners crowded the District's roads: as Brigadier General David Payson put it, "the time has arrived when it becomes the indispensable duty of the militia to fly to arms." Units flooded into Portland, Bath, Wiscasset, and Camden, filling the streets with martial music, and mounted officers and cavalry videttes galloped madly through the countryside carrying orders. A militia officer wrote of Portland, "no stores open, and the finest houses are used for barracks for militia." Moses Davis, who lived near Fort Edgecomb, recorded that the militia "made everything in confusion" and "Soldiers coming & going all the time." An army officer in Saco noted approvingly that the citizens were "uniting with great energy." However, this illusion of unity and effectiveness soon evaporated. The activated militia was expensive and badly organized, and its officers bickered incessantly with their army counterparts.[1]

STRINGBEANERS ACTIVATED

Individuals responded in various ways to the call for militia. One young drummer recalled being awoken at midnight and told to report to a unit the next day with three days' worth of provisions. On rising, he found his mother cooking biscuits and doughnuts to fill his knapsack and listened to a neighboring Black man offer advice based on his experiences in the Revolution. In Skowhegan, a mother unconsciously paraphrased the women of ancient Sparta, cautioning her three sons, "don't come home shot in the back." Some stringbeaners feigned illness, shirking their military duty even as friends and neighbors marched. Others took the military crisis less seriously. A Portland diarist mocked a militia officer who did not know a "cartridge from a cigar," ridiculing how the officer constantly glanced at his own and others' epaulets to ensure he had his properly placed.[2]

While numerous, the militiamen were ill equipped for combat. An observer described Oxford County's stringbeaners as "undisciplined, badly armed, miserably provided, and worse commanded." A Lincoln County militiaman estimated that only half of the firearms in his company could fire. One officer claimed that just one in three of his men had operable muskets, which he described as "miserable weapons of self-destruction." The musket shortage was particularly vexing because both the state and federal governments had sent many to the District, but town selectmen had not distributed them for fear of being charged for lost guns. Many companies had little experience with their arms. For instance, the Skowhegan men knew so little about their weapons that they cleaned their musket locks by boiling them in a large kettle. This was a problem, given that every musket was handmade, with no interchangeable parts. Local tradition has it that they spent an entire night matching locks to guns. Ammunition supplies were also low and of poor quality, and Camden's militia reportedly had to melt spoons to make bullets. It is said that some men left their statutory twenty-four cartridges at home to avoid being fined for not having ammunition at the subsequent year's muster. The cartridges they did bring were often old or deficient because their town selectmen had purchased the cheapest gunpowder possible.[3]

While awaiting British attack, the militia busied themselves building fortifications. Most were simple earthworks with a fieldpiece or two, but a few were more complex, such as Portland's Fort Burrows, which had a battery of nine cannons and barracks equipped with bunks and a kitchen. Portland's Committee of Safety called on residents to donate labor and material, even authorizing a suspension of church services so that work could continue on the Sabbath. Despite this, one Congregational minister insisted on holding services and reported a large attendance. The militia built two substantial forts in Lincoln County at the direction of Major General William King. One was an earthwork on a hill overlooking the Kennebec River's entrance; the other was placed on the northern end of Jeremysquam Island (modern Westport), opposite Fort Edgecomb. It had walls made of earth and logs, with a wooden gun platform and a magazine. South of the earthworks was a *chevaux de frise*, a row of sharpened wooden stakes that ran from shore to shore across the island.[4]

When not monitoring the construction of fortifications, officers did their best to keep idle hands busy. At Edgecomb, the day began with a roll call at which the men received a gill of whiskey, followed by a breakfast of salt beef and hardtack (often wormy) and coffee issued in buckets and served from a tin dipper. Drill took up the morning hours, followed by a noon meal. Afternoons were mainly free, and in the evening the troops underwent another inspection, when officers praised or criticized their performance. Absence without leave was frequent, but militiamen generally returned after completing chores or harvesting crops. Deserters faced various unorthodox punishments; one found himself bound to the skeleton of a horse while his comrades paraded past him. Theft was a problem in Portland: one company was infamous for stealing any iron that might be useful on a farm, and farmers near militia camps cut their corn early "to keep the soldiers from destroying of it."[5]

COMMAND AND CONFUSION

Massachusetts and the federal government continued to disagree about the militia, and those issues came to a head in 1814. Much of the confusion was linked to the problem of having two parallel command structures: one federal and one state. Moreover, the region's military commander, Henry Dearborn, and the Commonwealth's governor, Caleb Strong, loathed one another. No insult was forgotten, and every transgression was returned.

The federal government placed New England north of Cape Cod under Dearborn's command. Petulant and overweight, he was too old for field service and too quarrelsome for this sensitive posting. Already disliked by Massachusetts Federalists, he antagonized militia officers further by reorganizing detached militia into hundred-man companies. Previously, Massachusetts militia had had companies of sixty-four men, and Dearborn's reorganization meant that fewer officers were now needed. In July 1814 Dearborn wrote to Strong, asking him to provide detached militia and closing with a disingenuous insistence that regulations did not permit him to deviate from his reorganization plan. Strong concurred with the July request; but when Dearborn asked for more detached militia in September, he refused, pointing out that the reorganization had created too many problems.[6]

Brigadier General John Chandler commanded the regular forces in Maine. A Revolutionary veteran, he was a political appointee and a personal friend of Dearborn's. Chandler was notoriously stiff of bearing, bad-tempered, and brusque of speech, and his language frequently devolved into profanity. Like Dearborn, he was not a successful field general: in the battle of Stoney Creek, fought in Ontario in 1813, he had stumbled into enemy lines and had remained in British captivity until early 1814. As a commander, Chandler was indecisive and hesitant, seldom acting without consulting Dearborn first. Still suffering from wounds received in 1813, he refused to leave Portland for fear that the British would attack. He also proved to be high-handed in his dealings with the militia. After Governor Strong refused to detach militia as requested, Chandler announced that he would only feed militiamen who conformed to the hundred-man company organization. He also expelled talented Federalist militia officers such as Major Lemuel Weeks, who was commanding the detached militia at Fort Scammel and was one of Portland's leading citizens. Without notice, Chandler replaced Weeks with a regular officer.[7]

The Massachusetts military bureaucracy functioned under the ponderous title of "Board of Commissioners for the Protection of the Sea Coast," and this board was tasked with coordinating and supplying the militia. To accomplish that task, Governor Strong picked three reliably Federalist Revolutionary War veterans. The first, Major General David Cobb, succeeded George Ulmer as commander of the Tenth Division. Cobb was frequently ill and never traveled further east than Portland, but he was a Federalist stalwart and an opponent of what he called "this damnable War." The second, Adjutant General John Brooks, was a physician and a moderate Federalist, and he was already popular with Mainers. The third was Timothy Pickering, a former U.S. senator, secretary of war, and secretary of state during the Adams administration. Pickering was an ardent Federalist, a vocal critic of the war, and a leading proponent of New England secession. Despite their Federalist politics generally, the board and Governor Strong fostered good relations with U.S. Army officers. For example, Brooks urged Portland's militia officers to avoid any "collision between the government of this State and that of the United States," and he and Strong both praised William King for his energy and economy in defending Lincoln County. Notably, Massachusetts officials claimed that they could work with every federal officer sent to New England except for Dearborn.[8]

The Board of Commissioners faced numerous problems along the Massachusetts coast; but once Boston seemed to be secure, they focused their attention on the chaos in Maine. Three issues dominated. First, the enemy had completely knocked out the Tenth Division, and most of its officers were now absent or on parole. A handful of the Tenth's stringbeaners remained on duty, including the regiment from the Belfast area under the command of Jacob Ulmer, who now held the rank of colonel. After the British withdrew, he marched troops into Belfast, but locals would not provide provisions, which forced him to dismiss his command.[9]

Second, it was difficult to coordinate militia in the regions that were not under British occupation. William King was the District's most dynamic militia commander. Though he had minimal military experience, he possessed what an observer called a "Gigantic Mind," and he acted with energy and enterprise. Everywhere communities were clamoring for protection, but King exercised economy in calling out his units and dismissed them again as soon as possible. After the Hampden debacle, he marched two regiments from Lincoln County to Belfast and urged his old nemesis, Henry

Sewall, to march his own units from Kennebec County to Bangor or Hampden. To King's disappointment, however, Sewall ignored the request, mobilizing only when the Wiscasset Committee of Safety sent an urgent message that a British fleet was at the mouth of the Sheepscot River. The messenger found Sewall in church, and the commander immediately ordered his troops to march, though the warning turned out to be a false alarm.[10]

Third, the Board of Commissioners had to coordinate with federal officials. It happily supported the officers who commanded the navy yards in Charlestown, Massachusetts, and Kittery, Maine. Yet even at this moment of crisis, working with Dearborn was almost impossible.[11]

A BRAHMIN GALLOPS EAST

Reports from the District were confusing, so Governor Strong and the Board of Commissioners sent Lieutenant Colonel William Hyslop Sumner to Maine to sort them out. Sumner was a devoted Federalist, an outspoken advocate of the militia, and a firm opponent of standing armies, which he believed were "dangerous to civil liberty." He blamed the invasion of Maine on the federal government's lack of preparation and sneered that its fortifications were mere "embargo forts," strong enough to keep American merchant shipping bottled up in the harbors but insufficient for repelling British attacks. Given that Henry Dearborn had overseen the construction of these forts, his reaction was an omen of disagreement.[12]

The mission was complex and delicate. Sumner received two sets of instructions, one from the board and one from the governor. The commissioners discouraged the building of breastworks at likely landing places, rationalizing that the "best defence will be the firm breasts of our citizens, with the light artillery and small arms for their weapons." This instruction contravened Dearborn's suggestion that York County's militia should build exactly such breastworks. The commissioners also told Sumner to make certain that the militia was putting arms in order, preparing ammunition, and undergoing drills, including practice in scattering and regrouping.

The board believed that this would instill confidence in the men and enable them to defeat the enemy. In addition, they authorized Sumner to purchase supplies, even as they continued to hope that the federal government would provide fuel, straw, and forage. For his part, Strong instructed the District's militia generals to confer with Sumner. Given Maine's opposition to the governor, Sumner expressed reservations, but Strong was insistent and urged him to make haste for Portland, and the governor emphasized that the militia should make no effort to drive the British out of Castine.[13]

Sumner galloped first to Portsmouth, where he summoned Major General Ichabod Goodwin, who commanded York County's militia. Goodwin demurred, claiming that he had to be in court. But Sumner reminded him that the war required his attention, so Goodwin appeared on the following day. The two visited Captain Isaac Hull at the Kittery Naval Yard as well as the commander of Fort Constitution, noting that New Hampshire's militia seemed to be completely disorganized. New Hampshire officials urged Sumner to provide Massachusetts militia to garrison Portsmouth's forts. Sumner agreed, recommending that two hundred militiamen should be headquartered at Fort McClary in Kittery, which oversaw Portsmouth Harbor. Then Sumner rode northward into York, where he found several hundred militia milling around a tavern. After encouraging them to fire on the enemy from behind stone walls and trees, he continued on to Biddeford and Saco. The towns' selectmen complained that Governor Strong was doing nothing to defend them, but Sumner had no time for "those whose only objects are to produce discord and dissatisfaction" and spurred his horse on.[14]

In Portland, Sumner rode into military chaos: 2,000 militiamen were milling around without quarters or food while militia officers and federal officers bickered about who was in charge. Sumner helped the militia's leader, Brigadier General John Chandler, hammer out an agreement with the regular army's leader, Major General Alford Richardson, whereby the state would detach 2,000 militiamen into federal service. Most would be stringbeaners from inland Oxford County, a move that would allow the coastal militiamen to act as a reserve. Sumner reported to Strong that the agreement should satisfy everybody, including "the defenders and the defended, the economists and the alarmists," and the Board of Commissioners congratulated Sumner for leaving Portland "in so tranquil a state." They should not have been so smug. Dearborn was already moving to undo his mission; but unaware that trouble was brewing, Sumner rode for Wiscasset.[15]

Dearborn scuttled the Portland agreement by ordering Chandler to Portsmouth. Sumner was shocked, pointing out that Portsmouth already had a talented commander: "What reason could there have been for such a change?" Malice was the reason, and Dearborn's efforts to humiliate Sumner continued, reaching their lowest point in an incident that involved sending arms to Sebec, a tiny backwoods community. Ezekiel Chase of Sebec had appealed to Sumner for muskets, but he denied the request, noting that because Massachusetts had found itself in a war "without its consent or approbation" the states had to defend themselves, and the Commonwealth had no weapons to spare. This answer displeased Chase, who showed the letter to Dearborn. Deeply offended by Sumner's commentary that Massachusetts found itself in a war it opposed, Dearborn vented his ire to the Board of Commissioners. Its members hastened to assure him that Sumner had not intended to cause a rupture, but even Chandler realized that his superior had blundered in taking Sumner's comments personally. As he departed for Portsmouth, Chandler left a final order, asking every officer to "exert himself in preserving harmony between the different Corps called out for the defence of their Country." He should have saved his ink: foment, and even mutiny seethed in the ranks of Portland's detached militia.[16]

"MOST SOVEREIGN CONTEMPT"

On September 24, Major General Richardson, who commanded Cumberland County's militia, received a memorial signed by thirty of his officers complaining that the arrangement to defend Portland was unconstitutional and was subverting Massachusetts's sovereignty. Among their complaints was that, once the militia was under the command of regular officers, President Madison would be able to order the units to march to Canada. Furthermore, they declared that regular officers held their militia counterparts "in the most sovereign contempt. They have no regard to their local habits or feelings." Part of the problem lay in society's low regard for professional soldiers. Militiamen believed they were the superior force because they fought *pro aris et focis*—for hearth and home—as opposed to professional soldiers, who presumably fought for pay. Deeply insulted by the regular army's attitude toward them, many of Oxford County's militia officers said that they would resign their commissions before submitting to what they called "conscription." The militia's rank and file expressed a similar "spirit of disaffection," and one company actually marched for home—an odd reaction because Oxford County was notoriously Republican and therefore pro-war. With many of his officers threatening insubordination, Richardson's command rapidly eroded. He recognized, however, that arresting or discharging them would be pointless because he could not replace them, so he ordered the militia to remain under state control and requested Sumner's immediate return to Portland.[17]

Richardson needed Sumner's advice, especially about how to get his troops to garrison Fort Scammel, which lay exposed to enemy attack. But Sumner had lost patience with the "refractory troops" and demanded obedience, preferably through policy but, "if that do not answer, by force." He suggested that Richardson send his troops to Fort Scammel, ostensibly on fatigue duty, and then haul their tents to the site to keep them there. If that tactic failed, Richardson should order the Portland regiment to "compel the execution of your orders and arrest the first officer who refuses and as many as refuse."[18]

Dearborn stirred the pot by insisting on reorganizing the militia according to the War Department's directions. Governor Strong refused to agree to this reorganization, placing regular officers in an awkward spot. Now they had no authority over the militiamen who were serving at their posts. Fort Scammel's commander, Major Daniel Lane, used threats, leniency, and praise to convince the drafted militia to conduct vital construction work. When two militiamen overstayed their passes, he lectured them that the punishment for absence was death, but in the end he released them with just a warning. Almost in the same breath, he complained that the militia's murmuring about regulations must stop and threatened that "Gross Violation of rules & regulations & of Military Discipline will not be overlooked."[19]

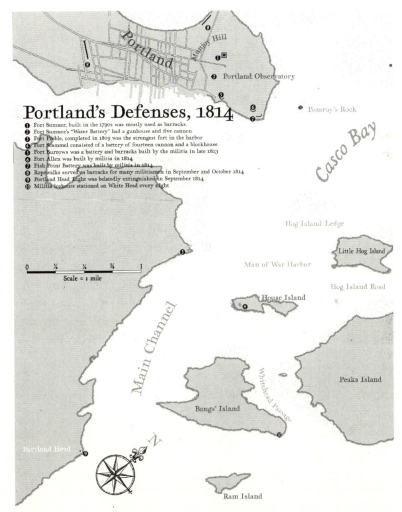

FIGURE 7. Portland had several fortifications but only a handful of federal troops to garrison them. In September 1814, militia flooded into the town to defend it against an anticipated naval attack, but the units often refused to cooperate with regular army officers. Their behavior led to general chaos and a near mutiny. Map by the author.

Yet even as the militia problems continued, there was one bright note: on October 1, the navy launched its seventy-four-gun ship of the line at Kittery. Christened *Washington*, it was, as Hull proudly wrote, "one of the best ships in the world." Within a week, he had the vessel's bottom coppered, armed it with cannons borrowed from *Congress*, and crewed it with sailors from the *Adams* who had walked to Kittery from Hampden after the battle there. Soon, however, funds ran out, and work on both *Washington* and *Congress* ground to a halt.[20]

"INFINITE MISCHIEF"

William King performed a balancing act in the second half of 1814, placating his superiors in Boston and cooperating with regular military officers and Dearborn. Most of King's units were concentrated in Wiscasset and Edgecomb, and several of Sewall's regiments also camped there. When Sumner arrived in Wiscasset on September 19, he singled out Sewall's Eighth Division for fulsome praise, reporting that it marched as well as Boston's uniformed companies did. Sumner then brokered an arrangement whereby Sewall would mobilize much of his division to support King, and he gave Sewall, the older and more experienced officer, command. King objected that the troops would be serving within the limits of his own division, but to no avail.[21]

King was usually diplomatic, but he erred in confiding to Chandler: "the economy of the general government has already cost us near half the district and if it is continued without state interference, Sir John Sherbrooke will have the whole before winter sets in." Dearborn caught wind of King's comment and was deeply wounded. Sumner then stepped in to widen the divide between the two Republicans, pointing out that Governor Strong had difficulties only with General Dearborn. King scrambled to mend the relationship by blaming most of the difficulties on former Secretary of War John Armstrong, whom Dearborn detested.[22]

While courting Dearborn's favor, King sidestepped the issue of organizing the detached militia along federal lines by working with Colonel Denny McCobb, the commander of the Forty-fifth U.S. Infantry, headquartered at Bath. McCobb had also retained his commission as a brigadier general in King's Eleventh Division of militia. When King suggested that McCobb should be able give orders in both capacities, Sumner was initially dubious, reporting to Boston that "Resistance is already spoken of. Officers cheerfully obey the orders of General McCobb as a militia officer, but do not wish to see those of Colonel McCobb of the U.S. Army." Nonetheless, the unorthodox arrangement worked, and McCobb successfully commanded 1,800 detached militia until he dismissed them in November.[23]

King and Sumner convinced the initially reluctant commander of Fort Edgecomb to share essential items such as gunpowder, tents, and camp kettles, although tensions continued. For example, when two militiamen enlisted into the Fortieth U.S. Infantry without notifying their superiors, their militia brigadier general seized and confined them. Fort Edgecomb's commander threatened to retaliate by arresting two other militiamen. King intervened, but Sumner grumbled about the army's recruiters: "these Camp Suckers are at every post, where the militia are stationed, using their every artifice, at their recruiting revels, to entice men to enlist." By the end of autumn, however, the onset of cold weather had made the issue moot. The British were unlikely to attack in winter, and it was costly to feed and pay the detached and state militia. The state militia went home in late October, followed by the detached militia in November.[24]

Yet just as the militia was breaking camp, the Madison administration and its supporters were considering how to oust the British from eastern Maine. Vice-President Elbridge Gerry was calling for a force of 15,000 to drive them out and to cow New England's Federalists, whom he had long suspected of treasonous intent. The Republican attorney Samuel K. Whiting of Bangor insisted that many men would volunteer if the federal government would fund an expedition. But Whiting had little idea of the military realities: the federal government had no funds, and the Massachusetts governor had no intention of supporting an expedition.[25]

Nonetheless, the administration went forward with plans and preparations to eject the British from Castine—even, perhaps, to make a feint at Fredericton, New Brunswick. Secretary of War James Monroe believed that taking Castine was "not only a practicable, but an easy attainment; provided it be managed, in the preparatory Steps, with discretion, and executed with promptitude, activity & boldness." The administration eventually decided that King was the man to lead the effort. Dearborn confided that he expected King to raise 3,000 to 4,000 men for the proposed expedition and promised three hundred regulars to support him, including a hundred artillerists. King went through the motions of asking for money and supplies and even inquired who would set the attack's route. Still, his tone betrayed his lack of confidence, and he warned Monroe that "failure would produce infinite mischief."[26]

President Madison called on Massachusetts to support this expedition with troops and financial support. In response, Governor Strong pointed out that the Commonwealth had borne the expense of calling out the troops in September to defend the coast and thus had no funds. Recalling the Penobscot expedition's bitter experience in 1779, when the British had destroyed an entire fleet of Massachusetts naval vessels, privateers, and troop transports, he pointed out the futility of an attack without naval control of Penobscot Bay. Strong leaked the story to the Federalist press, who derided the proposed attack as a farce. The British, too, heard about King's expedition. One rumor suggested that George Ulmer had somehow entered Castine to spy out its strengths and weaknesses; another claimed that King himself had entered the village twice in disguise. Castine's commander called for reinforcements from Halifax, which duly arrived. After Monroe received reports of these British preparations, he reluctantly wrote to King on January 2 to suspend the operation.[27]

In any case, King was more comfortable in the political sphere. His preferred approach was to defame the District's Federalist leadership via poison-pen campaigns. Jesse Appleton, the president of Bowdoin College, received an anonymous letter from King demanding to know why he had visited the British at Castine. King took an interest in the activities of Sheriff John Cooper of

Machias and was probably responsible for the newspaper articles accusing him of collaboration. He also publicly criticized Governor Strong for keeping Major General Cobb in Boston and lashed out at Brigadier Generals Blake and Brewer of the Tenth Division for essentially becoming British subjects. Finally, he took Major General Sewall to task for not joining him in marching to the Penobscot River after the battle at Hampden.[28]

"TEARS IN THEIR EYES"

Unfortunately, when the detached militia at Fort McClary withdrew in November, they brought the dreaded spotted fever back to their homes. Several had already died while in garrison, deaths that physicians attributed to changes in diet or exposure to cold. One observer thought the culprit might have been fumes from clothing or close bodily contact, pointing out that militia crowded into barracks were especially susceptible.[29]

The winter of 1814–15 was harsh, and the soldiers suffered terribly. At Fort Preble, officers complained that the barracks were cold and their blankets too small. When the privateer *Mammoth* brought 10,000 captured blankets into Portland, officers clamored for permission to procure them, claiming that they were twice the size of the ones they already had. Firewood was scarce, so some soldiers broke up and burned their bunks. Unlike the British military, the U.S. Army did not issue greatcoats to every soldier, instead providing watch coats only to sentries. Several soldiers from the Thirty-fourth Infantry faced trial for tearing the flannel lining out of those heavy coats to make caps. Lack of money created more misery: some soldiers had not received their enlistment bounties, and none had received pay for many months. As a result, a corporal at Fort Preble refused to go on duty. His officers responded with a swift court-martial that reduced him to the ranks, made him ride a "horse" for four hours, confined him to Fort Scammel for thirty days, and revoked two months' worth of pay.[30]

Sometimes the troops threatened mutiny, as at the Damariscotta battery, where some thirty men from the Forty-fifth U.S. Infantry refused to do duty. When an officer arrived, representatives "with tears in their eyes" claimed that many of the soldiers had not received their bounty or been paid for ten months. Their families had nothing to live on and had to beg for bread or starve, and the mutineers feared they would have to go on town support, an almost insufferable shame. The officer persuaded them to return to duty, but they begged him for money so their families would not "come on the Town." Yet there was no money for pay: officers often had to purchase straw and firewood for their troops out of their own pockets.[31]

For many soldiers, the answer was desertion. On occasion, these escapes could be violent, as when one stabbed a soldier who was pursuing him. More alarmingly, sergeants and corporals began to desert, an act that would once have been almost unthinkable. Henry Dearborn complained that laws regarding the harboring of deserters needed to be stronger, but the real problem was money and supplies.[32]

Most desertions occurred on weekends and in company with someone else, presumably a friend. In one case, a pair who absconded together were both French, probably previous deserters from the polyglot British army. Most deserters brought their haversacks with them, which suggests that leaving was not a spur-of-the-moment decision. The chance of capture was low, and those unlucky enough to be caught often ran away again. One soldier deserted from Fort Preble's hospital on November 11, 1814, but was apprehended a month later. Undeterred, he decamped again in March.[33]

Desertion became such a problem that the District's military authorities decided to make an example out of two absconders, William Furbush and Josiah Bailey of the Thirty-fourth U.S. Infantry, who had deserted from Fort Sumner on separate occasions. A court-martial held at Portland condemned them to death by firing squad, and soldiers from Forts Preble and Scammel joined others from mainland posts to witness the Sunday-morning execution. A cart carried the condemned men and their coffins to the appointed spot on Munjoy Hill, where soldiers forced the prisoners to kneel on their coffins beside their graves, their heads covered with white hoods. A mounted officer appeared just before the appointed time, holding a commutation in his hand. Furbush's father had written directly to President Madison, pointing out that his son had a wife and three small children and that "he has never absented himself but to go to the arms of a wife he loves and to embrace his tender offspring." Congressman Cyrus King had also taken up the cause, writing to Richard Cutts and James Monroe that Furbush had a family in Belfast and had deserted only because of his "extreme anxiety to see them." In other words, the graveside commutation was military theater: Portland's commanding officer had arranged to have the last-minute pardons delivered in the most dramatic way imaginable, thereby demonstrating the wisdom and kindness of the Madison administration.[34]

"YANKEE DOODLE UPSET"

Garrison duty was proverbially dull, and the snowbound tedium of a Maine winter only made it worse. British officers set up a theater in Castine, complete with costumes and props brought in from Halifax. In true Shakespearean style, officers played the roles of both men and women. But despite such entertainments, young officers could be troublesome, and sometimes they brawled with locals. One idle subaltern used his diamond ring to etch the words "Yankee Doodle Upset" on a window, along with a crude drawing of a British ensign over an American flag.[35]

Adventurers and merchants crowded into the village, each paying the British military $5 in coin for a pass to enter and stay. Among those holding such a pass was William Vaughan of Hallowell. In September 1814, he was commanding a militia regiment at Wiscasset, but by January 1815, he had received permission to stay in Castine for thirty days, almost certainly to engage in illicit trade. The pass fees went to the garrison's commissary officer, who placed them in the "military chest." Given the prevailing spirit of free enterprise, it is no surprise to learn that a military clerk embezzled nearly £1,000 from this chest. Castine's merchants took advantage of the business. In his daybook, one seller, John Lee, faithfully recorded the name, rank, and regiment of those who bought goods. For example, Captain Merrill of the *Hero* transport ship bought port wine, and Lieutenant Colonel Ximines of the Sixty-second Regiment bought flannel and two dozen handkerchiefs. Lee also recorded the names of Americans who bought British textiles; they included Francis Anderson of Belfast and his neighbors John Angier, Benjamin Whittier, and Ralph C. Johnson.[36]

Like the Americans, the British soldiers sometimes acted out or deserted. At one parade, an entire regiment displayed "shameful drunkenness." Soldiers sold their bread rations in return for alcohol and frequently became so intoxicated that they could not find their way back to their barracks. Many of these veterans grumbled that they had not enlisted to fight in America, and desertion was common. Yankees routinely facilitated the absconders, and the District's weavers were eager to hire the Scots and the Irish to work their looms. American recruiters welcomed British deserters into the U.S. Army as "good likely fellows." A Wiscasset man even urged President Madison to offer British soldiers a cash reward for desertion as an economical means of sapping the enemy's forces. Yet American citizens who encouraged desertion did so at considerable peril to themselves, as when a Cape Rosier farmer allowed a deserter to take his rowboat to escape a search party. The penalties were severe: British authorities publicly whipped two Americans who had assisted deserters in Eastport, giving them two hundred lashes while their mothers watched. At Castine, a court-martial tried a local and sent him to prison in Halifax for abetting desertion.[37]

British soldiers frequently risked death by deserting, as in August 1814, when four men drowned at Eastport while trying to swim to freedom. In October, British sentries in Machias shot and killed a deserter as he fled over the bridge crossing the Machias River. For locals, the bloodstains on the bridge's planking exemplified the brutality of their occupiers, as did the handling of the deserter's corpse, which was thrown into a rough wooden box and unceremoniously dumped into Machias Bay. In another instance, a sentry shot and killed a deserter as he attempted to cross Castine's canal.[38]

Deaths by firing squad were rare but memorable events. In one case, British officers apprehended two privates who had attempted to desert from Castine. Given his isolated situation,

General Gosselin bypassed the usual rules and ordered the men to be shot. The bloody affair took place on December 5, 1814. A platoon fired at the two, and then several soldiers advanced and discharged their muskets into their heads "to extinguish any spark of life which might have remained." American newspapers made much of the deserters scampering out of Castine, but the figures were not unusual. The Sixty-second Regiment of Foot recorded 130 desertions between 1798 and 1817; they peaked in 1814, when twenty-four deserted from Castine. Desertion was not usually a shooting offense in the Sixty-second; thirty-three deserters had returned to the regiment between 1798 and 1817, suffering a reduction in rank and probably a fierce flogging. Courts-martial often condemned deserters to transportation for life in Australia. Something must have set these two men apart; perhaps they absconded while on guard duty, or with their arms, or perhaps they told someone they intended to join the American army.[39]

Chapter 9
WINTER OF DISCONTENT

As winter settled into the District in late 1814, its communities were fracturing and quarrelling. The British invasion and occupation had created a new level of despair, one that was often manifesting as neutrality or open collaboration. Unsurprisingly, secession was also in the air. Some believed that New England should split from the United States, while others thought Maine should break its bond with Massachusetts and seek statehood. Both Federalists and Republicans found themselves discussing the possibility of armed civil war.

"NETTICUT VENTION"

After his falling out with Henry Dearborn, Governor Caleb Strong realized that Massachusetts would have to foot the militia bill. On September 7, 1814, he ordered the General Court to convene a special session in October to authorize funding for the militia, which would cost roughly $200,000 per month, and discuss the war in general. Dearborn expected the session to produce "a regular and systematic opposition to the Genl. Government." In the meantime, the Commonwealth's moderate Federalists were devising a plan to prevent the proceedings from getting out of hand.[1]

Strong opened the special session with a speech in which he described the state's situation as "peculiarly dangerous and perplexing." He called the war "unnecessary and unjust" and lamented the federal government's inability to defend the coast. Maine was underrepresented at the session, with only 57 out of its 120 delegates attended, including some from British-occupied territory. The gathering's most outspoken delegate was undoubtedly John Low of Lyman. Born in old Massachusetts, he had served in the American Revolution and had moved to the District in the 1780s. Although not well educated, he was a powerful force in his town, establishing its Congregational church and usually representing the community in the General Court. Now, alarmed by the Madison administration's mishandling of the war, Low rose and proposed a motion that Massachusetts should communicate with the other New England states and together send representatives to Washington to demand the president's resignation. Jeffersonians were incredulous at this proposal. The *New York Columbian* called Low insane, even after he withdrew the motion. The *Eastern Argus* accused him of playing the "tune of rebellion." But Low was not the only such Mainer. It is little wonder that the historian Samuel Eliot Morison later wrote that the District was the "hottest part of the anti-war bloc."[2]

Harrison Gray Otis of Boston responded to Low's radical speech much as he had responded to Samuel Fessenden's earlier in 1814. By refuting the words of rural Federalists, he was able to present himself as a thoughtful moderate. On October 8, Otis submitted a report that found "no force or means, bearing any proportion to the emergency, have been provided by the national government" for the Commonwealth's defense. His report called for a New England convention to discuss the war and consult about the states' mutual defense, and it raised the possibility of a constitutional convention. On October 18, the General Court voted to call for a New England convention to discuss the war. State Senator John Holmes of Alfred, Maine, arguably the most influential Republican currently serving in the General Court, spoke against the convention but to no avail. Maine's delegates narrowly favored the measure, thirty-four to twenty-three. The legislature then selected twelve delegates for a convention to be held at Hartford, Connecticut, doing so without the Republicans, who walked out of the proceedings. Two representatives came from Maine, both of them college-educated Federalist attorneys: Judge Samuel S. Wilde of Hallowell and Stephen Longfellow, Jr., of Portland. They were not backwoods rabble rousers like Fessenden or Low, and they were far more discreet than their brother attorney Cyrus King. In his comments Longfellow certainly played on regional pride, but he stopped short of calling for secession. He also advocated strongly for keeping the convention's proceedings secret, though his wife Zilpah objected. She thought secrecy "gave more plausibility to the cry of treason."³

Republicans were again alarmed when, on October 20, Governor Strong approved an act authorizing the Commonwealth to raise an army of 10,000 men, 1,000 of whom would go into service immediately. These would not be militia troops but a regular state army similar to the one that had been raised during the Revolution. Because the army would be funded entirely by the state, Strong was empowered to pick its officers, thus ensuring that they would all be Federalists. Again, a Maine representative, Albion K. Parris, offered the greatest resistance to the move, although he did not say aloud that raising this force was a step toward secession.⁴

Maine's Republicans were dismayed by the Hartford Convention. Representatives from towns such as Buckfield addressed the Massachusetts legislature and begged it to stop fanning sectional discord, expressing fears about "civil war and effusion of blood." The residents of Waterford resolved that those who were loyal to the national government should organize themselves into military units. An Oxford County convention declared that Massachusetts officials had conducted themselves in a manner "unbecoming the representatives of a free people" and resolved that Maine should remain a part of the Commonwealth only so long as it remained a part of the United States. In Republicans' view, not only had the legislature displayed cowardice, but its inertia in expelling the enemy from Maine was a "reproach to the valor and intrepidity of the militia, and a disgrace to the Commonwealth." Maine soldiers serving on the Canadian front also expressed outrage at the "damnable Corruption of New England, [that] has weakened the beliefs and publick Virtue."⁵

Federalists responded by lampooning Republican outrage in doggerel verse:

> *There's a "Netticut Vention" from three or four states*
> *They're going to undo us if we don't prevent,*
> *I can tell you no more. Sirs, my knowledge is spent.*
> *But I'll fight like the d——, I'll get me a sword*

And I'll mow them down level smack smooth by the board;
We must turn out to a man, sirs, and drive them like fury
We'll shoot and stab Feds, sirs, without judge or jury.[6]

This politized humor was not far from the truth. Maine's Republicans were indeed thinking about creating a military force, ostensibly to retake Castine but also to suppress Federalism.

THE PORTLAND CONFERENCE

Even as District Republicans were moving to separate Maine from Massachusetts, antiwar Federalist politicians were threatening to support the secession of New England from the federal union. One issue revolved around complaints that the General Court's special session had not mentioned Maine's defense. On October 19, District delegates Mark Langdon Hill, John Holmes, and Albion K. Parris suggested that a committee should examine the possibility of driving the British from Maine. But the legislature, firmly in the hands of the Federalists, ignored this request as well as a similar one in November. The Federalists expressed no interest in fighting to recover eastern Maine. Governor Strong even stated that the Commonwealth had no claim to recover Eastport. Timothy Pickering thought northeastern Maine should be traded for continued access to the fishing grounds off Nova Scotia and Newfoundland. Others believed that the people of Hancock and Washington counties were happy under British rule.[7]

In December, the District's Republicans, led by William King, met in Portland's customshouse to discuss the faltering war effort. With him was Joshua Wingate, Jr., a Bath merchant and a confederate in King's illicit trade, who, importantly, also happened to be Henry Dearborn's son-in-law. Several federal customs collectors and inspectors attended, including Josiah Hook, Jr., of Castine, Joseph Farley of Waldoborough, Isaac Ilsley of Portland, Jeremiah Bradbury of South Berwick, and James Carr of Bangor, who worked for Hook. Federal tax collectors attended, such as James Irish and the attorney Woodbury Storer, who had suppressed the tax revolt in North Yarmouth. In general, however, attorneys were underrepresented, with only three others present: William Pitt Preble, the federal district attorney; Benjamin Greene of South Berwick; and Samuel K. Whiting of Bangor. Joseph C. Boyd, the paymaster for the regular troops stationed in the District, joined the meeting, as did a number of merchants involved in maritime trade, among them Moses Carlton, Asa Clapp, and Matthew Cobb. Other attendees included a pair of former congressmen: William Widgery, who presided over the meeting, and Samuel Ayer, who frequently wrote for the *Eastern Argus*.

The meeting's focus was the District's sad plight in the war. Whiting led a committee that had drawn up an appeal to President Madison, complaining that state authorities had abandoned Maine to the enemy and blaming Governor Strong for "tamely submitting to the invasion of his territory, without making one effort to repel the Foe." The committee summarized, "Thus abandoned by the state authority, we view with serious alarm the situation in which we are placed—having the enemy in the bosom of our country—and an extensive seaboard unprotected; we shall soon become an easy prey to the savage attacks of our foe." The committee also addressed smuggling, pointing out that "the most unrestrained and unlimited intercourse with the enemy is carried on. We have become the general thorough-fare through which the unprincipled carry on the most illicit traffic—and thru which our domestic foes carry on their 'traitorous correspondence.'" The influence of customs officers on the committee was clearly apparent: "The Collectors on our Frontier, in vain raise the arm of Authority: our Revenue laws, are too inefficient to Support them. The Officers of the Militia, in vain call upon their troops: Govr Strong controuls their opperation." The committee proposed reviving the discredited volunteer system: "Nothing can arrest this treasonable traffic, which is so rapidly destroying the vital resources of our Country—which is sapping the foundation of our dearest rights; but the aid of the Genl. Govt. by a military force." With Madison's support and 4,000 volunteers, it claimed, Maine could "rise superior to Surrounding difficulties—defend our Towns from conflagration—and present an unshaken Phalanx, between our Foreign Foes and internal traitors."[8]

Whiting's committee saw federal authority as the only means of breaking the misused power of Massachusetts: "If Massachusetts won't cooperate and the Federal government is unable to, then the crisis has arrived when the District of Maine ought to Legislate for herself. Released from the thraldom of Boston influence, we would not suffer this Eastern section of this country to sink into insignificance.... If we can get no assistance let us make an effort ourselves." But Federalists mocked the calls for statehood, and Boston newspapers warned darkly that Maine's inhabitants should beware the "insidious arts" of those pushing for Maine's separation, for there was "nothing to gain, but much to lose by such a course." On February 25, the state senate voted down a motion introduced by Albion K. Parris authorizing a convention to consider Maine's statehood. Nevertheless, the idea grew in strength, even if old Massachusetts was not ready to let the District go.[9]

THE BOUNDS OF PROPRIETY

The war exacerbated political tensions in the District, and Federalists proposed increasingly radical measures, including New England secession. In late September, residents of North Yarmouth proposed a convention of New England states to consider how to end the war. The editor of the Federalist *Portland Gazette* picked up the theme, complaining that the federal government's forts at Castine and Machias were good only for enforcing the hated embargoes but were "not worth a straw in time of war." The paper further criticized the Madison administration and its followers as "traitors, after *destroying our commerce & fleecing us of our money* by a land tax, shop tax, stamp tax, and by *exhausting* the Banks by obtaining money of these institutions and squandering it on Canada expeditions, Henry plots, and a host of pimps, spies, and other tools and partizans of the Executive."[10]

The District's most influential antiwar Federalist was Saco attorney Cyrus King, a congressman and William King's youngest brother. He had long despised the Republicans' "Anti-commercial, restrictive Virginia system." He had even voted against accepting Thomas Jefferson's book collection to rebuild the Library of

Congress, arguing that the volumes would disseminate an "infidel philosophy." King's extremism reflected that of his supporters—for instance, Jeremiah Hill, who called Republicans "d——d Demos," "cursed children," "servants of corruption," and "Lovers of the wages of unrighteousness." King was a fiery orator who declared that the Madison administration's handling of New England was akin to British oppression before the Revolution. He was a leading opponent of militia reform, which he denounced as "calculated to destroy the militia system, and . . . the sovereignty of the States." A proposed conscription bill especially enraged him; he called it a move to "kidnap the people, as you would slaves."[11]

In his most famous speech, given in October 1814, King thundered, "If a simple King of England, by his corrupt servants, chastised New England with whips [before the Revolution]—this Administration have chastised her with scorpions." Throughout his time in office, King remained a thorn in the side of the Madison administration. Denouncing the ineptitude that allowed the British to capture and loot Washington, D.C., he also pointed out that President Madison had recalled Dearborn from Canada in disgrace yet had now put him in command of coastal New England. He reminded Congress that General Chandler had allowed a handful of British soldiers to capture him. Little wonder, he concluded, that "our militia officers would think themselves disgraced, and throw off their commissions, if they were ordered under such commanders." Yet for all his extremism, King did not advocate for New England's secession. Instead, he threw the issue back to the Madison administration: "But union, it seems, is now the watch-word. Does the administration desire it? Do the majority in this house desire it? Have either made the least advance or concession for it? Though urged by the nation, has Mr. Madison called round him the wise and the good without distinction of party?" These were difficult questions, and ones that the Madison administration did not dare to answer. Although moderate Federalists believed that King was exceeding "the bounds of propriety" in his bitter attacks on the federal government, his many supporters applauded his spirit.[12]

King's speeches were harsh, but they were only words. Governor Strong went a step further by sending a secret emissary to Sir John Coape Sherbrooke at Halifax. Strong's representative inquired about British support, should New England secede from the United States. The representative traveled via Castine, where he announced he had important business with Sherbrooke and received a pass to travel to Halifax. His identity was not revealed, but it was almost certainly George Herbert of Ellsworth, a Federalist and a vocal critic of the Madison administration. Like Strong, he was an attorney and his discretion could be relied on. Furthermore, he had worked with Sherbrooke after the British had occupied Castine, and Sherbrooke's notes indicate that he had previously met Strong's emissary, though they carefully withheld his name. Sherbrooke sent information about the meeting to his superiors in the Colonial Office, who responded warily because the emissary had not offered any written credentials.[13]

The Massachusetts legislature seemed to be taking a radical step when it voted for a convention of the New England states. However, it sent moderate representatives to Hartford who were unlikely to support rash measures. The only controversial matter discussed at the convention was that New England should raise an army to protect its coast. Moderate Federalists hoped that reason would rule at Hartford; as George Thatcher wrote, the representatives "must be firm, but prudent and moderate." At the same time, they expressed fierce regional loyalties, as when a Portland diarist declared, "let the buckskins [westerners] lift but a finger against us by way of violence & they shall find we have the mettle of our fathers: our swords are not rusty nor our hands feeble." As it turned out, the Hartford Convention was a remarkably mild event. Its report did not call for secession but opposed military conscription and the enlistment of minors and asked for better funding for regional defense. It also called for a constitutional convention to address various regional complaints. Both Massachusetts and Connecticut's legislatures accepted the report and sent representatives to Washington to procure more defense funding. Yet by the time they got there in February 1815, news had arrived that would make their efforts utterly unnecessary.[14]

"THE SWORD IS RETURNED TO THE SCABBARD"

Diplomats signed the Treaty of Ghent on December 24, 1814. In the United States, news of the war's end came in the same way that news of its beginning had arrived: with the clatter of hooves. A mounted courier arrived at the offices of the *Eastern Argus* at 11 p.m. on February 13, 1815. Official notification had arrived in New York City just thirty-eight hours previously, and a messenger covered the final leg from Boston to Portland in just thirteen hours. Portland celebrated with joyful cannon fire, pealing church bells, shouts and hurrahs, and the prominent display of flags. Bonfires, toasts to peace, and thanksgiving church services were common. A Portland citizen noted, "every face was merry, every foot step light, the day was the happiest I ever beheld." In Gorham, townspeople burned the beacon erected to warn of a British attack. In Norway, boys celebrated with firecrackers and toy cannons and by burning a tar barrel, which they mounted on a sled and pulled through the street. In Augusta, young men dressed as sailors crewed a boat mounted on a sled pulled by oxen through the streets, an appropriate response to the end of a war that had ostensibly been fought over sailors' rights. In Saco and Biddeford, the better-off raised a fund for the towns' destitute families "that all Hearts might rejoice together in the return of Peace to our beloved country." The District's U.S. marshal hosted a "Peace Ball" to celebrate with music and dancing, as did the people of Livermore. Celebrants handed out liquor liberally: in Bath, bodies of the dead-drunk littered the floor of the North Meetinghouse, and even in backwoods Sebec, the inhabitants drank and made merry. Undoubtedly the first morning of peace was a painful one for many imbibers. The more religiously inclined flocked to churches in hopes of ascribing some meaning to their recent sufferings. The General Court declared a day of thanksgiving on February 22, while the Madison administration proclaimed April 13 to be a national day of thanks.[15]

Most people were indeed thankful for the end of the war. A Norway schoolteacher recalled, "all were united in hailing with joy the news of peace." The Portland diarist expressed the common belief that the nation had escaped from the brink of ruin. Attorney William Freeman, a prominent Portland Federalist, addressed the townsfolk of Limerick to celebrate the peace. Like many, he sought to repair commercial ties with Britain, reminding Limerick's populace that "The hatchet is buried—the sword is returned to the scabbard.... We have fought like lions. Now let us lie down like lambs."[16]

"NEVER WAS TREATED WITH LESS CIVILITY"

Now that the war over, the question was how to reoccupy the third of the District that the British still held. It was a protracted process, with the last British soldiers departing from Moose Island in 1818, three and a half years after the war ended. While John Coape Sherbrooke had dangled the prospect of keeping eastern Maine, his old comrade, the Duke of Wellington, had scoffed at the idea, and thus any British effort to retain the lands vanished. British negotiators acceded to returning all of it, except for Moose Island, which international arbitration would address.[17]

The immediate concern was repossessing Castine. Who would be the American representative to take formal possession? George Ulmer fished for the honor, as did William King. However, Brigadier General James Miller ordered Lieutenant Colonel Horatio Stark of the Thirty-third U.S. Infantry to notify the British commander that the war was over. Stark arranged an appointment with General Gerard Gosselin and later reported that he "never was treated with less civility by any person who pretended to call himself a gentleman than by General Gosselin—I was not even asked to take a seat." The two exchanged angry words in an interview that lasted for only ten minutes, before Stark left "in perfect disgust." Gosselin claimed he could not permit any U.S. interference until he received evacuation orders. Yet Stark noted that it was "common conversation" in Castine that British soldiers had dismantled the batteries on the mainland side of the peninsula.[18]

While Castine remained in British possession, the garrison commander on Moose Island insisted that he had the right to pursue British subjects as far east as the Penobscot River. So at the end of April, six British soldiers and a sergeant set out in a boat to pursue deserters at Machias. Once there, two of the soldiers themselves deserted, taking the boat with them. Facing a long walk back to Eastport, the remaining men bumped into Lieutenant Samuel Morse. He enticed the sergeant to desert with his entire party, promising them generous bounties to join the American army. The sergeant eventually succumbed, and Morse seems to have helped other deserters escape as well.[19]

The British spent ten weeks packing up at Castine, and they took pains to carry off their loot, including ships. By the treaty's terms, the British retained all of the ships they had seized between the Penobscot River and Passamaquoddy Bay. Up until they left Castine, they continued to look for hidden vessels and to levy ransoms on ships still on the stocks. But when a shipowner resisted, threatening to use force to defend his vessel, Gosselin declined to force the issue, leaving the Americans to handle it, as required by the treaty's terms.[20]

The last British troops embarked on April 27, 1815, and that same day Lieutenant Colonel Stark and some thirty American soldiers landed and hoisted the Stars and Stripes over Fort George. Now the U.S. Army confronted the task of collecting any vessels claimed by the British, as required by the Treaty of Ghent. Henry Dearborn's aide, Major Samuel D. Harris, arrived to undertake the task but was perplexed to find that locals would not give up their vessels. Furthermore, the army had not collected the craft in Castine Harbor as ordered. Harris reported that he did not have enough troops to pursue the issue and recommended that the War Department hand over the matter to the State Department.[21]

The State Department fared no better than Harris or the army, and American shipowners who had lost their vessels to the British remained upset about their losses. Jeremiah O'Brien believed that the treaty meant that the British would return his schooner *Washington*. He sent his claim to the U.S. agent at Castine, but the British refused it because their courts had condemned the vessel before February 17.

Stung by this financial loss, O'Brien noted that *Washington* was often seen in Passamaquoddy Bay and schemed to retake it, although he never acted on his plan. As late as 1816, shipowners were continuing to write to the State Department about their vessels.[22]

The weapons the British military had seized were another annoying issue. Many had belonged to private individuals, others to the state or the federal government. The British took a literal interpretation of the treaty's provisions for returning weapons, restoring field pieces to the Commonwealth but retaining the rammers and other associated equipment. The question of small arms such as muskets was even more contentious. Shortly after news of the peace arrived, Judge Job Nelson of Castine asked Gosselin to return them, but Gosselin brushed him off. Then, on the morning he embarked, he told Nelson that Stark had the key to the storehouse with the arms. Stark unlocked the storehouse shortly after the British had left, but locals and other bystanders walked away with the weapons, and few went back to their rightful owners.[23]

The British soldiers at Robbinston withdrew at the end of March. However, by the terms of the first article of the Treaty of Ghent, Moose Island remained in British hands until an international arbitration determined whether it was in British or American territory. A British garrison remained in charge of the island until June 1818, ruling the island by martial law, and locals found the experience intensely uncomfortable. In March, several Eastport merchants defaulted on bonds due to the British government and fled to the mainland, and soldiers pursued them into nearby communities. One of the defaulters escaped thanks to the quick thinking of a Lubec woman, who hid him in a brick oven. In Robbinston, British soldiers raided John Brewer's house in his absence. Though they failed to find the men they were seeking, the intrusion angered locals. When one Lubec man asked by what authority they were searching his house in the middle of the night, an officer pointed a loaded pistol at him and growled, "by this authority, damn you." For his part, Brewer threatened to call out the militia if the British landed troops on the mainland again.[24]

The uncertainty of the boundary meant that suppressing illicit trade was difficult. The navy ordered the brig *Prometheus* to patrol Maine's coastline, especially at Quoddy. Its commander, Alexander Wadsworth of Portland, had fought at Hampden as the first lieutenant of the *Adams*. Now he found himself pursuing smuggling vessels, among them the pink-sterned schooner *Stranger*. Wadsworth complained that the crew had "so painted on her sides that if you should see one side to day and the other side tomorrow you would not know her to be the same vessel; on one side, the bows were black spotted with yellow and the quarters black, on the other side the bows were black and the quarters black spotted with yellow." *Prometheus* cruized the Maine coast seeking smugglers without much success, until the ship suffered mass desertion on Christmas Day 1815 while Wadsworth was ashore in Portland. The federal government replaced *Prometheus* in 1816 with a revenue cutter stationed in Portland.[25]

Despite naval vessels and revenue cutters, Quoddy remained a troublesome area to patrol against smuggling. Lemuel Trescott continued as the region's customs collector and reported several incidents in which smugglers took refuge on Moose Island, beyond his reach. For example, Trescott had seized the schooner *Salome* in Cobscook Bay and placed it under guard at Lubec. Two days later, an armed party took the schooner from the guards in the dead of night and sailed it to Moose Island. Federal efforts to serve a court summons to smugglers such as Jabez Mowry failed because the men simply crossed to British jurisdiction to evade federal officials.[26]

DARTMOOR MASSACRE

The war left many Americans bitter, but the Dartmoor Massacre of April 1815 cemented their hatred of Britain. During the war, the British imprisoned almost 6,000 Americans in a remote English prison facility called Dartmoor, a "gloomy solitary place." Roughly five hundred of the inmates had Maine connections. Most were privateersmen, but some were simply commercial seafarers, a handful were navy men. Some were men of color, such as Robert Sanders of Portland, but most, like Benjamin Kinsley of Nobleborough, were white Yankees. About twenty Maine men died in Dartmoor, mostly from disease, but one from injuries sustained while attempting to escape. Three Portland sailors were among a scant handful who successfully escaped from the facility.[27]

Perez Drinkwater, Jr., frequently wrote to his family in North Yarmouth, detailing Dartmoor's constant rain or snow, the prison's inadequate food, and the thousands of "creepers" (bedbugs and lice) that tormented the prisoners. Drinkwater was extremely bitter, expressing his desire to kill an Englishman and drink his blood and labeling the British as the "worst of all the human race for their [*sic*] is no crimes but what they are guilty of." He whiled away his time by drawing a detailed rendition of the prison and complained, "I am tired of stying heir in this Lothsom Prison for Lothsom it is and a retched place it is to put people in you may depend."[28]

The problems at Dartmoor came to a head in early April. Although the war was over, the British were having trouble finding transports for the prisoners, who became increasingly surly and impatient, taunting their guards and sometimes rioting. The Royal Navy captain who commanded the prison, Thomas G. Shortland, overreacted to one incident and ordered his soldiers to open fire. The soldiers fired several volleys into the mass of men, leaving seven dead and dozens wounded. No Maine men died in the incident, but two had limbs amputated due to their injuries, and several were wounded. Drinkwater wrote to his parents:

> Dowtless you have heird of the marcichre [massacre] of Dartmoor in which ther was 7 killed and 38 wounded, it was done on the 6th of this month, the soldiers fired on us when we were all in the yard about 5000 they fired on us in all directions and after we was in the prison [building] they killed a number in the prison. It was one of the most retched things that ever took place Amonghts the savages much more amonghts peple that are the bullworks of our religion. I had the good fortin to escape their fury, but they killed some while begging for mercy after being wounded they likewise kicked and mangle the dead right before our faces.

Charles Holmes of Camden escaped by diving among the crowd's legs while his fellow townsman, Paul Thorndike, jumped through a window. A guard attacked privateersman Lot Davis of Baldwin as he lay sick in his hammock, bayoneting his head and then breaking his leg with his musket butt. Another stabbed Robert Tadley of Bath in "the privates."[29]

The United States and Britain launched an investigation into the massacre. The American representative was Charles King, son of the Federalist senator Rufus King and nephew of William and Cyrus King. In conjunction with a British representative, King blandly blamed both sides, refusing to hold the commander and his guards accountable. Recently freed mariners from York responded with "surprise and indignation" to King's report, calling down the "choicest curses of Heaven upon the head of that murderous miscreant, the infamous Shortland." Like Drinkwater, these mariners now hated the British.[30]

The Dartmoor Massacre was a wound that refused to heal, and it fostered Anglophobia for decades. The event was widely commemorated in the United States, as with a large diorama of Dartmoor that was displayed in Portland in 1825. A museum charged patrons twenty-five cents to see it. One wonders how many of its former inmates viewed the model, whether they discussed it with other survivors or tried to explain their experiences to family and friends. As late as the 1850s, the "Dartmoorians" or "Dartmoor Graduates" were functioning as an advocacy group, selling engravings of the prison to fund their work.[31]

Chapter 10
APRÈS LA GUERRE

The postwar period was difficult in Maine. Because of the nation's war debt, federal taxes remained high. Farm production had suffered during the notoriously cold summer of 1816, and later that year massive fires burned thousands of acres. Landed proprietors continued to demand high prices from settlers for Maine's marginally productive land. In response, backcountry residents voted with their feet: some 20,000 caught "Ohio fever" and left for the fertile West. The maritime trades, especially shipbuilding, did remain strong, but worldwide peace after 1815 meant that larger ports were edging the District's out of international trade. Increasingly, Maine-built ships sailed for Boston and New York owners on coastal routes.[1]

The inhabitants retained a good deal of bitterness against the British. Dartmoor and the war had bred a generation of Anglophobes, and the animosity continued for decades. Perhaps the strangest manifestation of this was the 1818 abduction of a British girl in the midcoast town of Bristol. A local customs officer seized her from a ship and "swore he would keep her as a *slave*" to avenge his losses during the war. A crowd prevented the girl's father from rescuing her, and we still do not know how the case resolved itself.[2]

Hatred for the British extended to those who had opposed the war. The town of Deer Isle, which had hosted many smugglers and collaborators during the conflict, remained in an uproar for decades. Its church congregation abandoned their pro-British minister, and he soon died, reportedly insane. Thirty years after the war had ended, the issue of collaboration was enough to prevent a candidate from being elected to office. A local political pamphlet asked, "Who are the Federal leaders in Bucksport? . . . Let these treasonable proceedings answer!" Yet not all communities harbored such ill-will. An army officer visiting Castine in 1817 was mystified to find that its judges, clergymen, customshouse officers, tavernkeepers, drovers, and women "had an exalted opinion of British generosity."[3]

In these same years, however, the war's opponents were founding an enduring peace movement. They included Bowdoin College's president, Jesse Appleton, and Maine's most famous pacifist, William Ladd of Minot. In 1819, Ladd, who had recently experienced a religious conversion, visited Appleton, then on his deathbed. Like many of those who were involved in creating the Maine Peace Society, Appleton and Ladd were Federalists and Congregationalists. Just before speaking with Ladd, Appleton had sent a memorial from the Maine Peace Society to President Monroe in which he had condemned privateering on various grounds, deriding its pursuit of personal gain without honor or patriotism as well as its role in hardening young sailors' hearts to crime. Now Appleton recruited Ladd into the society, and the retired sea captain soon became its leader. By 1828, he had proposed an audacious plan that would stitch together various state peace societies into a national one, the American Peace Society, which still exists today.[4]

On the whole, the war had drawn Maine's inhabitants closer to the federal government. Pensions, trade policies, fishing bounties, even infrastructure such as lighthouses increasingly signified that the United States was a benevolent institution looking out for its citizenry's interests. Yet in the eyes of the District, Massachusetts could do no right.

WIDOWS' WEEDS

At the war's end, veterans poured back into the District. Unusually, more than 90 percent of them chose to stay in Maine, a remarkable figure given the outmigration associated with Ohio fever. One possibility is that the recruiting bonuses and land titles lavished on recruits was helping them purchase farms or pay off mortgages. Yet many had been wounded or were otherwise disabled, and their battered presence perpetuated communities' Anglophobia. One militiaman, wounded at the battle of Hampden, now had a forearm and hand that were "shriveled stiff and useless." Another stringbeaner at the same battle had taken a gunshot through the thigh and had been held prisoner for two months. By 1821, he applied for a pension because he had been reduced to wretchedness and want. A sailor on board *Enterprise* had sustained a remarkable injury during its battle with *Boxer*. A spent ball had hit him in the forehead, leaving an open hole that remained open and leaking pus for twenty-five years.[5]

Much more than combat, diseases killed or maimed soldiers and sailors. The army's camps and posts were notoriously sickly, and naval vessels were no better. Measles killed many and left others partially blind. Exposure to bad weather contributed to illness and rheumatism. A particularly sad story involved Lemuel Worster, who in 1814, when only twelve years old, marched with his father's militia company to Fort McClary. A "smart, active lad," he caught the dreaded spotted fever and barely survived, blind in one eye, deaf, and unable to speak, a burden to his family for the next forty years.[6]

The war left many widows and orphans. Their economic prospects were grim, and mothers and widows sometimes spent years wresting back pay from the federal government. Town officials, anxious to remove these women from relief rolls, petitioned members of Congress on their behalf. Many widows did not know the fate of their husbands. Lucy George of Norway wrote a heart-wrenching letter to A. J. Dallas, the acting secretary of war, begging for information: "My anxiety is grate as well as my children to know whether my Husband is living or not." Widows of mariners such as George Roberts, who had sailed from Portland on the privateer *Dash* in January 1815, were often left in limbo. When *Dash* disappeared with all hands, more than a dozen women were widowed. Hannah Roberts awaited news of her husband, but it never came. She put on widows' weeds, the traditional black garb of mourning, and wore them to the end of her days, never remarrying, living in part off a federal pension. Her refuge was religion: she attended a Methodist church daily and carried religious writings with her as a source of solace. As a further injustice, those who did take second husbands were not entitled to land bounties unless their previous husbands had died in battle.[7]

Veterans banded together in the decades after 1815, demanding that Congress provide them with more benefits. By 1850, all War of 1812 veterans, most of whom had served in the militia, were eligible for land grants. These and other benefits increasingly bound veterans to the federal government. During the Civil War, this relationship between service and loyalty became explicit: the government denied benefits to veterans if they had been disloyal to the Union cause. Those who wanted them had to formally swear that they had remained loyal. In one instance, veterans gathered to take this oath en masse, and an observer noted the emotion of the moment: "They were old, and wrinkled, and gray, for they were near the end of their life's campaign. When these old veterans raised their hands to Heaven and swore to their identity and service, the spectators were visibly affected." In 1871, Congress provided cash pensions for service, regardless of injury or disability. That year, eighty persons drew War of 1812 pensions in Bangor alone. As late as 1883, there were 2,135 War of 1812 pensioners on the rolls in Maine. Not all of these applications were legitimate. Robert Bowden, for instance, attempted to claim that he had served at the battle of Hampden. His father may well have fought in that battle, but Bowden was only nine years old in 1814 and was known as a teller of tales. Nonetheless, a neighbor cynically observed that he "deserves a pension as much as some that gets it in this vicinity."[8]

"WE ARE ONE PEOPLE"

A postwar highlight was President James Monroe's visit to New England in 1817. In Maine, he traveled as far east as Portland. While in Kennebunk, Monroe spoke in a spirit of mutual conciliation and declared that his New England tour confirmed "how much we are one people, how strongly the ties, by which we are united, do in fact bind us together; how much we possess in reality a community, not only of interest, but of sympathy and affection." Southern Maine joyfully welcomed Monroe with speeches and militia salutes. Several communities constructed evergreen arches over the highway. The one at Scarborough was artfully interwoven with roses that read "UNITED WE STAND"; but Westbrook, Scarborough's neighbor to the north, trumped that display by installing nineteen arches, one for each state. Portland's reception was no less enthusiastic. At a dinner with the town's prominent Republicans, Monroe received delegations or messages from towns further east, and he expressed regret he could not travel to Castine. Even the most obdurate Federalists could not help but be awed and pleased by the presence of the president. Among them was Judge David Sewall of York, who hosted a breakfast for Monroe and his entourage at his own home. Sewall was so impressed by the president that he reportedly refused to sit down in his presence. Even old Massachusetts welcomed Monroe: the crusty editor of the Federalist *Columbian Centinel* coined the term "Era of Good Feelings" to reflect the ebbing political partisanship.[9]

Monroe's visit was one manifestation of a series of benevolent federal actions that benefited the District of Maine. These included negotiating the border with British North America as well as protectionist measures linked to tariffs, cabotage, bounties, and fishing rights in Canadian waters. While not entirely successful, they demonstrated that the national government was actively attempting to better the lot of ordinary Americans.

The fourth article of the Treaty of Ghent required British and American commissioners to determine which nation held jurisdiction over the islands in Passamaquoddy Bay, including Moose Island (Eastport), which was still under military occupation. John Holmes of Alfred led the American delegation. Earlier in his life, Holmes had worked as a lawyer for the landed proprietors, and his politics had been Federalist. In 1811, however, he became a Republican, earning the scorn of Federalists, though Maine's Republicans hesitated to trust him. While serving as a state senator during the war, he was an influential critic of Governor Strong and his supporters and a strident promoter of Maine statehood. The Madison administration rewarded his loyalty by making him the American commissioner who would work with British counterparts after collecting documents, maps, and affidavits. The Americans attempted to claim all of the islands in Passamaquoddy Bay, even Grand Manan. The British made similar claims, but ultimately they came to an agreement based on negotiations that had taken place in 1807. The United States would receive Moose, Dudley, and Frederick islands while the British would retain Campobello, Deer, and Grand Manan islands. The British evacuated without incident, and on June 30, 1818, the American flag flew over Eastport, with locals giving six hearty cheers as it rose. Brigadier General James Miller represented the United States, with the attendance of Lieutenant Colonel Henry Sargent, who represented the Commonwealth's interests—essentially an afterthought. Eastport residents publicly thanked the last British garrison commander. The newly created local newspaper explained that it was "martial law, and a FOREIGN FLAG that was obnoxious to us,—not the English officers *personally.*"[10]

Another commission was created to determine the inland border between Maine and Canada. The process involved numerous difficulties, including bad weather, rugged terrain, fierce mosquitoes, supply problems, and personality clashes. The United States claimed that Maine extended almost to the Saint Lawrence River, whereas the British were anxious to preserve the crucial communication route between New Brunswick and Lower Canada that ran through Madawaska. Both sides conceded that a survey was needed, so each nation supported surveyors, chainmen, instrument bearers, blazers, and axmen, who began their slow work in 1817. Curiously, neither side relied on Native Americans, who could have shared firsthand knowledge about the area. Instead, they depended on expensive, time-consuming exploring parties and balky scientific instruments. The process dragged on through the 1820s, and eventually King William I of the Netherlands became the arbitrator. But the arrival of Yankee settlers in the Madawaska region in 1817 further complicated matters, and Britain and the United States did not resolve the border's location until after the bloodless Aroostook War of 1839.[11]

"PRECISELY WHAT IS WANTED"

Congressional protectionist policies benefited Maine's coastal communities, drawing them further into the American economy and away from British trade. During much of the Jefferson and Madison administrations, the District's coastal communities had resented commercial restrictions such as Jefferson's long embargo of 1808–9 and Madison's nonintercourse efforts and shorter embargoes in early 1812 and late 1813. But even President Madison was calling for American trade protections in 1815; and by 1816, Republicans had adopted many Federalist ideas about commerce. Still, a few opponents remained, among them Cyrus King, who rejected the "Era of Good Feelings" and blasted the Tariff Act of 1816 as more taxation.[12]

Many saw the tariff as a measure to protect the nascent American textile industry and assumed that shipping interests would oppose it because it would lessen foreign trade. Yet U.S. shipping patterns were transitioning to coastal trade, so the tariff had little impact. In fact, by 1820, the nation's coasting tonnage had, for the time, exceeded deep-sea tonnage, meaning that Americans now traded more among themselves than with foreign markets. In Maine, shipbuilding, too, remained largely unaffected, even though the tariff punished the importation of foreign-made ironware, because the District had competitive labor rates. This meant that the shipyards simply handed the expenses to buyers. Likewise, the tariff benefited Maine's growing fishing industry because it imposed a tax of $1 or $2 per barrel on Canadian fish, essentially excluding foreign-caught fish from American markets.[13]

However, protectionism would have little effect if the fishermen could not pursue fish off the coasts of Labrador, Newfoundland, Nova Scotia, and New Brunswick. The Treaty of Ghent was silent on this issue, so American fishermen assumed they could resume working those waters under the authority of the Treaty of Paris of 1783. In 1815, Maine fishing boats like the *Hiram* of Bristol appeared in Nova Scotia harbors, to the consternation of provincial officials, who claimed the Yankees were destroying their fishing grounds and polluting their harbors. Admiral Edward Griffith ordered Royal Navy ships to seize American fishing vessels close to the Maritime provinces. However, the Halifax vice-admiralty court found no grounds for such seizures, and the Colonial Office ordered Griffith's commanders to exercise moderation in their patrols. Griffith told his officers to "prevent by every lenient measure, the interference of the American fishermen in the fisheries of His Majesty's colonies." Nonetheless, Yankee fishermen sometimes resisted these "lenient" reminders, as when a Bucksport (recently renamed from Buckstown) fishing boat's crew overwhelmed the Royal Navy sailors who were taking them to Halifax.[14]

The Madison administration's secretary of state, James Monroe, responded vigorously to British aggression against American fishermen, asking John Quincy Adams, the American minister to Britain, to take steps to stop the harassment. It had been Adams's father, President John Adams, who had worked so diligently to gain American fishing privileges in the 1783 Treaty of Paris. When Monroe became president in 1817, Adams became secretary of state, and the two continued to pressure the British to reinstate American fishing privileges. In 1818, the American and British governments entered into a convention whereby Yankee fishing skippers could legally work in the waters of British North America so long as they remained outside of settled harbors. This requirement was frequently honored in the breach, and the British regularly seized American fishing craft, among them the *White Oak* of Kittery, owned by the widow Lydia Follett.[15]

Since 1814, Congress had been promoting the American cod fishery through a bounty system, but during the war it had little impact on the industry. Furthermore, the system had favored the owners of large schooners, which operated primarily out of Massachusetts. In 1819, Congress reconfigured the bounty's rate structure so that it was more generous and favored the medium-sized craft used by Maine's fishermen. The impact was immediate: by 1820, Maine's share of the cod fishery had doubled to 20 percent of the national catch.[16]

Congress also linked Maine's shipping community to the developing American economy through protectionist legislation that even the acerbic Cyrus King liked. William King recognized that regulations that excluded British-flagged ships from the Maritime provinces would profit shipowners like himself. The Navigation Act of 1817 enacted a cabotage policy, meaning that foreign vessels could not engage in coastal trade along the American seaboard. Cabotage favored American shipbuilding and mariners, and Maine had plenty of shipyards and seafaring communities. The District owned 50,000 tons of coastal shipping (more than 10 percent of the country's coastal tonnage) that employed as many as 3,000 seamen. However, as William King realized, the Navigation Act could have benefited the statehood movement if it had removed restrictions on the coastal trade that required frequent port calls. As he wrote to his stepbrother Rufus, a navigation bill to address the coastal trade "is precisely what is wanted" to win over port towns, many of which had repeatedly rebuffed the statehood movement.[17] Under existing regulations, As long as Maine remained a part of Massachusetts, its ships could venture as far south as New Jersey without mandatory port stops that cost time and money. But if Maine were to become a separate state, its coasting schooners would have to put into a Massachusetts port to allow a customs officer to check its cargo manifest and do the same in every other state as it proceeded down the coast. King set forth on a trip to Washington to promote a new coasting law that would loosen these regulations. He targeted Secretary of the Treasury William H. Crawford, who was in charge of enforcing the laws related to maritime commerce. Crawford, who had presidential ambitions, was anxious to assist him. King's stepbrother Rufus, a nationally influential Federalist and a senator from New York, was another critical ally. Both Crawford and Rufus King supported changing the coasting law and pushed legislation through Congress in early 1819. Now Maine vessels were permitted to sail as far south as Georgia before putting into port. King had successfully cut the commercial tie to Massachusetts and had removed the last impediment to statehood.[18]

SKUNK IN THE MEETINGHOUSE

After 1815, the federal government enacted policies that favored Maine's development and attachment to the nation. In the same period, the Massachusetts ideal of an orderly Boston-oriented society lingered on in Maine but suffered embarrassing setbacks.

Federalist officials fared poorly, the Congregationalist faith lost much of its prestige, and the militia's popularity waned.

Among Maine's Federalist officials, Sheriff Moses Adams fell the furthest. First came his widely mocked smuggling misadventure, and then a second disaster awaited him. On May 12, 1815, one of his children discovered his dead wife in their Ellsworth home; she had been beaten severely with a bootjack and hacked with an ax. Suspicion fell on the sheriff, who was arrested and imprisoned in the Castine jail over which he had so recently presided. Adams does not seem to have been popular locally, perhaps due to his collaboration with the British or rumors that he abused his wife and kept a mistress. In June, a court tried him in the Castine meetinghouse, where spectators crowded in so tightly that the second-story galleries almost collapsed. During their hasty evacuation, the crowd broke a window and nearly tore a door off its hinges. When the trial resumed, Adams pled not guilty, and the jury agreed with him after deliberating for only two hours. But one more indignity awaited him: as he left the meetinghouse, the crowd hissed. Ruined in reputation and purse, the ex-sheriff moved to the backcountry village of Acton, where he reportedly spent many hours by his fireplace, cheek in hand, twirling a set of fire tongs as he contemplated his downfall. It was a cruel comedown for this exemplar of the Massachusetts ideal.[19]

The Congregational ideal also fared poorly, and community displeasure with the church revealed itself in numerous ways. In August 1816, for instance, a man left a putrid skunk corpse in the pulpit of Camden's Congregational meetinghouse. But even by 1815 there were signs of stress. In North Yarmouth, the Reverend Francis Brown, who had repeatedly blasted the war in sermons, gave up his position to become president of Dartmouth College. His successor, the Reverend Joseph Waite Curtis, took the pulpit of the ancient meetinghouse at a ceremony attended by hundreds. The structure, dating back to 1729, groaned under the weight of the crowd, and some plaster fell onto a pew. As in Sheriff Adams's trial, much of the crowd made a mad dash for the doors, while others tried to calm them with calls of "No danger!" The new minister leaped out of a window before it became clear that the building would not collapse. His reaction was an ill portent for his success as pastor, and he resigned a few months later. More typical was the experience of Charles Emerson of Machias. Raised as a Congregationalist, he decided to join a local church and carefully interviewed both Congregationalist and Baptist ministers. Despite pressure from his neighbors, he joined the Baptist church and underwent baptism with his wife. They were not alone in shifting away from Congregationalism, which continued to grow but at a slower pace than the Baptist and Methodist churches did. At the same time Maine's evangelical sects became more moderate, abandoning foot washing, raucous meetings, and women preachers for more restrained forms of worship. Colleges and seminaries rose to meet their demand for better-trained ministers, among them the Maine Literary and Theological Institute (now known as Colby College) and the Bangor Theological Seminary.[20]

The Federalists fared no better with the militia, whose lackluster wartime performance had tarnished its reputation. Postwar squabbles only worsened the situation. Lieutenant Colonel Andrew Grant charged Brigadier General John Blake with neglect that had led to the defeat at Hampden. After a court of inquiry packed with Federalist militia officers and presided over by Major General Henry Sewall found no grounds to support the charge, Blake laid countercharges against his subordinate officers, Lieutenant Colonel Grant and Major Joshua Chamberlain, charging both with cowardice and conduct unbecoming an officer. The court cleared Chamberlain but suspended Grant from militia service for two years. Public opinion was less kind to Blake than the court had been. A year after the battle, he and his son were obliged to attend Hampden's annual muster, an event they viewed with trepidation—so much so that the elder Blake claimed to be ill and left the duty to his son. On arriving at the muster, the younger Blake was confronted by his father's effigy mounted on a mock-heroic horse, complete with a wooden sword and a large military hat labeled "Black Jack" on one side and "Traitor" on the other. When the son attempted to review the troops, the unit performed a right face away from him and paraded the straw general as if it were doing the review. A bonfire on the common capped the performance: stringbeaners hanged the dummy general, shot it, and then threw it into the flames. Massachusetts Federalists managed to ignore these proceedings; and the year after Blake's acquittal, Governor Strong promoted him to major general in command of the Tenth Division. Republican newspapers howled, but political appointments remained in the hand of old Massachusetts. However, Blake resigned after less than a year.[21]

The last hurrah for the old militia system was in 1818, when John Brooks, the new governor of Massachusetts, visited the District. A moderate Federalist, Brooks was popular even in Maine, where two towns now bear his name. The governor traveled as far east as Hancock County. He touted his visit as a military review calculated to "excite a spirit of laudable emulation" for the stringbeaners, but Republicans grumbled that it was an "electioneering tour." Still, it excited considerable excitement among Federalists who continued to see Boston as the hub of their universe, such as Henry Sewall, who advertised the event in the *Hallowell Gazette*. Brooks's presence would be a golden moment for Sewall, allowing him to parade the best units of his division in front of an esteemed governor and reinforce his prized links to Boston.[22]

Though the governor's visit was plagued with bad weather from the start, Sewall had the Hallowell muster field cleared with care and encouraged the militiamen to put extra effort into their appearance. When the day arrived, they gathered in the pouring rain, but no adoring crowds attended to admire the troops or governor. A local historian described the militia as a "doleful looking little army. Officers and soldiers could exhibit only their drooping plumes, soiled uniforms and muddy boots and ruined gaiters." Brooks and Sewall rushed through the inspection, which was followed by a hasty salute, and then everyone went home. The sodden parade was a portent of things to come. The institutions that were supposed to bind Maine to Massachusetts would continue to erode, even as Maine's Republicans moved to weaken them further.[23]

MAINE BECOMES A STATE

After the war, William King and his followers pursued a vigorous statehood agenda, and part of that effort involved discrediting Massachusetts. John Holmes tore into the Commonwealth's decision to withhold militia during the war, rebuked clergy who had taken "their stand in favor of the enemy," and blamed the state for devising and promoting a scheme for New England's "final separation." The *Eastern Argus* produced a steady flow of articles reminding readers that Massachusetts did not act for the benefit of Maine. Meanwhile, Massachusetts newspapers simply ignored the issue of separation. As Benjamin Vaughan of Hallowell concluded in 1819, "I think the old State is full as anxious to get rid of us." Among notable Massachusetts Federalists, only two, Josiah Quincy and John Adams, objected to Maine's statehood. Neither wanted to abandon the District's Federalists; and Adams worried that King, whom he called a "bold, daring, ardent genius with talents capable of inspiring the people with his own enthusiasm and ambition," would "tear off Maine from old Massachusetts and leave her in a state below mediocrity in the union." Harrison Gray Otis was more typical of Massachusetts Federalists: he believed that if a clear majority of Maine's people wished for statehood, they should have it. Of course, he was not an entirely disinterested party. Otis was a speculator in District lands and King's partner as proprietor of three townships. The two men hoped that statehood would bring a wave of settlers to Maine.[24]

King was well suited to the task of pursuing statehood. Colleagues recognized him as exceptionally intelligent, and he alone among the Massachusetts militia generals had emerged as an active and capable officer. But the experience that may have best prepared him to lead the District to statehood was his illicit maritime trade. As Maine's wealthiest shipowner, King had successfully navigated the tangle of laws and policies that had complicated maritime trade during the Napoleonic wars. Indeed, he seemed to thrive on bending or defying rules and regulations, including American embargoes, British blockades, French spoliation, and Swedish naturalization laws. His political success was less notable than his commercial success. After the war, King ran on the Republican ticket for lieutenant governor of Massachusetts with his old mentor Henry Dearborn running for governor. Neither candidate was popular in old Massachusetts, which remained firmly Federalist in politics, and the moderate Federalist Brooks handily won the governorship in 1817. In a replay of the 1812 gubernatorial election, Dearborn and King underperformed, barely winning the majority even in overwhelmingly Republican Maine.[25]

Maine's Republicans now realized that Dearborn was a liability, and they sensed that their counterparts in old Massachusetts would not help them. Dearborn's son-in-law, Joshua Wingate, Jr., suspected that Massachusetts Republicans would sooner support a Federalist than a Republican candidate from Maine, and he called on the District's inhabitants to move to protect their rights and privileges or "become the vassals and slaves of Mass't. proper."[26]

King and his colleagues, now known as the "Junto," worked diligently to erode Mainers' allegiance to Massachusetts. They published a stream of pamphlets and newspaper articles, relying on flattery, half-truths, and lies to make their case. The pamphlet *An Appeal to the People of Maine* argued that Massachusetts had attempted to slow Maine's economic growth because it was jealous of its prosperity. An item in the *Bangor Weekly Register* argued that "Massachusetts is a tyrannical stepmother, who wishes to cramp your energies, fleece you of your wealth, and reduce you to the most abject state of colonial vassalage." The *Eastern Argus*, the Junto's primary organ, optimistically declared, "The 'colony of Maine,' in contempt of all opposition, is by nature destined to become a populous, wealthy, and powerful country." These screeds received little reaction from Massachusetts proper, nor even much interest. The few published responses were mild, as when the *Boston Daily Advertiser* noted that "a man must be blind or perverse who does not see or admit, that Maine was a sort of Province or colony with distinct feelings."[27]

Many prominent Federalists were in favor of statehood. William King's brother Rufus King, arguably the most respected

Federalist in the nation, supported it, believing that separation would allow old Massachusetts to maintain its "ancient institutions." Their acid-tongued brother Cyrus, despite being an extreme Federalist, was also an advocate of statehood until his untimely death in 1817. While professing to venerate the institutions of Massachusetts, he often waxed sentimental about Maine, birthplace of himself and of his children. Nor did the Federalist-dominated Massachusetts legislature obstruct the statehood movement, though it did impose rigorous requirements to ensure that Maine's people actually did want separation. As William King was pleased to note, statehood was not a partisan issue in Massachusetts proper. In fact, the most vigorous opposition came from within the District, primarily Federalists associated with Bowdoin College, the *Hallowell Gazette*, and absentee proprietors.[28]

By the spring of 1819 an increasingly confident King was reporting that opposition to statehood had almost ceased. His confidence was well placed: after an 1819 vote overwhelmingly favored statehood, the Massachusetts legislature approved a separation, which would take place on March 15, 1820, provided the U.S. Congress approved the decision by March 4. Statehood seemed to be assured—until the question arose of Missouri's admission to the union as a slave state. Now, suddenly, Maine's statehood was in doubt. Advocates such as Daniel Cony of Augusta, who had worked toward separation for thirty years, feared they would not live to see it. Cony's distress was provincial: although he had never been to Missouri, he was incredulous that "the civilized populous State of Maine (300000 free inhabitants)" should be linked to its "trackless regions," "dreary wastes," and "sable tribes." William D. Williamson, a pro-statehood attorney and historian from Bangor, wrote that Maine's people were indignant that Maine's and Missouri's statehoods had been crammed into a single bill.[29]

The Missouri debate turned into a political melee. Speaker of the House John Clay and other proslavery "doughfaces" opposed Maine statehood unless Missouri could enter the union as a slave state. Rufus King, an adamant opponent of slavery, seemed to be willing to sacrifice Maine's statehood in order to keep slavery out of Missouri. Congressman John Holmes abandoned his antislavery stance and said that he would be willing to accept it in Missouri as the price of Maine's statehood; he even garnered supporting words from Thomas Jefferson. The House ultimately forged a compromise that permitted slavery in Missouri while forbidding it north of latitude 36 degrees 30 minutes in the rest of the Louisiana Purchase. The Senate approved the measure on March 3, 1820, beating the deadline set for Maine statehood by mere hours.[30]

In April, the new state's voters overwhelmingly chose William King to be Maine's first governor. Out of 22,014 votes, he received 21,083. In his maiden speech, he noted the friendly manner in which Massachusetts and Maine had parted. King's first year in office was unremarkable. However, he reneged on his deal to give one-third of all offices to Federalists and failed to pass legislation that would allow Maine to buy all of the remaining Massachusetts lands or create a tax break for nascent manufacturing establishments. The reasons for those failures were linked to Maine's demographics: the population remained overwhelmingly agricultural, and it was dominated by Jeffersonians who could not stomach the thought of tax incentives to "privileged classes." King resigned just after his 1821 reelection.[31]

CONSTITUTIONS

Both Maine and Massachusetts faced changes because of separation, especially in terms of state constitutions. Maine required a new constitution, while Massachusetts had to adjust its 1780 constitution to exclude provisions made for Maine's representation in the General Court. Maine's new constitution was a cautious affair, closely modeled on the Commonwealth's 1780 model, with minor deviations. Massachusetts's new version was downright conservative, a last-ditch attempt to preserve the Massachusetts ideal.

Representatives hammered out a constitution for Maine at a convention held in Portland in 1819. It was almost exclusively a Republican event, with the District's most prominent Federalists conspicuous by their absence. Attendees dutifully elected William King as president and produced a document that looked a great deal like the one from old Massachusetts. William Pitt Preble, the District's federal district attorney, was primarily responsible for this cautious approach, persuading the convention that the 1780 constitution was "already rooted in the good feelings and affections of the people." Nonetheless, Maine's constitution deviated from the Massachusetts model in several ways, none of them radical departures but all of them more egalitarian. Notably, it called for absolute freedom of religion; one delegate even advocated for the right of Muslims, Jews, and Hindus to worship freely. More importantly for the near future of the state, Catholics received equal status with Protestants, despite the misgivings of some representatives. (Anti-Catholic prejudice continued to persist for decades.) Another difference was universal suffrage for men over age twenty-one, "excepting paupers, persons under guardianship and Indians not taxed," with no mention of property qualifications.[32]

Like Massachusetts's, Maine's constitution laid out provisions for a state militia. It empowered the governor to act as "commander in chief" but inserted the wording "except when called into the actual service of the United States," thereby recognizing the federal government's primacy in military affairs. It also sharply limited the categories of people who could claim exemption from militia service, meaning that justices, firefighting companies, and clergy now had to attend musters or face fines. There was considerable grumbling in newspapers that the new provisions unfairly allowed justices and county officials to avoid service if they paid an annual fee of $6 whereas mechanics had to pay $13. The exemption clause, proposed by militia officer Abel W. Atherton, was one of the few notably Federalist provisions in the constitution. But King supported the measure, hoping to fire the militia with new zeal in their duties as citizen soldiers. Statehood also meant that officers holding Massachusetts commissions had to turn them in for new ones issued by Maine.[33]

Maine's statehood affected the Massachusetts constitution. In 1820 Commonwealth voters approved a call for a constitutional convention to consider any needed amendments. In contrast to Mainers' cautious expansion of personal liberties, Massachusetts

Federalists buttressed the Massachusetts ideal, preserving Boston's overrepresentation in the state's senate, state-supported religion, deference, property rights, and property qualifications for voting. Although John Adams refused to preside over the proceedings, his influence ensured that few changes would be made to the "old Fabrick" of the 1780 constitution. The convention's leaders were among the most outspoken members of the Boston-based status quo, and they included Josiah Quincy and Daniel Webster, who had moved to Boston from his native New Hampshire. Massachusetts Republicans had little opportunity, or perhaps will, to resist or propose more liberal ideas. One sounded almost like a Federalist when he wrote that "the Constitution should be approached with great reverence, and that we should proceed with great caution." Among the few Republican successes was a motion put forward by Henry Dearborn, who had left Maine and now lived in Boston. He proposed that Massachusetts should follow Maine in apportioning senate districts according to population, not wealth, and the recommendation passed overwhelmingly. Other minor changes included abolition of a religious test for office and property qualifications to vote. One significant change permitted chartering communities as cities. Boston led the way in this regard, abandoning its ancient system of selectmen in favor of a mayor. The Commonwealth's electorate approved the measure by a mere sixty-two votes, although Bostonians overwhelmingly supported it.[34]

Partings

Maine's statehood was not inevitable, nor was it led by heroes. Massachusetts did not put up much resistance; but even in Maine, the statehood movement did not attract widespread support until the vote of 1819. Afterward, the two states frequently cooperated on regional issues, such as reimbursement for 1814 militia expenses, prosecuting illegal timber operations in the new state's northern reaches, and aggressively pushing Maine's border as far north as possible.

Once achieved, statehood changed very little. John Adams sneered, "However ardent they were for the separation, now, when they have so peaceably obtained it, they seem to care little about it & perhaps even regret it." Maine did not become populous and wealthy as the proponents of statehood predicted it would, nor was the cost of governance reduced. Unlike Massachusetts, Maine did not industrialize to any considerable degree before the Civil War. Despite its admirable state motto, *Dirigo* (I lead), Maine was not much of a leader. Yet it did not succumb to the mediocrity that Adams had foreseen. In general terms, it was an underpopulated frontier much like the western states, with an economy based on agriculture and resource extraction (primarily timbering and fishing), which were augmented by the coasting trade and shipbuilding. Politically, it remained very much a New England state, with town meetings dominating the political calendar. Culturally, it continued to look to Boston for cues, retaining a love-hate relationship with the regional metropolis.[1]

Only a handful of Federalists had strenuously objected to Maine's statehood. Major General Henry Sewall, unable to reconcile himself to statehood or its first governor, resigned his militia commission on June 2, 1820. Governor William King, his old nemesis, immediately accepted the resignation. Judge David Sewall enjoyed muttering about the new state's governance with his Harvard classmate John Adams. Judge Sewall continued his membership in the Massachusetts Historical Society because no one had the nerve to point out that its bylaws now excluded him. Judge Samuel Sumner Wilde was one of the few Federalists who left the state, recognizing that his position on the Massachusetts Supreme Court was more prestigious and remunerative than any that Maine could provide.[2]

Like most statehood advocates in the nation's history, the leaders of Maine's statehood movement, the Junto, were accused of being ruthlessly ambitious and unprincipled as well as not exceptionally competent. Certainly, William King used statehood to launch his political ambitions. Though he adopted radical rhetoric to attract the squatters' votes, his actions indicate that he himself benefited from land speculation. While posturing as a patriotic military officer, he engaged in smuggling and traded with the enemy. None of this escaped the attention of newspaper editors, but the electorate overlooked these shortcomings. King achieved his goal and became the state's first governor. Yet like many insurgents, he found governing to be uninteresting, and he resigned after serving for little more than a year. A few years later, the controversy over his smuggling career exploded in a pamphlet war. Among other members of the Junto, John Holmes was arguably the most contentious. His willingness to accept the spread of slavery as the price of Maine's statehood outraged many antislavery leaders, including Rufus King, who called him a "contemptible and vulgar fellow." Other statehood advocates, such as Orchard Cook, an inveterate office seeker, did not live long enough to see the project through to completion. More happily, Daniel Cony of Augusta, a Federalist who had supported statehood since the 1790s, not only lived to see statehood but also saw his hometown become the state capital in 1831. This move away from Portland to a more central location reflected the democratic ideal of making governance more accessible to the electorate. However, the new capitol building, while constructed of local granite, was designed by a Boston architect and closely modeled after the Massachusetts statehouse. Although more egalitarian than Massachusetts, Maine continued to imitate it in many ways.[3]

The new state struggled to control three issues related to land ownership: squatters, Native Americans, and the northeastern boundary. First, Maine did little to relieve the suffering of its squatters, the so-called "White Indians." The new state's legislature gave people incentives to settle in wilderness lands and taxed nonresident proprietors and settlers at the same rate. Otherwise, it legislated harsh laws that discouraged squatter resistance. Second, Maine's Native Americans did not benefit from statehood. The Penobscots hastened to establish formal relations and secured a treaty similar to their 1818 treaty with Massachusetts. However, this document included a proviso wherein the new state claimed guardianship status. After 1820, the state managed Indigenous resources as it saw fit, whether the Natives agreed or not. Despite treaties, the Yankees disregarded Native American rights, engaging in intimidation, coercion, physical aggression, theft, vandalism, arson, and even murder. Third, illegal timber cutting on the state's wilderness lands was an ongoing problem. Per the Act of Separation, Massachusetts retained half of Maine's wilderness lands. Both states had land offices that competed in selling land to settlers or timber interests. Both states worked together to prosecute illegal timber cutting on public lands, but with little success. When agents attempted to stop illegal logging, loggers disguised as Natives beat them.[4]

Both Massachusetts and Maine sought to profit from selling land or the right to cut timber and thus cooperated in aggressively pushing Maine's boundary as far north as possible. Even before 1820, Yankees had moved into Madawaska and the Aroostook Valley to cut timber. New Brunswick officials believed they had jurisdiction there and complained to imperial authorities. The British government was less interested in timber than in defending the Madawaska communications route to Lower Canada. Maine attempted to push the issue as one involving states' rights and sent militia north in 1839. This bloodless engagement, in which Maine soldiers glowered at New Brunswick militia and British regulars, became known as the Aroostook War. Eventually, the federal government intervened to prevent a war with Britain and reached an amicable resolution of the border in the 1842 Webster-Ashburton Treaty.[5]

By now, Washington had also successfully curbed Massachusetts on the issue of states' rights. James Monroe, who had been secretary of war in 1814–15, had long objected to Caleb Strong's views about control of the militia. Even before the War of 1812 ended, he declared that Strong had pushed the idea of states' rights "further than I have ever known it to be carried." In 1817, the Commonwealth sent James Lloyd and William H. Sumner, both Federalists, to Washington to submit claims for reimbursement, but their reception was frosty. After being elected president, Monroe refused to consider paying the debt until Massachusetts conceded that the president had control over the militia in wartime. Meanwhile, as part of the separation act, Maine acquired one-third of Massachusetts's war debt. For years the two states struggled to persuade Congress to reimburse the expense of calling out the militia. Massachusetts believed that the federal government owed it more than $500,000, while Maine demanded more than $320,000, but Monroe, declared that Governor Strong had behaved in a manner "repugnant to the Constitution." Then, in 1824, Massachusetts voters elected William Eustis as their first Republican governor since Elbridge Gerry. Like Monroe, Eustis had served as secretary of war, and he soon set aside Federalist objections about national control of the militia. By renouncing the state's insistence on controlling the militia, Eustis cleared the way for Congress to reimburse Massachusetts and Maine. As he announced to the legislature, "Massachusetts is at length restored to the American family."[6]

However, the Massachusetts polity was never content to be a family member: it wanted to lead. This seemed unlikely in 1815, as the Commonwealth was facing a crisis in confidence. The Hartford Convention had discredited the Massachusetts ideal; its vaunted militia had been revealed as a paper tiger, and its political influence waned as the number of western and southern congressmen increased. To reassert its authority, Massachusetts drew on its intellectual and moral capital, presenting itself as not only the future of the American republic but as the very essence of the American historical experience. Daniel Webster and the founders of the Pilgrim Society, such as Alden Bradford, stumbled into this new approach to American exceptionalism. Webster gave a speech on the two hundredth anniversary of the 1620 landing at Plymouth Rock in which he made the case that New England no longer held itself distinct from the rest of the United States. Instead, Massachusetts, through the Pilgrims, represented the nation's actual foundation and its way forward. But Webster warned that there was a stain on the nation: slavery. He called on all to "pledge ourselves here, upon the rock of Plymouth, to extirpate and destroy it. It is not fit, that the land of the Pilgrims should bear the shame longer." In this way, Massachusetts relentlessly built a mythology of historical preeminence, from the Pilgrims to Bunker Hill. Henry Wadsworth Longfellow, the Maine-born son of a representative to the Hartford Convention, contributed to this mythmaking with his poem "Paul Revere's Ride."[7]

Massachusetts shook off the elements of the Massachusetts ideal relatively rapidly after 1820. In 1833, the Commonwealth disestablished state support for religion without struggle. In 1840, the General Court abolished compulsory militia service in favor of voluntary service. The last fragment of the Massachusetts ideal was the town meeting, which persists as a rural institution. Coincident with the disappearance of the Massachusetts ideal, the Commonwealth transformed itself into an industrial powerhouse. Tentatively at first, but with growing confidence and protected by tariffs, business leaders built textile mills on the state's rivers. In contrast, Maine's industrialization lagged until after the Civil War.[8]

Statehood was only one legacy of the War of 1812. The last of Maine's War of 1812 pensioners died in the 1890s, with a handful of widows enduring into the twentieth century. Even in the twenty-first century, the federal government acts to preserve and honor their memory. As recently as 2012, the Portland grave of a Black navy veteran finally received an official marker. The war's memory lingers on, and bicentennial celebrations in Canada and the United States commemorated that history. Nonetheless, it seems doubtful that a conflict as murky as the War of 1812 will ever fit comfortably into a simplistic and exceptionalist national narrative clouded by insistence on American success. This is especially true in Maine, a state born out of the war's many miseries.[9]

NOTES

ABBREVIATIONS

1812/LLIU: War of 1812, MSS 1776–1879, Lilly Library, Indiana University, Bloomington.

1812/WLC: War of 1812 Collection, William L. Clements Library, University of Michigan, Ann Arbor.

AAS: American Antiquarian Society, Worcester, MA.

ABO: Anonymous British Officer Journal, Special Collections and Archives, Nimitz Library, U.S. Naval Academy, Annapolis, MD.

ACP: Alexander Cochrane Papers, National Library of Scotland, Edinburgh.

ADM1: Admiralty Correspondence, 1660–1976, British National Archives, Kew.

ADM51: Admiralty: Captains' Logs, British National Archives, Kew.

ADM103: Admiralty: Navy Board and Predecessors: Prisoner of War Department and Predecessors: Registers of Prisoners of War, British National Archives, Kew.

ASP:C: *American State Papers, Claims* (Washington, DC: Gales and Seaton, 1834).

ASP:CN: *American State Papers: Commerce and Navigation* (Washington, DC: Gales and Seaton, 1832).

ASP:F: *American State Papers: Finance* (Washington, DC: Gales and Seaton, 1832).

ASP:FR: *American State Papers: Foreign Relations* (Washington, DC: Gales and Seaton, 1833).

ASP:MA: *American State Papers: Military Affairs* (Washington, DC: Gales and Seaton, 1832).

ASP:NA: *American State Papers: Naval Affairs* (Washington, DC: Gales and Seaton, 1834).

BCP: Benjamin Cushing Papers, DeGolyer Library, Southern Methodist University, Dallas.

BPL: Rare Books and Manuscripts Department, Boston Public Library, Boston.

CDB: Coast Defense Books, 1812–15, Massachusetts State Archives, Boston.

CHT: Charles Henry Taylor Collection of Privateering Papers, 1718–1928, MS Am 1087, Houghton Library, Harvard University, Cambridge, MA.

CHW: U.S. Customs House, Waldoboro, Maine, Letterbook, 1803–16, Maine Historical Society, Portland.

CKP: Cyrus King Papers, Rare Book and Manuscript Library, Columbia University, New York.

ABBREVIATIONS

CHM: Center for the History of Medicine, Countway Medical Library, Harvard University Medical School, Boston.
CO41: Colonial Office and Predecessors: Bermuda, Miscellanea, British National Archives, Kew.
CO188: Colonial Office and Predecessors: New Brunswick Original Correspondence, British National Archives, Kew.
CO217: Colonial Office and Predecessors: Nova Scotia and Cape Breton Original Correspondence, British National Archives, Kew.
CTP: Cutts-Thornton Papers, Maine Historical Society, Portland.
CUST34: Board of Customs: Papers Relating to Plantations, British National Archives, Kew
FMDO: First Military District Orders, 1813–15, Massachusetts Historical Society, Boston.
JMP: James Madison Papers, Library of Congress, Washington, DC.
HCA45: High Court of Appeals for Prizes: Case Books, British National Archives, Kew.
HCC: Hebdomary, Hebdomary Soar or Sink Hebdomary Memoranda: Diary, 1811–ca. 1890 (Mss 0034–022), Special Collections, College of Charleston, Charleston, SC.
HDL: Henry Dearborn Letterbooks, New-York Historical Society, New York.
HLH: Houghton Library, Harvard University, Cambridge, MA.
HPB: Henry P. Binney Family Papers, Massachusetts Historical Society, Boston.
HSP: Henry Sewall Papers, Maine State Archives, Augusta.
IHL: Isaac Hull Letterbooks, New-York Historical Society, New York.
ILP: Isaac Lane Papers, Maine Historical Society, Portland.
JLJ: Joseph Leavitt Journal, Bangor Public Library, Bangor, ME.
LoC: Library of Congress, Washington, DC.
M6: Letters Sent by the Secretary of War Relating to Military Affairs, 1800–89, National Archives Records Administration, Washington, DC.
M124: Letters Received by the Secretary of the Navy: Miscellaneous Letters, 1801–84, National Archives Records Administration, Washington, DC.
M125: Letters Received by the Secretary of the Navy: Captains' Letters, 1805–61, National Archives Records Administration, Washington, DC.
M147: Letters Received by the Secretary of the Navy from Commanders, 1804–86, National Archives Records Administration, Washington, DC.
M148: Letters Received from Commissioned Officers below the Rank of Commander and from Warrant Officers, 1802–86," National Archives Records Administration, Washington, DC.
M149: Letters Sent by the Secretary of the Navy to Officers, 1798–1868, National Archives Records Administration, Washington, DC.

ABBREVIATIONS

M179: Miscellaneous Letters of the Department of State, 1789–1906, National Archives Records Administration, Washington, DC.
M221: Letters Received by the Secretary of War, Registered Series, 1801–70, National Archives Records Administration, Washington, DC.
M222: Letters Received by the Secretary of War, Unregistered Series, 1789–1861, National Archives Records Administration, Washington, DC.
M558: U.S. Department of State: War of 1812 Papers, National Archives Records Administration, Washington, DC.
M566: Letters Received by the Office of the Adjutant General, 1805–21, National Archives Records Administration, Washington, DC.
M601: Letters Sent by the Postmaster General, 1789–1836, National Archives Records Administration, Washington, DC.
M625: Area File of the Naval Records Collection, 1775–1910, National Archives Records Administration, Washington, DC.
MaCC/RG21: Massachusetts Federal Circuit Court Records, National Archives Records Administration Northeast, Waltham, MA.
MaDC/RG21: Massachusetts Federal District Court Records, National Archives Records Administration Northeast, Waltham, MA.
MeCC/RG21: Maine Federal Circuit Court Records, National Archives Records Administration Northeast, Waltham, MA.
MeDC/RG21: Maine Federal District Court Records, National Archives Records Administration Northeast, Waltham, MA.
MDD: Moses Davis Diary, Maine State Library, Augusta.
MeHS: Maine Historical Society, Portland.
MeSA: Maine State Archives, Augusta.
MeSM: Maine State Museum, Augusta.
MHS: Massachusetts Historical Society, Boston.
MSA: Massachusetts State Archives, Boston.
MSB: Mary Sewall Buck Journals, Bucksport Historical Society, Bucksport, ME.
NARA: National Archives and Records Administration, Washington, DC.
NEHGS: New England Historic Genealogical Society, Boston.
NHHC: Naval History and Heritage Command Library, Washington, DC.
NYPL: Manuscripts and Archives Division, New York Public Library, Astor, Lenox, and Tilden Foundations, New York.
PAG: Carl D. Prince, ed., *Microform Edition of the Papers of Albert Gallatin* (Philadelphia: Rhistoric, 1969).
PEM: Peabody Essex Museum, Salem, MA.
RCP: Richard Cutts Papers, Albert and Shirley Small Special Collections Library, University of Virginia, Charlottesville.
RG1: Commissioner of Public Records, Nova Scotia Archives and Records Management, Halifax.
RG8/C: British Military and Naval Records, Libraries and Archives Canada, Ottawa.

ABBREVIATIONS

RG8/IV: Halifax Vice-Admiralty Court Records, Libraries and Archives Canada, Ottawa.

RG15: War of 1812 Pension and Bounty Land Warrant Application Files, National Archives and Records Administration, Washington, DC.

RG153: Records of the Office of the Judge Advocate General, Federal Court Martials, National Archives and Records Administration, Washington, DC.

RS7: Records of the Executive Council, Papers, 1784–1877, Provincial Archives of New Brunswick, Fredericton.

RS8: Records of the Executive Council, Miscellaneous 1, Aliens, Provincial Archives of New Brunswick, Fredericton.

RS24: Journals of the House of Assembly, Provincial Archives of New Brunswick, Fredericton.

RS33: Records of Lieutenant Governor George Stracey Smyth, Provincial Archives of New Brunswick, Fredericton.

RS588: Records of the Regular Military, Provincial Archives of New Brunswick, Fredericton.

RKP: Rufus King Papers, MS 1660, New-York Historical Society, New York.

SCA: George J. Mitchell Department of Special Collections and Archives, Hawthorne-Longfellow Library, Bowdoin College, Brunswick, ME.

SFLAC: Sherbrooke Fonds, Library and Archives Canada, Ottawa.

SJC: Supreme Judicial Court Records, Maine State Archives, Augusta.

T967: Copies of Presidential Pardons and Remissions, 1794–1893, National Archives and Records Administration, Washington, DC.

TBP: Thomas Barclay Papers, New-York Historical Society, New York.

TGT: Thomas G. Thornton Papers, Maine Historical Society, Portland.

TGT2: Thomas Gilbert Thornton Papers, MSS 98, R. Stanton Avery Special Collections, New England Historic Genealogical Society, Boston.

UMSC: University of Maine Special Collections, Fogler Library, University of Maine, Orono.

VFP: Vaughan Family Papers, Massachusetts Historical Society, Boston.

WBJ: William Begg Journals, 1812–14, Historical Society of Pennsylvania, Philadelphia.

WDP: William D. Patterson Papers, Maine Historical Society, Portland.

WKP: William King Papers, Maine Historical Society, Portland.

WKP2: William King Papers, Maine State Library, Augusta.

WO25/1298: War Office and Predecessors:Secretary at War, Secretary of State for War, and Related Bodies, Registers Muster Rolls, Sixty-second Regiment of Foot, British National Archives, Kew.

ZKH: Zebulon K. Harmon Papers, Maine Historical Society, Portland.

INTRODUCTION

1. Charles E. Clark and James S. Leamon, "Introduction: Maine in the New Nation," in *Maine in the Early Republic: From Revolution to Statehood*, ed. Charles E. Clark, James S. Leamon, and Karen Bowden (Hanover, NH: University Press of New England, 1988), 1; Gordon S. Wood, *Empire of Liberty: A History of the Early Republic, 1789–1815* (New York: Oxford University Press, 2009), 268–71.
2. James M. Banner, Jr., *To the Hartford Convention: The Federalists and the Origins of Party Politics in Massachusetts, 1789–1815* (New York: Knopf, 1970), 84, 115–21, 168–69; Henry Adams, *History of the United States of America during the Administration of Thomas Jefferson* (New York: Literary Classics of America, 1986), 62; Alan Taylor, *Liberty Men and Great Proprietors: The Revolutionary Settlement on the Maine Frontier, 1760–1820* (Chapel Hill: University of North Carolina Press, 1990), 110; Richard R. Westcott and Edward O. Shriver, "The Separation Movement in the Federal Period," in *Maine: The Pine Tree State from Prehistory to the Present*, ed. Richard W. Judd, Edwin A. Churchill, and Joel W. Eastman (Orono: University of Maine Press, 2011), 178–79.
3. Banner, *To the Hartford Convention*, 110–11; David Hackett Fischer, *The Revolution of American Conservatism: The Federalists in the Era of Jeffersonian Democracy* (New York: Harper and Row, 1965), 175–76; Richard Buel, Jr., *America on the Brink: How the Political Struggle over the War of 1812 Almost Destroyed the Young Republic* (New York: Palgrave Macmillan, 2005), 23–24.
4. The standard work on Maine's statehood is Ronald F. Banks, *Maine Becomes a State: The Movement to Separate Maine from Massachusetts, 1785–1820* (Middletown, CT: Wesleyan University Press, 1970). Also see James S. Leamon, "In Shays's Shadow: Separation and Ratification of the Constitution in Maine," in *In Debt to Shays: The Bicentennial of an Agrarian Rebellion*, ed. Robert A. Gross (Boston: Colonial Society of Massachusetts, 1993), 285–86; and Richard W. Judd, "Introduction," in Judd et al., *Maine*, 7.
5. Donald R. Hickey, "The War of 1812: Still a Forgotten Conflict?" *Journal of Military History*, 65, no. 3 (2001): 768; Samuel E. Morison, "Our Most Unpopular War," in *Dissent in Three American Wars*, ed. Samuel E. Morison, Frederick Merk, and Frank Freidel (Cambridge, MA: Harvard University Press, 1970), 43–44; Banks, *Maine Becomes a State*, chap 4.; Donald Graves, "The Many Wars of 1812," *Journal of the War of 1812*, 8, no. 2 (2004): 1–4; Judd, "Introduction," 6.

CHAPTER 1: "AN EXCEEDINGLY DIRTY AND NASTY PEOPLE"

1. John Adams, letter to Abbé de Mably, 1782, in *The Works of John Adams*, ed. Charles Francis Adams (Boston: Little, Brown, 1851), 5:492–96; James M. Banner, Jr., *To the Hartford Convention: The Federalists and the Origins of Party Politics in Massachusetts, 1785–1815* (New York: Knopf, 1970), 84–85; George Washington, letter to Lund Washington, August 20, 1775, in *The Writings of George Washington from the Original Manuscript Sources, 1745–1799*, ed. John

Clement Fitzpatrick and David Maydole Matteson (Washington, DC: U.S. Government Printing Office, 1931), 3:433; David Bell, *Loyalist Rebellion in New Brunswick* (Halifax, Nova Scotia: Formac, 2013), 137–38; Thomas Jefferson, letter to Henry Dearborn, March 17, 1815, in Brian Steele, "Thomas Jefferson, Coercion, and the Limits of Harmonious Union," *Journal of Southern History* 74, no. 4 (2008): 831; Martyn J. Bowden, "New England Yankee Homeland," in *Homelands: A Geography of Culture and Place across America*, ed. Richard L. Nostrand and Lawrence E. Estaville (Baltimore: Johns Hopkins University Press, 2001) 2, 6, 12–13.

2 Henry Adams, *History of the United States of America during the Administration of Thomas Jefferson* (New York: Literary Classics of America, 1986), 96.

3 Sean Condon, *Shays's Rebellion: Authority and Distress in Post-Revolutionary America* (Baltimore: Johns Hopkins University Press, 2015), 6–11; Peter S. Onuf, "Federalism, Republicanism, and the Origins of American Sectionalism," in *All Over the Map: Rethinking American Regions*, ed. Edward L. Ayers, Patricia Nelson Limerick, Stephen Nissenbaum, and Peter S. Onuf (Baltimore: Johns Hopkins University Press, 1996), 11–37; Banner, *To the Hartford Convention*, 53–54; David Sewall, letter to George Thatcher, November 2, 1785, in *Massachusetts Historical Society Proceedings*, 3rd ser., 58 (October 1924–June 1925): 194; David Hackett Fischer, *The Revolution of American Conservatism: The Federalist Party in the Era of Jeffersonian Democracy* (New York: Harper and Row, 1965), 2–6; Kevin M. Gannon, "Escaping 'Mr. Jefferson's Plan of Destruction': New England Federalists and the Idea of a Northern Confederacy, 1803–1804," *Journal of the Early Republic* 21, no. 3 (2001): 413–43.

4 Richard Buel, Jr., *America on the Brink: How the Political Struggles over the War of 1812 Almost Destroyed the Young Republic* (New York: Palgrave Macmillan, 2005), 25; Ronald P. Formisano, *The Transformation of Political Culture: Massachusetts Parties, 1790s–1840s* (New York: Oxford University Press, 1983), 127–28; James S. Leamon, Richard R. Westcott, and Edward O. Schriver, "Separation and Statehood, 1783–1820," in *Maine: The Pine Tree State from Statehood to the Present*, ed. Richard W. Judd, Edwin A. Churchill, and Joel W. Eastman (Orono: University of Maine Press, 2011), 171–72.

5 Buel, *America on the Brink*, 25; William Pencak, "The Fine Theoretical Government of Massachusetts Is Prostrated to the Earth: The Response to Shays's Rebellion Reconsidered," 121–43, and James S. Leamon, "In Shays's Shadow: Separation and Ratification of the Constitution in Maine," 281–96, both in *In Debt to Shays: The Bicentennial of an Agrarian Rebellion*, ed. Robert A. Gross (Boston: Colonial Society of Massachusetts, 1993); Leamon et al., "Separation and Statehood," 177–78.

6 Leamon et al., "Separation and Statehood," 178–79; C. Edward Skeen, *1816: America Rising* (Lexington: University of Kentucky Press, 2003), 157; John Adams, letter to Daniel Cony, February 1, 1819, in John Adams Papers, MHS.

7 Patricia Q. Wall, *Lives of Consequence: Blacks in Early Kittery and Berwick in the Massachusetts Province of Maine* (Portsmouth, NH: Portsmouth Marine Society, 2017); Bryan C. Weare, "Slaves and Free Blacks in Mid-Eighteenth to Mid-Nineteenth Century Cape Neddick, Maine," *Maine History* 51, no. 3

(2017): 203–27; Jean M. O'Brien, *Firsting and Lasting: Writing Indians Out of Existence in New England* (Minneapolis: University of Minnesota Press, 2010); Micah A. Pawling, *Wabanaki Homeland and the New State of Maine: The 1820 Journal and Plans of Survey of Joseph Treat* (Amherst: University of Massachusetts Press, 2007); Thomas B. Wait, letter to George Thatcher, January 24, 1810, in William C. di Giacomantonio, ed., *The Insurgent Delegate: Selected Letters and Other Writings of George Thatcher* (Boston: Colonial Society of Massachusetts, 2019), cix.

8   Orchard Cook, letter to John Farley, Peleg Tallman, William King, and George Ulmer, February 27, 1806, WKP.

9   Moses Greenleaf, *A Statistical View of the District of Maine* (Boston: Cummings and Hilliard, 1816), 46; Andrew Sherburne, *Memoirs of Andrew Sherburne: A Pensioner of the Navy of the Revolution* (Providence: Brown, 1831), 217. The root of the couple's suspicion was based on First Chronicles 21:1–4, "And Satan stood up against Israel, and provoked David to number Israel." Also see Paul Goodman, *The Democratic-Republicans of Massachusetts: Politics in a Young Republic* (Westport, CT: Greenwood, 1964), 119.

10 Silas Lee, letter to George Thatcher, May 9, 1788, Silas Lee Correspondence, BPL.

11 Stephen Marini, "Religious Revolution in the District of Maine, 1780–1820," in *Maine in the Early Republic: From Revolution to Statehood*, ed. Charles E. Clark, James S. Leamon, and Karen Bowden (Hanover, NH: University Press of New England, 1988), 121–28; George Augustus Wheeler, *History of Brunswick, Topsham and Harpswell, Maine: Including the Ancient Territory Known as Pejepscot* (Boston: Mudge and Son, 1877), 736–37; Mary Ellen Chase, *Jonathan Fisher: Maine Parson, 1768–1847* (Boston: Macmillan, 1948), 70; Elizabeth Mancke, *The Fault Lines of Empire: Political Differentiation in Massachusetts and Nova Scotia, Ca., 1760–1830* (New York: Routledge, 2005), 117–19.

12 Lawrence Delbert Cress, *Citizens in Arms: The Army and the Militia in American Society to the War of 1812* (Chapel Hill: University of North Carolina Press, 1982), chaps. 5 and 6; C. Edward Skeen, *Citizen Soldiers in the War of 1812* (Lexington: University Press of Kentucky, 1999), 178–79; commentary in *Eastern Argus* (Portland), July 12, 1805, and July 5, 1806; William H. Sumner, *An Inquiry into the Importance of the Militia to a Free Commonwealth in a Letter from William H. Sumner to John Adams, Late President of the United States; with His Answer* (Boston: Cummings and Hilliard, 1823), 7–8, 32.

13 Edward M. Coffman, "The Duality of the American Military Tradition: A Commentary," *Journal of Military History*, 64, no. 4 (2000): 967–980; Adjutant General, "General Orders, July 7, 1800," in Broadsides, LoC; Banner, *To the Hartford Convention*, 55–56; Sumner, *An Inquiry into the Importance of the Militia*, 38–39.

14 Joshua M. Smith, "The Yankee Soldier's Might: The District of Maine and the Reputation of the Massachusetts Militia, 1800–1812," *New England Quarterly* 84, no. 4 (2011): 247. For complaints regarding militia training, see anonymous, letter to James Madison, December 16, 1809, M221. Also see *Portland Gazette*, February 11, 1811.

15 Jonathan Fisher, diary entry, October 31, 1811, Jonathan Fisher Journal, AAS; William L. Welch, "Hanging Ebenezer Ball," *Maine History* 45, no. 2 (2010): 151–67; Chase, *Jonathan Fisher*, 190–91.

16 Ronald F. Banks, *Maine Becomes a State: The Movement to Separate Maine from Massachusetts, 1785–1820* (Middletown, CT: Wesleyan University Press, 1970), 7–11; Greenleaf, *Statistical View*, 82–84; Frederick S. Allis, Jr., ed., *William Bingham's Maine Lands, 1790–1820* (Boston: Colonial Society of Massachusetts, 1954), chap. 1, passim.

17 Greenleaf, *Statistical View*, 33; Laurel Ulrich, *A Midwife's Tale: The Life of Martha Ballard, Based on Her Diary, 1785–1812* (New York: Knopf, 1990), 77–80; United States and Tench Coxe, *Tabular Statements of the Several Branches of American Manufactures* (Philadelphia: Cornman, 1813), 3–7, 22. For an overview of Maine economic activity, see James B. Vickery, Richard W. Judd, and Sheila McDonald, "Maine Agriculture, 1783–1861," in Judd et al., *Maine*, 242–61.

18 Wayne M. O'Leary, *Maine Sea Fisheries: The Rise and Fall of a Native Industry, 1830–1890* (Boston: Northeastern University Press, 1996), 83, 86. For opinions regarding fishermen and lumbermen, see "The American Fisherman," *Freeman's Friend* (Portland), October 7, 1809; and Allis, *William Bingham's Maine Lands*, 14–15

19 Alan Taylor, *Liberty Men and Great Proprietors: The Revolutionary Settlement of the Maine Frontier, 1760–1820* (Chapel Hill: University of North Carolina Press, 1990), 75–78, 14–18, 21–29. For shock in old Massachusetts that Maine voters rejected elitists such as Henry Knox as their political leaders, see *Newburyport (MA) Herald*, June 8, 1804. For shifting attitudes on squatters, see John Lowell, Jr., letter to Timothy Pickering, December 3, 1814, in Henry Adams, ed., *Documents Relating to New England Federalism* (Boston: Little, Brown, 1877), 410; "Alarm!," *Democrat* (Boston), January 4, 1809; "Squatters," *Eastern Argus*, March 20, 1809; and *Boston Patriot*, March 7, 1810

20 G. A. Rawlyk, *The Canada Fire: Radical Evangelicism in British North America, 1775–1812* (Kingston, Ontario: McGill-Queen's University Press, 1994), 129–40; Marini, "Religious Revolution," 122, 129–40; Mancke, *Fault Lines of Empire*, 119–20; Shelby M. Balik, *Rally the Scattered Believers: Northern New England's Religious Geography* (Bloomington: Indiana University Press, 2014), 88–89; Ulrich, *A Midwife's Tale*, 296–300.

21 Louis Clinton Hatch, *History of Bowdoin College* (Portland, ME: Loring, Short, and Harmon, 1927), 19; Neal, *Wandering Recollections*, 66. For hostility to Methodist preachers, see Abel Stevens, *Memorials of the Introduction of Methodism into the Eastern States* (New York: Carlton and Phillips, 1854), 160–61; and Marie L. Sacks, "The Two Faces of Ballstown: Religion, Governance, and Cultural Values on the Maine Frontier, 1760–1820," *Maine History* 43, no. 1 (2007): 56.

22 Abraham Cummings, letters to Alexander McLean, August 7, 1803, and January 18, 1804, in Alden Bradford Reports, Boston Athenaeum; Abraham Cummings, *Immortality Proved by the Testimony of Sense* (Portland, ME: Lovell, 1859); William Batchelder, letter to John Peak, February 7, 1805, in Edmund

Worth, *Centennial Discourse Delivered on the One-Hundredth Anniversary of the Baptist Church in North Berwick, Me.* (Biddeford, ME: Butler, 1868), 18–19.

23   Stephanie Kermes, *Creating an American Identity: New England, 1789–1825* (New York: Palgrave Macmillan, 2008), 172; Joseph A. Conforti, *Imagining New England: Explorations of Regional Identity from the Pilgrims to the Mid-Twentieth Century* (Chapel Hill: University of North Carolina Press, 2001), 113, 153–54.

24   For David Cobb's activities, see Banks, *Maine Becomes a State*, 49; and David Cobb, letter to Henry Knox, August 30, 1795, in Allis, *William Bingham's Maine Lands*, 533–34; Taylor, *Liberty Men*, 55–56.

25   Samuel S. Wilde, letter to David Cobb, January 2, 1802, in Allis, *William Bingham's Maine Lands*, 1141–42; anonymous, "Col. John Black and Family," *Bangor Historical Magazine* 4, no. 4 (1888): 61–65.

26   Adams, *Documents Relating to New-England Federalism*, 283–84; Banner, *To the Hartford Convention*, 53–54; Fischer, *Revolution of American Conservatism*, 2–6, 258; Abraham Cummings, *The Present Times Perilous. A Sermon, Preached at Sullivan, on the Annual Fast, April 25, 1799* (Castine, ME.: Waters, 1799), 13; Jonathan J. Den Hartog, *Federalist Politics and Religious Struggle in the New American Nation* (Charlottesville: University of Virginia Press, 2015), 80–82; David Sewall, letter to George Thatcher, November 2, 1785, in *Massachusetts Historical Society Proceedings*, 3rd ser., 58 (October 1924–June 1925): 194.

27   Samuel Eliot Morison, "Memoir of Alden Bradford," *Proceedings of the Massachusetts Historical Society* 55 (October 1921–June 1922): 153–64; Alden Bradford, *An Oration, Pronounced at Wiscasset, on the Fourth of July, 1804* (Wiscasset, ME: Babson and Rust, 1804), passim.

28   Banner, *To the Hartford Convention*, 129–30; Banks, *Maine Becomes a State*, 42, 50–51; Goodman, *Democratic-Republicans*, 154–55; Taylor, *Liberty Men*, 215–17.

29   Goodman, *Democratic-Republicans*, 138–39; Taylor, *Liberty Men*, 211–12. On the low regard Federalists initially had for runners, see *Gazette of Maine* (Buckstown), April 10, 1806; Noble E. Cunningham, Jr., *The Jeffersonian Republicans in Power: Party Operations, 1801–1809* (Chapel Hill: University of North Carolina Press, 1963), 136–37; Bradford, *An Oration, Pronounced at Wiscasset*, 8–9; *Boston Centinel*, April 3, 1809; Peleg Tallman, letter to Denny McCobb, March 23, 1804, in William M. Emery, *Honorable Peleg Tallman: His Ancestors and Descendants* (Boston: Thomas Todd, 1935), 37–38; and Fischer, *Revolution of American Conservatism*, 267. On Federalist runners, see *Eastern Argus*, April 30, 1812.

30   Goodman, *Democratic-Republicans*, 146, 149; Wilde, letter to Cobb, January 2, 1803. For commentary on Dearborn's patronage, see *Columbian Centinel* (Boston), August 29, 1804; and *Eastern Argus*, October 14, 1824. Also see Joshua Shaw, letter to Orchard Cook, January 13, 1806, M418; and petitioners, letter to Albert Gallatin, January 12, 1806, M418.

31   Theodore J. Crackel, *Mr. Jefferson's Army: Political and Social Reform of the Military Establishment, 1801–1809* (New York: New York University Press, 1987), 37–40; William B. Skelton, *An American Profession of Arms: The Army*

Officer Corps, 1784–1861 (Lawrence: University Press of Kansas, 1992), 25–29, 75, 77–78. On Knox's construction efforts in Newport, see *Rhode-Island Republican* (Newport), September 18, 1802; and *New England Palladium* (Boston), March 1, 1803, and September 23, 1803.

32 Carl D. Prince, *Federalists and the Origins of the U.S. Civil Service* (New York: New York University Press, 1977) 37–40, 42, 206–7, 235; Gideon Granger, letter to Horatio Balch, and Gideon Granger, letter to James Thomas, both July 20, 1808, M601. On the postmaster's tribulations, see *Eastern Argus*, June 19, 1806, and May 11, 1809.

33 Prince, *Federalists and the Origins of the U.S. Civil Service*, 149–50; Goodman, *Democratic-Republicans*, 122, 124, 146–47; Levi Lincoln, letter to Thomas Jefferson, February 26, 1808, in Papers of Thomas Jefferson, LoC; Frederick Gardiner Fassett, *A History of Newspapers in the District of Maine* (Orono: Maine University Press, 1932), 107; Banks, *Maine Becomes a State*, 44–46; Richard Cutts, letter to Thomas G. Thornton, November 14, 1803, CTP.

34 John Binney, letter to Amos Binney, May 7, 1811, HPB; Taylor, *Liberty Men*, 219–20.

35 Goodman, *Democratic-Republicans*, 155–58; Banks, *Maine Becomes a State*, 54–55; Taylor, *Liberty Men*, 218–25.

36 George Ulmer, letter to William Donnison, May 6, 1807, in Adjutant General Correspondence, MSA. Newspaper editors avidly followed militia politics: for Wardwell, see "Court Martial," *Portland Gazette*, October 28, 1805; for Ulmer's appointment as colonel, see "Communicated," *Portland Gazette*, February 9, 1807; for general commentary on the politicization of Maine's militia, see "Lincoln, Hancock, and Washington," *Portland Gazette* March 7, 1807. Also see "Complaint," *Freeman's Friend* (Portland), October 30, 1805; "Court-Martial," *Eastern Argus*, October 25, 1805; and "Division Orders," *Gazette of Maine*, March 20, 1806.

37 On the militia mutiny against Sewall and its aftermath, see *Portland Gazette*, February 9, 1807, February 23, 1807, and March 9, 1807; and *Gazette of Maine*, March 26, 1807. On the furor over appointing King as a militia general, see *Portland Gazette*, February 29, 1808; *Columbian Centinel*, March 4, 1807; and *Democrat*, May 23, 1807.

38 The standard work on the embargo is Burton Spivak, *Jefferson's English Crisis: Commerce, Embargo, and the Republican Revolution* (Charlottesville: University Press of Virginia, 1979). Also see Henry Sewall, letter to James Sullivan, July 22, 1807, in Adjutant General Correspondence, MSA; *ASP:NA*, 1:168; *ASP:MA*, 1:221. On Henry Dearborn's son and fortifications, see *Eastern Argus*, May 26, 1808, June 2, 1808, November 30, 1808, and March 16, 1809. Also see Crackel, *Mr. Jefferson's Army*, 169–71; Robert W. Coakley, *The Role of Federal Military Forces in Domestic Disorders, 1789–1878* (Washington, DC: U.S. Army, Center of Military History, 1989), 83–84; and Leonard W. Levy, *Jefferson and Civil Liberties: The Darker Side* (Cambridge, MA: Belknap, 1963).

39 Joyce Butler, "Rising Like a Phoenix: Commerce in Southern Maine, 1775–1830," in *Agreeable Situations: Society, Commerce, and Art in Southern Maine*,

1780–1830, ed. Laura Fecych Sprague (Boston: Northeastern University Press, 1987), 27–28; David Cobb, letter to Charles W. Hare, April 16, 1808, in Allis, *William Bingham's Maine Lands*, 1228–29; George Herbert, letter to Daniel Webster, March 13, 1809, in *The Papers of Daniel Webster*, vol. 1, *Correspondence, 1798–1824*, ed. Charles M. Wiltse and Harold D. Moser (Hanover, NH: University of New England Press, 1974), 107–8; Steele, "Thomas Jefferson," 836, 843; James Madison, letter to Thomas Jefferson, August 10, 1808, in Thomas Jefferson Papers, LoC; Levy, *Jefferson and Civil Liberties*, 104–5, 108–9.

40 Leonard D. White, *The Jeffersonians: A Study in Administrative History, 1801–1829* (New York: Macmillan, 1959), 440–42, 455–56; Douglas Lamar Jones, "'The Caprice of Juries': The Enforcement of the Jeffersonian Embargo in Massachusetts," *American Journal of Legal History* 24 (1980): 319–20. On Sewall instructing a jury, see *Eastern Argus*, September 22, 1808;.

41 Charles Morris, letter to Lemuel Morris, October 7, 1808, in Miscellaneous Manuscripts, NYHS; Christopher McKee, *A Gentlemanly and Honorable Profession: The Creation of the U.S. Naval Officer Corps, 1794–1815* (Annapolis, MD: Naval Institute Press, 1991), 214, 464; John Smith, letter to Robert Smith, June 25, 1808, M147. On tarring and feathering, see *Portland Gazette*, December 12, 1808. On gunboats enforcing the embargo in Casco Bay, see *Freeman's Friend*, June 25, 1808, and July 9, 1808. Also see William Bainbridge, letters to Robert Smith, July 9, 1808, and August 18, 1808, M125; Isaac Ilsley, letter to William Bainbridge, November 1, 1808, M125; William Bainbridge, letter to Robert Smith, November 1, 1808, M125; William Bainbridge, letter to Robert Smith, November 21, 1808, M125; "Report on the state and condition of Gunboat 79, November 2, 1808, M125; William Eustis, letter to Richard Cutts, November 13, 1808, 1812/WLC; Henry Dearborn, letter to Albert Gallatin, October 29, 1808, PAG; Isaac Ilsley, letter to Daniel Ilsley, November 6, 1808, PAG; and William Widgery, letters to Richard Cutts, December 8, 1808, and December 24, 1808, RCP.

42 W.G. Pillsbury, letter to commanders of the U.S. ships *Chesapeake, Wasp, Argus*, November 15, 1808, M149; Joseph Chandler, letter to Henry Dearborn, December 6, 1808, M221; Joseph Chandler, letter to Henry Dearborn, November 19, 1808, M221.

43 Henry Dearborn, letter to state governors, January 17, 1809, in Thomas Jefferson Papers, LoC; J. C. A. Stagg, *Mr. Madison's War: Politics, Diplomacy, and Warfare in the Early American Republic, 1783–1830* (Princeton, NJ: Princeton University Press, 1983), 138–39. For complaints regarding how the militia were called out, see *Portland Gazette*, January 2, 1809, and March 6, 1809. Also see Don Higginbotham, "The Federalized Militia Debate: A Neglected Aspect of Second Amendment Scholarship," *William and Mary Quarterly*, 3rd ser., 55, no. 1 (1998), 54–55; Abiel Wood, Jr., letter to William King, December 1, 1808, WKP; and Buel, *America on the Brink*, 72–79.

44 Jotham Sewall, letter to Henry Sewall, January 15, 1809, HSP; "Company Rolls of Captains Andrew Grant and John Whiting, January 20, 1809," UMSC; "Claims for Services and Expenses in Assisting to Enforce the Embargo Laws

in Massachusetts, in 1809," *ASP:C*, 1:382–83; Coakley, *Role of Federal Military Forces*, 88–90. For Belfast complaints, see "Belfast Town Meeting," *Portland Gazette*, March 6, 1809, and April 3, 1809. Also see William Duane, letter to James Madison, December 1, 1809, JMP; and White, *The Jeffersonians*, 466–467; .

45 Banks, *Maine Becomes a State*, 57. On the quandary in which Maine's Republicans found themselves, see *Freeman's Friend*, October 15, 1808; *Eastern Argus*, November 3, 1808; *Essex Register* (Salem, MA), June 22, 1808; and *Portland Gazette*, December 19, 1808, and May 29, 1809. Also see George Henry Haynes, "Letters of Samuel Taggart, Part I," *Proceedings of the American Antiquarian Society*, new ser., 33 (April–October 1923): 333; Goodman, *Democratic-Republicans*, 194–95; and Orchard Cook, letter to William King, February 12, 1809, WKP.

46 John Binney, letter to his wife, April 27, 1809, in William D. Patterson, *Proceedings of the Four Hundred and Nineteenth Quarterly Meeting of the Wiscasset Fire Society* (Wiscasset, ME: Sheepscot Echo, 1905), 17–19.

47 Henry Sewall, letter to James Sullivan, July 22, 1807, in Adjutant General Correspondence, MSA; James W. North, *The History of Augusta, from the Earliest Settlement to the Present Time* (Augusta, ME: Clapp and North, 1870, 356–83); Ulrich, *A Midwife's Tale*, 318–20.

48 Taylor, *Liberty Men*, 193, 224, 227; di Giacomantonio, *The Insurgent Delegate*, xcii–xciii.

49 Stanley Elkins and Eric McKitrick, *The Age of Federalism: The Early American Republic, 1788–1800* (New York: Oxford University Press, 1993), 556–58; George Athan Billias, *Elbridge Gerry: Founding Father and Republican Statesman* (New York: McGraw-Hill, 1976), 314–15; Formisano, *Transformation of Political Culture*, 72–74.

50 Goodman, *Democratic-Republicans*, 142–43; Banner, *To the Hartford Convention*, 287–88, 364; Formisano, *Transformation of Political Culture*, 34, 37; Taylor, *Liberty Men*, 211. For the quotation about Maine squatters, see *Eastern Argus*, April 21, 1818.

51 David Cobb, letter to G. W. Hare, August 7, 1814, in David Cobb Papers, MHS; Billias, *Elbridge Gerry*, 316–23; Buel, *America on the Brink*, 144–49.

52 For newspaper coverage of Cobb's incautious remarks, see *Eastern Argus*, March 8, 1810; and *Castine Eagle*, March 8, 1810. Also see Stephen Marini, "Religious Revolution," 121–28, 140; and Mancke, *Fault Lines of Empire*, 119–20.

53 Shelby M. Balik, *Rally the Scattered Believers: Northern New England's Religious Geography* (Bloomington: Indiana University Press, 2014), 94–95; Conrad Wright, "The Dedham Case Revisited," *Proceedings of the Massachusetts Historical Society* 100 (1988): 36–37; Johann N. Neem, "The Elusive Common Good: Religion and Civil Society in Massachusetts, 1780–1833," *Journal of the Early Republic* 24, no. 3 (2004): 381–417; Goodman, *Democratic-Republicans*, 164–66.

54 Thomas Jefferson, letter to Henry Dearborn, August 14, 1811, in *The Papers of Thomas Jefferson*, Retirement Series, vol. 4, *18 June 1811 to 30 April 1812*, ed. J. Jefferson Looney (Princeton, NJ: Princeton University Press, 2007), 82–84; Billias, *Elbridge Gerry*, 316–17; Abiel Wood, letter to William King, April 9, 1809, WKP. For Bradford's prolix response to his dismissal, see "To His Excellency Elbridge Gerry, Esquire, Governor of Massachusetts," *Boston Commercial Gazette*, October 21, 1811. For his supporters outrage, see *Herald of Liberty* (Augusta), October 29, 1811.

55 Banks, *Maine Becomes a State*, 44–47; Petty Vaughan, letter to William O. Vaughan, March 9, 1812, in Petty Vaughan Letterbook, VFP; Henry Sewall, diary entry, May 5, 1812, in Henry Sewall Diary, MHS; Elbridge Gerry, letter to James Madison, April 5, 1812, in Elbridge Gerry Papers, MHS; Elbridge Gerry, letter to James Madison, May 19, 1812, JMP.

56 Richard Cutts, letter to James Madison, April 8, 1812, JMP; Formisano, *Transformation of Political Culture*, 57–58; Alden Bradford, *History of Massachusetts, from 1790 to 1820* (Boston: Eastburn, 1829), 119–20; Banner, *To the Hartford Convention*, 275–76; Stagg, *Mr. Madison's War*, 254–57; di Giacomantonio, *The Insurgent Delegate*, cvi.

57 Billias, *Elbridge Gerry*, 310–11, 324. On Federalists mocking Gerry's views, see Buel, *America on the Brink*, 147–49. Also see Jonathan J. Den Hartog, *Patriotism and Piety: Federalist Politics and Religious Struggle in the New American Nation* (Charlottesville: University of Virginia Press, 2015), 86–88.

58 Alden Bradford, *Biography of the Honorable Caleb Strong, Several Years Governor of the State of Massachusetts* (Boston: West, Richardson, and Lord), 1820.

59 On the ill-fated Seventeenth Division, see *American Advocate*, May 26, June 25, July 7, and July 9, 1812. Also see Massachusetts General Court, "Commonwealth of Massachusetts. Council Chamber, June 19th, 1812," in Broadsides, LoC; and Thomas Fillebrown, letter to Samuel Currier, December 27, 1813, in Charles B. Fillebrown, *Genealogy of the Fillebrown Family, with Biographical Sketches* (Boston, 1910), 34–35.

CHAPTER 2: WAR COMES TO MAINE

1 For criticism of Widgery's speeches, see "Widgery . . . again," *Portland Gazette*, January 13, 1812. For a defense of his speeches, see *Eastern Argus* (Portland), February 20, 1812.

2 Ronald F. Banks, *Maine Becomes a State: The Movement to Separate Maine from Massachusetts, 1785–1820* (Middletown, CT: Wesleyan University Press, 1970), 378–79). For Widgery's unconventional speeches and aphorisms, see *Eastern Argus*, January 30, 1812; and "Mr. Widgery," *Boston Repertory*, January 10, 1812.

3 Donald R. Hickey, *The War of 1812: A Forgotten Conflict, Bicentennial Edition* (Urbana: University of Illinois Press, 2012), 31–32; J. C. A. Stagg, *Mr. Madison's War: Politics, Diplomacy, and Warfare in the Early American Republic, 1783–1830* (Princeton, NJ: Princeton University Press, 1980), 87, 148; Kevin D. McCranie, *Utmost Gallantry: The U.S. and Royal Navies at Sea in the War of 1812* (Annapolis, MD: Naval Institute Press, 2011), 19.

4   For recruiting ads, see "Liberal Encouragement," *Eastern Argus*, January 16, 1812. Also see Henry Dearborn, letter to E. Ripley, June 5, 1812, in Papers of Henry Dearborn, 1801–14, Ohio State University, Columbus; and William B. Skelton, "High Army Leadership in the Era of the War of 1812: The Making and Remaking of the Officer Corps," *William and Mary Quarterly*, 51, no. 2 (1994): 253–74.

5   Denver Brunsman, "Subjects vs. Citizens: Impressment and Identity in the Anglo-American Atlantic," *Journal of the Early Republic* 30, no. 4 (2010): 572. For accounts of impressed Mainers, see *Eastern Argus*.

6   Diggio's impressment is detailed in "Impressment of Seamen," *Portland Gazette*, May 13, 1811; and "List of Wrongs. Impressment!," *Eastern Argus*, May 16, 1811. Also see Thomas Barclay and George Lockhart Rives, *Selections from the Correspondence of Thomas Barclay* (New York: Harper, 1894), 294–96; and Andrew Lambert, *The Challenge: Britain against America in the Naval War of 1812* (London: Faber and Faber, 2012), 41–46.

7   Paul Gilje, *Free Trade and Sailors' Rights in the War of 1812* (Cambridge: Cambridge University Press, 2013), chap. 12, passim; Joyce Butler, "Rising Like a Phoenix: Commerce in Southern Maine, 1775–1830," in *Agreeable Situations: Society, Commerce, and Art in Southern Maine, 1780–1830*, ed. Laura Fecych Sprague (Boston: Northeastern University Press, 1987), 24, 27.

8   *ASP:FR*, 3:10–12; "British Friendship," *Eastern Argus*, June 25, 1807; H. F. Pullen, "The Attempted Mutiny Onboard HM Sloop *Columbine* on 1 August 1809," *Nova Scotia Historical Quarterly* 8, no. 4 (1978): 309–18; Keith Mercer, "Northern Exposure: Resistance to Naval Impressment in British North America, 1775–1815," *Canadian Historical Review* 91, no. 2 (2010): 199–232.

9   Samuel Eliot Morison, "The Henry-Crillon Affair of 1812," *Proceedings of the Massachusetts Historical Society*, 3rd ser., 69 (October 1947–May 1950): 207–31; Stagg, *Mr. Madison's War*, 92–95.

10 William Girod, letter to John Wentworth, May 28, 1808, in David W. Parker, "Secret Reports of John Howe, 1808," *American History Review* 17 (October 1911): 74–75; John Wentworth, letter to Lord Castlereagh, October 26, 1807, CO 217/140 "Nancy," letter to G. C. Berkeley, January 18, 1808, 1812/LLIU.

11 For Nye's defiance of the Bostonians, see "Outrage," *Essex Register* (Salem, MA), June 27, 1812; and "From Hallowell, July 7," *Boston Patriot*, July 11, 1812.

12 "Declaration of War, by Express!!!," *Eastern Argus*, June 23, 1812; Moses Davis, diary entry, June 23, 1812, MDD; Henry Dearborn, letter to Jacob Eustis, September 28, 1812, 1812/WLC.

13 The original issue of Augusta's *Herald of Liberty* newspaper has yet to be found, but other newspapers picked the story; see *Boston Repertory*, July 7, 1812. Also see James W. North, *The History of Augusta, from the Earliest Settlement to the Present Time* (Augusta, ME: Clapp and North, 1870), 407–8.

14 Anonymous, diary entry, June 26, 1812, HCC; Joseph Leavitt, diary entry, April 4, 1812, JLJ; Mary Sewall Buck, diary entry, June 1812, MSB; "From the

Inhabitants of Portland, Massachusetts," July 6, 1812, HDL; "From the Inhabitants of Boothbay, District of Maine, July 7, 1812," HDL; Henry Dearborn, letter to James Madison, June 26, M221; petition from the citizens of Belfast, July 7, 1812, M625; inhabitants of Bristol, letter to Paul Hamilton, August 24, 1812, M124; Boothbay Committee of Safety, letter to Paul Hamilton, November 5, 1812, M124; Orchard Cook, letter to Paul Hamilton, July 12, 1812, M124; Joseph Farley, letter to Paul Hamilton, August 27, 1812, M124; Joseph Storer et al., letter to John Armstrong, April 10, 1813, M221; Henry Dearborn, letter to Jacob Eustis, June 30, 1812, HDL; Henry Dearborn, letters to Moses B. Porter, July 6, 1812, and July 9, 1812, HDL; Henry Dearborn, letter to Jacob Eustis, July 17, 1812, HDL.

15   Duncan McColl, "Memoir," quoted in Harold A. Davis, *An International Community on the St. Croix, 1604–1930* (Orono, ME, 1950), 104–5; Samuel Cook, letter to S. Kendall, July 12, 1812, in William H. Houlton and Family Papers, Minnesota Historical Society, Saint Paul.

16   Amasa Loring, *History of Piscataquis County, Maine: From its Earliest Settlement to 1880* (Portland, ME: Hoyt, Fogg, and Donham, 1880), 222–23; John Stuart, *Laugh and Grow Fat: Incidents in the Life of Capt. John Stuart* (Boston: Smith & Brother, 1874), 13–15; John F. Pratt, "Petition of Inhabitants of Penobscot River above Orono, 1812," *Bangor Historical Magazine* 5 (1890): 163–64; orders, Tenth Division, Massachusetts Militia, July 3, 1812, in Eastport Militia Papers, private collection.

17   Tribal conference, October 3, 1812, CO 188/19; Jonathan Odell, memorandum concerning tribal neutrality, July 10, 1812, in Records of George Stracey Smyth, RS 33: Records of the Executive Council, Papers, 1784–1877; War of 1812 Proclamations, July 10, 1812, RS7: George Stracey Smyth, letter to Earl Bathurst, August 31, 1812, in Indian Affairs Documents, Special Collections, Harriet Irving Library, University of New Brunswick, Fredericton; statement of Penobscot neutrality, February 6, 1813, in Council Files, MSA; David Owen, letter to Francis Joseph, October 3, 1812, CO 188/19

18   Elias Hutchins and William M. Bryant, *The Old Sailor: A Thrilling Narrative of the Life and Adventures of Elias Hutchins* (Cape Porpoise, ME: Atlantic Fireman's Educational Association, 1853), 24–25, 30–32. For John Nichols's deposition and his tribulations, see *Eastern Argus*, August 5, 1813. Also see Henry Otis Thayer, *Second War with England: Sundry Papers* (Bath, ME: Times Company, n.d.), 20–21; and Mathew Carey, *The Olive Branch, or, Faults on Both Sides, Federal and Democratic: A Serious Appeal on the Necessity of Mutual Forgiveness and Harmony* (Freeport, NY: Books for Libraries Press, 1969), 217.

19   Dwight F. Henderson, *Congress, Courts, and Criminals: The Development of Federal Criminal Law, 1801–1829* (Westport, CT: Greenwood, 1985), 99–101. For an example of Thornton's announcements, see *Eastern Argus*, July 30, 1812. Also see Edward T. McCarron, "Facing the Atlantic: The Irish Merchant Community of Lincoln County, 1780–1820," in *They Change Their Sky: The Irish in Maine*, ed. Michael C. Connolly (Orono: University of Maine Press, 2004), 73–74; John Dormer, statement, September 4, 1812, TGT2; and Augustus Davison, statement, November 17, 1812, TGT2.

20 George L. Hosmer, *An Historical Sketch of the Town of Deer Isle, Maine* (Boston: Stanley and Usher, 1886), 155–56; Petty Vaughan, letter to Messrs. Richards & Jones, March 2, 1813, VFP; Petty Vaughan, letter to Samuel G. Perkins, June 4, 1813, VFP; Joseph Farley, letter to William Jones, January 31, 1814, CHW; Joseph Farley, letter to George Washington Campbell, October 10, 1814, CHW.
21 Thomas G. Thornton, letter to John Mason, November 29, 1813, TGT; Frederick G. Fassett, Jr., *A History of Newspapers in the District of Maine, 1785–1820* (Orono: Maine University Press, 1932), 168–69.
22 Philip J. Lampi, "The Federalist Party Resurgence, 1808–1816: Evidence from the New Nation Votes Database," *Journal of the Early Republic* 33, no. 2 (2013): 268; Joseph Leavitt, diary entry, November 2, 1812, JLJ.
23 *Weekly Visitor* (Kennebunk, ME), October 3, 1812; Henry S. Burrage, "Some Letters of Richard Cutts," *Collections and Proceedings of the Maine Historical Society*, 2nd ser., 9 (1898): 39–41; Cyrus King, letter to Rufus King, December 17, 1812, RKP.
24 For insults to Widgery and Carr, see *Weekly Messenger*, April 17, 1812; *Eastern Argus*, July 23, 1812; *Essex Register*, July 22, 1812; and *Boston Repertory*, July 24, 1812. Also see T. H. Haskell, *The New Gloucester Centennial, September 7, 1874* (Portland, ME: Hoyt, Fogg, and Donham, 1875), 80; and J. K. Whitney, letter to John Holmes, October 11, 1814, in Charles A. Flagg, "Relating to the War of 1812," *Sprague's Journal of Maine History* 6 (November 1918–January 1919): 126–28.
25 "From the Republicans of Frankfort, District of Maine," July 4, 1812, JMP; "From the Republican Citizens of York County, District of Maine," September 10, 1812, JMP; letter from the inhabitants of Lyman, July 13, 1812, M179; Biddeford selectmen, letter to James Madison, July 27, 1812, M179; town of Wells, letter to James Madison, July 27, 1812, M179; "Columbia; War of 1812," *Machias (ME) Union*, September 6, 1881. For North Yarmouth's response to the war, see *Portland Gazette*, July 27, 1812.
26 "Meeting of the Delegates of the different towns in the County of Lincoln," August 3, 1812, 1812/LLIU; William Crosby, *An Address to the Electors of the County of Hancock with the Resolutions Adopted at the Convention, Held at Buckstown, September 15th, 1812* (Castine, ME: Hall, 1812); "Civil War Threatened," *Portland Gazette*, September 28, 1812.
27 Tobias Lord, letter to Richard Cutts, December 1, 1812, RCP; Josiah Fickett, letter to Paul Hamilton, February 10, 1812, M124; Asa Clapp and Matthew Cobb, letter to Paul Hamilton, April 16, 1812, M124; Francis Cook, letter to Paul Hamilton, July 21, 1812, M124.
28 For a full report of the cattle-smuggling affair, see "Communication," *American Advocate*, October 29, 1812; and *Grand Jury Indictment v. Christopher Thompson et al.*, and *United States v. 26 Fat Oxen*, both December 1812, MeDC/RG 21. Also see Joshua Wingate, letter to Albert Gallatin, November 7, 1812, M222; Benjamin Sawin, letter to Thomas G. Thornton, October 7, 1812, TGT; and William Little, *History of Warren, A Mountain Hamlet, Located among the White Hills of New Hampshire* (Concord, NH: McFarland and Jenks, 1854), 392–93.

29 Frederick Spofford, letter to Charles Spofford, September 4, 1812, 1812/WLC; Joshua Barney, letter to James Monroe, October 30, 1812, M179.
30 Brigade orders, July 23, 1812, in Chamberlain Collection, UMSC; Stagg, *Mr. Madison's War*, 259; Henry Dearborn, letter to James Madison, April 6, 1812, JMP; Joseph Wheaton, letter to James Madison, June 27, 1812, JMP; Aaron Rogers, letter to William King, September 13, 1812, WKP.
31 Henry Dearborn, letter to James Madison, September 30, 1812, JMP; George Ulmer, letter to John Blake, June 26, 1812, in Massachusetts Secretary of State, Executive Correspondence, 1802–54, MSA.
32 Stagg, *Mr. Madison's War*, 258–60; general orders, July 3, 1812, in Commonwealth of Massachusetts, *Considerations and Documents Relating to the Claim of Massachusetts for Expenditures during the Late War* (Washington, DC: de Krafft, 1818), 26.
33 Elbridge Gerry, letters to James Madison, July 5, 1812, and July 13, 1812, JMP; Stagg, *Mr. Madison's War*, 260–65; Brian Steele, "Thomas Jefferson, Coercion, and the Limits of Harmonious Union," *Journal of Southern History* 74, no. 4 (2008): 847.
34 Jeremiah O'Brien, letter to William Eustis, July 11, 1812, M221; list of prisoners landed at Machias, July 14, 1812, U.S. privateer *Fair Trader*, monition no. 73, vol. 122, RG8/IV; Henry Dearborn, letter to Jacob Eustis, July 17, 1812, HDL; John Binney, letter to Amos Binney, August 20, 1812, HPB.
35 Oliver Shead, letter to William Donnison, September 12, 1812, CDB; Oliver Leonard, letter to John Blake, September 14, 1812, in Charles M. Blake, "Gen. John Blake's Letters," *Bangor Historical Magazine* 6, nos. 7–9 (1891): 163–64.
36 General orders, August 5, 1812, in Adjutant General's Office, General Division, Brigade, and Regimental Orders, MSA; Caleb Strong, letter to William Eustis, August 5, 1812, in *ASP:MA*, 3:70–71; George Ulmer, letter to William King, September 15, 1812, WKP.
37 Jacob Ulmer, letter to Amasa Davis, September 19, 1812, in Quartermaster Correspondence, MSA; Joshua Chamberlain, letter to Jacob Ulmer, September 2, 1812, in Original Papers, Massachusetts Resolves, 1813, chap. 63, MSA; brigade orders, August 28, 1812, CDB; Amasa Stetson, letter to William Eustis, September 23, 1812, M221; Henry Sewall, letter to John Blake, October 30, 1812, in Blake, "Gen. John Blake's Letters," 139; Oliver Leonard, letter to John Blake, September 14, 1812, in ibid., 163–64; William Donnison, letter to John P. Boyd, September 26, 1812, M222; John P. Boyd, letter to William Donnison, September 27, 1812, M222.
38 For accusations of borderland misconduct, see the Federalist *Boston Repertory*, August 11, 1812; the Republican *Boston Patriot*, January 4, 1815; and Sherman Leland, letter to William King, September 17, 1812, WKP.
39 Jacob Ulmer, letter to William King, November 29, 1812, WKP; George Stracey Smyth, letter to John Coape Sherbrooke, November 2, 1812, SFLAC. For a lively account of efforts to suppress active warfare, see Robert L. Dallison, *A Neighbourly War: New Brunswick and the War of 1812* (Fredericton, NB: Goose Lane Editions, 2012).

40 British Admiralty, orders to Herbert Sawyer, May 9, 1812, 1812/LLIU; Hickey, *War of 1812*, 38–40; Orchard Cook, letter to James Madison, August 11, 1812, JMP.
41 Herbert Sawyer, letter to Andrew Allen, August 5, 1812, M625; Horatio Balch, letter to William King, July 29, 1820, WKP.

CHAPTER 3: "A MONGREL BREED OF SOLDIER"

1 "Money Lost by the Commander of a Company of Volunteers in 1813," in *ASP:C*, 1:499–501; supporting papers about the Westcott incident, in HR13A-G1.1, NARA; petition to the Senate and House of Representatives, June 15, 1813, M222.
2 Joseph Westcott, letter to William King, January 10, 1813, WKP; John Comings [Cummings], letter to William King, January 25, 1813, WKP.
3 George Ulmer, letter to John P. Boyd, December 26, 1812, M221; George Ulmer, letter to William King, March 19, 1813, WKP.
4 J. C. A. Stagg, *Mr. Madison's War: Politics, Diplomacy, and Warfare in the Early American Republic, 1783–1830* (Princeton, NJ: Princeton University Press, 1983), 148; Henry Dearborn, letter to William King, July 20, 1812, WKP; Henry Dearborn, letter to William King, August 7, 1812, WKP2.
5 William Duane, letter to James Madison, September 20, 1812, JMP; James Madison, letter to Henry Dearborn, October 7, 1812, JMP; Joseph Wheaton, letter to James Madison, June 27, 1812, JMP; Elbridge Gerry, letters to James Madison, July 5, 1812, July 13, 1812, and July 22, 1812, JMP; William King, letter to Denny McCobb, July 27, 1812, WKP; William Widgery, letter to William King, December 1, 1812, WKP; William King, letter to Henry Dearborn, July 27, 1812, WKP.
6 William Eustis, letter to William King, July 29, 1812, M6; William King, letter to William Eustis, August 6, 1812, WKP; George Ulmer, letter to William King, July 28, 1812, WKP; William King, letter to William Eustis, December 6, 1812, WKP; William King, letter to Denny McCobb, July 27, 1812, WKP; Samuel Dana, letter to James Monroe, November 30, 1814, M221; J. D. Learned, letter to John P. Boyd, December 18, 1812, M221; volunteer officers, letter to James Madison, December 16, 1812, M221; John Leavitt, letter to James Madison, December 16, 1812, M221; George Ulmer, letter to Eustis, August 27, 1812, M221; Jacob Kimball et al., letter to James Madison, December 16, 1812, JMP; Joshua Wingate, Jr., letter to James Madison, March 1, 1813, JMP; Henry Dearborn, letter to James Madison, March 22, 1813, JMP; Stagg, *Mr. Madison's War*, 87–88, 263.
7 Isaac Lane, letter to John Armstrong, March 12, 1813, M566; Donald R. Hickey, *The War of 1812: A Forgotten Conflict, Bicentennial Edition* (Urbana: University of Illinois Press, 2012), 71; John Blake, letter to William King, February 20, 1813, WKP2.
8 John Coape Sherbrooke, letter to Earl Bathurst, September 16, 1812, CO 217/147 Joseph C. Boyd, letters to Richard Cutts, January 28, 1813, and June 5,

1813, RCP; A. W. Atherton, letter to William King, May 24, 1813, WKP2; Joseph E. Smith, letter to Edwin Smith, August 5, 1812, 1812/LLIU.

9   James Campbell, letter to William King, August 31, 1812, WKP; Oliver Herrick, letter to William King, September 3, 1812, WKP; Francis Carr, Sr., letter to William King, September 3, 1812, WKP; Noah Miller, letter to William King, September 2, 1812, WKP. For a description of men volunteering, see "Patriotism. The Spirit of '76 in Nobleboro," *Eastern Argus*, September 10, 1812.

10 "Plan for an efficient Volunteer Corps," *American Advocate*, October 8, 1812.

11 For Federalist newspapers opposed to the volunteer program, see *Boston Commercial Gazette*, September 10, 1812; and "Volunteers," *Columbian Centinel* (Boston), September 16, 1812. Also see John Lowell, *Perpetual War, the Policy of Mr. Madison Being a Candid Examination of His Late Message to Congress* (Boston: Stebbins, 1812), 96; John Chandler, letter to William King, July 31, 1812, WKP; Benjamin Adams, letters to Ebenezer Warren, August 15, 1812, and October 8, 1812, VFP; "Plan for an efficient Volunteer Corps," *American Advocate*, October 8, 1812; and Sherbrooke, letter to Bathurst, September 16, 1812.

12 For the "ARMED MOB" quotation, see *Columbian Centinel*, September 23, 1812. Also see Lowell, *Perpetual War*, 94–96; and Stagg, *Mr. Madison's War*, 264–65. For Federalist criticism of Republican officers, see *Portland Gazette*, January 4, 1813; and William Donnison, letter to William King, November 2, 1812, WKP.

13 Charles Vaughan, letter to "my dearest nephew," January 17, 1813, VFP; Joseph Donnison, letter to Ebenezer Warner, February 11, 1813, VFP; petition of Oliver Herrick, Term Papers, March Term 1813, RG 21/MeDC; Benjamin Cushing, letters to Nathaniel Cushing, February 18, 1813, March 29, 1813, April 4, 1813, BCP; anonymous, diary entry, November 1812, HCC.

14 Comings, letter to King, January 25, 1813. For Federalist newspapers' commentary, see "A New Baltimore in the East," *Columbian Centinel*, July 24, 1813; and *Portland Gazette*, January 4, 1813.

15 James Madison, letter to Henry Dearborn, October 7, 1812, JMP; "The Spirit of '76 in Nobleboro," *Eastern Argus* (Portland), September 10, 1812; "Volunteers!," *Eastern Argus*, October 8, 1812; Daniel Rose, letter to William King, September 26, 1812, WDP; "Schedule of the Payments made and sums necessary to complete the first allowance of pay towards clothing the Volunteer Corps in the District of Maine," c. 1812, M222. For a sample of one such association, see "Inhabitants of New Gloucester, Maine," in 1812/WLC. Also see Stephen Brewer, letter to William Eustis, November 28, 1812, M221; Smith Elkins, letters to William King, November 25, 1812, and December 4, 1812, WKP. For recruiting ads, see *American Advocate*, October 22, 1812.

16 John Binney, letter to William King, December 10, 1812, WKP; John Binney, letter to William Eustis, October 24, 1812, M221; John Binney, letter to William King, December 13, 1812, WDP; John Binney, letters to Amos Binney, August 20, 1812, September 10, 1812, and November 19, 1812, HPB.

17 Anonymous, *A Short and Thrilling Narrative of a Few of the Scenes and Incidents That Occurred in the Sanguinary and Cruel War of 1812–14, between England*

and the United States (Norway, ME: Advertiser Press, 1853), 5–7. For the prisoners of war who landed at Portland, see "The CARTEL, or a Miniature of the "Jersey prison-ship,'" *Eastern Argus*, January 7, 1813; *Eastern Argus*, January 14 and February 12, 1813; and *Portland Gazette*, February 8 and February 15, 1813.

18 Thomas G. Thornton, letter to James Monroe, March 2, 1813, M558; William Pinkney, letter to the secretary of state, March 5, 1813, in Benjamin F. Hall, *Official Opinions of the Attorneys General of the United States* (Washington, DC: Robert Farnham, 1852), 1:107.

19 Stephen Longfellow, letter to George Wadsworth, March 19, 1813, in Stephen Longfellow Correspondence, MeHS; ration accounts, in "Records from Capt. Bailey Bodwell's Company of U.S. Volunteers," UMSC; anonymous, *A Short and Thrilling Narrative*, 6–9.

20 William Eustis, letter to John Parker Boyd, October 27, 1812, in "General Order Book of Military District No. 1," BPL; Silas Parlin, Jr., letter to William King, December 9, 1812; Joseph Donnison, James Collins, and Dan Stewart, Jr., letter to William Widgery, October 8, 1812, forwarded by Widgery to William King, October 12, 1812, WKP; Silas Parlin, Jr., letter to William King, April 7, 1813, WKP; Joshua Wingate, Jr., letter to Albert Gallatin, November 7, 1812, M222; William King, letter to Henry Dearborn, December 25, 1812, in James Monroe Papers, LoC; John Binney, letter to Amos Binney, November 19, 1812, HPB. On volunteers pilfering livestock, see "COMMUNICATION," *American Advocate*, March 11, 1813. Also see Thornton, letter to Monroe, March 2, 1813. On Boothbay's volunteers skirmishing with the Royal Navy, see "Extract of a letter from Capt. W. M. Read, dated Boothbay, April 5," *Boston Repertory*, April 17, 1813; and "Return of prisoners of war delivered to Capt. John Binney, from April 4 to May 10, 1813," TGT.

21 David R. Williams, speech, December 29, 1812, in *Debates and Proceedings of the Congress of the United States: 12th Congress, 2nd Session* (Washington, DC: Gales and Seaton, 1853), 462; Isaac Lane, John Holmes, and Daniel Lane, letter to Richard Cutts, January 6, 1813, RCP; John Holmes, letter to Richard Cutts, January 12, 1813, RCP; Isaac Lane, letter to Richard Cutts, January 23, 1813, RCP.

22 William Wingate, letter to James Madison, January 1, 1813, in James Madison Papers, NYPL.

23 John Parker Boyd, letter to T. H. Cushing, December 2, 1812, M566; George Ulmer, letter to William Eustis, August 27, 1812, M221; George Ulmer, letters to William King, September 15, 1812, and November 29, 1812, WKP2. For Canadian newspaper reports of King's presence in Eastport, see *New Brunswick Royal Gazette* (Saint John), August 24, 1812; and George Ulmer, letter to Caleb Strong, September 26, 1812, in "Secretary of the Commonwealth. Commissions," MSA. The skirmish at Eastport is covered in "Memoranda," *New England Palladium*, December 8, 1812.

24 George Ulmer, letters to William King, December 6, 1812, and December 12, 1812, WKP; George Stracey Smyth, to John Coape Sherbrooke, December 2, 1812, SFLAC.

25 George Ulmer, letters to William King, December 12, 1812, and January 10, 1813, WKP; Henry Dearborn, letter to John P. Boyd, December 20, 1812, HDL; Joseph Gubbins, letter to John Coape Sherbrooke, March 3, 1813, SFLAC.
26 Ulmer, letter to King, December 12, 1812; James Byers, letter to John Armstrong, February 16, 1813, M221.
27 George Ulmer, letters to William King, December 6, 1812, and January 15, 1813, WKP; Lemuel Trescott, letter to William King, December 24, 1812, WKP.
28 George Ulmer, letters to William King, January 15, February 23, and March 19, 1813, WKP. Note that HMS *Nova Scotia* was formerly the American privateer *Rapid* of Portland until its capture in October 1812. Also see George Ulmer, letter to Henry Dearborn, March 3, 1813, M221. The capture of Lieutenant Maclay is described in *City Gazette* (Saint John, NB), April 17, 1813. For Mrs. Ulmer's near capture, see *Portland Gazette*, July 12, 1813.
29 George Ulmer, letter to John Armstrong, March 29, 1813, M221.
30 Deposition of Josiah Sawyer, *N. C. Kelley v. Holmes Nash*, June Term, 1816, Hancock County, SJC.
31 Ulmer, letter to Armstrong, March 29, 1813; Nathaniel Stanley, letter to William King, March 16, 1813, WKP; George Ulmer, letters to William King, February 12, 1813, and March 26, 1813, WKP; Lyndon Oak, *History of Garland* (Dover, ME: Observer Publishing Company, 1912), 161–62; John Armstrong, letter to George Ulmer, February 3, 1813, WKP2.
32 *U.S. v. Robert Nowlin*, May Term, 1813, RG 21/MeDC; deposition of George Manser, *United States v. William Hume et al.*, December Term, 1814, RG 21/MeDC; George Ulmer, letter to William King, December 27, 1812, WKP; J. Maule, letter to George Ulmer, March 1, 1813, M221; Ulmer, letter to Armstrong, March 29, 1813; George Ulmer, letter to Shubael Downs, February 24, 1813, M221; *Commonwealth v. John Campbell*, June Term, 1813, Hancock County, SJC; George Ulmer, letter to William King, May 3, 1813, WKP2.
33 George Ulmer, letter to Henry Dearborn, March 3, 1813, M221; George Ulmer, letter to John Armstrong, April 12, 1813, M221; Joseph D. Learned, letter to John Armstrong, May 18, 1813, M221; deposition of Josiah Sawyer, *Nathaniel Kelley v. Holmes Nash*, June Term, 1816, Hancock County, SJC; Jeremiah O'Brien, letter to Albert Gallatin, April 8, 1813, PAG; deposition of William Coney, *U.S. v. the Schooner Polly*, May Term, 1814, RG 21/MeDC; depositions of Frederick Crone, John Cummings, Jacob Ulmer, and William Sterne, *Leland v. Ulmer*, June Term, 1821, Hancock County, SJC; deposition of Reuben Branard, *Ulmer v. Leland*, June Term, 1818, Hancock County, SJC; William Stern, letter to William King, July 31, 1813, WKP.
34 Depositions of Jacob Ulmer, Lewis Petihew, Jr., and Newell Witherle, *Leland v. Ulmer*, June Term, 1821, Hancock County, SJC; deposition of Zachariah Lawrence, *Ulmer v. Leland*, June Term, 1818, Hancock County, SJC; testimony of John Spear, June 3, 1821, *Leland v. Ulmer*, June Term, 1821, Hancock County, SJC; Joseph D. Learned, letter to John Armstrong, May 18, 1813, M221.
35 George Ulmer, letter to John Armstrong, May 30, 1813, M221; Joseph D. Learned, letters to John Armstrong, May 10 and May 18, 1813, M221;

deposition of George Cummings, *Leland v. Ulmer*, June Term, 1821, Hancock County, SJC.

36 Petition titled "The Eastern Frontier," June 15, 1813, M222; *Commonwealth v. John Campbell*, June Term, 1813, Hancock County, SJC; Moses Adams, letter to Joseph Farnum, July 9, 1813, and Joseph Farnum, letter to Charles K. Tilden, July 9, 1813, both in "Original Papers, Massachusetts Resolves 1813," chap. 162, MSA.

37 "Resolve for paying the troops detached in July last, for protection of the Gaol in Castine, and for rations supplied by the town of Ellsworth," February 11, 1814, and "Resolve for paying a detachment from Captain Farnum's Company, for protection of the Gaol at Castine," February 21, 1814, both in "Resolves of the General Court of Massachusetts," MSA; Rebecca Robbins, "Colonel John Black of Ellsworth (1781–1856)," *Maine Historical Society Quarterly* 17, no. 3 (1978): 128–29; George Ulmer, letters to William King, July 22, 1813, and August 28, 1813, WKP. For a report of the attack on the jail, see *Boston Patriot*, August 21, 1813.

38 For an account of the Eastport riot, see "A New Baltimore in the East," *Columbian Centinel*, July 24, 1813. Also see Alan Taylor, "Center and Peripheries: Locating Maine's History," *Maine History* 39, no. 2 (2000): 7–8.

39 Depositions of Zachariah Lawrence and Sherman Leland to J. D. Learned, July 10, 1813, *Ulmer v. Leland*, June Term, 1818, Hancock County, SJC; Robert Sparks File, RG 15; district orders, July 31, 1813, case file, *Leland v. Ulmer*, June Term, 1821, Hancock County, SJC; George Ulmer, letter to Sherman Leland, July 28, 1813, M221.

40 George Ulmer, letters to Thomas H. Cushing, July 2, 1813, and July 11, 1813, M221; Prescott Currier, *The Jails of Lincoln County, 1761–1813* (Wiscasset, ME: Lincoln County Historical Association, 1992), 214–18; "Marshal's Advertisement," *Eastern Argus*, July 8, 1813; George Ulmer, letter to Thomas G. Thornton, July 11, 1813, CHT.

41 Deposition of Richard McAllister, *U.S. v. 4 Oxen*, and deposition of William Delesdernier, *U.S. v. 14 Oxen*, both December Term, 1813, RG 21/MeDC; Benjamin Adams et al., letter to Isaac Lane, May 4, 1813, ILP; Sherman Leland, letter to Isaac Lane, June 1, 1813, ILP; Abijah Gregory, letter to Isaac Lane, May 29, 1813, ILP; George Ulmer, letter to William King, July 22, 1813, WKP.

42 Samuel Putnam et al., letter to William King, June 18, 1813, and William King, letter to Samuel Putnam, June 21, 1813, both in no. 4807, "Senate Unpassed Legislation 1813," MSA.

43 Benjamin Ames and Joseph F. Wingate, Jr., *The Disclosure. No. 1. Documents Relating to Violations and Evasions of the Laws, During the Commercial Restrictions and Late War with Great Britain, Etc.* (Bath, ME: Torrey, 1824), 26. For examples of Bermuda licenses issued to Bath vessels, see case file, *Dantzig* and *Christina*, RG8/IV, vol. 103. Alan Taylor, "The Smuggling Career of William King," *Maine History* 17, no. 1 (1977): 19–38.

44 Charles Stewart, letter to William Jones, April 5, 1814, M179; contract and muster roll for the Swedish schooner *Oscar*, [December?] 1813, in John Crosby Papers, MeHS; For British customs records of Maine vessels entering Bermuda in 1813, see CO 41/10.

CHAPTER 4: WAR AFLOAT

1. Monition 1, *Malcolm*, RG8/IV, vol. 74; Herbert Sawyer, letter to John W. Croker, June 28, 1812, ADM 1/502; Andrew Lambert, *The Challenge: Britain against America in the Naval War of 1812* (London: Faber and Faber, 2012), 110; Herbert Sawyer, letter to John W. Croker, July 18, 1812, in Sir Herbert Sawyer Letterbooks and Order Book, NYPL; Faye M. Kert, *Privateering: Patriots and Profits in the War of 1812* (Baltimore: Johns Hopkins University Press, 2015), 60–64.
2. Thomas Jefferson, letter to unknown, July 4, 1812, in Benson J. Lossing, *Pictorial Field-Book of the War of 1812* (New York: Harper, 1869), 993; Lambert, *The Challenge*, 198–99; Michael Rutstein, *The Privateering Stroke: Salem's Privateers in the War of 1812* (Salem, MA, 2012), 25–27.
3. William Jewett, letter to Albert Gallatin, July 23, 1812, M558; Daniel O. Davis, "Portland Privateers in the War of 1812," in *Collections and Proceedings of the Maine Historical Society* (Portland: Maine Historical Society, 1895), 6:178–83.
4. Florence G. Thurston and Harmon S. Cross, *Three Centuries of Freeport, Maine* (Freeport, ME, 1940), 55–59; petition of Samuel Porter, *United States v. Sloop "Sally" of Freeport*, September Term, 1816, RG21/MeDC.
5. William Goold, *Portland in the Past* (Portland, ME: Thurston, 1886), 444–49; E. C. Plumer, "The Privateer *Dash*," *New England Magazine* 10, no. 5 (1894): 568–71.
6. Joseph Leavitt, diary entry, April 4, 1813, JLJ; anonymous, diary entry, July 10, 1812, HCC; Theodore Wells, *Narrative of the Life and Adventures of Theodore Wells of Wells, Me.* (Biddeford, ME: Butler, 1874), 7. For Federalist newspapers grumbling about the immorality of privateering, see "The Blessings of Privateering," *Portsmouth (NH) Oracle*, July 25, 1812. For Adams's speech against privateers, see *Eastern Argus* (Portland), July 16, 1812.
7. Eleanor Motley Richardson and Peter Tufts Richardson, eds., *The Ingraham Diaries, 1795–1815* (Rockland, ME: Red Barn, 2018), 113, 117.
8. *Fame* logbook entries, April 17, 1813, April 18, 1813, and May 17, 1813, PEM; *Dart* logbook entries, July 28, July 31, 1812, MeHS; *Lilly* logbook entry, November 19, 1812, MeHS; *Dash* logbook entries, August 30 and August 31, 1813, MeHS; monition 109, *Rapid*, RG8/IV, vol. 75.
9. *Rover* logbook entries, November 6, 1812, and November 14, 1812, MeHS; *Portland Gazette*, September 6, 1813; *Wasp* logbook entry, April 29, 1813, PEM.
10. *Stephen Richards v. Sloop Hero*, February Term, 1815, RG21/MaDC; *Favorite* logbook entries, September 11, and September 12, 1812, MeHS; *Polly* logbook entry, December 13, 1812, MeHS; *Frolic* logbook entries, June 14, and August 15, 1813, PEM; logbook entries, August 10 and August 12, 181, in Journal of Naval Operations, 1812/LLIU.
11. *Argus* logbook entry, July 12, 1812, RG8/IV, vol. 120; *Holker* logbook entry, October 8, 1813, PEM. For commentary on anti-privateering sentiment and actions in Maine ports, see *Nova Scotia Royal Gazette* (Halifax), July 22, 1812; and "Barbarity," *Eastern Argus*, January 28, 1813.

12   William Coney, letter to Thomas G. Thornton, July 4, 1812, TGT. *No. 46* seems to have been a reference to the number on *Jefferson*'s commission.
13   For Saint John's alarm at the appearance of American privateers, see "American Privateers," *City Gazette* (Saint John, NB), July 25, 1812.
14   Maine newspapers reported on the activities of Canadian privateers as an immediate threat to local shipping. See "Recent British captures on this coast," *Portland Gazette*, August 2, 1813; as well as *Eastern Argus*, April 8, July 1, and October 13, 1813. Newspapers in old Massachusetts picked up the story when Canadian privateers began operating south of Cape Cod or in Massachusetts Bay; see *New Bedford (MA) Mercury*, April 9, 1813; "Liverpool Packet," *Columbian Centinel* (Boston), May 5, 1813; Kert, *Privateering*, 112–17; and "List of the American vessels captured by the privateer schooner *Liverpool Packet*," CO 217/91. For the cargo of the *Mary*, see *Mary* of Bath RG8/IV, vol. 90; and S. G. Ladd, letter to Amasa Davis, August 11, 1812, 1812/WLC. For a newspaper account of *Mary*'s capture, see *Boston Repertory*, July 15, 1813.
15   Robert H. Osgood, letter to Edwin Smith, July 9, 1812, 1812/LLIU.
16   *Fame* logbook entry, July 22, 1812, PEM. On the one-legged Captain Snow, see *Portland Gazette*, July 12, 1813.
17   Goold, *Portland in the Past*, 434–36; Richard Saumarez, diary entry, November 1, 1814, in Richard Saumarez Journal, 1812/LLIU.
18   *Fame* logbook entry, October 31, 1812, PEM; *St. Michael* logbook entry, July 29, 1812, MeHS; deposition of Judson Josselyn, *U.S. v. Two Boats*, September Term, 1813, RG21/MeDC.
19   Both American and Canadian newspapers widely reported this skirmish; see *New Brunswick Royal Gazette*, July 3, 1813; *Portland Gazette*, July 5 and July 12, 1813; *Acadian Recorder* (Halifax, NS), July 17, 1813; and *Boston Patriot*, July 7, 1813. On the *Fly*'s complete career, see Rutstein, *Privateering Stroke*, 71–72.
20   *Increase* crew agreement, in Samuel Tucker Papers, vol. 3, HLH; John Hannibal Sheppard, *Life of Samuel Tucker, Commodore in the American Revolution* (Boston: Mudge and Son, 1868), 89–92.
21   For a Canadian account of the battle, see *New Brunswick Royal Gazette*, June 14, 1813. Also see "Return of prisoners of war delivered to Capt. John Binney, commander of Fort Edgecomb, from April 4 to May 10, 1813," TGT; and Samuel Tucker, letter to John Binney, May 29, 1813, Samuel Tucker Papers," vol. 3, HLH.
22   *Young Teazer*'s pilot reported the privateer had almost escaped when it blew up; see John Carlow, *A Journal of Adventures at Sea* (Portland, ME: Pennell, 1839), 58–65. Postwar accounts suggest that it was an innocent mistake by the crew working in the privateer's magazine; see Frederick Johnson Pension File, RG15.
23   H. H. Cogswell, letter to Rudolph Kreighton, July 1, 1813, RG1/140; monition 265, *Young Teazer*, RG8/IV, vol. 100; *Portland Gazette*, August 2, 1813.
24   George Lee Haskins and Herbert A. Johnson, *History of the Supreme Court of the United States*, vol. 2, *Foundations of Power: John Marshall, 1801–1815* (New York: Macmillan, 1981), 437.
25   "Pirateering," *Columbian Centinel*, July 15, 1812; "Barbarous Treatment," *Merrimack Intelligencer* (Haverhill, MA), July 18, 1812.

26 Rutstein, *Privateering Stroke*, 65–66. For the *Partridge* incident, see *Portland Gazette*, September 6, 1813; and *Portsmouth (NH) Oracle*, October 31, 1812.
27 *Fame* logbook entry, October 28, 1812, PEM. An unusually detailed account is in *Portland Gazette*, November 23, 1812. Also see *J. Downie apt. Sch. "Jefferson" v. Sch. "Lively" & Cargo*, October Term, 1812, RG21/MaCC.
28 "Barbarous Treatment," *Merrimack Intelligencer*, July 18, 1812; *Upton v. Carey*, May Term, 1814, MeDC/RG21. The case also went to local courts: see *Veazie v. Carey et al.*, May Term, 1814, Lincoln County Circuit Court of Common Pleas, Lincoln County Courthouse, Wiscasset, ME. For the sloop *William & Ann*, see "Modern Warfare," *New Bedford Mercury*, July 24, 1812. Also see *Commonwealth v. Hooper*, September Term, 1812, Hancock County SJC.
29 Monition 72, *Friendship*, RG8/IV, vol. 122. For Rich's death and burial, see *Acadian Recorder*, April 10, 1813. Also see George Ulmer, letter to John Armstrong, April 16, 1813, M221; and interrogatory of James Paul, *Andrew Tucker v. Sloop "Eliza Ann,"* December Term, 1813, MeDC/RG21.
30 "Memorial of Seward Porter to Admiral Sir John B. Warren and Sir John C. Sherbrooke, 1813," CO 217/92; extract of Lawrence Hartshorne, letter to unknown, n.d., CO 217/92; anonymous, letter to "Messrs. Clap & Agry," August 28, 1813, VFP. Halifax newspapers reported that the Porters had traded at Halifax throughout the war; see *Acadian Recorder*, September 24, 1814.
31 *Robinson v. Hook*, October Term, 1826, RG 21/MeCC; petition of David and Ebenezer Robinson, February 29, 1828, Sen. 20 A-G2, Senate Claims Committee, RG 46, NARA; Edward J. Martin, "Maine's Mode of Privateering: A Tale of Fraud and Collusion in the Northeast Borderlands, 1812–1815," *London Journal of Canadian Studies*, 28, no. 1 (2013): 37–40.
32 Joseph W. Porter, "Smuggling in Maine in 1813," *Bangor Historical Magazine* 3, no. 6 (1887): 105–8; deposition of John Robinson, *Robinson v. Hook*; "American Federalist," letter to James Madison, October 5, 1813, JMP; Joseph F. Wingate, letter to Thomas Agry, February 19 1814, VFP; Josiah Hook, letter to William Jones, September 26, 1813, *Robinson v. Hook*; James Monroe, letter to Joshua Wingate, November 4, 1813, M40. For a detailed account of this incident, see Edward J. Martin, "Defining the Acceptable Bounds of Deception: Policing the Prize Game in the Northeastern Borderlands, 1812–1815," in *Border Policing: A History of Enforcement and Evasion in North America*, ed. Holly M. Karibo and George T. Diaz (Austin: University of Texas Press, 2020), 32–35. Also see U.S. Department of State, circular, January 21, 1814, NHHC; and Joseph Farley, letter to William Jones, September 20, 1813, CHW.
33 Arthur McClellan, letter to Thomas Barclay, September 2, 1813, TBP.
34 Both Canadian and American newspapers expressed shock at the conduct of the *Weasel*'s officers and crew. See "Extract of a letter from Pennfield, dated 10th June, 1813," *New Brunswick Royal Gazette*, June 14, 1813; and *Portland Gazette*, July 19, 1813.
35 "Extract of a letter received by a gentleman in Halifax, dated Argyle, Nova Scotia," *Portland Gazette*, November 23, 1812. The sworn depositions and Swaine's confession are in CO 217/90.

36 On the misconduct of Canadian privateersmen, see *Portland Gazette*, July 26, 1813. On the Salem privateersman, see *Essex Register*, July 25, 1812; and confession of James Archibald, May 1, 1815, RG1/227.
37 Lambert, *The Challenge*, 104–5; Rutstein, *Privateering Stroke*, 56–57.
38 William R. Wells, "US Revenue Cutters Captured in the War of 1812," *American Neptune* 58, no. 3 (1998): 225–27; Joshua M. Smith, *Battle for the Bay: The Naval War of 1812* (Fredericton, NB: Goose Lane, 2011), 41–42.
39 Brian Arthur, *How Britain Won the War of 1812: The Royal Navy's Blockades of the United States, 1812–1815* (Rochester, NY: Boydell and Brewer, 2011), 69–74; Lambert, *The Challenge*, 84–86, 105–15; Sir John B. Warren, letter to John W. Croker, January 5, 1813, and John W. Croker, letter to Sir John B. Warren, February 10, 1813, both in *The Naval War of 1812: A Documentary History*, vol. 2, *1813*, ed. William S. Dudley (Washington, DC: Naval Historical Center, 1992), 3:11, 17–19.
40 British Admiralty, "Coast of America, Proposed Division of Ships & Their Stations," in Dudley, *Naval War of 1812*, 2:80; Smith, *Battle for the Bay*, 65–70, 76.
41 Lambert, *The Challenge*, 211–26, 244. After the death of his uncle in 1816, Griffiths assumed his last name so is often referred to as Edward Griffith Colpoys (Kert, *Privateering*, 32–35).
42 For accounts of the Boothbay skirmish, see "Extract of a letter from Capt. W. M. Read, dated Boothbay, April 5," *Boston Repertory*, April 17, 1813. On the loss of the *Alexander*, see *Boston Repertory*, May 24, 1813; *Columbian Centinel*, May 22, 1813; and *Weekly Visitor* (Kennebunk, ME), May 22 and May 29, 1813. On the battle at the Kennebec's mouth, see *Portland Gazette*, June 21, 1813.
43 *Lilly* logbook entry, December 2, 1812, MeHS; *Holker* logbook entry, October 3, 1813, PEM.
44 For the activities of the Fundy Squadron, see *Essex Register*, March 31, 1813; *Acadian Recorder*, May 15, 1813; *Columbian Centinel*, April 3, 1813; and *City Gazette*, April 24, 1813. On HMS *Bream*, see *Boston Repertory*, July 27, 1813. Also see *Jabez Mowry v. Samuel Todd*, May Term, 1815, Cumberland County, SJC; and William Begg, diary entry, July 18, 1813, WBJ.
45 "Petition of Biddeford to James Madison for naval protection," c. early 1813, NHHC; "Distressing situation of the District of Maine," *Merrimack Intelligencer*, May 15, 1813; Jonathan Fisher, diary entry, May 3, 1813, in Jonathan Fisher Journal, AAS; William Moody, letter to Richard Cutts, May 8, 1813, RCP; Joseph C. Boyd, letter to Richard Cutts, May 17, 1813, RCP; Jeremiah Russell, letter to William Russell, April 15, 1813, in "Local Hardships during War of 1812," *Lincoln County News* (Newcastle, ME), January 15, 1987; Benjamin Cushing, letter to Nathaniel Cushing, April 4, 1813, BCP; George Herbert, letter to Daniel Webster, April 28, 1813, in *The Papers of Daniel Webster*, vol. 1, *Correspondence, 1798–1824*, ed. Charles M. Wiltse and Harold D. Moser (Hanover, NH: University of New England Press, 1974), 135–137.
46 Isaac Hull, letter to William Jones, March 4, 1813, IHP.
47 Isaac Hull, letter to William Jones, July 24, 1813, in Dudley, *Naval War of 1812*, 2:195–96; Linda M. Maloney, *The Captain from Connecticut: The Life and Times of Isaac Hull* (Boston: Northeastern University Press, 1986), 216–19.

48 Isaac Hull, letter to William Jones, May 20, 1813, IHP; Seth Storer, Jr., letter to Cyrus King, May 22, 1813, CKP.

49 Timothy Upham, Horatio Hill, and Cyrus Barton, *Report of the Case of Timothy Upham against Hill & Barton* (Dover NH: Ela, 1830), 67; Isaac Hull, letter to Samuel J. Morrill, March 5, 1813, in Samuel J. Morrill Papers, NYHS; William Widgery, letter to Secretary of the Navy, December 18, 1812, M124; Isaac Hull, letter to William Harper, May 20, 1813, IHP.

50 William Jones, letter to Lloyd Jones, February 27, 1813, in J. C. A Stagg, *Mr. Madison's War: Politics, Diplomacy, and Warfare in the Early American Republic, 1783–1830* (Princeton, NJ: Princeton University Press, 1983), 292. For Portland's complaints about its defenselessness against the Royal Navy, see *Portland Gazette*, March 15, March 29, and April 5, 1813; "Committee of General Safety and Defence of the Town of Portland," letter to John Armstrong, April 10, 1813, in Records of the Committee of "General Safety and Defence of the Town of Portland," MeHS; and Charles Fox, letters to John Fox, April 5, 1813, and April 6, 1813, in John Fox Papers, MeHS.

51 Isaac Hull, letter to Daniel Tucker, May 6, 1813, IHP; Isaac Hull, letters to William Jones, June 23, and July 31, 1813, IHP; William Widgery, letter to James Monroe, May 10, 1813, M179. For complaints about the capture of local shipping and a dig at Widgery's vote for the war in 1812, see *Portland Gazette*, August 2, 1813; and Isaac Hull, letter to William Jones, June 24, 1813, in Dudley, *Naval War of 1812*, 2:160.

52 "Naval General Order," July 29, 1813, in Dudley, *Naval War of 1812*, 2:160; Isaac Hull, letter to William Jones, June 24, 1813, in ibid., 2:205–6; Isaac Hull, letter to William Burrows, August 28, 1813, in ibid., 2:233; Henry Otis Thayer, *Second War with England: Sundry Papers* (Bath, ME: Times Company, n.d.), 6; Kevin D. McCranie, *Utmost Gallantry: The U.S. and Royal Navies at Sea in the War of 1812* (Annapolis: Naval Institute Press, 2011), 191; David Hanna, *Knights of the Sea: The True Story of the "Boxer" and the "Enterprise" and the War of 1812* (New York: NAL Caliber, 2012), chap. 8, passim.

53 Hook, letter to Jones, September 26, 1813, *Robinson v. Hook*; depositions of George Smith, Ebenezer Perkins, and John Faxon, *U.S. v. Sloop "Traveller,"* October Term, 1813, RG 21/MeDC; Charles Tappan, letter to George H. Preble, September 9, 1873, in Porter, "Smuggling in Maine during the War of 1812," 201–3.

54 David McCrery, letter to Alexander Gordon, September 6, 1812, and Edward R. McCall, letter to Isaac Hull, September 7, 1813, both in Dudley, *Naval War of 1812*, 2:234–35; "The Affair of the *Enterprise* and *Boxer*," newspaper clipping, in Maine Historical Manuscripts, MeHS.

55 Dudley, *Naval War of 1812*, 2:237–38; George W. Emery, *In Their Own Words: The Navy Fights the War of 1812* (Washington, DC: Naval Historical Foundation, 2013), 36–37.

56 Anonymous, diary entry, September 11, 1813, HCC; J. Patten, letter to "Honored Parents," September 7, 1813, in Maine Historical Manuscripts, MeHS; Joseph T. Wood, letter to John Binney, September 7, 1813, in William D. Patterson, *Proceedings of the Four Hundred and Nineteenth Quarterly Meeting of the Wiscasset Fire Society* (Wiscasset, ME: Sheepscot Echo, 1905), 22.

57 Goold, *Portland in the Past*, 485–87; David McCreary, letter to Thomas Barclay, September 9, 1813, TBP; Isaac Hull, letter to William Jones, September 16, 1813, IHL; Isaac Hull, letter to Samuel Ayer, September 6, 1813, in Dudley, *Naval War of 1812*, 2:239; "Expenses for Capt. Blyth burial," 1813, TGT.

58 The correspondence between the British ships and American officials is found in *Eastern Argus*, September 16, 1813. The shock of Saint John's population after the defeat of *Boxer* is found in *City Gazette*, September 13, 1813. Also see Charles Hare, *Testimonials and Memorials of the Services of Lieut. Charles Hare, of the Royal Navy, 37 Years a Lieutenant* (Saint John, NB, 1848), 29–30.

59 Edward R. McCall, letter to Isaac Hull, September 11, 1813, in Dudley, *Naval War of 1812*, 2:241; William Harper, letter to William Jones, December 5, 1813, in ibid., 289–90, 292; Isaac Hull, letter to William Harper, March 23, 1814, IHP.

60 Logbook of HMS *Bream*, ADM 51/2150; William Mackenzie Godfrey, letter to John Borlase Warren, September 30, 1813, and October 19, 1813, ADM 1/504; John Lawrence, letter to John Borlase Warren, October 5, 1813, ADM 1/504.

61 Julian Gwyn, *Frigates and Foremasts: The North American Squadron in Nova Scotia Waters, 1745–1815* (Vancouver: University of British Columbia Press, 2003), 141–42; Lambert, *The Challenge*, 251–52, 306–7; Sir John B. Warren, letter to John W. Croker, December 30, 1813, in Dudley, *Naval War of 1812*, 2:307–30; McCranie, *Utmost Gallantry*, 214–17.

CHAPTER 5: "WICKED WAR"

1 J. C. A. Stagg, "Enlisted Men in the United States Army, 1812–1815: A Preliminary Survey," *William and Mary Quarterly*, 3rd ser., 43, no. 3 (1986), 630; William Widgery, letter to James Monroe, May 10, 1813, M179; Isaac Lane, letter to John Armstrong, March 12, 1813, M566; Benjamin Adams, letter to John Armstrong, April 23, 1813, M566.

2 Samuel Hodges, Jr., letter to adjutant general, March 21, 1814, M566; James Bates, letter to John Armstrong, April 2, 1814, M566; Josiah Snelling, letter to John B. Walbach, March 1, 1814, M566.

3 Volunteer officers, letter to James Madison, December 16, 1812, M221; John Leavitt, letter to James Madison, December 16, 1812, M221; Joshua Wingate, Jr., to James Madison, March 1, 1813, JMP; Joseph C. Boyd, letters to Richard Cutts, May 17, 1813, and June 5, 1813, RCP; Isaac Hodsdon, letter to James E. Heath, October 22, 1851, RG15; Thomas G. Thornton, letter to James Madison, March 19, 1814, JMP; Henry Dearborn, letter to John Armstrong, August 11, 1814, M566; Flavel Sabin, letters to Nancy Sabin, February 2, 1814, and June 10, 1814, in Charles McKinney Collection, Broome County Historical Society, Binghamton, NY; Benjamin Adams, letter to Isaac Lane, August 13, 1814, ILP.

4 "To the Patriotic Citizens of Portland," *Eastern Argus* (Portland), July 8, "U.S. Army," September 2 and December 9, 1813; J. D. Learned, letter to John

Armstrong, April 14, 1813, M221; J. D. Learned, letter to Benjamin Poland, June 11, 1813, in Vinson Papers, MHS.

5 Ellis B. Usher, *A Biographical Sketch of Hannah Lane Usher of Buxton and Hollis, Maine* (La Crosse, WI, 1903), 14–16; Isaac Lane, letter to John Armstrong, March 12, 1813, M566; Isaac Lane, John Holmes, and Daniel Lane, letters to Richard Cutts, January 6 and January 23, 1813, RCP

6 "RECRUITING!," c. January 10, 1814, in War of 1812 Collection, Oberlin College Special Collections, Oberlin, OH; J. C. A. Stagg, *Mr. Madison's War: Politics, Diplomacy, and Warfare in the Early American Republic, 1783–1830* (Princeton, NJ: Princeton University Press, 1983), 171; George Thatcher, Jr., letter to Cyrus King, June 19, 1813, CKP; *Eastern Argus*, May 27, 1813; Peter Pelham, letter to unknown, June 14, 1814, in Osborne Family Papers, Special Collections Research Center, Syracuse University Library, Syracuse, NY; Nathaniel Hawthorne, *Yarn of a Yankee Privateer* (New York: Funk and Wagnalls, 1926), 30.

7 Flavel Sabin, letter to Nancy Sabin, June 10, 1814, in Charles McKinney Collection; Noah Parkman, letter to Isaac Lane, September 17, 1814, ILP. On recruiting difficulties in Hallowell, see "ANOTHER OUTRAGE—in Hallowell," *Boston Repertory*, March 10, 1814; and "To the Editor of the Hallowell Gazette," *Hallowell Gazette*, March 16, 1814.

8 On how local physicians billed recruiters for examining recruits, see William Simmons, letters to Joel R. Ellis, October 12, 1813, and April 13, 1814, in Joel R. Ellis Correspondence, author's collection. Also see anonymous, diary entry, November 1812, HCC; Joseph Bryant, letter to Isaac Lane, August 11, 1813, ILP; Benjamin Adams, letter to Isaac Lane, August 13, 1814, ILP; Benjamin D. Gardner, letters to Isaac Lane, August 17 and August 22, 1813, ILP; Samuel Jordan, letter to Isaac Lane, January 13, 1814, ILP; Stephen Woodman, letter to Isaac Lane, September 5, 1813, ILP; and Stagg, *Mr. Madison's War*, 170–71.

9 Zina Hyde, diary entry, May 9, 1814, in Parker McCobb Reed, *History of Bath and Environs* (Portland, ME: Lakeside, 1894), 92; Isaac Hodsdon, letter to Isaac Lane, August 23, 1813, ILP. On the strutting recruit, see Benjamin Bolton File, RG15. Also see J. D. Learned, letter to James Monroe, February 2, 1816, M222; J. D. Learned, letter to Callender Irvine, May 22, 1813, RG153; testimonies of Thomas Bailey, Robert Douglass, and Joseph D. Learned's defense statement, November 29, 1814, in Joseph D. Learned's court-martial, RG153.

10 Samuel Tyler, *Memorial of Hon. Samuel Tyler* (privately printed, 1900), 8–11; "Damages for Enlisting a Minor," *ASPM:MA*, 1:669; Daniel Dyer, letter to Isaac Lane, September 29, 1814, ILP; Donald R. Hickey, *The War of 1812: A Forgotten Conflict, Bicentennial Edition* (Urbana: University of Illinois Press, 2012), 109–10, 250–51. On underage recruits from Maine, see Joseph A. Bentley, George Brooks, and William Andrews Files, RG15; petitions of Benjamin Woodman and Zenas Drinkwater, October Term, 1814, Cumberland County, SJC; Isaac Hull, letter to David Sewall, April 5, 1814, IHP; Isaac Hull, letter to William Jones, November 2, 1814, IHP; and Isaac Hull, letter to Horatio Quincy, November 5, 1814, IHP.

11 Robert Chase and Moses Frussel, letter to Thomas H. Cushing, April 10, 1813, M566; Harry Hayman Cochrane, *History of Monmouth and Wales* (East Winthrop, ME: Banner, 1894), 585–87.
12 Castine, town meeting minutes, August 1812, Castine Town Hall Archives, Castine, ME; Benjamin D. Gardner, letter to Isaac Lane, August 22, 1813, ILP; Henry Hayes, letter to Isaac Lane, November 24, 1814, ILP; "Extract of a letter from the Hon. Stephen Jones, Esq. of Machias, Me. to the Rev. Clark Brown, of Swanzey, dated March 19, 1814," *Constitutionalist* (Exeter, NH), May 24, 1814; "Charles Emerson Autobiography," RG 1247, American Baptist Historical Society, Atlanta. On young men seeking employment in Canada, see "Monarchy and all," *Eastern Argus*, May 5, 1814.
13 *Thomas M. Cargill v. Peter Taylor and Another*, in *Reports of Cases Argued and Determined in the Supreme Judicial Court of the Commonwealth of Massachusetts*, by Dudley Atkins Tyng (Newburyport, MA: Edward Little, 1812), 206–10; John Binney, letter to Silas Lee, May 15, 1813, in Flagg Family Papers, Library of Virginia, Richmond; Benjamin D. Gardner, letter to Isaac Lane, August 17, 1813, ILP; Benjamin D. Gardner, letter to Isaac Lane, August 17, 1813, ILP; Barnebas Palmer, letter to Isaac Lane, August 7, 1814, ILP; Stagg, *Mr. Madison's War*, 172–73; anonymous, diary entry, December 1812, HCC; William Moody, letter to Richard Cutts, May 8, 1813, RCP. For a description of the Thirty-third Regiment's march from Saco, see *Eastern Argus*, September 2, 1813.
14 William Woodman, letter to J. Woodman, c. June 1813, and William Woodman, letter to his parents, June 15, 1813, both in New Gloucester Historical Society Archives, New Gloucester, ME; Tyler, *Memorial of Hon. Samuel Tyler*, 8–11.
15 Garrison orders, Fort Preble, August 27, September 18, and September 24, 1814, FMDO. For glimpses into garrison life at Machias's Fort O'Brien, see Samuel A. Morse's court-martial, RG 153; William B. Tempest, letter to J. B. Walbach, May 19, 1814, M566; and William B. Tempest, letter to Daniel Parker, May 5, 1814, in Daniel Parker Papers, Historical Society of Pennsylvania, Philadelphia.
16 Garrison orders, Fort Scammel, October 14 and November 12, 1814, FMDO.
17 Benjamin Adams, letter to Isaac Lane, August 12, 1813, ILP. For a sample of soldiers injured at Maine military posts, see Thomas R. Carman, Samuel Adams, Joseph Barter, John Bennet, William Booden, and Elisha Bolton Files, all RG 15. Also see Enoch Manning, letter to Andrew Lewis, June 10, 1814, in Enoch Manning, "Letter from Eastport," *Bangor Historical Magazine* 3, no. 10 (1888): 200.
18 Garrison orders, Fort Preble, June 11, 1813, in "Muster Rolls and Company Records Volume, 34th U.S. Infantry," HSP; garrison orders, Fort Preble, November 13, 1814, FMDO; Josiah Snelling, letter to John B. Walbach, March 1, 1814, M566; Sylvanus Day, letter to the secretary of war, August 29, 1814, M566.
19 Garrison orders, Fort Preble, June 10 and June 29, 1813, in "Muster Rolls and Company Records Volume, 34th U.S. Infantry"; regimental orders, Portland, August 7, 1813, ibid. The amorous officer's misdeeds are recorded in John

Leonard's court-martial, RG 153. A good overview of army discipline in the War of 1812 is John R. Grodzinski, "'Bloody Provost': Discipline during the War of 1812," *Canadian Military History* 16, no. 3 (2007): 25–32.

20 On the birth at Fort Edgecomb, see Benjamin Bolton Pension File, RG 15. Also see garrison orders, Fort Preble, June 25, 1813, in "Muster Rolls and Company Records Volume, 34th U.S. Infantry"; Manning, letter to Lewis, June 10, 1814.

21 "William Dwelley," in *House Report* 87 (32–1), January 30, 1852; "James Mains," in *House Report* 624 (27–2), April 12, 1842.

22 Thomas M. Vinson, letter to Thomas G. Thornton, September 21, 1813, TGT; Hickey, *War of 1812*, 176–78; "The Commonwealth Gaols," *Boston Gazette*, January 31, 1814; Prescott Currier, *The Jails of Lincoln County, 1761–1813* (Wiscasset, ME: Lincoln County Historical Association, 1992), 213; Jonathan Cook, letter to Thomas G. Thornton, April 19, 1813, TGT; J. Mason, letter to Thomas G. Thornton, April 6, 1814, TGT; Thomas G. Thornton, letter to J. Mason, April 24, 1816, TGT; Jonathan Simpson, letter to Thomas Barclay, September 14, 1813, TBP; Francis Cook, letter to Thomas G. Thornton, September 2, 1813, TGT2. For a rare account of prisoner-of-war life in the Wiscasset jail, see "Yankee Prison," *Acadian Recorder* (Halifax, NS), June 25, 1814.

23 "Return of Prisoners of War Reported to Jonathan Cook, Dep'y Marshal and delivered to Cap't John Binney Commanding United States Garrison at Edgecomb from the Fourth of April to the 10th of May 1813," TGT; Francis Cook, letter to Thomas G. Thornton, May 24, 1814, TGT2; Jonathan Simpson, letter to Thomas Barclay, July 29, 1813, TBP; George S. Smith, letter to Thomas G. Thornton, February 26, 1814, CHT.

24 "Yankee Prison." See also Joshua M. Smith, "'Find a hell before you leave this world': Maritimers as Prisoners of War, 1812–1815," *Journal of the Royal Nova Scotia Historical Society* 18 (2015): 65–76.

25 Charles Tebbets, letter to Thomas G. Thornton, July 21, 1812, CHT; John Binney, letter to William King, December 10, 1812, WKP; "Return of Prisoners at Castine Fort, August 25, 1813," TGT; J. B. Swanton, letter to Thomas G. Thornton, August 24, 1813, TGT; "Return of prisoners taken by privateer *America*, July 21, 1813," TGT.

26 William King, letter to John Brooks, August 30, 1813, in Secretary of State Executive Correspondence," 1802–54, MSA; Stephen Benton Porter File RG 15; David McCreary, letter to Thomas Barclay, September 9, 1813, TBP; Isaac Hull, letter to William Jones, September 16, 1813, IHL; J. D. Learned, letter to Robert Douglass, [July 1814], in "Muster Rolls and Company Records Volume, 34th U.S. Infantry"; Isaac Hull, letter to Samuel Ayer, September 6, 1813, in *The Naval War of 1812: A Documentary History*, vol. 2, *1813*, ed. William S. Dudley (Washington, DC: Naval Historical Center, 1992), 239.

27 Anthony G. Dietz, " The Use of Cartel Vessels during the War of 1812," *American Neptune* 28 (July 1968): 165–94; Jonathan Cook, letter to Thomas G. Thornton, May 11, 1813, TGT; Jonathan Simpson, letter to James Barrett, August 19, 1813, TGT; Francis Cook, letter to Thomas G. Thornton, May 24,

1814, TGT2; James Barrett, letters to Thomas G. Thornton, August 18, 1813, and August 19, 1813, CHT; Thomas G. Thornton, letter to General Mason, August 19, 1813, CTP.

28 David Payson, letters to William King, August 27, 1813, and August 29, 1813, WKP; Moses Davis, diary entry, August 29, 1813, MDD; Francis Cook, letter to Thomas G. Thornton, September 2, 1813, TGT2; "The Commonwealth Gaols"; Jonathan Cook, letter to Thomas G. Thornton, June 20, 1813, TGT.

29 "Little Brief Authority," *Portland Gazette*, July 26, 1813; anonymous, diary entry, August 14, 1813, HCC. For the army's side of the story, see *Eastern Argus*, August 5, 1813; and Linda M. Maloney, *The Captain from Connecticut: The Life and Times of Isaac Hull* (Boston: Northeastern University Press, 1986), 241–42.

30 On the Castine incident, see Daniel Brazier File, RG15; and Samuel F. Jordan, entry ZKH, 43:154. On Hodsdon's legal problems, see "Capt. Hodgdon [*sic*] and Military Despotism," *Hallowell Gazette*, April 13, 1814; "Washingtonians," *Eastern Argus*, May 5, 1814; James Willey, letter to John Armstrong, October 14, 1813, M221; Isaac Hodsdon, petition to Congress, January 31, 1822, in Isaac Hodsdon Papers, MeHS; and Eric M. Freeman, *Making Habeas Work: A Legal History* (New York: New York University Press, 2018), chap. 4.

31 H. Henry Senhouse, "Narrative Respecting the Sloop *Venture*," n.d., SFLAC; Thomas Saumarez, letter to John Coape Sherbrooke, November 30, 1813, SFLAC; James Madison, letter to Congress, December 9, 1813, JMP; "Marcellus," letter to John Armstrong, received March 1814, M222; J. D. Learned, letter to Richard Cutts, January 25, 1814, RCP.

32 Rufus McIntire, letter to Rhoda Allan McIntire, April 11, 1813, in Philip W. McIntyre, "Presentation of Rufus McIntire's Sword," in *Collections of the Maine Historical Society*, 3rd ser. (Portland: Maine Historical Society, 1904), 187–90; Jackson Durant's court-martial, RG153.

33 Citizens of Wiscasset, letter to John Armstrong, June 7, 1813, M221; Elias Morse, letter to William King, August 30, 1813, WKP; Ezekiel P. Dodge, letter to William King, April 7, 1813, WKP; Portland Committee of Safety, letter to Caleb Strong, August 24, 1813, in Maine Historical Manuscripts, MeHS; John Brooks, letter to Caleb Strong, September 20, 1813, CDB.

34 For Federalist commentary, see *Portland Gazette*, November 22 and December 20, 1813. Also see "Abstract of Subsistence for two Companies of Massachusetts detached Militia of 2 B. 12 Divn. stationed at Jordan's Point Battery (Fort Burroughs) under the command of Capt. Abel W. Atherton," c. December 1813, in Early Militia Quartermaster Correspondence, MSA.

35 Caleb Strong, letter to House of Representatives, June 7, 1814, MSA; SC1/Series 230, House Unpassed Legislation, 1814, nos. 7701 and 7702, MSA; SC1/Series 231 Senate Unpassed Legislation, 1814, no. 4797, MSA.

36 "Fort Burrows," *Portland Gazette*, December 27, 1813; *Eastern Argus*, February 3 and February 17, 1814; Dudley Hubbard, letter to Cyrus King, January 30, 1814, in "Eminent Men of Maine," MeHS.

37 Cochrane, *History of Monmouth and Wales*, 631; Mary Sewall Buck, diary entry, April 7, 1814, MSB; J. H. Sheppard, *Reminiscences of the Vaughan Family and*

More Particularly of Benjamin Vaughan, LL.D. (Boston: Clapp and Son, 1865), 19; Alpheus S. Packard, *Address of Alpheus S. Packard, D.D.: Delivered on the Occasion of the Centennial Celebration of the Congregational Church at Wiscasset, August 6th, 1873* (Wiscasset, ME: Wood, 1873), 17.

38 William Gribbin, *The Churches Militant: The War of 1812 and American Religion* (New Haven, CT: Yale University Press, 1973), 20, 71–72, 85, 87; William Barrows, Jr., *An Oration, Pronounced at Fryeburg, Maine, on the 4th Day of July, 1812* (Portland, ME: Arthur Shirley, 1812), 15; Lawrence Delbert Cress, "'Cool and Serious Reflection': Federalist Attitudes toward the War of 1812," *Journal of the Early Republic* 7 (Summer 1987): 126–27; Winthrop Bailey, *National Glory: A Discourse Delivered at Brunswick on the Day of the National Fast, August 20, 1812* (Portland, ME: Arthur Shirley, 1812), 12; Nathan S. S. Beman, *A Sermon, Delivered at the Meeting House of the Second Parish in Portland, August 20, 1812, On the Occasion of the National Fast* (Portland, ME: Hyde, Lord, 1812), 5–11; Jonathan T. Den Hartog, *Patriotism and Piety: Federalist Politics and Religious Struggle in the New American Nation* (Charlottesville: University of Virginia Press, 2015), chap. 3, passim.

39 For Republican disgust, see "The Voice of Hancock!," *Eastern Argus*, September 17, 1812. For the toast, see *American Advocate*, July 16, 1814. Also see J. W. Hanson, *History of the Old Towns, Norridgewock and Canaan* (Boston, 1849), 173; George L. Hosmer, *An Historical Sketch of the Town of Deer Isle, Maine* (Boston: Stanley and Usher, 1886), 155–56; and Joshua Cushman, *An Oration, Pronounced at Waterville, July 4, 1814* (Waterville, ME: Cheever, 1814), passim.

40 Gribbin, *The Churches Militant*, 93; Daniel Merrill, *Balaam Disappointed: A Thanksgiving Sermon, Delivered at Nottingham-West, April 13, 1815* (Concord, NH: Isaac Hill, 1816), 26.

41 Parker Cleaveland, Sr., letter to Parker Cleaveland, Jr., December 23, 1812, in Parker Cleaveland Collection, SCA; Isaac Lyman, letter to Cyrus King, July 17, 1813, 1812/WLC; Sarah Vaughan, letter to William Vaughan, September 18, 1812, VFP; Joseph Leavitt, diary entry, September 11, 1814, JLJ; "For the Repertory," *Boston Repertory*, July 24, 1812.

42 Richard Buel, Jr., *America on the Brink: How the Political Struggle over the War of 1812 Almost Destroyed the Young Republic* (New York: Palgrave Macmillan, 2005), 190–91; "Embargo," *Boston Gazette*, January 31, 1814; James M. Banner, Jr., *To the Hartford Convention: The Federalists and the Origins of Party Politics in Massachusetts* (New York: Knopf, 1970), 313.

43 "Extract of a letter from the Hon. Stephen Jones, Esq. of Machias, Me. to the Rev. Clark Brown, of Swanzey, dated March 19, 1814"; George Thatcher, letter to Cyrus King, February 14, 1814, CKP. For an example of the memorials, see Castine's, printed in *Boston Daily Advertiser*, February 16, 1814. Also see Buel, *America on the Brink*, 204.

44 Richard D. Brown, "'No Harm to Kill Indians': Equal Rights in a Time of War," *New England Quarterly* 81, no. 1 (2008): 34–62.

45 "Synopsis of Mr. Fessenden's and Mr. Blake's Speeches in the Massachusetts Legislature," *Eastern Argus*, February 24, 1814; Samuel Eliot Morison, *The Life and Letters of Harrison Gray Otis, Federalist, 1765–1848* (Boston: Houghton Mifflin, 1913), 2:68; Banner, *To the Hartford Convention*, 318.

46 Thomas Cutts, letter to Richard Cutts, July 15, 1813, RCP; J. D. Learned, letter to Richard Cutts, January 25, 1814, RCP; William Moody, letter to Richard Cutts, May 8, 1813, RCP; Dudley Hubbard, letter to Cyrus King, January 30, 1814, in "Eminent Men of Maine"; "Embargo Popular in Maine," *Boston Patriot*, February 16, 1814; "Admiralty Bulls," *Portland Gazette*, October 25, 1813; *U.S. v. 13 Oxen, 1 Cow & 1 Heifer*, December Term, 1813, RG 21/MeDC; *Commonwealth v. John Whiting et al.*, June Term, 1814, Hancock County, SJC.

47 Samuel Emerson, letter to Cyrus King, January 12, 1814, CKP; "Effects of Mr. Madison's War," *Boston Repertory*, January 4, 1814; "Embargo Popular in Maine"; William Moody, letter to Richard Cutts, May 8, 1813, RCP.

48 Old Farmer [John Lowell], *The Road to Peace, Commerce, Wealth, and Happiness* (Boston, 1813), 10–11; David Sewall, letter to Cyrus King, June 30, 1813, CKP; Nathaniel Courant, letter to Cyrus King, November 14, 1814, CKP.

49 Francis Gould Butler, *A History of Farmington, Franklin County, Maine: From the Explorations to the Present Time, 1776–1885* (Farmington, ME: Knowlton, McLeary, 1885), 129; Amasa Loring, *History of Piscataquis County, Maine: From Its Earliest Settlement to 1880* (Portland, ME: Hoyt, Fogg, and Donham, 1880), 119; *Eastern Argus*, December 30, 1813; *ASP:F*, 3:44; Hickey, *War of 1812*, 118–19; Daniel Evans, letter to Thomas G. Thornton, November 7, 1814, TGT; *United States v. Samuel Tuttle*, December Term, 1817, RG21/MeDC.

50 William Berry Lapham and Silas P. Maxim, *History of Paris, Maine, from Its Settlement to 1880* (Paris, ME, 1884), 126–27. Opposers of the tax estimated that collecting Oxford County's share of $5,559.60 would cost $1,050; see "Land Tax!," *Portland Gazette*, August 22, 1814. Also see *ASP:F*, 3:41; Robert Bailey Thomas, *The Massachusetts Register and United States Calendar; for the Year of Our Lord 1815* (Boston: John West, 1815), 250, 252; William Burdick, *The Massachusetts Manual, or, Political and Historical Register* (Boston: Callender, 1814), 152; and Cyrus Eaton, *History of Thomaston, Rockland, and South Thomaston, Maine* (Hallowell, ME: Masters, Smith, 1865), 284. The details of the tax can be found in *Laws of the United States Related to Direct Taxes and Internal Duties* (Boston: Russell, Cutler, 1813).

51 Joseph Williamson, "U.S. Direct Tax, 1815," *Bangor Historical Magazine* 4 (July 1888–June 1889): 62; Brian Arthur, *How Britain Won the War of 1812: The Royal Navy's Blockades of the United States, 1812–1815* (Rochester, NY: Boydell and Brewer, 2011), 183. York County's list of late taxpayers can be found in *Weekly Visitor* (Kennebunk, ME), December 3, December 10, and December 17, 1814. Four towns in the county were not included in these lists: Parsonsfield, Newfield, Cornish, and Limington.

52 "Direct Tax," *Eastern Argus*, January 5, 1815; Francis Brown, *The Evils of War: A Fast Sermon Delivered at North-Yarmouth, April 7, 1814* (Portland, ME: Arthur Shirley, 1814), 20.

53 For the tax delinquents, see "Direct Tax," *Eastern Argus*, January 5 and February 9, 1815. For delinquent taxes remaining in 1816, see *Independent Chronicle* (Boston), March 4, 1816.

54 *ASP:F*, 2:854; "Taxes!—Taxes!—New Taxes!!!," *Portland Gazette*, October 17, 1814; John L. Locke, *Sketches of the History of the Town of Camden, Maine* (Hallowell, ME: Masters, Smith, 1859), 107–8.

55 For complaints about heavy-handed federal officials, see "To the Citizens of Oxford County," *Portland Gazette*, August 22, 1814. Also see "Picture of the Times," *Boston Gazette*, February 3, 1814; Andrew Sherburne, *Memoirs of Andrew Sherburne A Pensioner of the Navy of the Revolution* (Providence, RI: Brown, 1831), 222; and Reed, *History of Bath*, 128–29.

56 James Irish, Jr., letter to James Madison, May 22, 1813, JMP; Orchard Cook, letter to Paul Hamilton, July 12, 1812, M124; Orchard Cook, letter to William Eustis, July 22, 1811, M221; John Binney, letter to Amos Binney, May 24, 1811, in Henry P. Binney Family Papers, MHS. Cook was held in low regard by both Federalists and Democrats but was a political ally of Richard Cutts; see *Boston Repertory*, March 17, 1812.

57 "Embargo Law," *Essex Register* (Salem, MA), January 5, 1814; Joseph Leavitt, diary entry, August 1814, JLJ; J. D. Learned, letter to Richard Cutts, January 25, 1814, RCP; "Smuggling and Bonding," *Boston Patriot*, December 1, 1813.

58 On the sleigh chase, see *Portland Gazette*, November 15, 1813.

59 Joseph Leavitt, diary entry, August 1814, JLJ; "Port of Portland," *Portland Gazette*, October 25, 1813; "Horse Marine List," *Weekly Visitor*, November 6, 1813.

60 *United States v. Ebenezer McIntosh et al.*, December Term, 1814, RG21/MeDC. On the fight with smugglers on a Portland pier, see *Portland Gazette*, June 21, 1813. Also see "Smugglers Detected," *Eastern Argus*, January 27, 1814; and Daniel Remich and Carrie E. Remich, *History of Kennebunk from Its Earliest Settlement to 1890* (Portland, ME: Lakeside, 1911), 260–62.

61 Anonymous, diary entry, January 29, 1814, HCC; William T. Bucknam, letter to his sister, November 9, 1813, in Thomas Child Collection, NEHGS; Ezekiel Dodge, letter to Nathaniel Cushing, September 15, 1814, CHM; "Washington Benevolent Mob," *Eastern Argus*, April 14, 1814; William Parkman, Jr., to William Parkman, Sr., September 28, 1814, Concord Public Library Archives, Concord, MA.

CHAPTER 6: "HAMPDEN RACES"

1 On the Jonesport skirmish, see "Communication for the Patriot," *Boston Patriot*, March 9, 1814; and *City Gazette* (Saint John, NB), March 21, 1814. Also see U.S. House of Representatives, "John Allen," in House Report 61, 35th Congress, 2nd sess., January 7, 1859. On Allen's sword, see "Tribute to Merit," *Boston Patriot*, June 22, 1814; and Stuart C. Mowbray, "The Presentation Sword of Captain John Allen," *Man at Arms* 19, no. 1 (1997): 26–30;

2 Samuel L. Miller, *History of the Town of Waldoboro, Maine* (Wiscasset, ME: Emerson, 1910), 113–14. The Waldoboro men's imprisonment is verified in

the Royal Navy's register of prisoners of war; see ADM 103/90. Their cruel incarceration was long remembered; see *Maine Farmer* (Augusta), March 9, 1854; and Brian Arthur, *How Britain Won the War of 1812: The Royal Navy's Blockades of the United States, 1812–1815* (Rochester, NY: Boydell and Brewer, 2011), 113.

3 Kevin D. McCranie, *Utmost Gallantry: The U.S. and Royal Navies at Sea in the War of 1812* (Annapolis, MD: Naval Institute Press, 2011), 214–18; Alexander Cochrane, letter to James Monroe, August 14, 1814, in *ASP: FR*, 3:693; J. Mackay Hitsman and Donald E. Graves, *The Incredible War of 1812: A Military History* (Toronto: Robin Brass Studio, 1999), 237–38; Arthur, *How Britain Won the War of 1812*, 110–13; Andrew Lambert, *The Challenge: Britain against America in the Naval War of 1812* (London: Faber and Faber, 2012), 315, 320.

4 Alexander Cochrane, quoted in C. J. Bartlett, "Gentlemen versus Democrats: Cultural Prejudice and Military Strategy in Britain in the War of 1812," *War in History* 1, no. 2 (1994): 153; Lambert, *The Challenge*, 305; David Milne, letter to George Hume, September 6, 1814, in Edgar Erskine Hume, "Letters Written during the War of 1812 by the British Naval Commander in American Waters (Admiral Sir David Milne)," *William and Mary Quarterly* 10, no. 4 (1930): 294; Richard Saumarez, diary entry, September 5, 1814 entry, in Richard Saumarez Journal, 1812/LLIU; Henry Edward Napier and Walter Muir Whitehill, *New England Blockaded in 1814: The Journal of Henry Edward Napier, Lieutenant in H.M.S. "Nymphe"* (Salem, MA: Peabody Museum, 1939), 23, 26–27; William Begg, diary entry July 4, 1814, WBJ.

5 "Commitment for Treason," *Essex Register* (Salem, MA), June 25, 1814; James Byers, letter to John Armstrong, July 9, 1814, M221; *United States v. Tyler P. Shaw*, October Term, 1814, and May Term, 1823, MaCC/RG21. For Shaw's denial of wrongdoing, see "To the Public," *Columbian Centinel* (Boston), November 19, 1814.

6 Cyrus King, letter to unknown, June 17, 1814, in King-Hale-Douglass Family Papers, MHS; The best account of *Bulwark*'s operations on the Maine coast is Nathan R. Lipfert, "An Episode of the Blockade: Locally Referred to as The Alarm or Panic of 1814," unpublished manuscript, consulted courtesy of the author.

7 Eleanor Motley Richardson and Peter Tufts Richardson, eds., *The Ingraham Diaries, 1795–1815* (Rockland, ME: Red Barn, 2018), 163; William King, letter to John Brooks, June 27, 1814, in Commonwealth of Massachusetts, *Report of the Merits of the Claim of the State of Massachusetts on the National Government* (Boston: Russell and Gardner, 1822), 36–38.

8 William King, letter to John Brooks, June 24, 1814, in Commonwealth of Massachusetts, *Report of the Merits*, 21; William Begg, diary entry, July 7, 1814, WBJ; David Payson, letters to William King, May 13, 1814, June 21, 1814, and June 26, 1814, WKP; Samuel Veazie, letter to William King, June 22, 1814, WKP; John H. Sheppard, letter to his mother, June 25, 1814, 1812/WLC; Lipfert, "Episode of the Blockade," 19; .

9 William King, letter to John Brooks, July 4, 1814, in Commonwealth of Massachusetts, *Report of the Merits*, 40–41; William Begg, diary entry, July 2,

1814, WBJ; Francis Byron Greene, *History of Boothbay, Southport and Boothbay Harbor, Maine, 1623–1905* (Portland: Loring, 1906), 255; John Johnston, *A History of the Towns of Bristol and Bremen in the State of Maine, Including the Pemaquid Settlement* (Albany, NY: Joel Munsell, 1873), 410–12.

10 *Boston Repertory*, July 19, 1814; William Begg, diary entries, August 7, and August 10, 1814, WBJ; Bill Horner, "Dr. William Begg, HMS *Tenedos*, the War of 1812, and the 'Battle of Norwood Cove,'" *Chebacco* 21 (2020): 88–97.

11 William Begg, diary entry, July 1, 1814, WBJ; Boothbay selectmen, letter to Amasa Davis, April 6, 1814, in Coastal Defense Letters, MSA; Joseph Beath, letter to Robert Larrabee, July 1812, in *Boothbay Region Historical Sketches: Selections from Out of Our Past*, by Barbara Rumsey (Boothbay Harbor, ME: Boothbay Region Historic Society, 1999), 2:62–65.

12 John H. Sheppard, letter to his mother, June 25, 1814, 1812/WLC.

13 George Augustus Wheeler, *History of Brunswick, Topsham and Harpswell, Maine* (Boston: Mudge and Son, 1877), 736–37; Henry Wilson Owen and Edward Clarence Plummer, *The Edward Clarence Plummer History of Bath, Maine* (Bath, ME: Times Company, 1936), 148–49, 153–54; William Jenks, letter to Jesse Appleton, June 20, 1814, in Jesse Appleton Collection, SCA.

14 District orders, July 28, 1814, ILP; William Bainbridge, letter to Henry Dearborn, August 31, 1812, in Boston Customhouse Papers, MHS. On the Lubec skirmish, see "Extract of a Letter from Eastport," *New England Palladium* (Boston), May 10, 1814; and "Extract of Another Letter," *Boston Patriot*, May 11, 1814.

15 General orders, March 28, 1814, in "General Order Book of Military District No. 1," BPL; Thomas H. Cushing, letter to John Walbach, March 11, 1814, M566; division orders, June 21 and June 22, 1814, in "Massachusetts Militia—Eleventh Division. Copies of Division Orders Commencing Anno Domini 1811," ZKH; John Brooks, letter to William King, July 1, 1814, in Commonwealth of Massachusetts, *Consideration and Documents Relating to the Claim of Massachusetts for Expenditures During the Late War* (Washington: de Krafft, 1818), 37; William King, letters to John Brooks, June 27, 1814, and July 1, 1814, in ibid.; James Perry, letter to William King, July 28, 1814, and July 29, 1814, WKP; William King, letter to John Brooks, June 24, 1814, in Commonwealth of Massachusetts, *Report on the Merits*, 21; Henry S. Burrage, "Captain John Wilson and Some Military Matters in the War of 1812," *Collections and Proceedings of the Maine Historical Society*, 2nd ser., 10 (1899): 421–23.

16 William King, letter to Henry Dearborn, July 26, 1814, in Henry Dearborn Papers, MHS; Martin Kinsley, letter to Amasa Davis, July 28, 1814, CDB; Joseph Williamson, letter to Norman Williams, August 10, 1814, 1812/WLC.

17 J. D. Learned, letter to Callender Irvine, May 22, 1813, in Joseph D. Learned's court-martial, RG 153; John Neal, *Wandering Recollections of a Somewhat Busy Life: An Autobiography* (Boston: Roberts Brothers, 1869), 175. Learned moved to Baltimore, where he became known as an apologist for slave ownership. John Neal remembered him as an "amiable, kind-hearted, shiftless, clever man, who was sadly perplexed and bothered all his life through, and up to the very

last, for 'presuming to be ambitious'" (ibid.). Also see Portland Committee of Safety, letter to Caleb Strong, June 22, 1814, *ASP:MA*, 3:865–67; Portland Committee of Safety, letter to Alford Richardson, August 6, 1814, ibid., 866–67; Lemuel Weeks, letters to Amasa Davis, August 8, 1814, August, 9, 1814, and August 19, 1814, CDB; Martin Kinsley, letter to Amasa Davis, July 28, 1814, CDB; William King, letter to Henry Dearborn, July 26, 1814, in Henry Dearborn Papers, MHS; Henry Dearborn, letter to John Armstrong, June 19, 1814, M221; Charles M. Blake, "Letter from the Committee of Safety, in Penobscot, 1814," *Bangor Historical Magazine* 2, no. 10 (1887): 203; William Abbott, letter to John Blake, June 30, 1814, and John Blake, letter to Caleb Strong, July 7, 1814, both in Charles M. Blake, "Gen. John Blake's Letters," *Bangor Historical Magazine* 6, nos. 7–9 (1891): 140–41.

18 "A Republican," letter to James Monroe, August 9, 1814, in James Monroe Papers, LoC; David Cobb, letter to G. W. Hare, August 7, 1814, in David Cobb Papers, MHS.

19 George Cranfield Berkeley, letter to William Marsden, August 14, 1807, CO 217/81; Nathaniel Atcheson, *American Encroachments on British Rights, or, Observations on the Importance of the British North American Colonies and on the Late Treaties with the United States* (London: Butterworth, 1808); "Joint Address to his Royal Highness from the Council and House concerning the New Brunswick-Maine boundary line," March 2, 1814, RS24.

20 John Coape Sherbrooke, letter to Earl Bathurst, July 9, 1814, CO 217/93 For more about Pilkington's life, see "A Memoir of Lieutenant-General Sir Andrew Pilkington, K.C.B., 1774–1853," n.d., unpublished manuscript, LAC.

21 John Swett, letter to Amasa Davis, July 2, 1814, CDB; George H. Hight, letter to James Monroe, December 31, 1814, M222; Thomas M. Hardy and Andrew Pilkington, letter to the officer commanding U.S. troops, July 14, 1814, in *Select British Documents of the Canadian War of 1812*, ed. William Wood (Toronto: Champlain Society, 1920–28), 3:301–5; George F. W. Young, *The British Capture and Occupation of Downeast Maine, 1814–1815/18* (Castine, ME: Penobscot Books, 2014), 1–6. On the soldiers who fled, see Samuel A. Morse's court-martial, RG153.

22 Charles Faxon, letter to his parents, July 28, 1814, in Manchester-Phetteplace-Stone Family Papers, Rhode Island Historical Society, Providence; John Brewer, letter to John Armstrong, July 16, 1814, M221; Henry Dearborn, letter to John Armstrong, Boston, July 25, 1814, M221; Rufus King, letter to Gouvernor Morris, February 15, 1815, RKP; John Brooks, letter to John Brewer, August 29, 1814, CDB.

23 McCranie, *Utmost Gallantry*, 201–2.

24 Charles Morris, letter to William Jones, September 20, 1814, M148; William J. Rogers, letter to William Jones, August 19, 1814, M148; Charles Morris, *The Autobiography of Charles Morris, U.S. Navy* (Annapolis, MD: Naval Institute, 1880), 68–69.

25 John L. Locke, *Sketches of the History of the Town of Camden, Maine* (Hallowell, ME: Masters, Smith, 1859), 112–16. The pilot received a presidential pardon after the war; see "Moses Thorndike," July 7, 1816, T967.

26 W. E. Campbell, *The Road to Canada: The Grand Communications Route from Saint John to Quebec* (Fredericton, NB: Goose Lane Editions, 2005), 47–48, 61–63; George Prévost, letter to John Coape Sherbrooke, July 15, 1814, SFLAC; Thomas Saumarez, letter to George Prévost, November 16, 1813, vol. 284, RG8/C; Thomas Saumarez, letter to Noah Freer, April 26, 1814, and June 7, 1814, vol. 284, RG8/C.

27 Campbell, *The Road to Canada*, 59–62. For an impressive first-person account of the 104th's march, see Donald E. Graves, ed., *Merry Hearts Make Light Days: The War of 1812 Journals of Lieutenant John Le Couteur, 104th Foot* (Ottawa: Carleton University Press, 1993). See also John R. Grodzinski, *The 104th (New Brunswick) Regiment of Foot in the War of 1812* (Fredericton, NB: Goose Lane Editions, 2014), 44–54; and Hugh Francis Pullen, *The March of the Seamen: The story of H.M. Armed Schooner "Tecumseth* Occasional Papers Nos. 8 and 9 (Halifax, NS: Maritime Museum of Canada, 1961), passim.

28 John R. Grodzinski, *Defender of Canada: Sir George Prévost and the War Of 1812* (Norman: University of Oklahoma Press, 2014), 146–47; George F. G. Stanley, *The War of 1812: Land Operations* (Toronto: Macmillan of Canada, 1983), 364–65; George Prévost, letter to John Coape Sherbrooke, July 15, 1814, SFLAC; John Coape Sherbrooke, letter to Earl Bathurst, August 18, 1814, CO 217/93 W. Cottnam Tonge, letter to M. G. Skerret, October 12, 1807, CO 217/81.

29 Earl Bathurst, letter to John Coape Sherbrooke, July 15, 1814, vol. 685, RG8/C; John Coape Sherbrooke, letter to George Prévost, August 2, 1814, vol. 685, RG8/C; Alexander Cochrane, letter to Earl Bathurst, July 14, 1814, in *Naval War of 1812, 1813–1814*, ed. Michael J. Crawford (Washington, DC: Naval Historical Center, 2002), 3:132; Edward Griffith, letter to John Croker, August 25, 1814, ADM 1/506; Edward Griffith, letter to Alexander Cochrane, August 23, 1814, ACP; John Coape Sherbrooke, to Earl Bathurst, August 26, 1814, CO 217/93.

30 John Coape Sherbrooke, letter to Earl Bathurst, September 10, 1814, and Edward Griffith, letter to Alexander Cochrane, September 9, 1814, both in Wood, *Select Documents of the Canadian War of 1812*, 3:308–22; Richard Saumarez, diary entry, September 1, 1814, in Richard Saumarez Journal, 1812/LLIU; Begg, diary entries, August 31 and September 1, 1814, Benjamin Cushing, letter to Nathaniel Cushing, September 2, 1814, BCP; David Payson, letter to John Brooks, August 31, 1814, *ASP:MA*, 3:876.

31 William Begg, diary entries, August 31 and September 1, 1814, WBJ; entry, February 14, 1814, in "General Order Book of Military District No. 1, July 14, 1812–June 14, 1814," BPL.

32 Francis Stanfell, letters to Edward Griffith, September 1, and September 4, 1814, in Francis Stanfell Papers, NYPL; anonymous, diary entry, September 1, 1814, ABO; Richard Saumarez, diary entries, September 1 and September 4, 1814, in Richard Saumarez Journal, 1812/LLIU. The Twenty-ninth Regiment was well known for its Black drummers; see J. D. Ellis, "Drummers for the Devil? The Black Soldiers of the 29th (Worcestershire) Regiment of Foot, 1759–1843," *Journal of the Society for Army Historical Research* 80 (2002): 186–202.

33 Robert Barrie, letter to Edward Griffith, September 3, 1814, enclosure in Edward Griffith, letter to Alexander Cochrane, September 9, 1814, ACP; Robert K. Sutcliffe, *British Expeditionary Warfare and the Defeat of Napoleon, 1793–1815* (Woodbridge, UK: Boydell, 2016), 144–45.

34 Stanfell, letters to Griffith, September 1 and September 4, 1814; Barrie, letter to Griffith, September 3, 1814; Henry John, letter to John Coape Sherbrooke, September 3, 1814, in Wood, *Select British Documents* 3:314–15; Erasmus Archibald Jones, *History of Frankfort* (Winterport, ME: Advertiser Job Print, 1897), 16–18.

35 John Blake, letter to John C. Calhoun, July 1820, in Charles M. Blake, "Memoir of General John Blake of Brewer, and His Descendants," *Bangor Historical Magazine* 2, no. 1 (1886): 3–6; *History of Penobscot County, Maine; With Illustrations and Biographical Sketches* (Cleveland: Williams, Chase, 1882), 351.

36 Epaphras Hoyt, *Practical Instructions for Military Officers: Comprehending a Concise System of Military Geometry, Field Fortification and Tactics of Riflemen and Light Infantry* (Greenfield, MA: John Denio, 1811), 92; brigade orders, July 23, 1812, in Chamberlain Collection, UMSC.

37 Henry John, letter to John Coape Sherbrooke, September 3, 1814, SFLAC; John Blake, letter to Caleb Strong, September 7, 1814, in John Blake File, RG 15. Blake's account is largely corroborated by Charles Morris in his official report to William Jones, September 20, 1814, M124; testimony of Jonathan Knowles, in John Blake's court of inquiry, MSA.

38 Isaac Maltby, *The Elements of War* (Boston: Wait and Company, 1813), xxi; *ASP:MA*, 3:890; Charles Morris's court-martial October 11, 1814, M273; Joseph Williamson, letter to George Williamson, September 7, 1814, accession 72.34.1, MeSM.

39 Joseph W. Porter, "Address on the Incorporation of Orrington," *Maine Historical Magazine* 7, nos. 10–12 (1892): 198; Jones, *History of Frankfort*, 18.

40 Testimony of Francis Carr and Simeon Stetson, in John Blake's court of inquiry, MSA.

41 Charles Morris's court-martial, October 11, 1814, M273; John Carlow, *A Journal of Adventures at Sea, Before and During the Late War between Great Britain and the United States of America* (Portland, ME: Pennell, 1839), 34; Williamson, letter to Williamson, Bangor, September 7, 1814.

42 Morris, *Autobiography*, 71; Isaac Cobb File, RG 15.

43 Richard Saumarez, diary entry, September 1, 1814, in Richard Saumarez Journal, 1812/LLIU; testimony of Francis Carr, John Blake's court of inquiry, MSA; Jones, *History of Frankfort*, 21–22.

44 Testimony of Oliver Leonard John Blake's court of inquiry, MSA. The phrase "Hampden Races" was a reference to the bigger and better-known battle of Bladensburg in Maryland, in which a British expedition also swept aside a hastily composed force of militia, sailors, and regulars on August 24, 1814.

45 Young, *British Capture and Occupation*, 32–41.

46 Morris, *Autobiography*, 71–72; Moses Appleton, letter to Nathan Appleton, September 10, 1814, in Appleton Family Papers, MHS; Isaac Hull, letter to William Jones, September 11, 1814, M124; Morris, *Autobiography*, 72; "List of the Officers and Crew of the U.S. Ship *Adams*," MeSA.

47 Faxon, letter to his parents, July 28, 1814; John Brewer, letter to John Armstrong, July 16, 1814, M221; Henry Dearborn, letter to John Armstrong, July 25, 1814, M221; John Brooks, letter to John Brewer, August 29, 1814, CDB; Samuel A. Morse's court-martial, January 1815, RG153; George H. Hight, letter to James Monroe, December 31, 1814, M222; Jeremiah O'Brien, letter to A. J. Dallas, November 17, 1815, M222; William Sanborn, letter to A. J. Dallas, November 17, 1814, M222.

48 "Extract of a letter received by a gentleman in this town, dated Machias, August 8, 1814," *Eastern Argus*, August 25, 1814; "To Gen. John Cooper Sheriff of the County of Washington," *Boston Patriot*, January 4, 1815.

49 Stephen Richardson Pension File, RG15; Michael Rutstein, *The Privateering Stroke: Salem's Privateers in the War of 1812* (Salem, MA, 2012), 224–27; Thomas Masterman Hardy, memorandum, July 17, 1814, in *Samuel Leach v. Chebacco Boat "S."* of Belfast, October Term, 1814, MeDC/RG21; *New Brunswick Royal Gazette* (Saint John), August 29, 1814; William D. Williamson, *The History of the State of Maine: from its first discovery, A.D. 1602, to the separation, A.D. 1820* (Hallowell, ME: Glazier, Masters, 1837), 641; Lemuel Trescott, letter to Henry Dearborn, July 30, 1814, in William Hull Papers, HLH; George H. Hight, letter to James Monroe, December 31, 1814, M222; William Sanborn, letter to A. J. Dallas, November 17, 1814, M222; *New England Palladium* (Boston), September 13, 1814; David Zimmerman, *Coastal Fort: A History of Fort Sullivan, Eastport, Maine* (Eastport, ME: Border Historical Society, 1984), 50–56.

50 William Begg, diary entries, September 10, 1814, and September 11, 1814, WBJ; Andrew Pilkington, letter to John Coape Sherbrooke, September 14, 1814, in Wood, *Select British Documents*, 3:329–334; anonymous, diary entries, September 10, and September 11, 1814, ABO; "Return of Ordnance, Arms, Ammunition taken by the troops of Lt. Col. Pilkington, Sept. 11th 1814," SFLAC. For the officer's comments on the cattle he found, see *Portland Gazette*, October 6, 1814.

51 Richard Saumarez, diary entry, September 11, 1814, in Richard Saumarez Journal, 1812/LLIU.

52 Anonymous, letter to William King, January 14, 1815, WKP; John Cooper, letter to Caleb Strong, September 17, 1814, in *Narrative of the Town of Machias, the Old and the New, the Early and Late*, by George Washington Drisko (Machias, ME: Press of the Republican, 1904), 306–9; Machias capitulation, September 12, 1814, SFLAC.

53 Anonymous, diary entry, September 12, 1814, ABO; William Begg, diary entry, September 12, 1814, WBJ; "Heroic and Interesting Incidents in War of 1812," *Machias (ME) Union*, March 9, 1897.

54 John Coape Sherbrooke, letter to George Prévost, September 23, 1814, in Sir John Coape Sherbrooke Out-Letter Book, SFLAC; receipt, dated Machias Bay, September 15, 1814, in Francis Stanfell Letter Book, NYPL; William Begg, diary entry, September 14, 1814, WBJ; anonymous, diary entry, September 14, 1814, ABO.

CHAPTER 7: "ONE AGAINST ANOTHER"

1 Eleanor Motley Richardson and Peter Tufts Richardson, eds., *The Ingraham Diaries, 1795–1815* (Rockland, ME: Red Barn, 2018), 174.
2 Joseph Williamson, letter to Norman Williams, October 25, 1814, 1812/WLC.
3 Joseph Williamson, letter to George Williamson, September 7, 1814, accession 72.34.1, MeSM.
4 Samuel K. Whiting, letter to John Holmes, October 11, 1814, in Charles A. Flagg, "Relating to the War of 1812," *Sprague's Journal of Maine History*, 6, no. 3 (1918–19): 126–28; "British Outrage," *Eastern Argus* (Portland), October 27, 1814; statement of John Godfrey, October 4, 1814, M625; *George Halliburton v. the Inhabitants of Frankfort*, June Term, 1817, Hancock County, SJC; Erasmus Archibald Jones, *History of Frankfort* (Winterport, ME: Advertiser Job Print, 1897), 22–23.
5 "Accounts from the Eastward," *New England Palladium* (Boston), September 13, 1814; "British Outrage"; Williamson, letter to Williamson, September 7, 1814; Joseph Williamson, "British Officers on the Penobscot," *Bangor Historical Magazine*, 3, no. 1 (1887): 27; Williamson, letter to Williams, October 25, 1814; Flagg, "Relating to the War of 1812," 126–28; George H. Witherle, "Letter from Castine, Relating to Its History, 1814, and Prior," *Bangor Historical Magazine* 3 (July 1887–June 1888): 216.
6 Mary Sewall Buck, diary entry, September 4, 1814, MSB.
7 Melatiah Jordan, letter to George W. Cambell, September 29, 1814, RG178; "Bonds for Seized Property at Moose Island," vol. 129, RG8/IV; John Coape Sherbrooke, letter to Earl Bathurst, February 25, 1815, CO 217/96. Halifax currency, also known as Nova Scotia currency, was worth less than British currency, which was based on pounds sterling.
8 Williamson, letter to Williamson, September 7, 1814; Edward Griffiths, letter to commander of HMS *Bulwark*, September 2, 1814, in Witherle, "Letters from Castine," 218; "Abstract of Decrees of Property Condemned at Penobscot," SFLAC; Jordan, letter to Cambell, September 29, 1814; permit for *Penobscot Packet*, September 16, 1814, in John Crosby Papers, MeHS; Jeremiah O'Brien, letter to James Monroe, July 4, 1815, M179; *George Bacon v. Schr. "Thinks-I-To-Myself*," December Term, 1814, RG21/MeDC.
9 Samuel K. Whiting, letter to John Holmes, October 11, 1814, in Flagg, "Relating to the War of 1812," 126–28; Williamson, letter to Norman Williams, October 25, 1814.
10 Monition 607, brig *Favorite*, and monition 616, ship *Betsy*, vol. 135, RG8/IV.
11 Robert Barrie, letter to Dolly Gardner Clayton, November 11, 1814, in *Naval War of 1812, 1813–1814*, ed. Michael J. Crawford (Washington, DC: Naval Historical Center, 2002), 3:340.
12 *Clement Cathell v. "General Kutousoff" and Cargo*, May Term, 1814, RG21/MeDC; "Arrival of a good Prize," *Eastern Argus*, June 2, 1814.
13 David Milne, letter to selectmen of Frankfort, September 14, 1814, in C. E. French Collection, MHS; David Milne, letter to commanding officer, Portland, September 20, 1814, in ibid; "In the District of Maine," *Columbian Centinel*,

September 24, 1814; David Milne, letter to officer commanding the District of Massachusetts, September 16, 1814, M221; Henry Dearborn, letter to David Milne, September 24, 1814, M221; Jones, *History of Frankfort*, 24–26. See also "The *Galloway*," HCA 45/70/33.

14 Anonymous, diary entry, November 15, 1814, ABO; HMS *Adder*, logbook entry, November 15, 1814, ADM 51/2087.

15 George Monkhouse, letter to Harris W. Hailes, January 14, 1815, RS8; Ezekiel Dodge, letter to Nathaniel Cushing, September 15, 1814, in Ezekiel G. Dodge Collection, CHM.

16 General order, September 15, 1814, Nova Scotia Council, September 23, 1814, RG1/227, PANS.

17 Gerard Gosselin, letter to the selectmen of Brewer, November 1, 1814, in Chamberlain Collection, UMSC; David Morgan, letter to Gerard Gosselin, November 14, 1814, in Maine Historical Manuscripts, MeHS; Paul Dudley Sargent, letter to Samuel Dana, November 4, 1814, enclosure in Samuel Dana, letter to James Monroe, November 30, 1814, M222.

18 Abishai Bolton, letters to Nathaniel Bolton, August 29, and September 14, 1814, in Nathaniel Bolton Papers, AAS; William B. Sprague, *Annals of the American Pulpit* (New York: Carter and Brothers, 1857), 310; Joseph Leavitt, diary entry, October 1814, JLJ.

19 William Black, letter to John Crosby, November 19, 1814, in John Crosby Papers, MeHS. On the Perkins family's trade with Bermuda during the war, see Bermuda customs records, CO 41/10.

20 John Coape Sherbrooke, letter to Earl Bathurst, September 8, 1814, CO 217/93; George Herbert, letter to John Coape Sherbrooke, September 10, 1814, CO 217/93; Edward Griffiths, letter to Alexander Cochrane, September 9, 1814, ACP.

21 William Begg, diary entries, July 1, August 7, and September 12, 1814, WBJ; *U.S. v. A Boat & Lading*, December Term, 1814, RG21/MeDC; Hickey, *War of 1812*, 234–35; Jacob Ulmer, letter to John Brooks, September 29, 1814, in *History of the City of Belfast in the State of Maine*, vol. 2, 1875–1900, by Joseph Williamson and Alfred Johnson (Boston: Houghton Mifflin, 1913), 439; Alexander Milliken, letter to the U.S. secretary of state, October 26, 1814, M179.

22 George Ulmer, letter to Henry Dearborn, September 26, 1814, in King-Dearborn-Little Papers, MHS; Ezekiel G. Dodge, letter to Nathaniel Cushing, September 15, 1814, in Ezekiel G. Dodge Collection, CHM; John Comings, Joseph Gowin, and Moses Burly, letter to William King, October 3, 1814, WKP.

23 *U.S. v. 13 Oxen, 1 Cow & 1 Heifer*, December Term, 1813, RG21/MeDC; *Commonwealth v. John Whiting et al.*, June Term, 1814, Hancock County, SJC; U.S. Congress, Committee of Claims, *Report of the Committee of Claims on the Bill from the Senate, for the Relief of Josiah Hook, Jun.* (Washington, DC: Gales and Seaton, 1824); "Criminal Intercourse," *Boston Patriot*, January 4, 1815.

24 Anonymous, letter to William King, November 26, 1814, WKP.

25 Anonymous, letter to William King, January 14, 1815, WKP; Andrew Pilkington, letter to John Coape Sherbrooke, September 14, 1814, in *Select*

British Documents of the Canadian War of 1812, ed. William Wood (Toronto: Champlain Society, 1920–28), 3:329; John Cooper, letter to Caleb Strong, September 17, 1814, in *Narrative of the Town of Machias, the Old and the New, the Early and Late*, by George Washington Drisko (Machias: Press of the Republican, 1904), 306–9; John Cooper, letter to Josiah Harris, September 13, 1814, 1812/WLC; Peter E. Vose, "General John Cooper," *Bangor Historical Magazine* 2, no. 1 (1886): 33–35; "To Gen. John Cooper, Sheriff of Washington County," *Boston Patriot*, January 4, 1815.

26 "Federalism of the 'Boston Stamp,' or Sheriff Adams of Smuggling Memory," *Eastern Argus*, March 9, 1815; "The Double-Bottomed Waggon," *Boston Patriot*, November 9, 1814; "Sheriff Adams and his False-Bottom Waggon," February 8, 1815; *United States v. A Horse, Waggon, & Lading*, December Term, 1814, RG21/MeDC.

27 George Stracey Smyth, letter to John Coape Sherbrooke, December 26, 1814, SFLAC; complaint of James Bentley, February 10, 1815, Notary Public Records, in Ward Chipman Papers, New Brunswick Museum, Saint John; "Transcripts of civil and military cases in St. John, New Brunswick," 221–326, 1812/LLIU; George L. Hosmer, *An Historical Sketch of the Town of Deer Isle, Maine* (Boston: Stanley and Usher, 1886), 234–35.

28 Isaac Hull, letter to Samuel Storer, October 10, 1814, IHL; Isaac Hull, letters to William Jones, October 10, 1814, and November 28, 1814, IHL; Isaac Hull, letter to J. B. McCulloch, November 4, 1814, IHL; Charles Morris, letter to William Jones, September 20, 1814, M124; Isaac Hull, letter to Jones, November 4, 1814, M625; Hugh D. McLellan and Katherine B. Lewis, *History of Gorham, Me.* (Portland, ME: Smith and Sale, 1903), 161; Samuel Storer, letter to William Jones, December 19, 1814, in Samuel Storer Letterbook, personal collection of George Emery; inhabitants of Hampden, petition to U.S. Congress, September 19, 1814, M625; certificate of George B. McCulloch, October 3, 1814, M625; deposition of Simeon Stetson, October 5, 1814, M625; copy of certificate permitting Hampden committee to salvage *Adams*, n.d., M625; Isaac Hull, letter to William Jones, October 10, 1814, M625; "Report of Property saved from the wreck of the U.S. late ship *Adams*," [October 1814], M625.

29 Williamson, *History of the State of Maine*, 655; Simeon Stetson, letter to John Crosby, Sr., December 3, 1814, in John Crosby Papers, MeHS.

30 John Blake, letter to the Massachusetts General Court, February 14, 1815, Unpassed Legislation, 1814, no. 7937A, MSA; John Coape Sherbrooke, memorandum about the Penobscots, September 9, 1814, CDB; John Blake, report, January 31, 1815, in Fannie Hardy Eckstorm Collection, UMSC; Gerard Gosselin, letter to John Coape Sherbrooke, February 10, 1815, SFLAC.

31 John Chandler, letter to James Monroe, November 21, 1814, M221; Elbridge Gerry, letter to Henry Dearborn, November 17, 1814, M221.

32 Passports of John Suckley and John G. Smith, RG1/227; *U.S. v. 1 Trunk Merchandise*, May Term, 1815, RG 21/MeDC; D. C. Harvey, "Pre-Agricola John Young, or A Compact Family in Search of Fortune," *Collections of the Nova Scotia Historical Society* 32 (1959): 135.

33 Joshua M. Smith, *Borderland Smuggling: Patriots, Loyalists, and Illicit Trade in the Northeast* (Gainesville: University Press of Florida, 2006), 88–89; "Amos Proctor," House Report 474 *(28–1)*, May 15, 1844, 43–44; Lewis Tappan, *The Life of Arthur Tappan* (New York: Hurd and Houghton, 1870), 46–56; *United States v. 11 Bales Merchandise* and *United States v. 16 Bale Merchandise*, both February Term, 1815, RG21/MeDC; "Remission of Forfeitures" *ASP:F*, 3:112; Cornelius Peter Van Ness, *Claim of C. P. Van Ness* (Washington, DC, 1852), 18.

34 Brian Arthur, *How Britain Won the War of 1812: The Royal Navy's Blockades of the United States, 1812–1815* (Rochester, NY: Boydell and Brewer, 2011), 176–78, 230, 241; John Coape Sherbrooke, letter to Earl Bathurst, January 6, 1815, CO 217/96; Samuel K. Whiting, letter to William King, December 21, 1814, WKP; John Chandler, letter to James Monroe, November 21, 1814, M221; "Look Out for British Spies," *Eastern Argus*, November 17, 1814. Further comments on the Castine smuggling trade appear in *Eastern Argus*, November 24, 1814. Also see "A loop hole, or the Blockade partially removed," *Portland Gazette*, November 21, 1814.

35 "Amos Proctor," 41–42; "Accommodating Stage," *Hallowell Gazette*, January 4, 1815; *United States v. Charles Hayward et al.* October Term, 1817, RG21/MaCC; deposition of John Crosby Jr., *United States v. 6 Bales Goods*, September Term, 1816, RG21/MeDC.

36 Josiah Hook, Jr., letter to A. J. Dallas, November 24, 1814, *Robinson v. Hook*, October Term, 1826, RG21, MeCC; "Amos Proctor," 11, 31–32.

37 Joseph Farley, letter to Henry Dearborn, November 1, 1814, CHW; Benjamin Ames and Joseph F. Wingate, Jr., *The Disclosure. No. 1. Documents Relating to Violations and Evasions of the Laws, During the Commercial Restrictions and Late War with Great Britain, Etc. Part the First. (Further and Still More Important Suppressed Documents.)* (Bath, ME: Torrey, 1824), 23–25; William King, letters to James Monroe, October 30 and December 27, 1814, M221.

38 "Amos Proctor," 14. Proctor apparently kept a detailed journal of his adventures, but it has yet to come to light. In 1844, Congress awarded Proctor $27,446.63 for his role in the seizure, but by that time he had died. For public notices of seizures, see the "Marshal's Sales" ads, *Eastern Argus*, February 16, February 20, and February 23, 1815. Also see *United States v. William Dawes, Josiah L. James, and Offen B. Palmer*, Special Term, February 1815, RG21/MeDC; and *United States v. 1 Hogshead Rum*, May Term, 1815, RG21/MeDC.

39 "Extract of a letter, dated Castine, November 21, 1814," *New Brunswick Royal Gazette* (Saint John), December 19, 1814; "Loss of the sch'r ANN, Capt. M'Donald, from Halifax to Castine," *Acadian Recorder* (Halifax, NS), November 5, 1814; Jesse Page, letter to Thomas G. Thornton, October 15, 1814, TGT; libel of Jonathan Low, Jr., et al., October 19, 1814, *United States v. Schooner "Ann,"* December Term, 1814, RG21/MeDC; deposition of George Coombs, January 26, 1820, M625; Joseph Farley, letter to David Sewall, October 17, 1814, M625; Joseph Farley, letter to Jonathan Low, Jr., November 21, 1814, M625; Nicholas Emery, letter to Jonathan Low, Jr., November 12, 1814, M625.

40 John L. Locke, *Sketches of the History of the Town of Camden, Maine* (Hallowell, ME: Masters, Smith, 1859), 135–44; "Noah Miller," House Report 120, (33–1),

February 16, 1854, 1–9; "West Drinkwater and Others," *House Report* 10, (34–1), March 31, 1856, 1–22. For a highly detailed account of the *Mary's* capture, see *Acadian Recorder*, April 22, 1815.

41 William Mounsey, letter to Camden selectmen, November 3, 1814, M221; Erastus Foote, letter to Asa Hill, November 4, 1814, M221; Benjamin Cushing, letter to Nathaniel Cushing, December 22, 1814, BCP.

42 A. Eustiphive, letter to W. P. Preble, December 3, 1814, M179; W. P. Preble, letter to A. J. Dallas, January 27, 1815, M179.

43 *U.S. v. Thomas Cunningham*, December Term, 1815, RG 21/MeDC; *Commonwealth v. Daniel Whittier*, June Term, 1815, Hancock County, SJC; "Pension to a Revenue Officer Disabled in Service," *ASP:C*, 1:523.

44 Harvey, "Pre-Agricola John Young," 131; Alexander Milliken, "An Interesting Historical Document," *Collections and Proceedings of the Maine Historical Society*, 2nd ser. (Portland: Maine Historical Society, 1891), 2:332 (in the document, the name of the ship *Fame* has been mistakenly transcribed as *Fawn*); *Alexander Milliken v. Schooner "Industry" & Cargo*, February Term, 1815, RG21/MeDC; Richardson and Richardson, *The Ingraham Diaries*, 177.

45 Log entry, December 25, 1814, in "Journal of Proceedings onboard the Private Armed Schooner *Cumberland*," 1812/LLIU; Robert Rockfort, letter to John W. Croker, December 28, 1814, ADM 1/509; log entries, February 4, February 5, and February 7, 1815, in "Logbook of the Privateer Schooner *Fly* of Portland," MeHS.

CHAPTER 8: YANKEE CONFUSION

1 Henry Dearborn, letter to Caleb Strong, September 4, 1814, in Commonwealth of Massachusetts, *Considerations and Documents Relating to the Claim of Massachusetts for Expenditures during the Late War* (Washington, DC: De Krafft, 1818), 46–47; Otis Robbins, Jr., letter to his brother, September 17, 1814, in *History of Thomaston, Rockland, and South Thomaston, Maine*, by Cyrus Eaton (Hallowell, ME: Masters, Smith, 1865), 299–300; Moses Davis, diary entries, September 2, 9, 11, and 21, 1814, MDD; Simon Walworth, letter to Jonas Simonds, September 22, 1814, 1812/LLIU.

2 "Drummer Burrill," *Pemaquid Messenger* (Bristol, ME), March 20, 1890; Louise Helen Coburn, *Skowhegan on the Kennebec* (Skowhegan, ME: Independent Reporter Press, 1941), 589; Charles F. Whitman, *A History of Norway, Maine: From the Earliest Settlement to the Close of the Year 1922* (Norway, ME, 1924), 100; anonymous, diary entry, September 17, 1814, HCC.

3 William H. Sumner, letter to John Brooks, September 19, 1814, in Commonwealth of Massachusetts, *Considerations and Documents*, 50–55; William H. Sumner, letter to John Brooks, October 28, 1814, CDB; Coburn, *Skowhegan on the Kennebec*, 589.

4 Lemuel Weeks, letter to Amasa Davis, August 8, August 9, and August 19, 1814, CBD; William H. Sumner, letter to John Brooks, September 28, 1814, CDB; William Goold, *Portland in the Past* (Portland, ME: Thurston and

Company, 1886), 440–41; David Payson, letter to William King, October 13, 1814, WKP.

5 "Extracts from an Orderly Book of Capt. Richard Hiscock," Boothbay Harbor Historical Society, Boothbay, ME; Henry P. Warren, *The History of Waterford, Oxford County, Maine* (Portland, ME: Hoyt, Fogg, and Donham, 1879), 127; Moses Davis, diary entries, September 24 and September 28, 1814, MDD.

6 Donald R. Hickey, *The War of 1812: A Forgotten Conflict, Bicentennial Edition* (Urbana: University of Illinois Press, 2012), 264–65; Henry Dearborn, letter to Caleb Strong, July 8, 1814, in Commonwealth of Massachusetts, *Considerations and Documents*, 27; Caleb Strong, letter to the secretary of war, September 7, 1814, *ASP:MA*, 3:73.

7 District orders, August 19, 1814, FMDO; George F. Talbot, "General John Chandler of Monmouth, Maine, with Extracts from His Autobiography," *Collections of the Maine Historical Society*, 1st ser. (Portland: Maine Historical Society, 1884), 9:167–205; Henry Dearborn, letter to John Armstrong, June 19, 1814, M221; John Chandler, letters to Henry Dearborn, September 2, 1814, and September 5, 1814, 1812/LLIU; John Chandler, letter to Henry Dearborn, September 4, 1814, in John Chandler Letters, 1714–1814, NYHS; William H. Sumner, letter to John Brooks, September 15, 1814, *ASP:MA*, 3:896–97; John Chandler, letter to the Portland Committee of Safety, September 11, 1814, *ASP:MA*, 3:895.

8 David Cobb, letter to Charles W. Hare, August 7, 1814, in David Cobb Papers, MHS; Abel Atherton, letter to John Brooks, December 20, 1813, *ASP:MA*, 3:894; John Brooks, letter to Abel Atherton, December 27, 1813, *ASP:MA*, 3:858–59; John Brooks, letter to William King, July 1, 1814, in Commonwealth of Massachusetts, *Considerations and Documents*, 38–39.

9 George Ulmer, letter to William King, September 13, 1814, WKP; Jacob Ulmer, letter to William King, September 16, 1814, WKP; George Watson, letter to William H. Sumner, September 23, 1814, CDB; Jacob Ulmer, letter to John Brooks, September 29, 1814, *ASP:MA*, 3:858–59.

10 William King, letter to Henry Sewall, September 8, 1814, in Henry Sewall Papers, MeHS; Samuel Dana letter, to James Monroe, November 30, 1814, M222; Wiscasset Committee of Safety, letter to Henry Sewall, September 11, 1814, HSP; Henry Sewall, letter to David Payson, September 11, 1814, 1812/WLC.

11 See the correspondence among Captain William Bainbridge, commander of the Charlestown Navy Yard; Governor Caleb Strong; and Adjutant John Brooks, in Commonwealth of Massachusetts, *Considerations and Documents*, 29–36.

12 William H. Sumner, *An Inquiry into the Importance of the Militia to a Free Commonwealth* (Boston: Cummings and Hilliard, 1823), 7–8; William H. Sumner, letter to John Brooks, September 19, 1814, in Commonwealth of Massachusetts, *Considerations and Documents*, 50–55. The most thorough account of militia problems at Portland is Donald R. Hickey, "New England's Defense Problem and the Genesis of the Hartford Convention," *New England Quarterly* 50, no. 4 (1977): 587–604.

13 Commissioners of the Sea-Coast Defense, letter to William H. Sumner, September 10, 1814, *ASP:MA*, 3:890; Henry Dearborn, letter to Isaac Hull, September 10, 1814, in Commonwealth of Massachusetts, *Considerations and Documents*, 61; William H. Sumner, *A History of East Boston: With Biographical Sketches of Its Early Proprietors, and an Appendix* (Boston: Tilton, 1858), 736–39.

14 William H. Sumner, letter to John Brooks, September 12, 1814, CDB; William H. Sumner, letter to John Brooks, September 15, 1814, *ASP:MA*, 3:892.

15 William H. Sumner, letter to John Brooks, September 19, 1814, in Commonwealth of Massachusetts, *Considerations and Documents*, 50–55; Henry Dearborn, letter to James Madison, September 6, 1814, JMP.

16 William H. Sumner, letter to John Brooks, September 22 and September 24, 1814, in Commonwealth of Massachusetts, *Considerations and Documents*, 56–57; William H. Sumner, letter to Ezekiel Chase, September 21, 1814, *ASP:MA*, 3:918; Henry Dearborn, letter to Thomas H. Perkins, September 27, 1814, *ASP:MA*, 3:918; Thomas H. Perkins to Dearborn, September 27, 1814, *ASP:MA*, 3:918; John Chandler, letter to Henry Dearborn, September 26, 1814, in Gunther Collection of War of 1812 Documents, Chicago History Museum; *Eastern Argus*, October 13, 1814.

17 District orders, September 23, 1814, FMDO; "To Major General Alford Richardson, commanding the militia called out for the defence of Portland," September 24, 1814, *ASP:MA*, 3:85–86; William H. Sumner, letter to John Brooks, September 25, 1814, *ASP:MA*, 3:85–86; Ricardo A. Herrera, *For Liberty and the Republic: The American Citizen as Soldier, 1775–1861* (New York: New York University Press, 2015), 87–88.

18 Alford Richardson, letter to William H. Sumner, September 30, 1814, *ASP:MA*, 3:900; William H. Sumner, letter to Alford Richardson, October 1, 1814, *ASP:MA*, 3:900.

19 Henry Dearborn, letter to John Brooks, September 28, 1814, in Commonwealth of Massachusetts, *Considerations and Documents*, 65; garrison orders, September 28, 1814, and September 29, 1814, FMDO.

20 William Jones, letter to James Madison, October 26, 1814, in *Naval War of 1812, 1813–1814*, ed. Michael J. Crawford (Washington, DC: Naval Historical Center, 2002), 3:633; Linda M. Maloney, *The Captain from Connecticut: The Life and Times of Isaac Hull* (Boston: Northeastern University Press, 1986), 254–57.

21 Division orders, September 8, 1814, in Eleventh Division Orderbook, MeHS; Samuel Dana, letter to James Monroe, November 30, 1814, M222; William King, letter to John Brooks, September 8, 1814, *ASP:MA*, 3:877; William H. Sumner, letter to John Brooks, September 19, 1814, in Commonwealth of Massachusetts, *Considerations and Documents*, 50–55; John Chandler, letter to William King, September 18, 1814, in ibid., 50–55; receipt from Captain James Perry, Fortieth U.S. Infantry, October 3, 1814, in Orders of Governor and Council and General Orders, MSA; agreement among Henry Sewall, William King, and William H. Sumner, September 22, 1814, in Henry Sewall Papers, MeHS; Sumner, *History of East Boston*, 742.

22 William King, letter to John Chandler, September 19, 1814, in Commonwealth of Massachusetts, *Considerations and Documents*, 55; William H. Sumner, letter to John Brooks, October 1, 1814, *ASP:MA*, 3:906; Hickey, *War of 1812*, 268–70; William King, letter to Henry Dearborn, October 6, 1814, WKP.

23 District orders, September 28, 1814, in John Wilson Papers, MeHS; orders, Sub-Military District Headquarters, Portsmouth, October 7, 1814, FMDO; William H. Sumner, letter to John Brooks, October 3, 1814, *ASP:MA*, 3:907.

24 William H. Sumner, letter to John Brooks, September 22, 1814, in Commonwealth of Massachusetts, *Considerations and Documents*, 56–57; receipt from Captain James Perry, 40th U.S. Infantry, October 3, 1814, "Orders of Governor and Council and General Orders," MSA; William H. Sumner, letter to John Brooks, October 28, 1814, CDB.

25 Elbridge Gerry, letter to Henry Dearborn, November 17, 1814, M221; Samuel K. Whiting, letter to William King, December 21, 1814, WKP; Ronald F. Banks, *Maine Becomes a State: The Movement to Separate Maine from Massachusetts, 1785–1820* (Middletown, CT: Wesleyan University Press, 1970), 60–61.

26 James Monroe, letter to Henry Dearborn, November 14, 1814, in James Monroe Papers, LoC; Henry Dearborn letter, to William King, December 22, 1814, in James B. Vickery Collection, UMSC; William King, letter to Henry Dearborn, December 23, 1814, 1812/WLC; William King, letter to James Monroe, December 27, 1814, M221.

27 Caleb Strong, letter to James Monroe, December 9, 1814, M221; George Stracey Smyth, letters to John Coape Sherbrooke, October 31, 1814, and December 24, 1814, SFLAC; George Prévost, letter to John Coape Sherbrooke, January 28, 1815, SFLAC. On Ulmer's rumored espionage, see *Columbian Centinel* (Boston) December 21, 1814; "The Expedition to Castine," *Hallowell (ME) Gazette*, January 11, 1815; and James Monroe, letter to William King, January 2, 1815, M222.

28 Banks, *Maine Becomes a State*, 63–66; *Eastern Argus*, March 2, and March 30, 1815; *Boston Patriot*, January 4, January 7, March 11, and March 15, 1815.

29 William Fogg, diary entries, November 5 and November 9, 1814, in J. L. M. Willis, "A Journal for the Year—1814," *Old Eliot* 3, no. 2 (1899): 15–19; "Spotted Fever," *Portsmouth (NH) Patriot*, February 4, 1815.

30 Henry Dearborn, letter to James Monroe, December 2, 1814, M221; Robert Ilsley, letter to John Chandler, November 29, 1814, 1812/LLIU; Robert Ilsley, letter to Henry Dearborn, April 7, 1815, M221; Thomas Buckminster, letter to Isaac Lane, February 2 and February 12, 1815, ILP; Nathaniel Gookin, letter to Isaac Lane, November 2, 1814, ILP; detachment orders, Portland, February 26, 1815, FMDO.

31 John J. Davis, letter to secretary of war, October 31, 1814, M221; James Perry, letter to secretary of war, January 14, 1815, M221; Timothy Upham, letter to James Monroe, December 17, 1814, M222.

32 "Ichabod Waymouth," *House Report* 102, (32–1), January 13, 1852; Perry, letter to secretary of war, January 14, 1815; Henry Dearborn, letter to James Monroe, December 8, 1814, M221.

33 "34th Regiment of Infantry. Capt. Thomas Bailey's Company. Fort Preble, Portland Harbor, Maine. U.S. Army Miscellaneous Collection," NYPL.

34 Garrison order, Fort Preble, February 4, 1815, FMDO; W. Byrd Powell, *The Natural History of the Human Temperaments* (Cincinnati: Phillips, 1849), 315–16; Isaac Furbush et al., letter to James Madison, January 9, 1815, M566; Cyrus King, letter to Richard Cutts, January 16, 1815, M566; Cyrus King, letter to James Monroe, January 16, 1815, M566; Samuel Emerson, letter to Cyrus King, January 10, 1815, CKP; pardons of Joseph Bailey and William Furbush, January 18, 1815, T967.

35 "From the East," *Boston Gazette*, January 5, 1815; George Augustus Wheeler, *History of Castine, Penobscot, and Brooksville* (Bangor, ME: Burr and Robinson, 1875), 74–75, 299–302.

36 "Extract from a letter dated Bangor, November 15th, 1814," *Boston Repertory*, November 21, 1814; "From Castine," *Acadian Recorder* (Halifax, NS), December 3, 1814; "Amos Proctor," House Report 474 (28–1), May 15, 1844, 42; permit to William Vaughan, January 30, 1815, VFP. On the "military chest," see *Public Ledger and Daily Advertiser* (London), December 12, 1817; and John Lee and Company's daybook, in Witherle Collection, Baker Library, Harvard Business School, Boston.

37 Wheeler, *History of Castine*, 301; "Deserters," *Portland Gazette*, November 7, 1814; Stephen Bean, letter to Isaac Lane, September 24, 1814, ILP. See John H. Cannon File, RG 15: Cannon enlisted under a false name "to avoid the vigilance of English emissaries, with which the country then abounded." Also see John Langdon, letter to James Madison, September 19, 1814, JMP; "30 Dollars Reward," *Eastern Argus*, December 1, 1814; Grace Limeburner et al., *Traditions and Records of Brooksville, Maine* (Auburn, ME: Merrill and Webber, 1936), 11–12; "British Barbarity," *Eastern Argus*, May 24, 1815; and "British Barbarity and Villainy," *Boston Patriot*, June 7, 1815. The local man tried for abetting desertion was probably Eben Hutchins of Penobscot, who had refused to take the British oath. See his obituary in the *Machias (ME) Union*, May 3, 1881.

38 Anonymous, letter to William King, January 14, 1815, WKP. For an older woman's recollection of the British occupation, see *Machias Union*, March 9, 1897. Also see David Zimmerman, *Coastal Fort: A History of Fort Sullivan, Eastport, Maine* (Eastport, ME: Border Historical Society, 1984), 56. For details of the execution of British deserters, see *Newburyport (MA) Herald*, December 30, 1814.

39 George Prévost, letter to John Coape Sherbrooke, January 28, 1815, SFLAC; Wheeler, *History of Castine*, 133, 159, 300. Privates Thomas Simpson and William West were "shot for Desertion"; see WO 25/1298.

CHAPTER 9: WINTER OF DISCONTENT

1 Henry Dearborn, letter to James Monroe, October 15, 1814, M221; Donald R. Hickey, "New England's Defense Problems and the Genesis of the Hartford Convention," *New England Quarterly* 50, no. 4 (1977): 598–600.

2   Caleb Strong, speech, October 5, 1814, in Commonwealth of Massachusetts, *Resolves of the Commonwealth of Massachusetts, 1814–1815* (Boston: Russell, Cutler, 1815), 558; Richard Buel, Jr., *America on the Brink: How the Political Struggle over the War of 1812 Almost Destroyed the Young Republic* (New York: Palgrave Macmillan, 2005), 215–17; Samuel Eliot Morison, "Our Most Unpopular War," in *Dissent in Three American Wars*, ed. Samuel Eliot Morison, Frederick Merk, and Frank Freidel (Cambridge, MA: Harvard University Press, 1970), 43–44.

3   Buel, *America on the Brink*, 215–18; Samuel Eliot Morison, *Life and Letters of Harrison Gray Otis* (Boston: Houghton Mifflin Company, 1913), 2:104, 140.

4   "An Act to Establish a Military Corps for the Defence of the Commonwealth of Massachusetts," passed October 20, 1814, chap. 77, *Laws of the Commonwealth of Massachusetts*, 6: 575–78. Intriguingly, this law called for the soldiers to be organized into hundred-man companies rather than the traditional sixty-four-man companies, thus complying with federal military regulations. For Parris's response, see *Eastern Argus*, October 27, 1814.

5   Alfred Cole and Charles Foster Whitman, *A History of Buckfield, Oxford County, Maine, from the Earliest Explorations to the Close of the Year 1900* (Buckfield, ME, 1915), 92; *Eastern Argus*, February 2, 1815. The entire proceedings of the Oxford Convention can be found in "Oxford Convention," *American Advocate* (Hallowell, ME), January 21, 1815. See also Jeremiah Goodwin, letter to John Holmes, December 25, 1814, Portsmouth Athenaeum, Portsmouth, NH.

6   Poem attributed to John Hunter of Strong, Maine, and titled "Farmington Convention," in Francis Gould Butler, *A History of Farmington, Franklin County, Maine* (Farmington, ME: Knowlton, McLeary, 1885), 126–27.

7   James Monroe, letter to governors of Massachusetts and Connecticut, September 17, 1814, in *ASP:MA*, 1:614; Ronald F. Banks, *Maine Becomes a State: The Movement to Separate Maine from Massachusetts, 1785–1820* (Middletown, CT: Wesleyan University Press, 1970), 61; Caleb Strong, letter to Timothy Pickering, October 17, 1814, in *Documents Relating to New England Federalism, 1800–1815*, ed. Henry Adams (Boston: Little, Brown, 1877), 399; Timothy Pickering, letter to Gouverneur Morris, October 21, 1814, in ibid., 402; John Lowell, Jr., letter to Timothy Pickering, December 3, 1814, in ibid., 413.

8   Samuel K. Whiting et al., letter to James Madison, December 8, 1814, M221.

9   Samuel K. Whiting, letter to William King, September 21, 1814, WKP; "To the Inhabitants of Maine," *Weekly Messenger* (Boston), December 30, 1814; Banks, *Maine Becomes a State*, 66.

10 On North Yarmouth's meeting, see *Portland Gazette*, September 26, 1814; and "Defending the Soil," *Portland Gazette*, October 3, 1814.

11 Quoted in W. Johnston, *History of the Library of Congress*, vol. 1, *1800–1864* (Washington, DC: Government Printing Office, 1904), 86; Jeremiah Hill, letter to Cyrus King, November 6, 1814, CKP.

12 Herbert T. Silsby, "A Secret Emissary from Down East," *Maine Historical Society Quarterly* 11, no. 7 (1972): 109–10; Cyrus King, speech, October 22, 1814, printed in full in the *Hallowell Gazette*, November 9, 1814; anonymous, diary entry, December 24, 1814, HCC; George Thatcher, letter to Cyrus King, November 17, 1814, in Calvin M. McClung Historical Collection, East Tennessee History Center, Knoxville.

13 Silsby, "A Secret Emissary," 109–10; J. S. Martell, "A Side-Light on Federalist Strategy during the War of 1812," *American Historical Review*, 43, no. 3 (1938): 554.

14 J. C. A. Stagg, *Mr. Madison's War: Politics, Diplomacy, and Warfare in the Early American Republic, 1783–1830* (Princeton, NJ: Princeton University Press, 1983), 480–82; Buel, *America on the Brink*, 226–27; Hickey, *War of 1812*, 279–83; anonymous, diary entries, November 12, November 19, and December 24, 1814, HCC.

15 Anonymous, diary entry, February 18, 1815, HCC; Hugh D. McLellan and Katherine B. Lewis, *History of Gorham, Me.* (Portland, ME: Smith and Sale, 1903), 310; David Noyes, *The History of Norway* (Norway, ME, 1852), 109–10; James W. North, *The History of Augusta, from the Earliest Settlement to the Present Time* (Augusta, ME: Clapp and North, 1870), 420; George Folsom, *History of Saco and Biddeford with Notices of Other Early Settlements* (Saco, ME: Putnam, 1830), 112–13; "Ratification of the Treaty," *American Advocate*, February 25, 1815; "Peace Ball," *American Advocate*, March 4, 1815; Henry Wilson Owen and Edward Clarence Plummer, *The Edward Clarence Plummer History of Bath, Maine* (Bath, ME: Times Company, 1936), 164; Amasa Loring, *History of Piscataquis County, Maine: From Its Earliest Settlement to 1880* (Portland: Hoyt, Fogg, and Donham, 1880), 227.

16 Noyes, *History of Norway*, 109–10; anonymous, diary entry, February 25, 1815, HCC; William Berry Lapham, *History of Rumford, Oxford County, Maine* (Augusta ME: Maine Farmer, 1890), 166; William Freeman, *An Address Delivered at Limerick, Me., February 1815, on the Celebration of Peace between Great Britain and the United States* (Bangor, ME: Smith and Sayward, 1846), 7.

17 Duke of Wellington, letter to Earl of Liverpool, November 9, 1814, in *Supplementary Despatches and Memoranda of Field Marshal Arthur, Duke of Wellington, K.G.*, vol. 9, *April 1814 to March 1815*, ed. Arthur Wellesley Wellington and Arthur Richard Wellesley Wellington (London: Murray, 1858), 426.

18 George Ulmer, letter to Daniel Parker, February 27, 1815, RG15; George Ulmer, letter to William King, February 27, 1815, WKP; William King, letter to James Monroe, February 20, 1815, M221; James Miller, letter to Horatio Stark, February 20, 1815, M221; James Miller, letter to William King, March 8, 1814, M221; James Miller, letter to secretary of war, March 24, 1815, M221; Horatio Stark, letter to James Miller, March 18, 1815, M221; Gerard Gosselin, letter to Horatio Stark, March 15, 1815, M221.

19 Anthony St. John Baker, letter to James Monroe, July 31, 1815, and enclosures, in *Diplomatic Correspondence of the United States: Canadian Relations, 1784–1860*, ed. William R. Manning (Washington, DC: Carnegie Endowment for International Peace, 1940), 1:724–27. The records refer to the lieutenant as "Moss," but undoubtedly this was Samuel A. Morse, who was both a resident of Machias and an officer in the Fortieth U.S. Infantry.

20 Gerard Gosselin, letter to Horatio Stark, April 25, 1815, M222; Horatio Stark, letter to Henry Dearborn, April 29, 1815, M221; Samuel Upton, Thomas Adams, Otis Little, and others, letter to A. J. Dallas, June 4, 1815, M221.

21 Jonathan R. Bell, letter to Eleazar W. Ripley, October 2, 1815, M179; Samuel D. Harris, letter to Henry Dearborn, May 29, 1815, M179; H.A.S. Dearborn, letter to A. J. Dallas, June 22, 1815, M179; "From Castine," *Boston Patriot*, April 22, 1815; A. J. Dallas, letter to James Madison, May 12, 1815, JMP; Bradford Perkins, *Castlereagh and Adams: England and the United States, 1812–1823* (Berkeley: University of California Press, 1964), 163–64.

22 Jeremiah O'Brien, letter to James Monroe, July 4, 1815, M179; James Caze and John Richaud, letter to James Monroe, August 21, 1816, M179.

23 Bradford Harlan, letter to quartermaster, June 19, 1815, in Quartermaster Correspondence, MSA; Job Nelson, letter to John Dickinson, July 20, 1815, in ibid.

24 On General Brewer's conduct, see *Eastern Argus*, April 26, 1815. Also see Jonathan D. Weston, letter to Cyrus King, March 30, 1816, CKP; Ichabod R. Chadbourne, letter to Cyrus King, November 25, 1815, CKP; and "Interesting Abstracts," *Boston Patriot*, April 15, 1815.

25 Alexander S. Wadsworth, letter to Benjamin Crowninshield, November 10, November 20, and December 28, 1815, M148; Irving A. King, *The Coast Guard under Sail: The U.S. Revenue Cutter Service, 1789–1865* (Annapolis: Naval Institute Press, 1989), 67–69.

26 Lemuel Trescott, letter to Joseph Gubbins, January 2, 1816, M179; Joseph Gubbins, letter to Lemuel Trescott, February 15, 1816, M179; Lemuel Trescott, letter to A. J. Dallas, February 5, 1816, M179; Jonathan Odell, letter to Earl Dalhousie, December 19, 1816, RS588; George Smith, letter to Thomas G. Thornton, August 29, 1815, CTP.

27 "Charles Emerson Autobiography," in American Baptist Historical Society Archives, Atlanta; Joseph Farley, letter to John Mason, June 17, 1814, CHW. The estimate of Maine men at Dartmoor is based on a database assembled by the late Ira Dye and going through British prisoner of war registers. Also see Robert Sanders's pension application, RG15. Note that Sanders also went by the name of Robert Willet.

28 "Sketch of Dartmoor Prison, 1815," MeHS; Charles Andrews, *Prisoners' Memoirs, or Dartmoor Prison* (New York, 1852), 101–2, 138–39, 144–51.

29 Paul A. Gilje, *Free Trade and Sailors' Rights in the War of 1812* (New York: Cambridge University Press, 2013), chap. 19; Perez Drinkwater, Jr., letter to his parents, April 8, 1815, in *Prisoners of War at Dartmoor*, by Trevor James (Jefferson, NC: McFarland, 2013), 177–78; Cyrus Eaton, *History of Thomaston, Rockland, and South Thomaston, Maine* (Hallowell, ME: Masters, Smith, 1865), 294; James Fairfield, letter to Lois Fairfield, April 25, 1815, in Captain James Fairfield Collection, Brick Store Museum, Kennebunk, ME; Lot Davis File, in MacArthur Files, SCA.

30 Gilje, *Free Trade and Sailors' Rights*, 269–75. For York seafarers' response to the king's report, see *Niles' Weekly Register* (Baltimore), October 28, 1815.

31 Daniel Brent, letter to Denny McCobb, March 10, 1819, M40; Glover Broughton, letters to Jonathan Talpey, March 22 and March 29, 1853, in Talpey Family Correspondence, Old York Historical Society, York, ME.

CHAPTER 10: APRÈS LA GUERRE

1 Moses Greenleaf, *A Survey of the State of Maine: In Reference to Its Geographical Features, Statistics and Political Economy* (Portland, ME: Shirley and Hyde, 1829), passim.
2 Paul Holland Searson, letter to James Monroe, February 27, 1819, M179; deposition of William Burns March 30, 1819, M179.
3 George L. Hosmer, *An Historical Sketch of the Town of Deer Isle, Maine* (Boston: Stanley and Usher, 1886), 156, 236; "Who are the Federal leaders in Bucksport?," n.d., 1812/LLIU; Benjamin Waterhouse, "Report of 1817 Tour," in Benjamin Waterhouse Letterbook, CHM.
4 Peter Brock, *Pacifism in the United States, from the Colonial Era to the First World War* (Princeton, NJ: Princeton University Press, 1968), 482–88; John Hemmenway, *Apostle of Peace, Memoir of William Ladd* (Boston: American Peace Society, 1872), 41; Calvin Montague Clark, *History of the Congregational Churches in Maine* (Portland : Southworth, 1935), 397–98.
5 James W. Oberly, "Westward Who? Estimates of Native White Interstate Migration after the War of 1812," *Journal of Economic History*. 46, no. 2 (1986): 433. For examples of veterans seeking pensions from the Maine legislature, see Elisha Douglass, 1821, GY 5-5, and John Carleton, 2nd, 1821, both RS 3-47, MeSA. Also see J. B. S. Jackson, *A Descriptive Catalogue of the Anatomical Museum of the Boston Society for Medical Improvement* (Boston: Ticknor, 1847), 18.
6 "Petition of Lemuel Worster," *Senate Report* 542 (33-2), February 26, 1855.
7 Lucy George, letter to A. J. Dallas, November 15, 1815, M566; Lora Altine Woodbury Underhill, *Descendants of Edward Small of New England and the Allied Families:* (Boston: Houghton Mifflin, 1934), 1086–88. For a widow's petition for a pension, see Hannah Swain, widow of John, vol. 48, 132, ZKH.
8 James W. Oberly, "Gray-Haired Lobbyists: War of 1812 Veterans and the Politics of Bounty Land Grants," *Journal of the Early Republic*, 5, no. 1. (1985): 37; Charles O. Stickney, "The Defense of Portland in 1814," *Eastern Argus* (Portland), January 19, 1895; "Certain Massachusetts Soldiers of War of 1812," in House Report 80, 40th Congress, 3rd sess. (40-1), January 15, 1881. Numbers thanks to Larry Glatz, who extrapolated them from U.S. Pension Bureau, *List of pensioners on the roll, January 1, 1883, giving the name of each pensioner, the cause for which pensioned, the post-office address, the rate of pension per month, and the date of original allowance* (Washington, DC: Government Printing Office, 1883), vols. 1–5. Also see Robert Bowden File, RG 15.
9 Noble E. Cunningham, Jr., *The Presidency of James Monroe* (Lawrence: University Press of Kansas, 1996), 36; Samuel Putnam Waldo, *The Tour of James Monroe, President of the United States* (Hartford, CT: Bolles and Company, 1818), 172–89; Christopher Gore, letter to Rufus King, November 30, 1817, RKP; Ronald P. Formisano, *The Transformation of Political Culture: Massachusetts Parties, 1790s–1840s* (New York: Oxford University Press, 1983), 119.
10 Ronald F. Banks, *Maine Becomes a State: The Movement to Separate Maine from Massachusetts, 1785–1820* (Middletown, CT: Wesleyan University Press, 1970),

71; Richard J. Buel, Jr., *America on the Brink: How the Political Struggle over the War of 1812 Almost Destroyed the Young Republic* (New York: Palgrave Macmillan, 2005), 204, 217; Francis M. Carroll, *A Good and Wise Measure: The Search for the Canadian-American Boundary, 1783–1842* (Toronto: University of Toronto Press, 2001), 35–46; Waterhouse, "Report of 1817 Tour," CHM; secretary of state, letter to James Miller, June 1, 1818, M40; *Eastport (ME) Sentinel*, August 31, 1818.

11 Carroll, *A Good and Wise Measure*, 47–69; Gary Campbell, *The Road to Canada: The Grand Communication Route from Saint John to Quebec* (Fredericton, NB: Goose Lane, 2005), 65–66; Howard T. Jones, "Anglophobia and the Aroostook War," *New England Quarterly* 48, no. 4 (1975): 519–39.

12 C. Edward Skeen, *1816: America Rising* (Lexington: University of Kentucky Press, 2003), 55–56.

13 William K. Bolt, *Tariff Wars and the Politics of Jacksonian America* (Nashville, TN: Vanderbilt University Press, 2017), 14–15; Gerald S. Graham, *Sea Power and British North America, 1783–1820* (Cambridge, MA: Harvard University Press, 1941), 259.

14 *Hiram*, RG8/IV, vol. 162; *New Brunswick Courier* (Saint John), February 24, 1816; *Free Press* (Halifax, NS), May 26, 1818; Henry Wright, letter to Britain's commissioners of customs, May 28, 1816, CUST34/6207; "Gallant Exploit," *American Advocate* (Hallowell, ME), July 18, 1818.

15 Graham, *Sea Power and British North America*, 260–61; petition of Lydia Follett, September 20, 1821, CUST34/6598; and Wayne M. O'Leary, *Maine Sea Fisheries: The Rise and Fall of a Native Industry, 1830–1890* (Boston: Northeastern University Press, 1996), 16–20, 40–48.

16 O'Leary, *Maine Sea Fisheries*, 42–43.

17 William King, letter to Cyrus King, December 30, 1816, RKP; William King, letter to Rufus King, April 13, 1818, RKP; Rufus King, letter to Christopher Gore, February 11, 1819, RKP; Banks, *Maine Becomes a State*, 35; Skeen, *1816*, 59.

18 William King, letter to Rufus King, February 11, 1819, RKP; Banks, *Maine Becomes a State*, 127–28.

19 "Shocking Murder!," *Eastern Argus*, June 7, 1815. For the hissing incident, see *Eastern Argus*, June 28, 1815. For rumors about Adams's spousal abuse and infidelity, see *Boston Patriot*, June 3, 1815. Also see Moses Adams, letters to Caleb Strong, May 20 and June 17, 1815, in Council Files, MSA; John Bulfinch, *The Trial of Moses Adams, High-Sheriff of the County of Hancock* (Boston: Tileston, 1815), passim; Joseph Williamson, "Capital Trials in Maine, before the Separation," *Collections and Proceedings of the Maine Historical Society*, 2nd ser. (Portland, ME: Maine Historical Society, 1890), 1:171–72; and Alan Rogers, "A Sailor 'By Necessity': The Life of Moses Adams, 1803–1817," *Journal of the Early Republic*, 11, no. 1 (Spring 1991): 19–50.

20 *Commonwealth v. Coburn Tyler*, September Term, 1816, Lincoln County, SJC, MeSA; Ellen Mason, "The Old Meeting House of North Yarmouth, Maine," *Old Times* 2, no. 2 (1878): 185; "Charles Emerson Autobiography," RG 1247, American Baptist Historical Society, Atlanta; Alan Taylor, *Liberty Men and*

Great Proprietors: The Revolutionary Settlement on the Maine Frontier, 1760–1820 (Chapel Hill: University of North Carolina Press, 1990), 237–38; Banks, *Maine Becomes a State*, 141–42.

21. James Brooks, letter to Cyrus King, April 15, 1815, in King-Hale-Douglass Family Papers, MeHS; Commonwealth of Massachusetts, general orders, May 15, 1813, and January 19, 1816, UMSC; John Blake, letter to Caleb Strong, August 26, 1815, in Mason Family Correspondence, Bangor Historical Society, Bangor, ME; Benson J. Lossing, *Pictorial Field-Book of the War of 1812* (New York: Harper and Brothers, 1869), 902; "Black Jack," *Eastern Argus*, October 25, 1815, "Commemoration of the Celebrated Battle at Hampden 1814," *Eastern Argus*, November 1, 1815; "Hero of Hampden!!," *Eastern Argus*, February 13, 1816; William Riddall, "Letter of Capt. and Major Riddall to Major General Gosseline [*sic*] at Castine, 181* Relating to Gen. John Blake," *Bangor Historical Magazine* 8, nos. 4–6 (1893): 92.

22. On Brooks's tour, see *Columbian Centinel* (Boston) September 16, 1818. For Federalist outrage regarding Republican slander of Brooks, see *Hallowell Gazette*, September 2, 1818; and Formisano, *Transformation of Political Culture*, 63–65, 103.

23. On Brooks's bad luck with weather, see *Weekly Visitor* (Kennebunk, ME), September 12, 1818; and Charles Elventon Nash, Martha Ballard, and Edith Lydia Hary, *The History of Augusta; First Settlements and Early Days as a Town* (Augusta, ME, 1904), 227.

24. John Holmes, *An Oration, Pronounced at Alfred, on the 4th of July, 1815, being the Thirty Ninth Anniversary of American Independence* (Boston, 1815), passim; Stephanie Kermes, *Creating an American Identity: New England, 1789–1825* (New York: Palgrave Macmillan, 2015), 151, 162; Benjamin Vaughan, letter to Martha Jefferson Randolph, June 23, 1819, in Thomas Jefferson Papers, MHS; Robert A. McCaughey, *Josiah Quincy, 1772–1864: The Last Federalist* (Cambridge, MA: Harvard University Press, 1974), 84–85; John Adams, letter to Daniel Cony, February 1, 1819, in John Adams Papers, MHS; Samuel Eliot Morison, *The Life and Letters of Harrison Gray Otis* (Boston: Houghton Mifflin, 1913), 2:234; James S. Leamon, Richard R. Westcott, and Edward O. Schriver, "Separation and Statehood," in *Maine: The Pine Tree State from Statehood to the Present*, ed. Richard W. Judd, Edwin A. Churchill, and Joel W. Eastman (Orono: University of Maine Press, 2011),184.

25. Banks, *Maine Becomes a State*, 118–19; Richard Alton Erney, *The Public Life of Henry Dearborn* (New York: Arno, 1979), 329–31.

26. Joshua Wingate, Jr., letter to William King, February 17, 1818, WKP.

27. Anonymous, *An Appeal to the People of Maine on the Question of Separation* (Boston, 1816), 4. For Massachusetts as an evil stepmother, see *Bangor Weekly Register*, April 13, 1816. For an optimistic view of Maine's future, see *Eastern Argus*, April 20, 1819. A more balanced view can be found in *Boston Daily Advertiser*, August 9, 1819.

28. Rufus King, letters to Christopher Gore, February 11, 1819, and November 5, 1816, RKP; Banks, *Maine Becomes a State*, 93–94, 134, 144.

29. William King, letter to Rufus King, May 10, 1819, RKP; Daniel Cony, letters to Rufus King, November 30, 1819, and February 7, 1820, RKP; William D. Williamson, letter to Rufus King, January 26, 1820, RKP.

30 Mark L. Hill, letter to William King, December 30, 1819, WKP; Matthew Mason, "The Maine and Missouri Crisis: Competing Priorities and Northern Slavery Politics in the Early Republic," *Journal of the Early Republic* 33, no.4 (2013): 691.

31 Richard R. Westcott and Edward O. Schriver, "Reform Movements and Party Reformation, 1820–1861," in *Maine: The Pine Tree State*, 196.

32 Kermes, *Creating an American Identity*, 166; Banks, *Maine Becomes a State*, 153–56; William Pitt Preble, letter to William King, August 5, 1819, WKP.

33 The militia issues were discussed in some depth by the new state's newspapers. See *Portland Gazette*, March 28 and May 2, 1820; *Eastern Argus*, July 4 and October 3, 1820; and *Bangor Weekly Register*, July 20, 1820.

34 Nathan Hale, *Journal of Debates and Proceedings in the Convention of Delegates, Chosen to Revise the Constitution of Massachusetts* (Boston: Daily Advertiser, 1821), passim; Harlow Walker Sheidley, "Preserving 'The Old Fabrick': The Massachusetts Conservative Elite and the Constitutional Convention of 1820–1821," *Proceedings of the Massachusetts Historical Society*, 3rd ser., 103 (1991): 114–37; Samuel Eliot Morison, *A History of the Constitution of Massachusetts* (Boston: Wright and Potter, 1917), 30, 34; Johann N. Neem, "The Elusive Common Good: Religion and Civil Society in Massachusetts, 1780–1833," *Journal of the Early Republic* 24, no. 3 (2004): 407–41.

PARTINGS

1 John Adams, letter to David Sewall, November 4, 1821, in Adams Family Papers, MHS; David Sewall, letter to John Adams, October 26, 1821, in John Adams Papers, MHS; Moses Greenleaf, *A Survey of the State of Maine: In Reference to Its Geographical Features, Statistics and Political Economy* (Portland, ME: Shirley and Hyde, 1829);

2 Henry Sewall, letter to William Sewall, July 31, 1820, in Sewall Family Letters, MeHS; David Sewall, letter to John Adams, October 6, 1819, in John Adams Papers, MHS; John Adams, letter to David Sewall, October 10, 1819, in ibid.; Charles Deane, "Notice of David Sewall," *Proceedings of the Massachusetts Historical Society* 1 (1791–1835): 390; J. Gardner White, *Memoir of Samuel Sumner Wilde* (Cambridge, MA: Wilson and Son, 1882), 10.

3 Benjamin Ames and Joseph F. Wingate, Jr., *The Disclosure. No. 1. Documents Relating to Violations and Evasions of the Laws, During the Commercial Restrictions and Late War with Great Britain, Etc.* (Bath, ME: Torrey, 1824); William King and Mark Langdon Hill, *Remarks Upon a Pamphlet Published at Bath, Me., Relating to Alleged Infractions of the Laws During the Embargo, Non-Intercourse, and War* (Bath, ME: Eaton, 1825); Rufus King, letter to Christopher Gore, April 9, 1820, RKP; Matthew Mason, "John Holmes and the Shifting Partisan Politics of Slavery in Maine," *Maine History* 53, no. 2 (2020): 5–8.

4 Alan Taylor, *Liberty Men and Great Proprietors: The Revolutionary Settlement on the Maine Frontier, 1760–1820* (Chapel Hill: University of North Carolina Press, 1990), 242–43; Micah A. Pawling, *Wabanaki Homeland and the New State of Maine: The 1820 Journal and Plans of Survey of Joseph Treat* (Amherst: University of Massachusetts Press, 2007), 1–66; Jacques Ferland, "Tribal

Dissent or White Aggression?: Interpreting Penobscot Indian Dispossession Between 1808 and 1835," *Maine History* 43, no. 2 (2007): 126, 163; Nancy W. Gordon, "Protecting the Public Interest: Land Agents vs. Loggers on the Eastern Frontier, 1820–1840," *Enterprise and Society* 3, no. 3 (2002): 462–81.

5 W. E. Campbell, *The Aroostook War of 1839* (Fredericton, NB: Goose Lane, 2013), 29–44; Francis M. Carroll, *A Good and Wise Measure: The Search for the Canadian-American Boundary, 1783–1842* (Toronto: University of Toronto Press. 2001), 198–202; J. Chris Arndt, "Maine in the Northeastern Boundary Controversy: States' Rights in Antebellum New England," *New England Quarterly* 62, no. 2 (1989): 205–23.

6 Commonwealth of Massachusetts. *Considerations and Documents Relating to the Claim of Massachusetts for Expenditures during the Late War* (Washington, DC: de Krafft, 1818); "On the Service of the Militia of Massachusetts" and "Speech of Governor Eustis to the Legislature of Massachusetts," *ASP:MA*, 3:8, 58.

7 Peter J. Gomes, "Pilgrims and Puritans: 'Heroes' and 'Villains' in the Creation of the American Past," *Proceedings of the Massachusetts Historical Society*, 3rd ser., 95 (1983): 2–5; Stephanie Kermes, *Creating an American Identity: New England, 1789–1825* (New York: Palgrave Macmillan, 2015), 169–70; Margaret Bendroth, *The Last Puritans: Mainline Protestants and the Power of the Past* (Chapel Hill: University of North Carolina Press, 2015), 27–29; Daniel T. Rodgers, *As a City on a Hill: The Story of America's Most Famous Lay Sermon* (Princeton, NJ: Princeton University Press, 2018), 191–92.

8 Peter S. Field, *The Crisis of the Standing Order: Clerical Intellectuals and Cultural Authority in Massachusetts, 1780–1833* (Amherst: University of Massachusetts Press, 1998), 209, 234; Robert F. McGraw, "Minutemen of '61: The Pre-Civil War Massachusetts Militia," *Civil War History* 15, no. 2 (1969): 101–15.

9 "Ceremony to Remember a Forgotten Man," *Portland Daily Sun*, September 14, 2012.

INDEX

Page numbers in *italics* indicate figures.

Acadian Recorder (Halifax), owner of, 46
Act of Separation, 235
Act Respecting Enemy Aliens (1798), 45
An Act to Establish a Military Corps for the Defence of the Commonwealth of Massachusetts (1814), 289n4
Adams, Abigail, 31
Adams, Henry, 1, 8
Adams, John: Henry Adams's relationship to, 1; and John Henry, 41; and Knox, 22; Massachusetts ideal of, 7–9; objections to Maine's statehood, 227, 232, 233; and Treaty of Paris, 222
Adams, John Quincy, 8, 222
Adams, Moses, 73, 80, 172, 224
USS *Adams*, 145–47, 149–53, 155–57, 173, 192, 212
HMS *Adder*, 167
African Americans: and American military recruitment, 109–10; as Baptists, 17; Black drummers of Twenty-ninth Regiment, 277n32; definitions for, 4; and Maine's relationship to Massachusetts, 9; official marker for War of 1812 veterans, 237; as privateer crews, 80
Agnes (British ship), 118
agriculture: postwar demographics of Maine, 230; poverty of backcountry settlers, 2, 15–17; and squatters, 15–16, 18–19, 23–24, 26, 30–31, 34, 234–35. *See also* fishing; timber industry
HMS *Alban*, 165

alcohol: American soldiers' use of, 108, 111, 114, 121; and British plundering of Maine, 162; distilleries, 15; taxation of, 130
Alexander (privateer), 96
Allen, John, 39, 136
Alline, Henry, 16
American Advocate, call for U.S. Volunteers, 58, 60, 61
American Encroachments on British Rights (1808 pamphlet), 144
American Peace Society, 216
American privateers. *See* privateers
Americans, defined, 4
Anderson, Francis, 198
Angier, John, 198
Ann (Canadian schooner), 178–79
An Appeal to the People of Maine (pamphlet), 228
Appleton, Jesse, 194, 216
Archibald, James, 93
Armstrong, John, 192
Arnold, Benedict, 58
Aroostook War (1839), 220, 235
Assembly (Massachusetts), defined, 4. *See also* General Court (Massachusetts)
Atcheson, Nathaniel, 144
Atherton, Abel, 59, 121, 231
Augusta Light Infantry, 26, 30–31
Ayer, Samuel, 204

HMS *Bacchante*, 149
Bailey, Josiah, 196
Bailey, Winthrop, 124
Baker, Samuel, 124–25
Ball, Ebenezer, 13–14
Bangor, British occupation of, 161–63, 165, 167, 171, 173–74
Bangor Theological Seminary, 225

Bangor Weekly Register, on statehood, 228
Banks, Ronald, 3
Banner, James M., Jr., 1, 35
Baptist Church: African American congregants, 17; Congregationalist converts to, 225; during postwar period, 225; Republican views of congregants, 35, 93; support of war, 124–25; Toleration Act, 33
Barclay, Thomas, 40
Baring Brothers, 19, 24, 169
Barnes v. Falmouth (1810), 33–34
Barrie, Robert, 150–51, 162–63, 165, 166
Bartlett, Samuel, 176
Bathurst, Earl, 148
Bell, Richard, 80
HMS *Belvidera*, 45, 77
Beman, Nathan S. S., 124, 128
Bermuda trade, 76, 260n43
Betsey (brig), 29
Betsy (British ship), 165
Betterment Act (1808), 24
Betterment Act (1810), 24
Bingham, William, 19, 24
Bingham Purchase, 24
Binney, John, 52, 63–64
Black, John, 19, 73–74
Black, William, 100, 169
Blacks. *See* African Americans
Bladensburg (Maryland), battle of, 278n44
Blake, John, Jr., 58–59, 143, 151–57, 167, 174, 195, 225–26, 278n37
Blakely, Johnston, 100
Blyth, Samuel, 95, 100–103
Board of Commissioners for the Protection of the Sea Coast (Massachusetts), 185–89
HMS *Borer*, 144
Boston Daily Advertiser, on Maine statehood, 228
Bowden, Robert, 218
Bowdoin, James, 9

Bowdoin College, 17, 125, 141, 194, 216, 229
Bowman, Isaac, 103
Bowman, William, 116
HMS *Boxer*, 69, 95, 97, 100–104, 117–18, 121, 217
Boyd, Joseph C., 106, 204
Bradbury, George, 47
Bradbury, Jeremiah, 203
Bradford, Alden, 19–20, 34, 35, 36, 236
HMS *Bream*, 86, 95–96, 103, 104, 136, 142
Brewer, John, 53, 195, 211
Britain: British Privy Council, 40; British subjects as naturalized Americans in Maine, 45–46; currency of, 280n7; espionage in American territory by, 39, 41; impressment by, 38–40, 45, 48; Napoleon defeated by, 161; Orders in Council, 40; Royal Navy's interactions with privateers, 77, 90, 93–104. *See also* British invasion of Maine; British occupation of Maine
British invasion of Maine, 136–60; *Adams* pursuit and destruction, 145–47, 149–53, 155–57, 173; fall of Machias, 158–60; "Hampden Races," 156, 278n44; Moose Island capitulation, 142–45, 171; Penobscot invasion, 151–57, *154*; Sherbrooke and capture of Castine, 147–51; skirmishes leading up to, 136–42, *137*, 217; veterans of, 216. *See also* British occupation of Maine
British occupation of Maine, 161–81, 182–99; British departure from Maine, 209–12; British desertions, 198–99; British ships harassed by American privateers, 172, 178–81; cocoa incident, 166–67; conflicting response by Massachusetts and federal government, 184–95, *191*; militia

INDEX

activated in response to, 182–84; militia desertions, 195–97; Milliken's "PROCLAMATION" of liberation, 180–81; neutrality oath required, 167–69, 172, 173; permits/bonds on ships, 164, 168, 173–74; plunder of Maine communities, 161–67; pro-British sentiment by Federalists, 169–74; smuggling operations, 174–81
Brooks, John, 145, 186, 226
Brown, Francis, 132, 224
Brown, John G., 175
Buck, Mary Sewall, 163–64
Buckskin (privateer), 85
HMS *Bulwark*, 138–41
Burrows, William, 100–102, 121

cabotage policy, 222–23
Campobello Island, New Brunswick, 44, 82, 84, 85, 92
Canada: American invasion plans, 38–39, 52–54; Canadians, defined, 4; currency of, 280n7; Eastern Frontier and U.S. Volunteers, 58, 66–69, 67; Eastern Frontier of, 58, 66–69, 67; geographic names, 5; Loyalists in exile in, 7; postwar border negotiation, 219, 220, 234–35; privateers of, 83, 85–86, 90–93, 96, 99, 262n14; U.S. Volunteers and invasion plans, 57, 60
Cand, John, 45
Cannon, John H., 288n37
capital punishment: by American military, 196–97; by British military, 198–99; by Commonwealth of Massachusetts, 13–14, 127; by Nova Scotia, 93
Carlton, Moses, 204
Carr, Francis, 47, 155, 156, 163
Carr, James, 203
Castine: American repossession of, 209; battery, 56, 67, 117;
British desertions from, 198–99; capture of, 147–51; early British occupation of Maine, 164–65, 168, 170; Fort George, 13; and Moose Island capitulation, 142–43; postwar goodwill to Britain in, 215–16; smuggling and illicit operations in, 175–81, 197; and U.S. Volunteers, 73–74
cattle smuggling, 49–50, 120, 129, 171
Cayford, John, 124
Chamberlain, Joshua, 155, 225
Chandler, John, 34, 37, 60–61, 185, 188–89, 206
Chase, Ezekiel, 189
Chase, Roger, 49
USS *Chesapeake*, 26, 148
Cheverus, John, 17
child soldiers, 74, 119, 217
Christina (Swedish sloop), 176
Clapp, Asa, 204
class issues. *See* Maine's statehood movement
Clay, Henry, 38
Clay, John, 229
Clements, Lydia, 93
Cobb, David: Black family and relationship to, 73, 169; in Boston, 195; on British invasion of Maine, 144; and District of Maine's relationship to Massachusetts, 18–19, 24, 30, 32–33, 36; as Tenth Division commander, 185–86
Cobb, Matthew, 204
Cochrane, Alexander, 104, 137–39, 148
cocoa incident, 166–67
Colby College, 225
collusive capture by privateers, 87, 90–92
Columbian Centinel, on "Era of Good Feelings," 219
HMS *Columbine*, 41
Commodore Barry (revenue cutter), 94

A Compressed View of the Points to be Discussed with the United States (1814 pamphlet), 144
Coney, William, 70
Congregationalist Church: and British invasion of Maine, 141–42; lost prestige of postwar period, 224–25; on Massachusetts ideal, 16–20; on militia and British invasion, 141; and Toleration Act, 32–36; on war as God's punishment, 123–25, 132
USS *Congress*, 192
Congress (U.S.): Cyrus King elected to, 46–47; on indebted soldiers, 112; privateers commissioned by, 77–79; Second Enforcement Act, 28; U.S. Volunteers created by, 57–60; Volunteer Act (1812), 57–58, 65–66
USS *Constitution*, 76, 98
Cony, Daniel, 229, 234
Cook, Francis, 123
Cook, Orchard, 10, 29–30, 36, 133, 234, 273n56
Cooper, John, 11, 53, 158, 160, 164, 171–72, 194–95
Cottrill, Matthew, 17
Crabtree, William, 78
Crawford, William H., 223
Crevay, Nicholas, 126–27
Crosby, John, Sr., 76, 169, 174
Cross, Joseph, Jr., 78
Crown (Canadian privateer), 86
cruizing (patrolling), 95–96
Cummings, Abraham, 17, 19
Curtis, Joseph Waite, 224–25
Cushing, Thomas H., 75
customs. *See* privateers; smuggling
Cutts, Richard, 23, 29, 35, 106, 197, 273n56
Cutts, Thomas, 139

Dallas, A. J., 217
Damariscotta River battery, 121, 139, 195–96
Danzic (British brigantine), 173
Dart (privateer), 89
Dartmoor Massacre (April 1815), 212–14, 291n27
Dash (privateer), 78–79, 90, 217
Davis, Lot, 213–14
Davis, Moses, 182
Deane, Samuel, 12
Dearborn, Henry: appointed army's senior general, 38–39; and British invasion of Maine, 142, 143; and British occupation of Maine, 167; and conflicting response to British occupation by Massachusetts and federal government, 184–87, 189, 190, 192, 194, 196; Cyrus King on Madison's appointment of, 206; and District of Maine's relationship to Massachusetts, 21–23, 26–27, 32, 34, 37; as gubernatorial candidate, 228; and Hartford Convention, 200; and Maine's reaction to breakout of war, 43, 50–51; and political patronage, 22; and Portland Conference, 203, 210; on senate districts, 232; and Treaty of Ghent, 210; on U.S. Volunteers, 57–58, 60, 62
De Lancey, James, 151–52
Diggio, John, 40
Diligence (British transport), 70, 72, 94
disease: among soldiers, 113; vs. deaths from combat, 217; superstition about, 123
District of Maine, 7–37, 38–55; Act Respecting Enemy Aliens, 45; British reaction to outbreak of war, 54–55; Canada invasion plans, 38–39; declaration of war, 38–42; declaration of war and Maine's reaction, 42–46; defined, 4–5; Eastern Frontier of, 58, 66–69, 67; effect of embargo (1807–1810) on, 26–31, 48; Federalists'

victory in 1812 elections, 46–48; gubernatorial election and voting patterns (1812), 31–37, *35*; inconsistency with Massachusetts ideal, 7, 8–10, 12, 135; and Massachusetts militia's role in, 12–14; military installations in, *109* (*see also individual names of forts*); militia and partisan politics, 50–54; population growth of, 10, *11*; population image of, 14–19; postmasters of, 22–23; religious rejection of Massachusetts ideal, 10–14, 16 18, 245n9; Republican ideology of, 19–25; War of 1812 opposed by, 3–4. *See also* British invasion of Maine; British occupation of Maine; Maine's statehood movement; trade
Dolphin (privateer), 88
Donnison, William, 52–53
HMS *Dragon*, 150, 162
Drinkwater, Perez, Jr., 213
Dwight, Timothy, 7, 15

Eastern Argus (Portland): on army expansion and recruitment, 106; and Ayer, 204; on John Low, 201; on religious leaders' criticism of war, 124; on statehood, 227, 228; on tax delinquents, 132; on Treaty of Ghent, 208; on Widgery, 38
Eastern Cemetery (Portland), 103
Eastern Frontier, U.S. Volunteers at, 58, 66–69, *67*
Eastern Station (Kittery Naval Yard), 98–99, 143
Eaton, Samuel, 12, 141
economic issues. *See* agriculture; financial issues; privateers; smuggling; trade
Eighth Militia Division, 23, 25, 34, 37, 192
Elbridge Gerry (privateer), 83

Eleventh Militia Division, 193
Eliza Ann (British sloop), 90
Ellsworth Light Infantry, 73
embargoes. *See* trade
Emerson, Bulkeley, 41
Emerson, Charles, 225
Emerson, Edward, Jr., 41
HMS *Emulous*, 95, 103, 104
USS *Enterprise*, 85, 99–104, 121, 217
Enterprize (schooner), 88
"Era of Good Feelings," 219
Eustis, William, 51, 58, 236
"The Evils of War" (sermon, F. Brown), 132

Falmouth Universalist church, 33
Fame (privateer), 81, 84–85, 180
HMS *Fantôme*, 104, 142
Farley, Joseph, 179, 203
Favorite (British brig), 165
Favorite (privateer), 81
Federalists: army and war criticized by, 111, 115, 118, 122, 125–29; and British occupation of Maine, 169–74; Congregationalist ministers as, 123, 125; customs criticized by, 134; declaration of war and Maine's reaction, 42–46; defined, 4; and Hartford Convention, 200–203, 207; Jefferson loathed by, 20; and Massachusetts ideal, 19–25, 248n36; militia and partisan politics, 50–54; in postwar period, 223–26, 233–34; privateers criticized by, 79–82; on taxation, 130–34; on U.S. Volunteers program, 57–63, 66, 73, 74, 76. *See also* King, Cyrus; *Portland Gazette*
Fessenden, Samuel, 127–28, 201
Fillebrown, John, 108, 149
financial issues: and American military problems, 109, 111; bonds and currency, 280n7; British plundering of Maine, 161–67;

financial issues (*continued*)
Hartford Convention and funding for militia, 200–203, 207; illicit activities by disgruntled soldiers in Castine, 197; incentives for U.S. Volunteers, 63; indebted soldiers, 62, 111–12; prison expenses, 116; soldiers' late/lost pay, 56–57, 71, 195–97; and starvation, 97–98, 128. *See also* privateers; smuggling; trade
Fisher, Jonathan, 12, 14
fishing: British ban/restrictions on, 137, 168, 203; as cover for privateers, 77, 79, 81, 91; federal government on, 216, 219; postwar growth of, 221–22, 233; and Tariff Act, 221
Fly (American privateer), 85, 181
Fly (Canadian privateer), 85, 93, 100
Follett, Lydia, 222
Fort Burrows (Portland), 121–22, 183
Fort Constitution (Portsmouth, NH), 98, 188
Fort Edgecomb (Wiscasset): and breakout of war, 42; and British invasion of Maine, 139; and conflicting response to British occupation by Massachusetts and federal government, 182, 184, 193; lack of soldiers at, 121; punishment and imprisonment at, 117, 118; U.S. Volunteers at, 63; women at, 114–15
Fortieth U.S. Infantry (Boston), 105, 142, 149, 158, 193
Fort McClary (Kittery), 98, 188, 195, 217
Fort O'Brien (Machias), 89, 158–60, 180
Fort Preble (Portland): army expansion and recruitment, 106; and conflicting response to British occupation by Massachusetts and federal government, 195, 196; construction of, 26–28; lifestyle and duties of soldiers, 113, 115; and prisoners of war, 117, 118; sentries at, 119
Fort Scammel (Portland): and conflicting response to British occupation by Massachusetts and federal government, 185, 190, 196; construction of, 26; lifestyle and duties of soldiers, 113, 115; punishment and imprisonment at, 117–18; recruitment at, 106; sentries at, 119; U.S. Volunteers at, 63
Fort Sullivan (Eastport), 42, 68–69, 70, 75, 106, 115, 120, 144–45
Fort Sumner (Portland), 41, 63, 64, 106, 196
Forty-fifth U.S. Infantry (Bath), 105, 107, 110, 193, 195–96
France: British blockage against (1805–1807), 40–41; French Revolution, 19, 20; Lowell on Napoleonic France, 61
Frederick Island, 220
Freeman, William, 209
Friendship (brig), 88–90
Frolic (privateer), 81
Fundy Squadron, 95–98, 103, 104
Furbush, William, 196–97
HMS *Furieuse*, 179–80

Gallatin, Albert, 58
Gazette of Maine (Buckstown), owner of, 46
General Court (Massachusetts): counties created by, 11; defined, 4; on embargo of British trade, 126–28; gerrymandering of, 31–37, *35*; and Hartford Convention, 200–201, 203; and Maine's statehood, 230; on militia, 50, 237; Religious Freedom Act, 33; on Shays's Rebellion, 8–9; on Treaty of Ghent, 208

General Pike (privateer), 81
George, Lucy, 217
Germantown (privateer), 89–90
Gerry, Elbridge, 12, 31–37, 51, 175, 193, 236
gerrymandering, 31–37, 35
Gilman, John, 143
Girod, William "Nancy," 41
Goodwin, Ichabod, 188
Gordon, Alexander, 95, 96
Gore, Christopher, 30
Gosselin, Gerard, 168, 173–74, 199, 209, 211
Grant, Andrew, 225
Graves, Donald, 3
Great Britain. *See* Britain
Greene, Benjamin, 204
Greenleaf, Moses, 14
Griffith, Edward, 95, 148–50, 159, 160, 168, 170, 221–22
guerre de razzia (raiding warfare), 138–39
HMS *Guerriere*, 40, 98
Gulf of Maine, 77, 93–100

Hallowell Gazette, on Maine's statehood, 226, 229
Hamilton, Alexander, 19
Hammond, Charles, 156
"Hampden Races," 156, 278n44. *See also* British invasion of Maine
Hardy, Thomas, 144
Hare (Canadian privateer), 136
Harper, William, 99
Harriet (sloop), 56
Harris, Samuel D., 210
Hartford Convention (1814–1815), 200–203, 207, 236
Harvard College, 16
Haskell, Jonathan, III, 100
Hemmings, Sally, 20
Henry, John, 41
Herbert, George, 98, 170, 207
HMS *Herring*, 95
Hickey, Donald, 3
Hill, Jeremiah, 206
Hill, Mark Langdon, 203

Hiram (fishing boat), 221
Hodsdon, Isaac, 107, 108, 120
Holland, Anthony, 46
Holmes, Charles, 213
Holmes, John, 65, 201, 203, 219, 227, 230, 234
Hook, Josiah, Jr., 91, 164, 171, 178, 180, 203
"Horse Marine List" (newspaper article), 134
Houlton, 44, 129, 168
House Select Committee on Military Affairs, 65
Hull, Isaac: and army recruitment, 110; and British invasion of Maine, 143; and British occupation of Maine, 173, 188, 192; on British prisoners, 117; *Enterprise* and *Boxer* battle, 101–2; on sentries, 119; shipbuilding overseen by, 98–100
Hutchins, Eben, 288n37
Hutchins, Elias, 45
Hyder Ally (privateer), 165

Ilsley, Isaac, 178, 203
Ilsley, Robert, 78
Increase (privateer), 86
HMS *Indian*, 90, 94
Industry (British schooner), 181
Ingraham, Charles, 80
Ingraham, Henry, 80
Insurrection Act (1807), 26–27
Irish, James, Jr., 122, 133, 203

Jane, Henry, 94
Jefferson (privateer), 82–83, 89, 181
Jefferson, Thomas: and competition between Federalists and Republicans, 19–23; Cyrus King on book collection of, 205–6; and District of Maine's relationship to Massachusetts, 7, 19–23, 26–30, 32, 34; embargoes of, 221; and Henry, 41; and John Holmes, 230; Massachusetts's political class and criticism of, 2;

Jefferson, Thomas (*continued*)
  on privateers, 77; on state sovereignty vs. regional identity, 1
Jeffersonians. *See* Republicans
Jenks, William, 141–42
Jennings, Solomon, 75
Jewett, James, 78
Jewett, Ruth, 78
John, Henry, 150, 163
Johnson, Frederick, 86–87
Johnson, Ralph C., 198
Jones, William, 39
Jordans Point battery (Fort Burrows), 121–22
Junto, 228, 234

Kavanagh, James, 17
King, Charles, 214
King, Cyrus: and British occupation response, 197; Charles King's relationship to, 214; elected to Congress, 46–47; on embargo of British trade, 126; and Hartford Convention, 201; and New England secession threats, 205–7; on protectionist legislation, 222; on statehood, 229; on Tariff Act, 221; William King's relationship to, 3
King, Rufus, 47, 214, 223, 228–30, 234
King, William: and British invasion of Maine, 139, 142–44; and British occupation, 171, 178, 184, 186–87, 192–93, 194–95; brothers of, 47; and Castine's repossession, 209; Charles King's relationship to, 214; and District of Maine's relationship to Massachusetts, 21, 23–25, 29–30, 31, 32, 34, 36; land speculation by, 233; as Maine's first governor, 4, 233; and Maine's passage of statehood, 227–29, 234; and McCobb, 107; and Navigation Act, 222–23;
and Portland Conference, 203; Portland convention (1819), 230–31; on prisoners of war, 117; smuggling by, 40–41, 49–50, 55, 92, 227–28; and U.S. Volunteers, 57–62, 66, 71, 72, 75–76; War of 1812 supported by, 3, 4
Kinsley, Benjamin, 212
Kittery Naval Shipyard, 98–100, 143, 157, 192
Knox, Henry, 15–16, 22, 31
Kutusoff (ship), 166–67, 174

Ladd, William, 216
HMS *Landrail*, 181
Lane, Daniel, 107, 190–91
Lane, Isaac, 59, 65, 106, 112
Leamon, James, 2
Learned, Joseph D., 74, 105–6, 110, 120–22, 143, 272–76n17
Leavitt, Joseph, 169
Lee, John, 197–98
Lee, Silas, 11, 23
Leland, Sherman, 72–75, 106, 120
Leonard, Oliver, 156
Levy, Leonard, 27
Lewis, Andrew, 149, 152, 155
Liberty Men and Great Proprietors (Taylor), 16
Lilly (privateer), 80, 96
Lincoln, Levi, 28
HMS *Little Belt*, 40
Lively (schooner), 89
Liverpool Packet (Canadian privateer), 83
Lloyd, James, 236
Llufrio, Constantino, 175
Longfellow, Henry Wadsworth, 21, 237
Longfellow, Stephen, Jr., 21, 201–2
Longfellow, Zilpah, 202
Loring, Joseph, 105
Low, John, 47, 200–201
Low, Jonathan, Jr., 179
Lowell, John, Jr., 2, 61

INDEX

Lower Canada, 5, 57–58, 120, 147–48, 220
Lunenburgh (Canadian privateer), 93
Lydia (privateer), 91, 100

HMS *Macedonian*, 45
Machias: fall of, 158–60 (*see also* British invasion of Maine); Fort O'Brien, 89, 158–60, 180; Machias Bay vulnerability, 51–52
Maclay, Samuel, 53, 69
Madawaska region, 144, 147–48, 220, 235
Madison, James: and British invasion of Maine, 138, 184–95, *191*; criticized for military problems, 111, 120, 124, 127, 129, 133, 134; and declaration of war, 3, 38–47, 50, 52; and dissent of New Englanders at wars' end, 204, 206, 207, 208; and District of Maine's relationship to Massachusetts, 19, 23, 34; Massachusetts's political class and criticism of, 2; on privateers, 92; on state sovereignty vs. regional identity, 1; and U.S. Volunteers, 57–62, 65
Madison (privateer), 83
HMS *Maidstone*, 84
Maine (state): Act of Separation, 235; constitution of, 230–32; *Dirigo* state motto, 233; Junto of, 228, 234; passage of statehood, 227–30, 233; William King as first governor, 4, 233
Maine, District of. *See* District of Maine
Maine Literary and Theological Institute, 225
Maine Peace Society, 216
Maine's statehood movement: and competition between Federalists and Republicans, 21 (*see also* Federalists; Republicans); and Hartford Convention, 200–203, 207, 236; and New England secession threats, 203–8; regional vs. national identities in North America, 1–3; Shays's Rebellion and early push for, 8–9, 13, 18. *See also* British invasion of Maine; British occupation of Maine; District of Maine; War of 1812
Malcolm (brigantine), 77
Mammoth (privateer), 195
Manning, Enoch, 158, 166–67
Margaretta (Swedish brig), 100–101
HMS *Martin*, 104, 120
Mary (British sloop), 179–80
Mary of Augusta (sloop), 83
Mary of Waldoborough (sloop), 136–37
Massachusetts: Act of Separation, 235; An Act to Establish a Military Corps for the Defence of the Commonwealth of Massachusetts, 289n4; Board of Commissioners for the Protection of the Sea Coast, 185–89; "Commonwealth" or "old Massachusetts," defined, 4; conflicting response to British occupation by Massachusetts and federal government, 184–95, *191*; constitution of (1780), 7–9, 12, 230; constitution of (1820), 230–32; and Crevay's murder, 126–27; enlistment consent requirement, 110; Federalist ideology of, 19–25; Maine's passage of statehood, 227–30; Massachusetts ideal, 7–14, 16–25, 135, 245n9, 248n36; Massachusetts ideal and Hartford Convention, 200–203, 207, 236; New England states' call for war's end, 203–8; prisoners of war held in, 115–16, 118, 119; slavery ban in, 9;

Massachusetts (*continued*)
soldier burials, 111; Supreme Court, 51, 234; taxation, 8–9, 13, 18, 128–35, 221, 272n50; War of 1812 opposed by, 3–4, 105, 128. *See also* District of Maine; General Court (Massachusetts); militia; religion; Strong, Caleb
Massachusetts Historical Society, 20, 233
Matignon, Francis, 17
McCall, Edward, 101
McCobb, Denny, 107, 110, 193
McDonough (privateer), 78
Merrill (Captain of *Hero*), 197–98
Merrill, Daniel, 125
Merrill, James, Jr., 122
Merritt, Timothy, 125
Methodist Church: and Massachusetts religious orthodoxy, 17; during postwar period, 225; support of war, 124–25; Toleration Act, 124–25
militia: activated in response to British invasion of Maine, 136, 139–43, 145, 149–60, 182–84; and competition between Federalists and Republicans, 24–25, 248n36; conflicting response to British occupation by Massachusetts and federal government, 184–95, *191*; defense against privateers, 84; desertions from, 195–97; District of Maine bound to Massachusetts ideal, 12–14; District of Maine's squatters and property disputes, 16, 18–19; and embargo (1807–1810), 26–31, 48; Hartford Convention and funding for, 200–203, 207; Maine's constitution on, 231; Massachusetts General Court on (1840), 237; and Monroe on states' rights, postwar period, 236; during postwar period, 225; Shays's Rebellion, 8–9, 13, 18; stringbeaners, defined, 13; supply problems, 53–54; volunteer officers excluded from, 62. *See also* U.S. Volunteers
Miller, James, 209, 220
Miller, Noah, 179–80
Milliken, Alexander, 166, 170, 177, 180–81
Milne, David, 138–40, 166–67
Missouri Compromise (1820), 229–30
Mitchell, Ammi R., 132
modus vivendi ("way of living") directive, 66–69, *67*
Monroe, James: and American Peace Society, 216; and Cyrus King, 197; postwar presidential visit to Maine, 218–20, 222; as secretary of state, 222; as secretary of war, 178, 194; on states' rights, 235–36
Moose Island: British departure from, 209–12, 220; capitulation of, 142–45, 171; postwar occupation of, 219. *See also* British invasion of Maine
Morison, Samuel Eliot, 3, 201
Morris, Charles, 27–28, 145–47, 152–53, 155–57, 278n37
Morse, Jedidiah, 7
Morse, Samuel A., 158–60, 166–67, 210, 290n19
Morton, Perez, 13–14
Mowry, Jabez, 55, 172, 212
"myth of New England exclusiveness," 1

Napoleon Bonaparte, 40, 47, 61, 104, 123, 161
Native Americans: Crevay's murder, 126–27; defined, 4; fear of attacks in Maine, 44–45; and Maine's early relationship to Massachusetts, 9; Maine (state) on land ownership, 234–35. *See also individual names of tribes and nations*

INDEX

USS *Nautilus*, 95
naval warfare. *See* British invasion of Maine; privateers; smuggling; War of 1812; *individual names of ships*
Navigation Act (1817), 222–23
Neal, John, 17
Nelson, Job, 211
neutrality oath, 167–69, 172, 173
New Brunswick, Canada, 4, 64, 75, 95, 144, 147–48, 220
New England: "myth of New England exclusiveness," 1; regional vs. national identities in, 1–3; secession threats, 203–8. *See also* District of Maine; Maine (state); Maine's statehood movement; Massachusetts
New York Columbian, on John Low, 201
Nichols, John, 39–40, 45
Ninety-eighth Regiment of Foot (British), 148–50
HMS *Nova Scotia*, 69, 95, 259n28
Nye, Ansel, 42
Nyman, Johan, 177
HMS *Nymphe*, 138

Oakman, Tobias, 153, 156
Oates (Lieutenant), 144
O'Brien, Jeremiah, 51, 160, 165, 210–11
104th Regiment (New Brunswick), 147
"Order Book for Portland Forts," 114
Orders in Council (1807), 40, 54
Otis, Harrison Gray, 9, 128, 201, 227

Page, John, Jr., 49
Parker, Isaac, 13–14, 23
Parris, Albion K., 202, 203, 205
Parsons, Theophilus, 33–34
Partridge (privateer), 88
Passamaquoddy tribe, 44–45, 158
Patten, Amos, 174
Paul Jones (privateer), 173

"Paul Revere's Ride" (H. W. Longfellow), 237
Payson, David, 182
Peillon, Stephen J. M., 176
Penobscot Nation, 44, 127, 174, 235
Penobscot Packet (boat), 165
Penobscot River, invasion of, 151–57, 154. *See also* British invasion of Maine
Perkins family, 169
Perpetual War (Lowell), 61
Perry, Isaac, 149, 151
Perry, James, 142
HMS *Peruvian*, 146, 149
Peters, Sarah, 16–17
Pickering, Timothy, 1, 2, 8, 29, 186, 203
HMS *Pictou*, 160
Pilkington, Andrew, 144–45, 159, 160
Plessis, Joseph-Octave, 44
HMS *Plumper*, 94
HMS *Porgey*, 41
Porter, Samuel, 78–79, 263n30
Porter, Seward, 78–79, 90–91, 263n30
Portland: and British invasion of Maine, 143; burial of *Enterprise* and *Boxer* captains, 102; and embargo (1807–1810), 26–31, 48; Portland Conference (1814), 203–5; Portland convention (1819), 230; Portland Observatory, 117
Portland Gazette: on military protection, 99, 122; on New England secession threats, 205; on taxation, 132–33; on U.S. Volunteers, 63
Portsmouth Packet (privateer), 104
postwar period, 215–32; constitutions of Maine and Massachusetts, 230–32; Federalists' status during, 223–26, 233–34; land ownership, 234–35; Maine's hatred for British, 215–16; Maine's statehood, 227–30, 233;

postwar period (*continued*)
and Massachusetts ideal, 236–37; Monroe's visit to Maine (1817), 218–20; protectionist policies, 220–23; states' rights, 235–36; veterans, widows, and orphans in Maine, 216–18, 237; widows' weeds, defined, 217
Preble, William Pitt, 204, 231
USS *President*, 40
Prévost, George, 148
privateers, 77–104; American commission of, 77–79; British efforts to avoid escalation of war, 77; Canadian, 83, 85–86, 90–93, 96, 99, 262n14; collusive capture by, 87, 90–92; combat/capture by, 82–87; criticism of, 79–82; cruizing (patrolling) by, 95–96; *Enterprise* and *Boxer* battle, 100–104; harassment of British occupiers by (2014–2015), 172, 178–81; imprisonment of, 116–18; intentional beaching by, 96–97; lawsuits and arrests involving, 87, 89–90; and military recruitment problems, 107–8; naval warships and interactions with, 93–100; policing roles of, 87–89; privateer against privateer combat, 85–87; ransomed vessels, 97; "shaving mills," 79; theft and violence by, 92–93; and War of 1812 breakout, 41, 44, 46, 49–53
Proctor, Amos, 178
USS *Prometheus*, 211
property and property rights: direct tax of 1813, 128–35, 272n50; District of Maine's squatters and property disputes, 16, 18–19; postwar period land ownership in Maine, 234–35; squatters, 15–16, 18–19, 23–24, 26, 30–31, 34, 234–35

punishment and imprisonment: capital punishment, 13–14, 93, 127, 196–99; Dartmoor Massacre, 212–14, 291n27; of indebted soldiers, 62, 111–12; for militia desertions, 195–97; penalties for enlisted men, 114; prisoners of war, 115–19
Putnam, Perley, 144–45
HMS *Pylades*, 165

Quebec, 65
Quincy, Josiah, 227, 232

Rambler (privateer), 82
HMS *Ramillies*, 144
Rapid (privateer), 78, 84, 95, 259n28
HMS *Rattler*, 69, 95, 96, 99, 103
religion: criticism of taxes, 132; District of Maine and rejection of Massachusetts ideal, 10–14, 16–20, 245n9; Massachusetts on freedom of, 231, 237; support/criticism of War of 1812, 123–27; Toleration Act, 32–36. *See also* Baptist Church; Congregationalist Church; Methodist Church
Religious Freedom Act (1811), 32–36
Republicans: army and war influenced/supported by, 105–7, 122–26, 130–33; declaration of war and Maine's reaction, 42–46; defined, 4; District of Maine and opposition to Federalists by, 19–25, 248n36; and embargo (1807–1810), 26–31, 48; Massachusetts ideal opposed by, 20–21; militia and partisan politics, 50–54; New England secession threats by, 203–8; privateers supported by, 88; on U.S. Volunteers program, 57–62, 66, 73, 76. See also *Eastern Argus*; Jefferson, Thomas; King, William; Monroe, James

INDEX

Revenge (privateer), 84
Richardson, Alford, 122, 143, 188, 189–90
Ripley, Eleazar Wheelock, 39
Roberts, George, 217
Roberts, Hannah, 217
Robinson family, 91–92, 100
Rodgers, John, 40
Rover (privateer), 80

Saint Andrews, New Brunswick, 53–54, 70, 75, 82
Saint George battery, 121, 139
Saint John, New Brunswick, 5, 82, 175
Salisbury (privateer), 81
Salome (schooner), 212
Sanders, Robert, 212–13
Sargent, Henry, 220
Sargent, Paul Dudley, 169
Sawyer, Herbert, 77, 93–94
Second Enforcement Act (1809), 28
Senhouse, Henry Fleming, 104
Seventeenth Militia Division, 34
Sewall, David, 19, 27, 179, 219, 233–34
Sewall, Henry: and British occupation response, 186–87, 192, 195; on charges against Blake, 225–26; and District of Maine's relationship to Massachusetts, 23, 25, 26, 29, 30, 34, 37; and James Merrill, Jr., 122; on Maine's statehood, 233; refusal to mobilize militia, 50; refusal to supply militia, 53
Sewall, Samuel, 13–14
HMS *Shannon*, 93
"shaving mills," 79. *See also* privateers
Shaw, Tyler Porter, 138
Shays's Rebellion (1786–1787), 8–9, 13, 18
Shead, Oliver, 52
Sheffield (New Brunswick schooner), 171

Sherbrooke, John Coape: and British invasion of Maine, 144, 148–49, 159, 160; and British occupation of Maine, 163, 166, 168–70, 174, 192, 209; on forbearance by Britain, 54; and New England secession threats, 207
shipbuilding industry: Kittery Naval Shipyard, 98–100, 143, 157, 192; registration of ships built in Bath, 76, 260n43; Tariff Act, 221
Shortland, Thomas G., 213
Sixtieth Regiment (British), 148–49, 150
Sixty-second Regiment of Foot (British), 148–50, 199
slavery: Learned on, 272–76n17; Massachusetts ban on, 9; Webster on, 237
smuggling: and Bermuda trade, 76; during British occupation of Maine, 164, 171, 172, 174–81; of cattle, 49–50, 120, 129, 171; collusive capture by privateers and contraband, 92; military sentry roles, 119–20; Moses Adams and, 172, 224; and Treaty of Ghent, 210–11; U.S. Volunteers and policing roles, 64–73, 75
Smyth, George Stracey, 54, 148
HMS *Spartan*, 84
Spitfire (brig), 40
Spofford, Charles, 49
Spofford, Frederick, 49
squatters, defined, 16. *See also* property and property rights
Stark, Horatio, 209, 211
starvation, 97–98, 128
State Department (U.S.), 210–11
HMS *Statira*, 85
Stewart, Charles, 76
St. Michael (privateer), 85
Stoddard, Amos, 22
Stoodley, Nathaniel, 99
Storer, Woodbury, 132, 203–4

Strong, Caleb: and Blake, 226; and British invasion of Maine, 142–44; and British occupation response, 184–90, 192, 194–95; and District of Maine's relationship to Massachusetts, 19, 20, 24, 35–37; and Hartford Convention, 200, 202; and John Holmes, 219; and Monroe, 236; Moses Adams appointed sheriff by, 80; and New England secession threats, 203, 204, 207; on regionalism vs. national identity, 2; and U.S. Volunteers, 62; and War of 1812 military problems, 121, 122, 123, 125, 127; on war's breakout in Maine, 44, 47, 48, 50–53
suffrage (men over twenty-one), 231
Sullivan, James, 24, 25, 27, 28, 30
Sumner, William Hyslop, 187–89, 190, 192, 193, 236
Superb (privateer), 78
Surprise (privateer), 166
Sweden, Bath ships registered under, 76
Swiftsure (privateer), 81, 88

Tadley, Robert, 214
Talleyrand-Périgord, Charles de, 14
Tallman, Peleg, 47, 76
Tappan, Arthur, 176
Tappan, Charles, 100, 102
Tappan, John, 92, 176
Tappan, Lewis, 176
Tariff Act (1816), 221
taxation: criticism of, 128–35, 272n50; and Shays's Rebellion, 8–9, 13, 18; Tariff Act, 221
Taylor, Alan, 16
Tebbets, Charles, 177
HMS *Tenedos*, 97, 140–41
Tenth Militia Division, 36, 180, 186, 195, 226
Thatcher, George, 10, 13–14, 17, 19, 31, 126, 207

Thatcher, Samuel, 31
Thirty-fourth U.S. Infantry (Portland), 72, 75, 105–6, 114, 121, 195, 196
Thirty-third U.S. Infantry (Saco), 75, 105, 106–7, 112, 122
Thorndike, Paul, 213
Thornton, Thomas G., 23, 45, 46, 64, 116, 117, 118
timber industry: and Maine's statehood agreement with Massachusetts, 233, 235; postwar period, 235; and squatters, 15–16; trade of, 26, 77, 97, 128, 169, 171; War of 1812 breakout and Maine's reaction, 44–45
Toleration Act (1811), 32–36
trade: with Bermuda, 76, 260n43; British harassment of, 40–41, 44, 46, 48–55; cabotage policy, 222–23; embargoes, 26–31, 36, 38–39, 48, 99, 127–29, 205, 221, 227; merchant ships and defense against privateers, 84; by timber industry, 26, 77, 97, 128, 169, 171. *See also* privateers; smuggling
Traveller (schooner), 89
Treaty of Ghent (1814), 208–11, 219, 221
Treaty of Paris (1783), 221, 222
Trescott, Lemuel, 58, 212
Tucker, Samuel, 85
twelve-month Volunteers. *See* U.S. Volunteers
Twenty-first U.S. Infantry Regiment, 39, 107
Twenty-ninth Regiment of Foot (British), 148–50, 277n32
Tyler, Samuel, 110

Ulmer, George: and British occupation of Maine, 170, 179, 185–86, 194, 209; and District of Maine's relationship to Massachusetts, 36; as Hancock County sheriff, 66, 80; imprisonment of, 71–72, 81; U.S. Volunteers program commanded by, 57, 58, 69–76; War of 1812 military problems, 106; on war's breakout in Maine, 50, 53

Ulmer, Jacob, 54, 186

Unger, William P., 176, 177

Union (sloop), 176

U.S. Volunteers, 56–76; active service initiated by, 63–64; created by Madison and Congress, 57–60; at Eastern Frontier, 58, 66–69, 67; Federalists' opposition to, 60–63; Lowell on "mongrel breed of soldier citizen," 61; paid recruitment of, 72–73; paid soldiers and lost payroll, 56–57, 71; policing roles of, 64, 69–73, 75; poor morale of, 64–65; program failure, 65–66, 73–76, 105; supply problems of, 68–69, 70–71

Vaughan, Benjamin, 227
Vaughan, Charles, 45–46
Vaughan, Robert, 45–46
Vaughan, William, 197
Venture (ship), 120
Victory (British ship), 139, 174
Viper (privateer), 158–59
volunteer soldiers. *See* U.S. Volunteers
Vose, Josiah, 107, 108

Wadsworth, Alexander, 145, 212
War Department (U.S.), 51, 190, 210
Wardwell, Jeremiah, 25
War of 1812: American child soldiers, 74, 119, 217; British occupiers' departure from Maine, 209–12; British permits/bonds on American ships, 164, 168, 173–74; Dartmoor Massacre, 212–14, 291n27; disease outbreaks, 113, 123, 217; *guerre de razzia* (raiding warfare), 138–39; impressment of sailors, 38–40, 45, 48; Massachusetts's and Maine's opposing views of, 3–4; New England states' call for war's end, 205–7; regional vs. national identities and, 2; Treaty of Ghent, 208–11, 219. *See also* British invasion of Maine; British occupation of Maine; postwar period; U.S. Volunteers; War of 1812 and American military

War of 1812 and American military, 105–35; army expansion and recruitment, 105–12; District of Maine military installations, *109*; garrisons vs. militia, 119–22; lifestyle and duties of soldiers, 112–15; officers' disagreements, 122; parental consent for enlistment, 110; punishment and imprisonment during, 115–19; religious support/criticism of, 123–27; and taxation, 128–35, 272n50; uniforms and weapons supplied to soldiers, 110; as "wicked," 127–29. *See also* U.S. Volunteers

Warren, John Borlase, 94–95
USS *Washington*, 192
Washington (schooner), 165, 210–11
Washington (sloop), 42
Washington, George, 7, 42, 74, 151–52
Wasp (privateer), 81, 97
Waters, Kervin, 103
Weasel (American privateer), 92–93, 263n34
Weazle (Canadian privateer), 92
Webster, Daniel, 232, 236–37
Webster-Ashburton Treaty (1842), 235
Weeks, Joseph, Jr., 84
Weeks, Lemuel, Jr., 78, 185

Wellington, Duke of (Arthur Wellesley), 209
Westcott, Joseph, 56–57, 71, 73
White Oak (fishing boat), 222
Whiting, Samuel K., 193, 204–5
Whittier, Benjamin, 198
"wickedness" of war, 127–29
Widgery, William, 38, 47, 60, 99, 125–26, 204
Wilde, Samuel Sumner, 18–19, 22, 201, 234
William & Anne (ship), 89
William I (Dutch king), 220
Williamson, Joseph, 161–62, 163, 165
Williamson, William, 161–62
Williamson, William D., 229
Wilson, John, 47
Wily Reynard (privateer), 93
Wingate, Joseph F., Jr., 92
Wingate, Joshua, Jr., 203, 228
Wiscasset jail, 116–17, 118
women, at army installations, 114–15
Wood, Abiel, 47, 123
Worster, Lemuel, 217

Ximines (Lieutenant Colonel), 198

Yankees, defined, 4
Young, John, 175
HMS *Young Emulous*, 96
Young Teazer (privateer), 86–87